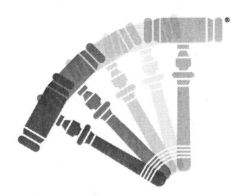

Casenote® Legal Briefs

TRADEMARK

Keyed to Courses Using

Ginsburg, Litman, and Kevlin's

Trademark and Unfair Competition Law: Cases and Materials

Fifth Edition

Copyright © 2014 CCH Incorporated. All Rights Reserved.

Published by Wolters Kluwer Law & Business in New York.

Wolters Kluwer Law & Business serves customers worldwide with CCH, Aspen Publishers, and Kluwer Law International products. (www.wolterskluwerlb.com)

No part of this publication may be reproduced or transmitted in any form or by any means, electronic or mechanical, including photocopy, recording, or utilized by any information storage and retrieval system, without written permission from the publisher. For information about permissions or to request permission online, visit us at wolterskluwerlb.com or a written request may be faxed to our permissions department at 212-771-0803.

To contact Customer Service, e-mail customer.service@wolterskluwer.com, call 1-800-234-1660, fax 1-800-901-9075, or mail correspondence to:

Wolters Kluwer Law & Business
Attn: Order Department
P.O. Box 990
Frederick, MD 21705

Printed in the United States of America.

1 2 3 4 5 6 7 8 9 0

ISBN 978-1-4548-4795-3

Certified Chain of Custody
Product Line Contains At Least
20% Certified Forest Content
www.sfiprogram.org
SFI-00756

About Wolters Kluwer Law & Business

Wolters Kluwer Law & Business is a leading global provider of intelligent information and digital solutions for legal and business professionals in key specialty areas, and respected educational resources for professors and law students. Wolters Kluwer Law & Business connects legal and business professionals as well as those in the education market with timely, specialized authoritative content and information-enabled solutions to support success through productivity, accuracy and mobility.

Serving customers worldwide, Wolters Kluwer Law & Business products include those under the Aspen Publishers, CCH, Kluwer Law International, Loislaw, ftwilliam.com and MediRegs family of products.

CCH products have been a trusted resource since 1913, and are highly regarded resources for legal, securities, antitrust and trade regulation, government contracting, banking, pension, payroll, employment and labor, and healthcare reimbursement and compliance professionals.

Aspen Publishers products provide essential information to attorneys, business professionals and law students. Written by preeminent authorities, the product line offers analytical and practical information in a range of specialty practice areas from securities law and intellectual property to mergers and acquisitions and pension/benefits. Aspen's trusted legal education resources provide professors and students with high-quality, up-to-date and effective resources for successful instruction and study in all areas of the law.

Kluwer Law International products provide the global business community with reliable international legal information in English. Legal practitioners, corporate counsel and business executives around the world rely on Kluwer Law journals, looseleafs, books, and electronic products for comprehensive information in many areas of international legal practice.

Loislaw is a comprehensive online legal research product providing legal content to law firm practitioners of various specializations. Loislaw provides attorneys with the ability to quickly and efficiently find the necessary legal information they need, when and where they need it, by facilitating access to primary law as well as state-specific law, records, forms and treatises.

ftwilliam.com offers employee benefits professionals the highest quality plan documents (retirement, welfare and non-qualified) and government forms (5500/PBGC, 1099 and IRS) software at highly competitive prices.

MediRegs products provide integrated health care compliance content and software solutions for professionals in healthcare, higher education and life sciences, including professionals in accounting, law and consulting.

Wolters Kluwer Law & Business, a division of Wolters Kluwer, is headquartered in New York. Wolters Kluwer is a market-leading global information services company focused on professionals.

Format for the Casenote® Legal Brief

Nature of Case: This section identifies the form of action (e.g., breach of contract, negligence, battery), the type of proceeding (e.g., demurrer, appeal from trial court's jury instructions), or the relief sought (e.g., damages, injunction, criminal sanctions).

Fact Summary: This is included to refresh your memory and can be used as a quick reminder of the facts.

Rule of Law: Summarizes the general principle of law that the case illustrates. It may be used for instant recall of the court's holding and for classroom discussion or home review.

Facts: This section contains all relevant facts of the case, including the contentions of the parties and the lower court holdings. It is written in a logical order to give the student a clear understanding of the case. The plaintiff and defendant are identified by their proper names throughout and are always labeled with a (P) or (D).

Palsgraf v. Long Island R.R. Co.

Injured bystander (P) v. Railroad company (D)

N.Y. Ct. App., 248 N.Y. 339, 162 N.E. 99 (1928).

Party ID: Quick identification of the relationship between the parties.

NATURE OF CASE: Appeal from judgment affirming verdict for plaintiff seeking damages for personal injury.

FACT SUMMARY: Helen Palsgraf (P) was injured on R.R.'s (D) train platform when R.R.'s (D) guard helped a passenger aboard a moving train, causing his package to fall on the tracks. The package contained fireworks which exploded, creating a shock that tipped a scale onto Palsgraf (P).

🏛 RULE OF LAW
The risk reasonably to be perceived defines the duty to be obeyed.

FACTS: Helen Palsgraf (P) purchased a ticket to Rockaway Beach from R.R. (D) and was waiting on the train platform. As she waited, two men ran to catch a train that was pulling out from the platform. The first man jumped aboard, but the second man, who appeared as if he might fall, was helped aboard by the guard on the train who had kept the door open so they could jump aboard. A guard on the platform also helped by pushing him onto the train. The man was carrying a package wrapped in newspaper. In the process, the man dropped his package, which fell on the tracks. The package contained fireworks and exploded. The shock of the explosion was apparently of great enough strength to tip over some scales at the other end of the platform, which fell on Palsgraf (P) and injured her. A jury awarded her damages, and R.R. (D) appealed.

ISSUE: Does the risk reasonably to be perceived define the duty to be obeyed?

HOLDING AND DECISION: (Cardozo, C.J.) Yes. The risk reasonably to be perceived defines the duty to be obeyed. If there is no foreseeable hazard to the injured party as the result of a seemingly innocent act, the act does not become a tort because it happened to be a wrong as to another. If the wrong was not willful, the plaintiff must show that the act as to her had such great and apparent possibilities of danger as to entitle her to protection. Negligence in the abstract is not enough upon which to base liability. Negligence is a relative concept, evolving out of the common law doctrine of trespass on the case. To establish liability, the defendant must owe a legal duty of reasonable care to the injured party. A cause of action in tort will lie where harm,

though unintended, could have been averted or avoided by observance of such a duty. The scope of the duty is limited by the range of danger that a reasonable person could foresee. In this case, there was nothing to suggest from the appearance of the parcel or otherwise that the parcel contained fireworks. The guard could not reasonably have had any warning of a threat to Palsgraf (P), and R.R. (D) therefore cannot be held liable. Judgment is reversed in favor of R.R. (D).

DISSENT: (Andrews, J.) The concept that there is no negligence unless R.R. (D) owes a legal duty to take care as to Palsgraf (P) herself is too narrow. Everyone owes to the world at large the duty of refraining from those acts that may unreasonably threaten the safety of others. If the guard's action was negligent as to those nearby, it was also negligent as to those outside what might be termed the "danger zone." For Palsgraf (P) to recover, R.R.'s (D) negligence must have been the proximate cause of her injury, a question of fact for the jury.

▶ ANALYSIS

The majority defined the limit of the defendant's liability in terms of the danger that a reasonable person in defendant's situation would have perceived. The dissent argued that the limitation should not be placed on liability, but rather on damages. Judge Andrews suggested that only injuries that would not have happened but for R.R.'s (D) negligence should be compensable. Both the majority and dissent recognized the policy-driven need to limit liability for negligent acts, seeking, in the words of Judge Andrews, to define a framework "that will be practical and in keeping with the general understanding of mankind." The Restatement (Second) of Torts has accepted Judge Cardozo's view.

Quicknotes

FORESEEABILITY A reasonable expectation that change is the probable result of certain acts or omissions.

NEGLIGENCE Conduct falling below the standard of care that a reasonable person would demonstrate under similar conditions.

PROXIMATE CAUSE The natural sequence of events without which an injury would not have been sustained.

Concurrence/Dissent: All concurrences and dissents are briefed whenever they are included by the casebook editor.

Analysis: This last paragraph gives you a broad understanding of where the case "fits in" with other cases in the section of the book and with the entire course. It is a hornbook-style discussion indicating whether the case is a majority or minority opinion and comparing the principal case with other cases in the casebook. It may also provide analysis from restatements, uniform codes, and law review articles. The analysis will prove to be invaluable to classroom discussion.

Issue: The issue is a concise question that brings out the essence of the opinion as it relates to the section of the casebook in which the case appears. Both substantive and procedural issues are included if relevant to the decision.

Holding and Decision: This section offers a clear and in-depth discussion of the rule of the case and the court's rationale. It is written in easy-to-understand language and answers the issue presented by applying the law to the facts of the case. When relevant, it includes a thorough discussion of the exceptions to the case as listed by the court, any major cites to the other cases on point, and the names of the judges who wrote the decisions.

Quicknotes: Conveniently defines legal terms found in the case and summarizes the nature of any statutes, codes, or rules referred to in the text.

Wolters Kluwer Law & Business is proud to offer *Casenote® Legal Briefs*—continuing thirty years of publishing America's best-selling legal briefs.

Casenote® Legal Briefs are designed to help you save time when briefing assigned cases. Organized under convenient headings, they show you how to abstract the basic facts and holdings from the text of the actual opinions handed down by the courts. Used as part of a rigorous study regimen, they can help you spend more time analyzing and critiquing points of law than on copying bits and pieces of judicial opinions into your notebook or outline.

Casenote® Legal Briefs should never be used as a substitute for assigned casebook readings. They work best when read as a follow-up to reviewing the underlying opinions themselves. Students who try to avoid reading and digesting the judicial opinions in their casebooks or online sources will end up shortchanging themselves in the long run. The ability to absorb, critique, and restate the dynamic and complex elements of case law decisions is crucial to your success in law school and beyond. It cannot be developed vicariously.

Casenote® Legal Briefs represents but one of the many offerings in Legal Education's Study Aid Timeline, which includes:

- *Casenote® Legal Briefs*
- *Emanuel® Law Outlines*
- Emanuel® *Law in a Flash* Flash Cards
- Emanuel® *CrunchTime®* Series
- *Siegel's Essay and Multiple-Choice Questions and Answers Series*

Each of these series is designed to provide you with easy-to-understand explanations of complex points of law. Each volume offers guidance on the principles of legal analysis and, consulted regularly, will hone your ability to spot relevant issues. We have titles that will help you prepare for class, prepare for your exams, and enhance your general comprehension of the law along the way.

To find out more about Wolters Kluwer Law & Business' study aid publications, visit us online at *www.wolterskluwerlb.com* or email us at *legaledu@wolterskluwer.com*. We'll be happy to assist you.

How to Brief a Case

A. Decide on a Format and Stick to It

Structure is essential to a good brief. It enables you to arrange systematically the related parts that are scattered throughout most cases, thus making manageable and understandable what might otherwise seem to be an endless and unfathomable sea of information. There are, of course, an unlimited number of formats that can be utilized. However, it is best to find one that suits your needs and stick to it. Consistency breeds both efficiency and the security that when called upon you will know where to look in your brief for the information you are asked to give.

Any format, as long as it presents the essential elements of a case in an organized fashion, can be used. Experience, however, has led *Casenote® Legal Briefs* to develop and utilize the following format because of its logical flow and universal applicability.

NATURE OF CASE: This is a brief statement of the legal character and procedural status of the case (e.g., "Appeal of a burglary conviction").

There are many different alternatives open to a litigant dissatisfied with a court ruling. The key to determining which one has been used is to discover *who is asking this court for what.*

This first entry in the brief should be kept as *short as possible.* Use the court's terminology if you understand it. But since jurisdictions vary as to the titles of pleadings, the best entry is the one that addresses who wants what in this proceeding, not the one that sounds most like the court's language.

RULE OF LAW: A statement of the general principle of law that the case illustrates (e.g., "An acceptance that varies any term of the offer is considered a rejection and counteroffer").

Determining the rule of law of a case is a procedure similar to determining the issue of the case. Avoid being fooled by red herrings; there may be a few rules of law mentioned in the case excerpt, but usually only one is *the* rule with which the casebook editor is concerned. The techniques used to locate the issue, described below, may also be utilized to find the rule of law. Generally, your best guide is simply the chapter heading. It is a clue to the point the casebook editor seeks to make and should be kept in mind when reading every case in the respective section.

FACTS: A synopsis of only the essential facts of the case, i.e., those bearing upon or leading up to the issue.

The facts entry should be a short statement of the events and transactions that led one party to initiate legal proceedings against another in the first place. While some cases conveniently state the salient facts at the beginning of the decision, in other instances they will have to be culled from hiding places throughout the text, even from concurring and dissenting opinions. Some of the "facts" will often be in dispute and should be so noted. Conflicting evidence may be briefly pointed up. "Hard" facts must be included. Both must be *relevant* in order to be listed in the facts entry. It is impossible to tell what is relevant until the entire case is read, as the ultimate determination of the rights and liabilities of the parties may turn on something buried deep in the opinion.

Generally, the facts entry should not be longer than three to five *short* sentences.

It is often helpful to identify the role played by a party in a given context. For example, in a construction contract case the identification of a party as the "contractor" or "builder" alleviates the need to tell that that party was the one who was supposed to have built the house.

It is always helpful, and a good general practice, to identify the "plaintiff" and the "defendant." This may seem elementary and uncomplicated, but, especially in view of the creative editing practiced by some casebook editors, it is sometimes a difficult or even impossible task. Bear in mind that the *party presently* seeking something from this court may not be the plaintiff, and that sometimes only the cross-claim of a defendant is treated in the excerpt. Confusing or misaligning the parties can ruin your analysis and understanding of the case.

ISSUE: A statement of the general legal question answered by or illustrated in the case. For clarity, the issue is best put in the form of a question capable of a "yes" or "no" answer. In reality, the issue is simply the Rule of Law put in the form of a question (e.g., "May an offer be accepted by performance?").

The major problem presented in discerning what is *the* issue in the case is that an opinion usually purports to raise and answer several questions. However, except for rare cases, only one such question is really the issue in the case. Collateral issues not necessary to the resolution of the matter in controversy are handled by the court by language known as *"obiter dictum"* or merely *"dictum."* While dicta may be included later in the brief, they have no place under the issue heading.

To find the issue, ask *who wants what* and then go on to ask *why did that party succeed or fail in getting it.* Once this is determined, the "why" should be turned into a question.

The complexity of the issues in the cases will vary, but in all cases a single-sentence question should sum up the issue. *In a few cases,* there will be two, or even more rarely, three issues of equal importance to the resolution of the case. Each should be expressed in a single-sentence question.

Since many issues are resolved by a court in coming to a final disposition of a case, the casebook editor will reproduce the portion of the opinion containing the issue or issues most relevant to the area of law under scrutiny. A noted law professor gave this advice: "Close the book; look at the title on the cover." Chances are, if it is Property, you need not concern yourself with whether, for example, the federal government's treatment of the plaintiff's land really raises a federal question sufficient to support jurisdiction on this ground in federal court.

The same rule applies to chapter headings designating sub-areas within the subjects. They tip you off as to what the text is designed to teach. The cases are arranged in a casebook to show a progression or development of the law, so that the preceding cases may also help.

It is also most important to remember to *read the notes and questions* at the end of a case to determine what the editors wanted you to have gleaned from it.

HOLDING AND DECISION: This section should succinctly explain the rationale of the court in arriving at its decision. In capsulizing the "reasoning" of the court, it should always include an application of the general rule or rules of law to the specific facts of the case. Hidden justifications come to light in this entry: the reasons for the state of the law, the public policies, the biases and prejudices, those considerations that influence the justices' thinking and, ultimately, the outcome of the case. At the end, there should be a short indication of the disposition or procedural resolution of the case (e.g., "Decision of the trial court for Mr. Smith (P) reversed").

The foregoing format is designed to help you "digest" the reams of case material with which you will be faced in your law school career. Once mastered by practice, it will place at your fingertips the information the authors of your casebooks have sought to impart to you in case-by-case illustration and analysis.

B. Be as Economical as Possible in Briefing Cases

Once armed with a format that encourages succinctness, it is as important to be economical with regard to the time spent on the actual reading of the case as it is to be economical in the writing of the brief itself. This does not mean "skimming" a case. Rather, it means reading the case with an "eye" trained to recognize into which "section" of your brief a particular passage or line fits and having a system for quickly and precisely marking the case so that the passages fitting any one particular part of the brief can be easily identified and brought together in a concise and accurate manner when the brief is actually written.

It is of no use to simply repeat everything in the opinion of the court; record only enough information to trigger your recollection of what the court said. Nevertheless, an accurate statement of the "law of the case," i.e., the legal principle applied to the facts, is absolutely essential to class preparation and to learning the law under the case method.

To that end, it is important to develop a "shorthand" that you can use to make marginal notations. These notations will tell you at a glance in which section of the brief you will be placing that particular passage or portion of the opinion.

Some students prefer to underline all the salient portions of the opinion (with a pencil or colored underliner marker), making marginal notations as they go along. Others prefer the color-coded method of underlining, utilizing different colors of markers to underline the salient portions of the case, each separate color being used to represent a different section of the brief. For example, blue underlining could be used for passages relating to the rule of law, yellow for those relating to the issue, and green for those relating to the holding and decision, etc. While it has its advocates, the color-coded method can be confusing and time-consuming (all that time spent on changing colored markers). Furthermore, it can interfere with the continuity and concentration many students deem essential to the reading of a case for maximum comprehension. In the end, however, it is a matter of personal preference and style. Just remember, whatever method you use, underlining must be used sparingly or its value is lost.

If you take the marginal notation route, an efficient and easy method is to go along underlining the key portions of the case and placing in the margin alongside them the following "markers" to indicate where a particular passage or line "belongs" in the brief you will write:

N (NATURE OF CASE)
RL (RULE OF LAW)
I (ISSUE)
HL (HOLDING AND DECISION, relates to the RULE OF LAW behind the decision)
HR (HOLDING AND DECISION, gives the RATIONALE or reasoning behind the decision)
HA (HOLDING AND DECISION, applies the general principle(s) of law to the facts of the case to arrive at the decision)

Remember that a particular passage may well contain information necessary to more than one part of your brief, in which case you simply note that in the margin. If you are using the color-coded underlining method instead of marginal notation, simply make asterisks or checks in the margin next to the passage in question in the colors that indicate the additional sections of the brief where it might be utilized.

The economy of utilizing "shorthand" in marking cases for briefing can be maintained in the actual brief writing process itself by utilizing "law student shorthand" within the brief. There are many commonly used words and phrases for which abbreviations can be substituted in your briefs (and in your class notes also). You can develop abbreviations that are personal to you and which will save you a lot of time. A reference list of briefing abbreviations can be found on page x of this book.

C. Use Both the Briefing Process and the Brief as a Learning Tool

Now that you have a format and the tools for briefing cases efficiently, the most important thing is to make the time spent in briefing profitable to you and to make the most advantageous use of the briefs you create. Of course, the briefs are invaluable for classroom reference when you are called upon to explain or analyze a particular case. However, they are also useful in reviewing for exams. A quick glance at the fact summary should bring the case to mind, and a rereading of the rule of law should enable you to go over the underlying legal concept in your mind, how it was applied in that particular case, and how it might apply in other factual settings.

As to the value to be derived from engaging in the briefing process itself, there is an immediate benefit that arises from being forced to sift through the essential facts and reasoning from the court's opinion and to succinctly express them in your own words in your brief. The process ensures that you understand the case and the point that it illustrates, and that means you will be ready to absorb further analysis and information brought forth in class. It also ensures you will have something to say when called upon in class. The briefing process helps develop a mental agility for getting to the *gist* of a case and for identifying, expounding on, and applying the legal concepts and issues found there. The briefing process is the mental process on which you must rely in taking law school examinations; it is also the mental process upon which a lawyer relies in serving his clients and in making his living.

Abbreviations for Briefs

acceptance	acp	offer	O
affirmed	aff	offeree	OE
answer	ans	offeror	OR
assumption of risk	a/r	ordinance	ord
attorney	atty	pain and suffering	p/s
beyond a reasonable doubt	b/r/d	parol evidence	p/e
bona fide purchaser	BFP	plaintiff	P
breach of contract	br/k	prima facie	p/f
cause of action	c/a	probable cause	p/c
common law	c/l	proximate cause	px/c
Constitution	Con	real property	r/p
constitutional	con	reasonable doubt	r/d
contract	K	reasonable man	r/m
contributory negligence	c/n	rebuttable presumption	rb/p
cross	x	remanded	rem
cross-complaint	x/c	res ipsa loquitur	RIL
cross-examination	x/ex	respondeat superior	r/s
cruel and unusual punishment	c/u/p	Restatement	RS
defendant	D	reversed	rev
dismissed	dis	Rule Against Perpetuities	RAP
double jeopardy	d/j	search and seizure	s/s
due process	d/p	search warrant	s/w
equal protection	e/p	self-defense	s/d
equity	eq	specific performance	s/p
evidence	ev	statute	S
exclude	exc	statute of frauds	S/F
exclusionary rule	exc/r	statute of limitations	S/L
felony	f/n	summary judgment	s/j
freedom of speech	f/s	tenancy at will	t/w
good faith	g/f	tenancy in common	t/c
habeas corpus	h/c	tenant	t
hearsay	hr	third party	TP
husband	H	third party beneficiary	TPB
injunction	inj	transferred intent	TI
in loco parentis	ILP	unconscionable	uncon
inter vivos	I/v	unconstitutional	unconst
joint tenancy	j/t	undue influence	u/e
judgment	judgt	Uniform Commercial Code	UCC
jurisdiction	jur	unilateral	uni
last clear chance	LCC	vendee	VE
long-arm statute	LAS	vendor	VR
majority view	maj	versus	v
meeting of minds	MOM	void for vagueness	VFV
minority view	min	weight of authority	w/a
Miranda rule	Mir/r	weight of the evidence	w/e
Miranda warnings	Mir/w	wife	W
negligence	neg	with	w/
notice	ntc	within	w/i
nuisance	nus	without	w/o
obligation	ob	without prejudice	w/o/p
obscene	obs	wrongful death	wr/d

Table of Cases

Prelude

Quick Reference Rules of Law

Top Tobacco, L.P. v. North Atlantic Operating Co., Inc.

Roll-your-own tobacco company (P) v. Roll-your-own tobacco company (D)

509 F.3d 380 (7th Cir. 2007).

NATURE OF CASE: Appeal from summary judgment for defendant in action for trademark infringement damages.

FACT SUMMARY: Top Tobacco, L.P. (Top Tobacco) (P), which sold tobacco to the roll-your-own, make-your-own (RYO/MYO) market using the mark "TOP," printed above a drawing of a spinning top, sought trademark damages against North Atlantic Operating Company, Inc. (North Atlantic) (D), which used a can to hold tobacco, also for the RYO/MYO market, that bore the phrase "Fresh-Top Canister." Top Tobacco (P) contended that none of its rivals could use the word "top" as a trademark, and that North Atlantic's (D) use caused impermissible trademark confusion and dilution.

🏛 **RULE OF LAW**

A mark holder cannot prevail on its action for trademark damages, where, as a matter of law, it cannot show that the defendant's use of the mark causes trademark confusion or dilution.

FACTS: Top Tobacco, L.P. (Top Tobacco) (P) sold tobacco to the roll-your-own, make-your-own (RYO/MYO) market using the mark "TOP," printed above a drawing of a spinning top. The mark was prominently displayed on its products and was well known to merchants and consumers. North Atlantic Operating Company, Inc. (North Atlantic) (D), was also in the RYO/MYO market. When North Atlantic (D) introduced a tobacco can with a pull-top lid, it used the phrase "Fresh-Top Canister" on the can. However, the phrase was not prominently displayed on the can, whereas North Atlantic's (D) "ZIG-ZAG" mark, with a picture of a Zouave soldier, were. The trade dress (including colors and typography) of each producer's can was distinctive. Top Tobacco (P) brought suit against North Atlantic (D) for trademark damages, asserting that Top Tobacco (P) had the exclusive right to the word "top" for use on tobacco in the RYO/MYO market, and that North Atlantic's (D) use caused trademark confusion and dilution. Specifically, Top Tobacco (P) asserted that consumers and merchants were confused by North Atlantic's (D) use of the word "top," and that Top Tobacco (P) had a famous mark that had been diluted by that use. The only evidence introduced were pictures of the respective producers' cans. The district court granted summary judgment to North Atlantic (D), and the court of appeals granted review.

ISSUE: Can a mark holder prevail on its action for trademark damages, where, as a matter of law, it cannot show that the defendant's use of the mark causes trademark confusion or dilution?

HOLDING AND DECISION: (Easterbrook, C.J.) No. A mark holder cannot prevail on its action for trademark damages, where, as a matter of law, it cannot show that the defendant's use of the mark causes trademark confusion or dilution. The principal purpose of trademark protection is to prevent consumer confusion by informing consumers of the origin of goods or services. Because the word "top" has many meanings, there is potential for confusion. However, here, Top Tobacco (P) has not demonstrated such confusion. Based on the pictures of the respective producers' cans, it is virtually impossible to believe that any consumer, however careless, would confuse these products. Although various tests have been developed to determine likelihood of confusion, here there is no need to rely on those tests—which are mere proxies for the likelihood of confusion—where it is clear from the evidence that there is no likelihood of confusion. Top Tobacco (P) argues that some merchants may have been confused by price lists that omitted the ZIG-ZAG brand but contained the phrase "Fresh-Top Can." This argument is not persuasive, not only because the price lists identified the producers of each product, but also because no evidence of actual merchant confusion has been presented. Finally, as to Top Tobacco's (P) claim that it has a "famous" brand that was diluted by the "Fresh-Top Canister" phrase, the word "top" which is widely used in the tobacco industry as a whole, has too many meanings and is too common and widely used, for any one firm to appropriate it. Further, even if Top Tobacco (P) could claim niche fame in the RYO/MYO market, the word "top" is not famously distinctive "as a designator of source" in any sensibly specified niche of tobacco products. Affirmed.

▶ **ANALYSIS**

In addition to articulating some fundamental trademark law principles, this case demonstrates the critical importance to a trademark action of the evidence presented. The court in this case acknowledged that judges are not perceptual psychologists or marketing experts and may misunderstand how trade dress affects purchasing decisions. Thus, it might have helped Top Tobacco's (P) case if it could have presented evidence in the form of consumer surveys or affidavits from consumers or merchants attesting to actual confusion. One suspects, however, that Top

Continued on next page.

Tobacco (P) could not have mustered such evidence, even if it wanted to, and that the court's decision was the correct one.

■■■

Quicknotes

DILUTION The diminishment of the capability of a trademark to identify and distinguish the particular good or service with which it is associated.

TRADE DRESS The overall image of, or impression created by, a product that a court may enforce as a trademark if it determines that such image has acquired secondary meaning and that the public recognizes it as an indication of source.

■■■

Concepts of Trademarks and Unfair Competition

Quick Reference Rules of Law

Cheney Bros. v. Doris Silk Corp.

Silk designer (P) v. Copier of designs (D)

35 F.2d 279 (2d Cir. 1929), *cert. denied*, 281 U.S. 728 (1930).

NATURE OF CASE: Petition in equity for an injunction.

FACT SUMMARY: Cheney Brothers (Cheney) (P), a designer and manufacturer of silks, brought suit against Doris Silk Corp. (D) for allegedly copying one of its designs and undercutting Cheney's (P) profits.

RULE OF LAW
There is no common-law rule of unfair competition that prevents one business from copying another business's product design.

FACTS: Cheney Brothers (Cheney) (P) makes silk products with designs. A designed product has a shelf life of one season. Cheney (P) cannot anticipate which of its designs will be popular, and not all are. Doris Silk Corp. (D) copied one of Cheney's (P) most popular designs, and set the price for its product lower than that of Cheney's (P). Cheney (P) sought an injunction to prevent Doris Silk Corp. (D) from copying its designs until the expiration of the season in which it was created.

ISSUE: Is there a common-law rule of unfair competition that prevents one business from copying another business's product design?

HOLDING AND DECISION: (Hand, J.) No. There is no common-law rule of unfair competition that prevents one business from copying another business's product design. First, Cheney's (P) request for an injunction limited in time is denied, because the equitable relief cannot be so limited where no relief is warranted. Cheney's (P) reliance on *International News Service v. Associated Press*, 248 U.S. 215 (1918), is not appropriate, since that case dealt with protection of news copy for the period in which it was initially distributed to the Associated Press's members, and it was limited to its facts. To extend that doctrine to all goods would encroach on the legislature's authority.

ANALYSIS

Scholars have stated that this court believed that the decision in *International News Service v. Associated Press*, 248 U.S. 215 (1918), was erroneous, but instead of addressing the issue head on simply held that its holding should not be interpreted to cover this case. The court believed that Cheney Brothers (P) should have had some protection, but the court found no statutory or common-law basis for it.

Copyright law eventually changed and currently allows designers to stop knockoffs.

■=■

Quicknotes

COPYRIGHT Refers to the exclusive rights granted to an artist pursuant to Article I, Section 8, Clause 8 of the United States Constitution over the reproduction, display, performance, distribution, and adaptation of his work for a period prescribed by statute.

■=■

Sears, Roebuck & Co. v. Stiffel Co.

Retailer (D) v. Lamp designer (P)

376 U.S. 225 (1964).

NATURE OF CASE: Action seeking damages for unfair competition.

FACT SUMMARY: Although Stiffel Co. (P) had obtained design and mechanical patents on a "pole lamp" it placed on the market, Sears, Roebuck & Co. (D) thereafter began to sell its own version at a much cheaper price.

🏛 RULE OF LAW
A state's unfair competition law cannot impose liability for, or prohibit, the copying of an article that is unprotectable under either federal patent or copyright laws.

FACTS: Having designed a pole lamp that it marketed, Stiffel Co. (P) obtained both design and mechanical patents thereon. In a short time, Sears, Roebuck & Co. (Sears) (D) came out with the same lamp, but it sold at a much cheaper price. As a result, Stiffel (P) brought an action seeking damages for unfair competition, but the court held that the patents Stiffel (P) had secured were invalid for want of invention. It nonetheless recognized that the lamps were substantially identical and, noting that customers might be confused, the court held that Sears (D) had engaged in unfair competition by marketing the confusingly similar lamps. From that decision, Sears (D) appealed, the court of appeals affirmed, and the United States Supreme Court granted certiorari.

ISSUE: If a particular article is one which neither the federal patent nor copyright laws protect, can a state's unfair competition law impose liability for or prohibit copying the article?

HOLDING AND DECISION: (Black, J.) No. Just as a state cannot directly encroach upon federal patent or copyright law, it may not use its own laws on unfair competition or any other subject to protect an article, which is left unprotected under the aforementioned federal laws. These federal systems of protection have occupied the field, and state law in those areas is preempted by the applicable federal scheme. Thus, where, as in this case, a state's unfair competition law clashes with the objectives of federal patent or copyright law, in providing a uniform system of protection while also preserving free competition where it is deemed appropriate, it must yield under the doctrine of preemption. Since Stiffel (P) was unable to obtain protection under the federal copyright or patent laws, its article was among those the federal scheme desired to leave unprotected, and the state cannot enter into the picture and extend protection. Reversed.

▶ ANALYSIS

The preemption doctrine, on which this case was decided, flows from the Supremacy Clause in Article IV of the Constitution, which makes federally enacted laws the supreme law of the land. The result is that when Congress passes laws that "occupy" a particular field, that action serves to "preempt" states from taking individual action in that area. It is an important concept in dealing with patents and copyrights, for a national system of protection could easily be thwarted and would be all but useless were inventors and authors uncertain whether their federal rights were effectively altered depending upon which state they were in. This type of uncertainty would have a damaging effect on the generation of new ideas and new products, which really depends on a nationwide standard of protection.

Quicknotes

CERTIORARI A discretionary writ issued by a superior court to an inferior court in order to review the lower court's decisions; the Supreme Court's writ ordering such review.

COPYRIGHT Refers to the exclusive rights granted to an artist pursuant to Article I, Section 8, Clause 8 of the United States Constitution over the reproduction, display, performance, distribution, and adaptation of his work for a period prescribed by statute.

ENCROACHMENT The unlawful intrusion onto another's property.

PATENT A limited monopoly conferred on the invention or discovery of any new or useful machine or process that is novel and nonobvious.

PREEMPTION Judicial preference recognizing the procedure of federal legislation over state legislation of the same subject matter.

UNFAIR COMPETITION Any dishonest or fraudulent rivalry in trade and commerce, particularly imitation and counterfeiting.

Bonito Boats v. Thunder Craft Boats

Boat designer (P) v. Manufacturer (D)

489 U.S. 141 (1989).

NATURE OF CASE: Review of order voiding state law prohibiting duplication of boat hulls.

FACT SUMMARY: Thunder Craft Boats, Inc. (D) contended that Florida's law prohibiting the duplication of unpatented boat hulls violated federal patent laws.

🏛 RULE OF LAW
States may not prohibit the duplication of unpatented or unpatentable articles.

FACTS: Florida enacted a law prohibiting the duplication of molded boat hulls. Bonito Boats, Inc. (Bonito) (P), which had designed a certain type of boat hull mold and had commercially exploited it, brought an action against Thunder Craft Boats, Inc. (Thunder Craft) (D). Bonito (P) alleged that Thunder Craft (D) had copied the design of its hull. The design was not patented. The trial court held the Florida law to be preempted by federal patent law and declared the law invalid. The appellate and Florida Supreme Courts affirmed, and the United States Supreme Court granted certiorari.

ISSUE: May states prohibit the duplication of unpatented or unpatentable articles?

HOLDING AND DECISION: (O'Connor, J.) No. States may not prohibit the duplication of unpatented or unpatentable articles. Federal patent law reflects a very careful balance between healthy competition and rewarding innovation. A person who meets the requirements of novelty, usefulness, and nonobviousness will be rewarded with a temporary monopoly; all other utilitarian articles may be exploited by the public. Federal patent laws, in order to determine what is protected, must also determine what is not protected. The balance struck in patent laws requires that all nonpatented, publicly known designs be freely traded. If states were free to grant de facto monopolies to unpatented or unpatentable articles, the balance struck in federal patent laws would be upset. Here, the Florida law is a good illustration. Bonito (P) did not apply for a patent. Consequently, federal patent law would permit any competitor to use its design. The Florida law prevents this. Consequently, the Florida law acts to upset the fine balance created in patent law. Since the law is inconsistent with federal law, it must fail. Affirmed.

▶ ANALYSIS

This case should not be taken to mean that there is no place for state laws in the law of intellectual property. State unfair competition laws have coexisted with federal law in this area for quite some time, with little evidence of incom-

patibility. In the instant case, the Court indicated it had no inclination to strike down state trade secret or unfair competition laws.

■■■

Quicknotes

CERTIORARI A discretionary writ issued by a superior court to an inferior court in order to review the lower court's decisions; the United States Supreme Court's writ ordering such review.

MONOPOLY A privilege or right conferred upon an individual or entity granting it the exclusive power to manufacture, sell and distribute a particular service or commodity; a market condition in which one or a few companies control the sale of a product or service thereby restraining competition in respect to that article or service.

PATENT A limited monopoly conferred on the invention or discovery of any new or useful machine or process that is novel and nonobvious.

PREEMPTION Judicial preference recognizing the procedure of federal legislation over state legislation of the same subject matter.

■■■

Trade-Mark Cases

United States (P) v. Trademark infringers (D)

100 U.S. 82 (1879).

NATURE OF CASE: Challenge to convictions for infringement.

FACT SUMMARY: Three trademark users were charged with infringement—two in New York, and one in Ohio—and the federal appeals courts in the various circuits disagreed about whether congressional legislation regarding trademarks was constitutional.

🏛 RULE OF LAW
Congress does not have power under the U.S. Constitution to regulate trademarks.

FACTS: Congress passed a law in 1870 entitled "An Act to revise, consolidate, and amend the statutes relating to patents and copyrights." Chapter 2, title 60 of the Act contained information relating to the registration of trademarks. In 1876, Congress also passed a law that punished by fine and imprisonment the fraudulent use, sale, and counterfeiting of trademarks registered under the previous statute. Three trademark users were charged with infringement—two in New York and one in Ohio—and the federal appeals courts in the various circuits disagreed about whether congressional legislation regarding trademarks was constitutional.

ISSUE: Does Congress have power under the U.S. Constitution to regulate trademarks?

HOLDING AND DECISION: (Miller, J.) No. Congress does not have power under the U.S. Constitution to regulate trademarks. Because the states have the power to regulate trademarks, any congressional power to regulate trademarks must derive from the U.S. Constitution, and the only two relevant clauses—Article I, Section 8, which specifically enumerates those powers granted to Congress, and the Commerce Clause—do not apply to trademarks. The first clause authorizes Congress "to promote the progress of science and useful arts," and Congress derives its power to regulate patents and copyrights by that clause, but trademarks differ from patents and copyrights, in that trademarks are neither scientific nor artistic. Trademarks are the adoption of something already in existence as the distinctive symbol of the party using it. They are not original, invented, discovered, scientific, or artistic, and are the result of accident rather than design. Therefore, the power to regulate trademarks cannot be inferred from the same clause that implies the power to regulate patents and copyright. In addition, because the legislation at issue was not limited to interstate transactions, Congress could not derive power to create it pursuant to the Commerce

Clause, the only other possible source of constitutional power to regulate trademarks.

▶ ANALYSIS

While not expressly stated in casebook excerpt, the Court expressly decided not to address the issue of whether trademarks relate to commerce in general terms, so as to bring it within congressional control.

■■■

Quicknotes

COMMERCE CLAUSE Article 1, Section 8, Clause 3 of the United States Constitution, granting Congress the power to regulate commerce with foreign countries and among the states.

INFRINGEMENT Conduct in violation of a statue or contract that interferes with another's rights pursuant to law.

■■■

Hanover Star Milling Co. v. Metcalf

Flour seller (P) v. Flour seller (D)

240 U.S. 403 (1916).

NATURE OF CASE: Appeal of dismissal of a trademark infringement action.

FACT SUMMARY: Hanover Star Milling Co. (D) used the same trademark as did Allen & Wheeler Co. (P), but in a different market area.

RULE OF LAW
A party is entitled to trademark protection only in the area in which his product is marketed.

FACTS: Hanover Star Milling Co. (Hanover) (D) employed a Tea Rose trademark. The use of the same mark by Allen & Wheeler Co. (P) antedated Hanover's (D) use thereof. Hanover (D) distributed its product, flour, in a wholly different market than did Allen & Wheeler Co. (P). The court of appeals held in favor of Hanover (D), and Allen & Wheeler Co. (P) sought certiorari.

ISSUE: Is a party entitled to trademark protection only in the area in which its product is marketed?

HOLDING AND DECISION: (Pitney, J.) Yes. A party is entitled to trademark protection only in the area in which its product is marketed. The purpose behind trade-marked protection is the assumption that a manufacturer or vendor has an important property interest in the goodwill of his business, and part of that goodwill is the mark with which the buying-public identifies his product. From this it follows that in an area where the mark is not identified in the public mind with the vendor's property, the purpose for protecting the vendor's trademark interest does not exist. Therefore, trademark protection cannot extend beyond a products area of distribution. Affirmed.

▶ ANALYSIS

Trademark law is relatively recent in origins. Patent and Copyright concepts predate the Constitution. Serious legal discussion of trademarks did not begin before the latter half of the 1800s in this country, and in England not long before. Trademark law is lumped together with patent and copyright law, but it does have features unique to itself, such as that discussed in the instant case.

■■■■

Quicknotes

TRADEMARK INFRINGEMENT The unauthorized use of another's trademark in such a manner as to cause a likelihood of confusion as to the source of the product or service in connection with which it is utilized.

■■■■

Stork Restaurant, Inc. v. Sahati et al.

New York club (P) v. San Francisco club (D)

166 F.2d 348 (9th Cir. 1948).

NATURE OF CASE: Petition for injunction.

FACT SUMMARY: Appellants (P), the owners of the famous "The Stork Club" in New York, sought to enjoin appellees (D), the owners of "The Stork Club" in San Francisco, from using its trade name. The lower court denied injunctive relief.

🏛 **RULE OF LAW**
The misleading of the public by the imitation of a trade name for the purpose of securing for the imitator some of the goodwill, advertising, and sales stimulation of the trade name is unlawful, even where there is no direct competition between the parties.

FACTS: Appellants (P), the owners of the famous "The Stork Club" at 3 East 53rd Street in New York City, spent millions through the years to advertise the club as one of the best in the world. Its patrons included celebrities, and it was featured in a movie. The club employs over 200 people, and has an annual gross income of more than $1 million. Appellees (D) opened a small bar called "The Stork Club" in San Francisco. It was a neighborhood tavern with ten stools and four employees. Appellants (P) sought to enjoin appellees (D) from using their trade name. The lower court denied injunctive relief.

ISSUE: Is the misleading of the public by the imitation of a trade name for the purpose of securing for the imitator some of the goodwill, advertising, and sales stimulation of the trade name unlawful, even where there is no direct competition between the parties?

HOLDING AND DECISION: (Garrecht, J.) Yes. The misleading of the public by the imitation of a trade name for the purpose of securing for the imitator some of the goodwill, advertising, and sales stimulation of the trade name is unlawful, even where there is no direct competition between the parties. This imitation is tantamount to "reaping where one has not sown," and neither the difference in the size of the operations nor the geographical distance between them, is sufficient to preclude the possibility that they might be confused, or thought to be related in some way. Further, while it may be true that a savvy traveler could not possibly confuse the two, one who is not world-wise might, and the law protects that person from deception. Finally, it is not necessary under California law for appellants (P) to show actual loss as a basis for an injunction. Appellants (P) merely want to prevent the dilution of the value of its purchased prestige. Reversed and remanded.

▶ **ANALYSIS**

The case clearly illustrates the concept of "dilution." The San Francisco bar's use of the trade name dilutes the goodwill that was bought by the New York operation through advertising, years of operation, world-renowned service, and all of the cost associated with it. The use of the name by another bar, however humble, borrows some of that goodwill, without having to pay for it, and injures the "source" through the dilution.

Quicknotes

TRADEMARK DILUTION The diminishment of the capability of a trademark to identify and distinguish the particular good or service with which it is associated.

Champion Spark Plug Co. v. Sanders

Spark plug manufacturer (P) v. Second hand spark plug dealer (D)

331 U.S. 125 (1947).

NATURE OF CASE: Petition of certiorari.

FACT SUMMARY: Sanders (D) reconditioned and resold spark plugs manufactured by Champion Spark Plug Co. (Champion) (P) without clearly indicating on the packaging that the plugs were reconditioned, and without removing Champion's (P) trademark.

🏛 RULE OF LAW
Equity does not necessarily require that a business that has infringed the trademark of another business refrain from further use of the trademark.

FACTS: Champion Spark Plug Co. (Champion) (P) manufactured spark plugs. The plugs were trademarked. Sanders (D) was in the business of reconditioning and reselling Champion (P) plugs, but Champion (P) was uninvolved with Sanders's (D) business, and Sanders (D) failed to clearly indicate on the packaging of the reconditioned plugs that the plugs were reconditioned, and failed to remove the Champion (P) trademark. In a suit by Champion (P), the trial court found that Sanders (D) had infringed the trademark but that there had been no fraud. It denied an accounting, but enjoined further infringement. The court of appeals affirmed, but contrary to the trial court, refused to require Sanders (D) to remove the Champion (P) trademark from the repaired or reconditioned plugs that they resell.

ISSUE: Does equity necessarily require that a business that has infringed the trademark of another business refrain from further use of the trademark?

HOLDING AND DECISION: (Douglas, J.) No. Equity does not necessarily require that a business that has infringed the trademark of another business refrain from further use of the trademark. Equity prohibits the use by a business of a trademark of another business. But the equities of this case are satisfied by a decree requiring that the word "repaired" or "used" be plainly and durably stamped on each plug, and that the packaging and literature used in connection with the sales clearly show that the plugs are used and reconditioned, and by whom, even though the decree does not require that the trademarks be removed. The second hand dealer gets some advantage from the trademark, but that is fine as long as the manufacturer is not identified with the inferior product.

▶ *ANALYSIS*

Clearly, requiring the second hand dealer to remove the Champion (P) trademark would be a more effective way to prevent confusion between the businesses. Disclosure might not be a fail-safe way of preventing confusion, because some purchasers of the refurbished plugs might not read the literature, and even if they do, could interpret the literature as stating that the plugs were reconditioned under the authority of Champion (P).

■■■

Quicknotes

TRADEMARK INFRINGEMENT The unauthorized use of another's trademark in such a manner as to cause a likelihood of confusion as to the source of the product or service in connection with which it is utilized.

■■■

CHAPTER 2

What Is a Trademark?

Quick Reference Rules of Law

1. *Kellogg Co. v. National Biscuit Co.* Sharing in the goodwill of an article unprotected by patent or trademark is the exercise of a right possessed by all. — 14

2. *Coca-Cola Co. v. Koke Co. of America.* The holder of a trademark does not lose all rights to claims in equity against infringement and unfair competition if the trademark in itself and the advertisements accompanying it make fraudulent representations to the public. — 15

3. *Peaceable Planet, Inc. v. Ty, Inc.* The rule that personal names are not protected as trademarks until they acquire secondary meaning is subject to exception where none of the purposes served by the rule is present, and application of the rule would impede rather than promote competition and consumer welfare. — 16

4. *Mishawaka Rubber & Woolen Manufacturing Co. v. S.S. Kresge Co.* To recover profits for trademark infringement, the trademark owner is not required to prove that the purchasers of goods bearing the infringing mark were induced by the infringing mark to believe that the goods were the goods of the trademark owner and purchased for that reason, and that they would otherwise have bought from the trademark owner. — 17

5. *Qualitex Co. v. Jacobson Products Co., Inc.* Color alone may be registered as a trademark. — 19

6. *TrafFix Devices, Inc. v. Marketing Displays, Inc.* An expired utility patent, determined to serve solely functional purposes, is not entitled to trademark protection. — 20

7. *Abercrombie & Fitch Co. v. Hunting World, Inc.* The extent to which trademark protection will be given depends on whether the term is generic, descriptive, suggestive, or arbitrary and/or fanciful. — 21

8. *In the Matter of the Application of Quik-Print Copy Shops, Inc.* A mark is merely descriptive if it immediately conveys to one seeing or hearing it knowledge of the ingredients, qualities, or characteristics of the goods or services with which it is used. — 22

9. *Zobmondo Entertainment, LLC v. Falls Media, LLC.* A mark is not "merely descriptive" as a matter of law where it reasonably may be inferred that a mental leap is required to understand the mark's relationship to the product, and where it reasonably may be inferred that competitors do not have to use the mark to fairly describe their goods or services. — 23

10. *Wal-Mart Stores, Inc. v. Samara Brothers, Inc.* An unregistered trade dress design under § 43 (a) of the Lanham Act, absent a showing of a secondary meaning, is not distinctive and, therefore, not protected from infringement. — 25

11. *American Waltham Watch Co. v. United States Watch Co.* A party may be enjoined from using the name of a geographic location on its product without some accompanying statement that clearly distinguishes the product from a product made by another party, whose name incorporates the name of the geographic location. — 26

12. *Board of Supervisors for Louisiana State University Agricultural and Mechanical College v. Smack Apparel Co.* An unregistered color scheme can receive trademark protection where the scheme has acquired secondary meaning. — 27

13. *Chrysler Group, LLC v. Moda Group, LLC.* A mark that is not inherently distinctive, and that has not acquired distinctiveness through a secondary meaning, is not entitled to trademark protection. — 29

Kellogg Co. v. National Biscuit Co.

Cereal company (D) v. Cereal company (P)

305 U.S. 111 (1938).

NATURE OF CASE: Appeal from decree enjoining unfair competition.

FACT SUMMARY: Kellogg Co. (D) appealed from a decree enjoining it from the manufacture and sale of the breakfast food known as "shredded wheat" under the name "Shredded Wheat," and from producing it in the same pillow-shaped form used by National Biscuit Co. (P).

🏛 RULE OF LAW
Sharing in the goodwill of an article unprotected by patent or trademark is the exercise of a right possessed by all.

FACTS: National Biscuit Co. (P) brought suit to enjoin unfair competition by the manufacture and sale of the breakfast food commonly known as "shredded wheat" by the Kellogg Co. (D) under the name "Shredded Wheat," and in the same pillow-shaped form as that used by National Biscuit Co. (P). Kellogg Co. (D) denied that National Biscuit Co. (P) was entitled to the exclusive use of the name or of the pillow shape; denied any passing off, as alleged by National Biscuit Co. (P); asserted that it had used every reasonable effort to distinguish its product from that of National Biscuit Co. (P), and contended that in honestly competing for a part of the market for shredded wheat it was exercising the common right freely to manufacture and sell an article of commerce unprotected by patent. Kellogg Co. (D) appealed the decree in favor of National Biscuit Co. (P).

ISSUE: Is sharing in the goodwill of an article unprotected by patent or trademark the exercise of a right possessed by all?

HOLDING AND DECISION: (Brandeis, J.) Yes. Sharing in the goodwill of an article unprotected by patent or trademark is the exercise of a right possessed by all. National Biscuit Co. (P) had no exclusive right to the use of the term "Shredded Wheat" as a trade name, for that is the generic term of the article, which describes it with a fair degree of accuracy and is the term by which the biscuit in pillow-shaped form is generally known by the public. The product was patented under the name "shredded wheat," and for many years there was no attempt to use the name as a trademark. Once the patent had expired, there passed to the public not only the right to make the article, but also to use the name by which it had become known. In addition, upon expiration of the patents, the pillow-shaped form was also dedicated to the public. There is no evidence of passing off or deception on the part of Kellogg Co. (D); and it has taken every reasonable precaution to prevent confusion or the practice of deception in the sale of its product. Reversed.

▶ ANALYSIS

In a portion of the *Kellogg* case not reported here, it is indicated that the National Biscuit Co. (P) claimed exclusive right to the name "Shredded Wheat" because it had "acquired the 'secondary meaning' of shredded wheat made by the plaintiff's predecessor." As indicated above, the Court found shredded wheat to be the "generic" term for the product. It would seem more difficult to establish a secondary meaning for a name like "shredded wheat," than for one like "Nu-Enamel." Although the *Armstrong Paint & Varnish* case, 305 U.S. 315 (1938), referred to "Nu-Enamel" as descriptive, the spelling "nu" is, at least, fanciful, and "new" enamel could, presumably, be distinguished from enamel that is "old." However, the words "shredded wheat," are the only ones which it is practical to use in describing the product; they in no way distinguish National Biscuit Co.'s (P) shredded wheat from that of Kellogg Co. (D).

■=■

Quicknotes

DESCRIPTIVE A descriptive mark has a dictionary meaning, or a meaning in common usage, that is used in connection with products or services directly related to, or suggestive of, that meaning. A descriptive mark is not entitled to trademark protection unless it has acquired distinctiveness over time.

GENERIC MEANING A term that encompasses a class of related products and lacks the requisite distinctiveness for federal trademark protection.

GOODWILL An intangible asset reflecting a corporation's favor with the public and expectation of continued patronage.

■=■

Coca-Cola Co. v. Koke Co. of America

Soda manufacturer (P) v. Soda manufacturer (D)

254 U.S. 143 (1920).

NATURE OF CASE: Grant of writ of certiorari.

FACT SUMMARY: Coca-Cola Company (P) sought an injunction against Koke Co. of America (D) to prevent infringement of its trademark Coca-Cola and unfair competition in selling soda. The district court granted the decree, and the court of appeals reversed.

🏛 RULE OF LAW
The holder of a trademark does not lose all rights to claims in equity against infringement and unfair competition if the trademark in itself and the advertisements accompanying it make fraudulent representations to the public.

FACTS: Before 1900, some of Coca-Cola Co.'s (Coca-Cola's) (P) goodwill was helped by the presence in the product's recipe of cocaine. It was eliminated from the recipe in 1906, and Coca-Cola (P) advertised extensively regarding the elimination of the chemical from the drink. Koke Co. of America (Koke) (D) later made and sold an imitation of Coca-Cola's (P) product. Koke (D) chose the name "Koke" in order to benefit from the success achieved by Coca-Cola (P) from the marketing and sales of its soft drink. The court of appeals found that the Coca-Cola trademark and the company's advertising of the trademark fraudulently represented to the public that the Coca-Cola soft drink contained cocaine, and because of that fraud, the company lost its claim to help from the courts.

ISSUE: Does the holder of a trademark lose all rights to claims in equity against infringement and unfair competition if the trademark in itself and the advertisements accompanying it make fraudulent representations to the public?

HOLDING AND DECISION: (Holmes, J.) No. The holder of a trademark does not lose all rights to claims in equity against infringement and unfair competition if the trademark in itself and the advertisements accompanying it make fraudulent representations to the public. The name Coca-Cola now indicates to most people the soft drink, not the elements contained in the recipe. It has taken on a secondary meaning in which the product is more emphasized than the producer. Before this suit was brought, Coca-Cola (P) had advertised to the public that it should not expect cocaine in the product, and that it did not exist in the product. The public is therefore not at significant risk of being defrauded, and because Coca-Cola's (P) position must be judged on facts as they were when the suit began, and not by the facts of an earlier time, it would be going too far to deny it relief on the basis of fraud.

▶ ANALYSIS

This case illustrates that the scope of protection afforded a word mark that has been used by its owner for decades is broad. Whatever benefit Coca-Cola Co. (P) received from the public's belief that the product contained cocaine, if any part of the public did so believe, became largely irrelevant in the Court's analysis, because the trademark had acquired over time a secondary meaning.

◼◼◼

Quicknotes

FRAUDULENT MISREPRESENTATION A statement or conduct by one party to another that constitutes a false representation of fact.

SECONDARY MEANING A word or mark that becomes associated with a particular merchant or product as its source of origin.

TRADEMARK Any word, name, symbol, device or combination thereof that is either currently utilized, or which a person has a bona fide intent to utilize, in commerce in order to distinguish his goods from those of another.

TRADEMARK INFRINGEMENT The unauthorized use of another's trademark in such a manner as to cause a likelihood of confusion as to the source of the product or service in connection with which it is utilized.

◼◼◼

Peaceable Planet, Inc. v. Ty, Inc.

Toy manufacturer (P) v. Toy manufacturer (D)

362 F.3d 986 (7th Cir. 2004).

NATURE OF CASE: Appeal of district court judgment.

FACT SUMMARY: Peaceable Planet, Inc. (P) manufactured and sold stuffed camels named "Niles." The company sold a few thousand camels. A year later, Ty, Inc. (D), which is a much more successful toy manufacturer, also began selling a camel named "Niles." Ty (D) sold almost two million in one year. Peaceable Planet (P) sued Ty (D).

🏛 RULE OF LAW
The rule that personal names are not protected as trademarks until they acquire secondary meaning is subject to exception where none of the purposes served by the rule is present, and application of the rule would impede rather than promote competition and consumer welfare.

FACTS: Ty, Inc. (D) makes stuffed toys shaped like animals, the most recognizable of which are known as "Beanie Babies." Peaceable Planet, Inc. (P) also makes stuffed toys in the shapes of animals, but with much less success than Ty (D). In 1999, Peaceable Planet (P) began selling a camel named "Niles," and it was packaged with information about camels and Egypt. The company sold a few thousand camels in that year. In 2000, Ty (D) began selling a camel, also named "Niles." Ty (D) sold almost two million in one year. The district court found that "Niles," a personal name, is a descriptive mark that the law does not protect without a secondary meaning, and that Peaceable Planet (P) failed to prove that consumers associated the name "Niles" with its camel.

ISSUE: Is the rule that personal names are not protected as trademarks until they acquire secondary meaning subject to exception where none of the purposes served by the rule is present, and application of the rule would impede rather than promote competition and consumer welfare?

HOLDING AND DECISION: (Posner, J.) Yes. The rule that personal names are not protected as trademarks until they acquire secondary meaning is subject to exception where none of the purposes served by the rule is present, and application of the rule would impede rather than promote competition and consumer welfare. The reasons for not protecting personal names in certain situations are distinct from the reasons for not protecting descriptive terms. Personal names generally are not protected for three reasons. First, the rule is designed to allow people to use their names in conjunction with their business. Second, the rule contemplates that some names are so common that consumers will not assume that two businesses with the same name are related simply because they share the same name, thereby avoiding the possibility of confusing the consumer. Finally, preventing someone from using his name to identify his business would deprive consumers of useful information. In this case, (1) "Niles" is not the Ty's (D) name, (2) "Niles" is a very uncommon name, and (3) consumers would not be deprived of information if Ty (D) had to choose another name for its camel. Therefore, Peaceable Planet (P) held a valid trademark in the name "Niles." The district court's judgment that "Niles," being a personal name, is a descriptive mark that the law does not protect unless and until it has acquired secondary meaning is reversed.

▶ ANALYSIS

This case draws a distinction between personal names and descriptive terms, and that distinction is based on the purpose for the rule: The Seventh Circuit's holding is based on the premise that the reasoning for not protecting personal names in some circumstances is entirely distinct from the reasoning for not protecting descriptive terms.

■=■

Quicknotes

DESCRIPTIVE A descriptive mark has a dictionary meaning, or a meaning in common usage, that is used in connection with products or services directly related to, or suggestive of, that meaning. A descriptive mark is not entitled to trademark protection unless it has acquired distinctiveness over time.

SECONDARY MEANING A word or mark that becomes associated with a particular merchant or product as its source of origin.

TRADEMARK Any word, name, symbol, device or combination thereof that is either currently utilized, or which a person has a bona fide intent to utilize, in commerce in order to distinguish his goods from those of another.

■=■

Mishawaka Rubber & Woolen Manufacturing Co. v. S.S. Kresge Co.

Shoe and rubber heel manufacturer (P) v. Seller of rubber heels (D)

316 U.S. 203 (1942).

NATURE OF CASE: Appeal from order directing trademark infringer to account for trademark holder's lost profits.

FACT SUMMARY: Mishawaka Rubber & Woolen Manufacturing Co. (Mishawaka) (petitioner) (P) obtained a judgment that S.S. Kresge Co. (Kresge) (respondent) (D) had infringed its trademark in a red circular plug that it placed in the rubber heels of shoes it manufactured. The lower courts ordered Kresge (D) to account to Mishawaka (P) for lost profits improperly accrued to Kresge (D) by reason of the infringement. Mishawaka (P) contended that its entitlement to such lost profits should not be limited to only those profits that it could affirmatively prove to have resulted from sales to purchasers that were induced to buy because they thought they were buying Mishawaka's (P) product and which sales Mishawaka (P) would have otherwise made.

🏛 RULE OF LAW
To recover profits for trademark infringement, the trademark owner is not required to prove that the purchasers of goods bearing the infringing mark were induced by the infringing mark to believe that the goods were the goods of the trademark owner and purchased for that reason, and that they would otherwise have bought from the trademark owner.

FACTS: Mishawaka Rubber & Woolen Manufacturing Co. (Mishawaka) (petitioner) (P) manufactured and sold shoes with rubber heels that had a circular red plug in them. Mishawaka (P) held a trademark in the red plug. S.S. Kresge Co. (Kresge) (respondent) (D) sold rubber heels of inferior quality to those made by Mishawaka (P). Some of those heels contained a red plug that the trial court found infringed Mishawaka's (P) trademark. However, there was no evidence that particular purchasers were actually deceived into believing that the heels sold by Kresge (D) were manufactured by Mishawaka (P). The trial court enjoined further infringement and ordered Kresge (D) to account to Mishawaka (P) for lost profits from sales "to purchasers who were induced to buy because they believed the heels to be those of plaintiff and which sales plaintiff would otherwise have made." Mishawaka (P) appealed, contending that this was the wrong standard for determining the profits that improperly accrued to Kresge (D) by reason of the infringement, as it incorrectly placed the burden on the trademark holder to prove its lost profits. The United States Supreme Court granted certiorari.

ISSUE: To recover profits for trademark infringement, is the trademark owner required to prove that the purchasers of

goods bearing the infringing mark were induced by the infringing mark to believe that the goods were the goods of the trademark owner and purchased for that reason, and that they would otherwise have bought from the trademark owner?

HOLDING AND DECISION: (Frankfurter, J.) No. To recover profits for trademark infringement, the trademark owner is not required to prove that the purchasers of goods bearing the infringing mark were induced by the infringing mark to believe that the goods were the goods of the trademark owner and purchased for that reason, and that they would otherwise have bought from the trademark owner. Once infringement has been proved, the burden is on the infringer to show that the infringement had no relation to his profits and had no cash value in sales made by him. Although the trademark owner is not entitled to profits that demonstrably did not occur as a result of infringement, where the infringer cannot show that the infringement had no cash value, the trademark owner is entitled to profits from the sale by the infringer of infringing goods. Although this standard may result in a windfall to the trademark holder where it is impossible to isolate the profits that are attributable to the infringing mark, to hold otherwise would potentially give the infringer a windfall. In such instances, it promotes honesty and comports with experience to assume that the infringer's profits from the sales of goods bearing the owner's mark resulted from the good will generated by that mark. [Reversed.]

▶ ANALYSIS

A dissent by Justice Black argued that in a case such as this, where there was no evidence of actual confusion by buyers, and there was no intent to fraudulently deceive, an injunction prohibiting further infringement was sufficient. Justice Black also argued that, under such circumstances, the majority's decision granted a windfall to Mishawaka (P) imposed a penalty on Kresge (D), neither of which were deserved nor justified by the Trademark Act.

Quicknotes

TRADEMARK Any word, name, symbol, device or combination thereof that is either currently utilized, or which a person has a bona fide intent to utilize, in commerce in order to distinguish his goods from those of another.

Continued on next page.

TRADEMARK INFRINGEMENT The unauthorized use of another's trademark in such a manner as to cause a likelihood of confusion as to the source of the product or service in connection with which it is utilized.

■═■

Qualitex Co. v. Jacobson Products Co., Inc.

Dry cleaning tool manufacturer (P) v. Dry cleaning tool manufacturer (D)

514 U.S. 159 (1995).

NATURE OF CASE: Appeal from judgment setting aside lower court determination of trademark infringement.

FACT SUMMARY: After Qualitex Co. (P) used greengold to color its pads for dry cleaning presses for 30 years, Jacobson Products Co., Inc. (Jacobson) (D) imitated the color on its pads, causing Qualitex (P) to register the color as its trademark and sue Jacobson (D) for infringement.

 RULE OF LAW
Color alone may be registered as a trademark.

FACTS: Qualitex Co. (P) sold green-gold pads for dry cleaning presses since the 1950s. In 1989, Jacobson Products Co., Inc. (Jacobson) (D), a rival of Qualitex (P), began selling similarly colored pads. In 1991, Qualitex (P) registered the green-gold color on press pads with the Patent and Trademark Office as a trademark and sued Jacobson (D) for infringement and unfair competition. Qualitex's (P) victory in district court was reversed by the Ninth Circuit because it held that the Lanham Act does not permit color alone to be a registered trademark. Because other circuit courts have allowed color trademarks (notably Owens-Corning's pink fiberglass), the United States Supreme Court granted certiorari.

ISSUE: Can color alone be registered as a trademark?

HOLDING AND DECISION: (Breyer, J.) Yes. Color alone may be registered as a trademark. The Lanham Act permits trademarks using words, names, symbols, devices or combinations thereof. Courts and the Patent Trademark Office have authorized shapes (Coca-Cola bottle), sounds (NBC's three chimes) and even smells (plumeria blossoms on sewing thread). Color is qualitatively no different and serves to identify and distinguish one source of goods from another just as well. Color does have the difficulty of being descriptive and thus unable to qualify as a mark without secondary meaning. But when the public identifies the feature with its source, such as Owens-Corning's pink fiberglass, a trademark is permissible. The functionality doctrine is not an obstacle here either because the color performs no nontrademark function. If it did, the province of patent would rule, and the perpetual nature of trademarks would deter advances in design and functionality. But here, the color does not put competitors at a disadvantage; it is just a color. Reversed.

▶ ANALYSIS

This case simply expands the scope of the Lanham Act protection to cover color, but it must pass muster under descriptive term analysis nevertheless. The case was reversed, but remanded to determine whether the color has acquired a secondary meaning.

■==■

Quicknotes

DESCRIPTIVE A descriptive mark has a dictionary meaning, or a meaning in common usage, that is used in connection with products or services directly related to, or suggestive of, that meaning. A descriptive mark is not entitled to trademark protection unless it has acquired distinctiveness over time.

LANHAM ACT Name of the Trademark Act of 1946 that governs federal law regarding trademarks.

SECONDARY MEANING A word or mark that becomes associated with a particular merchant or product as its source of origin.

TRADEMARK Any word, name, symbol, device or combination thereof that is either currently utilized, or which a person has a bona fide intent to utilize, in commerce in order to distinguish his goods from those of another.

TRADEMARK INFRINGEMENT The unauthorized use of another's trademark in such a manner as to cause a likelihood of confusion as to the source of the product or service in connection with which it is utilized.

■==■

TrafFix Devices, Inc. v. Marketing Displays, Inc.

Competitor (D) v. Road sign manufacturer (P)

532 U.S. 23 (2001).

NATURE OF CASE: Trade dress infringement.

FACT SUMMARY: Marketing Displays, Inc. (P) sued TrafFix Devices, Inc. (D) for trade dress infringement of a dual-spring mechanism designed to allow temporary road signs to remain standing in high gusts of wind.

> 🏛 **RULE OF LAW**
> An expired utility patent, determined to serve solely functional purposes, is not entitled to trademark protection.

FACTS: Robert Sarkinsian, an inventor, designed a dual-spring mechanism to attach to temporary road signs (e.g., "Road Work Ahead") so they would remain upright in high gusts of wind. He secured two utility patents for the design. Marketing Displays, Inc. (MDI) (P) obtained the patents and had a successful business manufacturing and selling road signs that utilized the dual-spring design under the name "WindMaster." Once the patents expired, TrafFix Devices, Inc. (TrafFix) (D) began selling road signs that incorporated a similar dual-spring mechanism under the name "Wind-Buster." MDI (P) sued TrafFix (D) for trade dress infringement. The district court found for TrafFix (D) and the court of appeals reversed. The United States Supreme Court granted certiorari.

ISSUE: Is the holder of an expired utility patent that is determined to be solely functional in nature entitled to trademark protection?

HOLDING AND DECISION: (Kennedy, J.) No. The holder of an expired patent that is determined to be solely functional in nature is not entitled to trademark protection. Under trade dress law, a "design or packaging of a product may acquire a distinctiveness which serves to identify the product with its manufacturer or source; and a design or package which acquires this secondary meaning, assuming other requisites are met, is a trade dress which may not be used in a manner likely to cause confusion as to the origin, sponsorship, or approval of the goods." Trade dress protection, however, may not prohibit the copying of goods and products, unless an intellectual property right protects those items. Here, the patent had expired. Where a trade dress patent has expired, the person who seeks to re-establish the patent must demonstrate that the feature of the patent in question is not solely functional by showing "that it is merely an ornamental, incidental, or arbitrary aspect of the device." The dual-spring design's main purpose is to keep the sign standing upright in heavy winds. This purpose was specifically stated in the patent applica-

tion. Further, the design is essential to the use of those specific road signs. Therefore, the design is decidedly functional. Due to its functionality, competitors do not need to significantly alter or hide the dual-spring design. The court of appeals decision is reversed and remanded.

▶ *ANALYSIS*

The Court has stated that copying is not always prevented or discouraged in the interest of promoting competition. When competitors are allowed to copy certain products, it not only promotes competition, but can also lead to modifications that promote advances in technology or goods.

∎≡∎

Quicknotes

TRADE DRESS The overall image of, or impression created by, a product that a court may enforce as a trademark if it determines that such image has acquired secondary meaning and that the public recognizes it as an indication of source.

TRADEMARK Any word, name, symbol, device or combination thereof that is either currently utilized, or which a person has a bona fide intent to utilize, in commerce in order to distinguish his goods from those of another.

PATENT A limited monopoly conferred on the invention or discovery of any new or useful machine or process that is novel and nonobvious.

∎≡∎

Abercrombie & Fitch Co. v. Hunting World, Inc.

Apparel merchant (P) v. Apparel merchant (D)

537 F.2d 4 (2d Cir. 1976).

NATURE OF CASE: Appeal of judgment canceling certain trademark registrations.

FACT SUMMARY: Abercrombie & Fitch Co. (P) sued Hunting World, Inc. (D) for infringement of several of its safari-related trademarks, but the court dismissed the complaint and canceled the trademark registrations.

RULE OF LAW
The extent to which trademark protection will be given depends on whether the term is generic, descriptive, suggestive, or arbitrary and/or fanciful.

FACTS: Abercrombie & Fitch Co. (A&F) (P) put out a line of safari-related apparel. Hunting World (D) also retailed safari-type clothing. A&F (P) brought an action to enjoin the use of some of the terms used by Hunting World (D) as violative of A&F's (P) trademarks. These included descriptions of boots, hats, and various other types of clothing. The district court not only dismissed the complaint, it canceled A&F's (P) trademarks. A&F (P) appealed.

ISSUE: Will the extent to which trademark protection is given depend on whether the term is generic, descriptive, suggestive, or arbitrary and/or fanciful?

HOLDING AND DECISION: (Friendly, J.) Yes. The extent to which trademark protection will be given depends on whether the term is generic, descriptive, suggestive, or arbitrary and/or fanciful. Court decisions and legislative enactments have created these four categories, although in any case, classification may be quite difficult. Generic descriptions can never be given trademark status, although arbitrary and/or fanciful names may always receive protection. Descriptive terms may be given trademark status only to the extent the description has become identified in the public mind with a particular product. The "suggestive" category, which allows greater trademark protection, is a somewhat vaguely defined class. A term is suggestive if it requires thought or imagination on the part of the individual perceiving the term.

▌ ANALYSIS

For the most part, a descriptive term cannot be given trademark status. The law does not permit one to prevent others from describing the goods they sell. It is for this reason that terms that are products of pure invention are best suited for trademark status, although if they become too successful, they run the risk of transforming into generic terms, the classic example being "aspirin," originally a brand name.

■══■

Quicknotes

DESCRIPTIVE A descriptive mark has a dictionary meaning, or a meaning in common usage, that is used in connection with products or services directly related to, or suggestive of, that meaning. A descriptive mark is not entitled to trademark protection unless it has acquired distinctiveness over time.

GENERIC MEANING A term that encompasses a class of related products and lacks the requisite distinctiveness for federal trademark protection.

■══■

In the Matter of the Application of Quik-Print Copy Shops, Inc.

Printer (P) v. Trademark board of registration (D)

616 F.2d 523 (C.C.P.A. 1980).

NATURE OF CASE: Appeal of denial of trademark registration.

FACT SUMMARY: The board of registration refused to register Quik-Print Copy Shops' (Quik-Print's) (P) name as a trademark, on grounds that the name of the shops were merely descriptive. Quik-Print (P) appealed.

🏛 RULE OF LAW
A mark is merely descriptive if it immediately conveys to one seeing or hearing it knowledge of the ingredients, qualities, or characteristics of the goods or services with which it is used.

FACTS: The board of registration refused to register Quik-Print Copy Shops' (Quik-Print's) (P) name as a trademark, on grounds that the name of the shops were merely descriptive. The board found that "Quik-Print" is equivalent to "Quick-Print," and that the simple definition of the latter, together with the company's advertising materials emphasize "same day service," indicate that the term is descriptive only. Quik-Print (P) appealed.

ISSUE: Is a mark merely descriptive if it immediately conveys to one seeing or hearing it knowledge of the ingredients, qualities, or characteristics of the goods or services with which it is used?

HOLDING AND DECISION: (Miller, J.) Yes. A mark is merely descriptive if it immediately conveys to one seeing or hearing it knowledge of the ingredients, qualities, or characteristics of the goods or services with which it is used. Registration under the Lanham Act will be denied if a mark is merely descriptive of any of the goods or services for which registration is sought. The term "Quik" describes one of the qualities or characteristics of the service provided by Quik-Print (P), namely the speed with which it is done. This characteristic comes immediately to mind, and the board's decision is affirmed.

▶ ANALYSIS

Even assuming that the term "Quik-Print" is suggestive, arbitrary, or fanciful for argument's sake, it still is descriptive only. There is no secondary meaning where the spelling of the words is simply modified, but there is no secondary meaning of the term beyond its obvious meaning.

Quicknotes

DESCRIPTIVE A descriptive mark has a dictionary meaning, or a meaning in common usage, that is used in connection with products or services directly related to, or suggestive of, that meaning. A descriptive mark is not entitled to trademark protection unless it has acquired distinctiveness over time.

SECONDARY MEANING A word or mark that becomes associated with a particular merchant or product as its source of origin.

Zobmondo Entertainment, LLC v. Falls Media, LLC

Board games publisher (P) v. Books and board games publisher (D)

602 F.3d 1108 (9th Cir. 2010).

NATURE OF CASE: Appeal from summary judgment denying a trademark infringement action and related claims.

FACT SUMMARY: Falls Media, LLC (D) contended that its registered trademark, "WOULD YOU RATHER . . . ?," was not merely descriptive, so that the trademark infringement claims it brought (in response to a suit initiated by Zobmondo Entertainment, LLC (P)) should not have been dismissed on summary judgment.

🏛 RULE OF LAW

A mark is not "merely descriptive" as a matter of law where it reasonably may be inferred that a mental leap is required to understand the mark's relationship to the product, and where it reasonably may be inferred that competitors do not have to use the mark to fairly describe their goods or services.

FACTS: Falls Media, LLC (Falls Media) (D) first used the mark "WOULD YOU RATHER . . . ?" in connection with books it published and with a website it used to promote those books. Five years later, Zobmondo Entertainment, LLC (Zobmondo) (P) used the mark on a board game it published. The books incorporated questions posing humorous, bizarre, or undesirable choices. When Falls Media (D) introduced a "Would You Rather?" board game, Zobmondo (P) filed a trademark suit, and then Falls Media (D) brought a trademark infringement action and related claims against Zobmondo (P). The cases were consolidated, and the parties filed cross-motions for summary judgment. The district court granted Zobmondo's (P) motion on the infringement claims, on the ground that the mark, "WOULD YOU RATHER . . . ?" was merely descriptive and lacked secondary meaning. Falls Media (D) appealed, contending it had raised genuine issues of material fact as to whether its mark was suggestive and deserving of trademark protection. The court of appeals granted review.

ISSUE: Is a mark "merely descriptive" as a matter of law where it reasonably may be inferred that a mental leap is required to understand the mark's relationship to the product, and where it reasonably may be inferred that competitors do not have to use the mark to fairly describe their goods or services?

HOLDING AND DECISION: (Gould, J.) No. A mark is not "merely descriptive" as a matter of law where it reasonably may be inferred that a mental leap is required to understand the mark's relationship to the product, and where it reasonably may be inferred that competitors do

not have to use the mark to fairly describe their goods or services. In general, two tests are used to determine whether a mark is suggestive or merely descriptive. The first test, known as the "imagination" test, asks whether "imagination or a mental leap is required in order to reach a conclusion as to the nature of the product being referenced." Here, the district court determined that under this test, no imagination or interpretive leap is necessary to understand that the phrase "WOULD YOU RATHER . . . ?" is the main aspect of the product to which it is affixed. Here, there is no literal meaning of the phrase, as the words precede an ellipse, so that it may be inferred that there is a question, but only imagination can inform a buyer that that question will serve up a bizarre or humorous choice. On the one hand, consumers who already understand the phrase "WOULD YOU RATHER . . . ?" to refer specifically to a game of questions involving bizarre or humorous choices might not consider the mark very suggestive as the name of a board game, but to consumers who do not share such an understanding, "WOULD YOU RATHER . . . ?" is simply the first three words of an open-ended question. For those consumers, the mark "WOULD YOU RATHER . . . ?" may not "describe" anything, except that a question is asked, and may indeed require imagination and multistage reasoning to understand the mark's relationship to the game to which it is affixed. Because all reasonable inferences must be made in Falls Media's (D) favor, the imagination test by itself is thus inconclusive to determine whether the challenged mark is suggestive or merely descriptive. The second common test for determining whether a mark is suggestive or merely descriptive, known as the "competitors' needs" test, focuses on the extent to which a mark is actually needed by competitors to identify their goods or services. If competitors have means of describing their products or services other than solely through use of the mark, this tends to indicate that the mark is merely suggestive. Here, the district court erred in failing to consider this test—which, it turns out, strongly favors Falls Media's (D) argument that "WOULD YOU RATHER . . . ?" is suggestive. Sufficient evidence was presented that its competitors do not need to use that phrase to fairly describe their products, and that there are alternative linguistic phrasings that can adequately do so. In fact, Zobmondo (P) itself identified 135 possible alternative names for its game during development. Because giving all reasonable inferences to Falls Media (D) raises a genuine issue of material fact under both the imagination test and the competitors' needs test as to whether

Continued on next page.

"WOULD YOU RATHER . . . ?" is suggestive or merely descriptive, the issue must be resolved at trial. [Reversed and remanded.]

▶ *ANALYSIS*

A third test used in determining whether a mark is suggestive or merely descriptive, known as the "extent-of-use" test, evaluates the extent to which other sellers in a similar commercial context have used the mark on similar merchandise or for a commercial service. As with the other tests used in this case—the imagination test and the competitors' needs test—this test merely presents criteria that offer guidance as to whether the mark is suggestive. No one test by itself is a controlling measure of trademark validity. Thus, for example, whether a summary judgment is disfavored by both the imagination test and the needs test, then extent of use at most could only be one factor to be considered, and could not command a summary judgment in the face of disputed facts about how a mark might be perceived by consumers.

■━━■

Quicknotes

DESCRIPTIVE A descriptive mark has a dictionary meaning, or a meaning in common usage, that is used in connection with products or services directly related to, or suggestive of, that meaning. A descriptive mark is not entitled to trademark protection unless it has acquired distinctiveness over time.

SUMMARY JUDGMENT Judgment rendered by a court in response to a motion made by one of the parties, claiming that the lack of a question of material fact in respect to an issue warrants disposition of the issue without consideration by the jury.

TRADEMARK Any word, name, symbol, device or combination thereof that is either currently utilized, or which a person has a bona fide intent to utilize, in commerce in order to distinguish his goods from those of another.

TRADEMARK INFRINGEMENT The unauthorized use of another's trademark in such a manner as to cause a likelihood of confusion as to the source of the product or service in connection with which it is utilized.

■━━■

Wal-Mart Stores, Inc. v. Samara Brothers, Inc.

Retailer (D) v. Clothing manufacturer (P)

529 U.S. 205 (2000).

NATURE OF CASE: Trade dress infringement.

FACT SUMMARY: Samara Brothers, Inc. (P) sued Wal-Mart Stores, Inc. (D) for, among other causes of action, infringement of an unregistered trade dress design under the Trademark Act of 1946.

🏛 RULE OF LAW
An unregistered trade dress design under § 43(a) of the Lanham Act, absent a showing of a secondary meaning, is not distinctive and, therefore, not protected from infringement.

FACTS: Samara Brothers, Inc. (Samara) (P) is a designer and manufacturer of children's clothes, its primary product being spring and summer one-piece seersucker clothes. Various stores sell this line of clothes. Wal-Mart Stores, Inc. (Wal-Mart) (D) is one of the largest and most well-known retailers in the United States. Wal-Mart (D) contracted with Judy-Philippine, Inc. (J-P), one of its suppliers, to manufacture a line of spring and summer children's clothes, sending J-P photographs of several of Samara's (P) garments upon which J-P was to base the clothes for Wal-Mart (D). J-P then copied, with minor modifications, 16 of Samara's (P) garments, many of which contained elements that were copyrighted. Wal-Mart (D) sold J-P's garments and earned over $1.5 million in gross profits from those sales. Samara (P) sent cease-and-desist letters to Wal-Mart (D), finally bringing suit for copyright infringement.

ISSUE: In an action for trademark infringement of an unregistered trade dress is a product's design, in and of itself, distinctive and therefore protected under § 43(a) of the Lanham Act?

HOLDING AND DECISION: (Scalia, J) No. In an action for trademark-infringement of an unregistered trade dress, a product's design, in and of itself, is not distinctive and is, therefore, not protected under § 43(a) of the Lanham Act. The relevant portion of § 43(a) gives a producer "a cause of action for the use by any person of 'any word, term, name, symbol, or device, or any combination there-of ... which ... is likely to cause confusion ... as to the origin, sponsorship, or approval of his or her goods ... '" 15 U.S.C. § 1125(a). Courts, in interpreting this section, have required a producer to demonstrate that a trade dress mark is distinctive. The producer can show distinctiveness in one of two ways: (1) that the mark's intrinsic nature identifies the mark as being from a particular source or (2) that in the minds of the general public, the mark has attained distinctiveness. This court has held that in regard to one category of a trademark—color—there is no inherent distinctness, so color could only be protected if the producer showed that the color had a secondary meaning. Here, Samara's (P) product design can be equated to color and, therefore, a consumer is not predisposed to equate the product design feature with Samara (P). As such, in an infringement of an unregistered trade dress suit, under § 43(a) of the Lanham Act, a product's design is only distinctive and protected if the producer can demonstrate that a secondary meaning is attached to that product. Samara (P) never adequately demonstrated any distinctiveness attributable to its children's clothing line. Reversed and remanded.

▶ ANALYSIS

In this ruling, the Court desired to avoid lower courts having to evaluate differences with product design or product packaging, which are sometimes difficult to ascertain. In short, the Court wanted to avoid a ruling that would encourage a "slippery slope" analysis when deciding if certain products are inherently distinctive.

■=■

Quicknotes

LANHAM ACT § 43(a) Federal trademark infringement statute.

TRADE DRESS The overall image of, or impression created by, a product that a court may enforce as a trademark if it determines that such image has acquired secondary meaning and that the public recognizes it as an indication of source.

■=■

American Waltham Watch Co. v. United States Watch Co.

Watchmaker (P) v. Watchmaker (D)

173 Mass. 85 (Mass. 1899).

NATURE OF CASE: Bill in equity for an injunction.

FACT SUMMARY: American Waltham Watch Co. (P) sought to enjoin United States Watch Co. (D) from conspicuously including the word "Waltham" on its watches. The trial court granted the injunction.

RULE OF LAW
A party may be enjoined from using the name of a geographic location on its product without some accompanying statement that clearly distinguishes the product from a product made by another party, whose name incorporates the name of the geographic location.

FACTS: American Waltham Watch Co. (P) sought to enjoin United States Watch Co. (D) from conspicuously including the word "Waltham" on its watches. Both parties made watches in Waltham, Massachusetts, and indicating the location of manufacture was considered to be commercially important by watchmakers. United States Watch Co. (D) did not want to include the word "Waltham" as part of its name, or as part of the name of its products, but wanted to indicate that its watches were made in Waltham, Massachusetts, without also including words to distinguish its watches from American Waltham Watch Co. (P) in the minds of the general public. The trial judge granted the injunction, and United States Watch Co. (D) appealed.

ISSUE: May a party be enjoined from using the name of a geographic location on its product without some accompanying statement that clearly distinguishes the product from a product made by another party, whose name incorporates the name of the geographic location?

HOLDING AND DECISION: (Holmes, J.) Yes. A party may be enjoined from using the name of a geographic location on its product without some accompanying statement that clearly distinguishes the product from a product made by another party, whose name incorporates the name of the geographic location. The arguments of both parties have merit. American Waltham Watch Co. (P) should not lose sales or goodwill by reason of a mistake in the mind of the consumer caused by United States Watch Co. (D). On the other hand, United States Watch Co. (D) should be able to tell the world that it makes watches in Waltham, Massachusetts, and while a person or company cannot generally appropriate a geographical name, the word "Waltham" as used in the name "American Waltham Watch Co." has become so closely associated with the American Waltham Watch Co. (P) product that American Waltham Watch Co. (P) is entitled to have United States Watch Co. (D) take reasonable precautions as are commercially practicable to prevent consumer confusion.

► ANALYSIS

The Court was careful to state that this was a "specific and concrete" question, which indicates that it meant not to create a general rule of law. Today, a party is generally allowed to include on its product the location of manufacture, without having to worry about trademark infringement.

■=■

Quicknotes

BILL IN EQUITY First pleading in a lawsuit in which a plaintiff seeks equitable remedies.

GOODWILL An intangible asset reflecting a corporation's favor with the public and expectation of continued patronage.

■=■

Board of Supervisors for Louisiana State University Agricultural and Mechanical College v. Smack Apparel Co.

University (P) v. Apparel company (D)

550 F.3d 465 (5th Cir. 2008).

NATURE OF CASE: Appeal from summary judgment for plaintiffs in trademark infringement action.

FACT SUMMARY: Smack Apparel Co. (Smack) (D) contended that four universities (Universities) (P) did not have protectible unregistered trademarks in their respective school color schemes, and that those color schemes had not acquired secondary meaning, so that it was error to grant summary judgment to the Universities (P) on their trademark infringement claims against Smack (D) for its use of those color schemes on t-shirts that referenced the respective Universities' (D) football games and championships.

RULE OF LAW
An unregistered color scheme can receive trademark protection where the scheme has acquired secondary meaning.

FACTS: Four universities (Universities) (P) brought a trademark infringement action against Smack Apparel Co. (Smack) (D), alleging that Smack (D) had violated their trademark rights in the school color schemes by using those schemes on t-shirts that also referenced the respective Universities' (D) football games and championships. Each of the Universities (P) used a distinct two-color scheme as its school colors, and had used its particular color scheme for over a hundred years in numerous areas associated with university life, including in connection with their athletic programs, particularly on team uniforms, resulting in wide-spread recognition of the colors among college sports fans. Each university operated a successful collegiate football program, and their football teams had made appearances on nationally televised football games viewed by millions of people. The Universities (P) granted licenses for retail sales of products, including t-shirts, that bore the university colors and trademarks. Collectively, the Universities (P) generated around $93 million annually in sales of such products. The Universities (P) did not, however, own registered trademarks in their color schemes. Smack (D) manufactured t-shirts targeted toward fans of college sports teams, and it used school colors and printed messages associated with the Universities (P) on its shirts. Smack's (D) shirts frequently appeared alongside those that had been officially licensed by the Universities (P). The district court granted summary judgment to the Universities (P) for trademark infringement. Smack (D) appealed, contending that the color schemes had not acquired secondary meaning, and,

therefore, were not trademark-protectible. The court of appeals granted review.

ISSUE: Can an unregistered color scheme receive trademark protection where the scheme has acquired secondary meaning?

HOLDING AND DECISION: (Reavley, J.) Yes. An unregistered color scheme can receive trademark protection where the scheme has acquired secondary meaning. The color schemes at issue are descriptive marks, which are protectible if they have acquired secondary meaning and are nonfunctional. The Universities (P) do not claim that every instance in which their school colors appear violates their respective trademarks. Instead, the claimed trademark is in the colors on merchandise that combines other identifying indicia referring to the Universities (P). Therefore, it is appropriate to consider not only the color but also the entire context in which the color and other indicia are presented on the t-shirts at issue here. Secondary meaning occurs when, in the minds of consumers, the primary significance of the mark is to identify the source of the product rather than the product itself. A multifactor test is used to determine whether a mark has acquired secondary meaning. The factors include: (1) length and manner of use of the mark or trade dress, (2) volume of sales, (3) amount and manner of advertising, (4) nature of use of the mark or trade dress in newspapers and magazines, (5) consumer-survey evidence, (6) direct consumer testimony, and (7) the defendant's intent in copying the mark or trade dress. Here, application of these factors, and consideration of the context in which the school colors are used, leads to the conclusion that the color schemes have acquired secondary meaning. The evidence shows that the Universities (P) have used their color schemes for over a century; the volume of sales of items branded with the school colors run into the tens of millions of dollars annually; the Universities (P) use the colors schemes in their promotional materials; the color schemes have been referenced multiple times in newspapers and magazines; and, although there was no consumer-survey evidence or direct consumer testimony, Smack (D) itself admitted it had incorporated the Universities' (P) color schemes into its shirts to refer to the Universities (P) and call them to the mind of the consumer, i.e., Smack (D) believed that the Universities' (P) color schemes had secondary meaning that could influence consumers. Based on this evidence, there is no genuine issue of

Continued on next page.

fact that when viewed in the context of t-shirts or other apparel, the marks at issue here have acquired the secondary meaning of identifying the Universities (P) in the minds of consumers as the source or sponsor of the products rather than identifying the products themselves. Smack (D) argues that the use by businesses in a college town of the color scheme of the local university means that consumers in college towns merely associate school colors with "support of the home team." Even if that were true, that fact does not create an issue of fact as to the secondary meaning of the colors used in merchandise that the Universities (P) indisputably produce. Further, merely because the Universities (P) may grant licenses to many licensees to sell authorized products does not negate the fact that the schools are still the sources of the marks. For all these reasons, the marks at issue have acquired secondary meaning and may receive trademark protection. Affirmed.

▶ *ANALYSIS*

It should be noted that the factors in the seven-factor test for determining secondary meaning in combination may show that consumers consider a mark to be an indicator of source even if each factor alone would not prove secondary meaning. For example, Smack (D) argued that the longstanding use of the school colors to adorn licensed products was not the same as public recognition that the school colors identified the Universities (P) as a unique source of goods. While this factor standing alone thus might not have shown secondary meaning, when the court considered it with the other factors in the test, along with the context in which the marks were used, the court concluded that the secondary meaning of the marks was inescapable.

■■■

Quicknotes

DESCRIPTIVE A descriptive mark has a dictionary meaning, or a meaning in common usage, that is used in connection with products or services directly related to, or suggestive of, that meaning. A descriptive mark is not entitled to trademark protection unless it has acquired distinctiveness over time.

SECONDARY MEANING A word or mark that becomes associated with a particular merchant or product as its source of origin.

SUMMARY JUDGMENT Judgment rendered by a court in response to a motion made by one of the parties, claiming that the lack of a question of material fact in respect to an issue warrants disposition of the issue without consideration by the jury.

TRADEMARK Any word, name, symbol, device or combination thereof that is either currently utilized, or which a person has a bona fide intent to utilize, in commerce in order to distinguish his goods from those of another.

TRADEMARK INFRINGEMENT The unauthorized use of another's trademark in such a manner as to cause a likelihood of confusion as to the source of the product or service in connection with which it is utilized.

■■■

Chrysler Group LLC v. Moda Group LLC

Car manufacturer (P) v. City promoter (D)

796 F. Supp. 2d 866 (E.D. Mich. 2011).

NATURE OF CASE: Motion to preliminarily enjoin the use of a certain phrase during the pendency of a trademark action.

FACT SUMMARY: Chrysler Group LLC (Chrysler) (P), a car manufacturer, sought to preliminarily enjoin Moda Group LLC (Pure Detroit) (D), a company promoting the city of Detroit and its culture, from using the phrase "IMPORTED FROM DETROIT" ("IFD"), claiming that Chrysler (P) had a protectable trademark in that phrase, based on its use of that phrase in a commercial, and on t-shirts that it sold on its website.

RULE OF LAW

A mark that is not inherently distinctive, and that has not acquired distinctiveness through a secondary meaning, is not entitled to trademark protection.

FACTS: Chrysler Group LLC (Chrysler) (P), a car manufacturer with offices and plants in Michigan and Canada, but not in Detroit, spent over $50 million on an ad campaign, which it introduced during a Superbowl. The ad featured one of Chrysler's (P) cars, and at the end of the ad, the words "IMPORTED FROM DETROIT" ("IFD") appeared on the screen for seven seconds. Because the ad generated significant interest on its website, Chrysler (P) began selling t-shirts with the IFD phrase through its website. Immediately after the commercial aired, Moda Group LLC (Pure Detroit) (D), a company located in Detroit, which promoted the city of Detroit and its culture, began making shirts featuring the IFD phrase. Pure Detroit's (D) shirts did not have the Chrysler (P) logo or name on them. Chrysler (P) started selling its t-shirts after Pure Detroit (D) had started selling its shirts. Rejecting Chrysler's (P) request to cease and desist using the IFD phrase, Pure Detroit (D) continued to sell the shirts, and also began selling tote bags and other variations of its t-shirt. Chrysler (P) brought a trademark action against Pure Detroit (D) and moved to preliminarily enjoin Pure Detroit (D) from using the IFD phrase during the pendency of the action.

ISSUE: Is a mark that is not inherently distinctive, and that has not acquired distinctiveness through a secondary meaning, entitled to trademark protection?

HOLDING AND DECISION: (Tarnow, J.) No. A mark that is not inherently distinctive, and that has not acquired distinctiveness through a secondary meaning, is not entitled to trademark protection. Primarily geographically descriptive marks are not entitled to trademark

protection, since they are not inherently distinctive, unless they have acquired secondary meaning. Chrysler (P) contends that the IFD phrase is inherently distinctive because it requires a "mental leap" to identify the underlying goods. This contention is rejected, since the phrase merely describes the geographical origin of the goods associated with the phrase. Accordingly, for purposes of satisfying the requirements necessary for the issuance of a preliminary injunction, it is unlikely that Chrysler (P) will be able to prove that the IFD phrase is inherently distinctive. Chrysler (P) alternatively argues that the phrase has acquired secondary meaning. To determine secondary meaning, a seven-factor test is used: (1) direct consumer testimony; (2) consumer surveys; (3) exclusivity, length, and manner of use; (4) amount and manner of advertising; (5) amount of sales and number of customers; (6) established place in the market; and (7) proof of intentional copying. No single factor is determinative and not all factors must be proven. Here, the first two factors have not been addressed by the parties. As to the third factor, only a short time has passed since Chrysler (P) introduced the IFD phrase. More than a short period of time is required to establish secondary meaning. The fact that Chrysler (P) spent over $50 million on the ad campaign, and had it viewed by more than 94 million people, does not by itself establish secondary meaning; this merely tends to show that Chrysler (P) wanted to establish secondary meaning—not necessarily that it succeeded. Nevertheless, this factor likely weighs in Chrysler's (P) favor. Another factor in Chrysler's (P) favor is that its IFD shirt was very popular and that it sold close to six thousand items with that phrase over a short time. However, as to the sixth factor, Chrysler (P) has failed to show that the IFD phrase was established in the marketplace prior to Pure Detroit's (D) use of it. Because Pure Detroit (D) started making its shirts the day after the commercial aired, Chrysler (P) would essentially have to show that the phrase acquired secondary meaning overnight. However, as a matter of law, secondary meaning cannot be established instantaneously. Finally, as to the seventh factor, although Pure Detroit (D) knew of Chrysler's (P) commercial, any intentional copying on its part was not done with the intent to derive a benefit from Chrysler's (P) reputation, but instead was done to promote pride in Detroit. Even if Pure Detroit (D) referenced Chrysler's (P) commercial in its advertising for the Pure Detroit t-shirts (by referring to IFD as a "tagline that is making headlines across America!," this factor weighs slightly in Pure Detroit's (D) favor. Weighing these factors, Chrysler (P) has not met

Continued on next page.

its substantial burden of establishing that the IFD phrase acquired secondary meaning. Accordingly, there is not a strong likelihood that it will succeed on the merits, and, for this reason, its motion for a preliminary injunction must be denied. [Motion denied.]

▶ *ANALYSIS*

As this case demonstrates, although the duration of use of a mark can establish secondary meaning, that duration must be more than a relatively short period. Here, the court rejected Chrysler's (P) contention that the phrase acquired secondary meaning within hours, or even days, after the commercial aired, finding that such a period was too short to establish secondary meaning.

■══■

Quicknotes

DESCRIPTIVE A descriptive mark has a dictionary meaning, or a meaning in common usage, that is used in connection with products or services directly related to, or suggestive of, that meaning. A descriptive mark is not entitled to trademark protection unless it has acquired distinctiveness over time.

PRELIMINARY INJUNCTION A judicial mandate issued to require or restrain a party from certain conduct; used to preserve a trial's subject matter or to prevent threatened injury.

SECONDARY MEANING A word or mark that becomes associated with a particular merchant or product as its source of origin.

TRADEMARK Any word, name, symbol, device or combination thereof that is either currently utilized, or which a person has a bona fide intent to utilize, in commerce in order to distinguish his goods from those of another.

■══■

Use and Ownership

Quick Reference Rules of Law

Thoroughbred Legends, LLC v. Walt Disney Co.

Trademark owner (P) v. Entertainment company (D)

2008 U.S. Dist. LEXIS 19960 (N.D. Ga. 2008).

NATURE OF CASE: Motion for summary judgment made by defendant in trademark infringement case.

FACT SUMMARY: The Walt Disney Company (Disney) (D) and its subsidiaries, American Broadcasting Companies, Inc. (ABC) (D), and ESPN Productions, Inc. (ESPN) (D) (collectively, Disney entities (D)), decided to make a movie about the famous racehorse Ruffian. Upon learning this, Thoroughbred Legends, LLC (Legends) (P) was created for the purpose of registering the trademark RUFFIAN, and Legends (P) obtained such registration. After the Disney entities (D) made the movie without licensing the RUFFIAN trademark from Legends (P), Legends (P) and others brought a trademark infringement action against the Disney entities (D). The Disney entities (D) contended that Legends (P) and the other plaintiffs were not entitled to trademark rights in RUFFIAN because they made no commercial trademark use of that mark.

🏛 **RULE OF LAW**
The owner of a mark is not entitled to trademark rights in the mark where the owner has not made commercial trademark use of the mark.

FACTS: The Walt Disney Company (Disney) (D) and its subsidiaries, American Broadcasting Companies, Inc. (ABC) (D), and ESPN Productions, Inc. (ESPN) (D) (collectively, Disney entities (D)), decided to make a movie about the famous filly racehorse Ruffian. After it was learned that the Disney entities (D) were interested in making the movie, Thoroughbred Legends, LLC (Legends) (P) was created for the purpose of registering the trademark RUFFIAN, and Legends (P) obtained such registration, which was for a service mark in the entertainment services, including production of motion picture films. The Disney entities (D) declined Legends' (P) invitation to license the RUFFIAN mark, and made the movie without such licensing. Legends (P) and some individuals who had been associated with Ruffian then brought a trademark infringement action against the Disney entities (D). The Disney entities (D) moved for summary judgment, contending that there was no genuine issue of material fact as to whether Legends (P) had ever made commercial trademark use of the RUFFIAN mark. The evidence showed that Legends (P) and its principal, Blum, had attempted to license the RUFFIAN mark, and had attempted to have a movie documentary made about Ruffian. However, in taking these actions, the evidence also showed that Legends (P) did not use the RUFFIAN mark to identify the source of any service, but merely described it

and claimed rights to the mark. There was also evidence that Legends (P) attempted to license the RUFFIAN mark for use on various items, but no such license agreement was entered into, and the RUFFIAN mark was not used by the prospective licensee, or in any other way connected with movie production.

ISSUE: Is the owner of a mark entitled to trademark rights in the mark where the owner has not made commercial trademark use of the mark?

HOLDING AND DECISION: (Martin, J.) No. The owner of a mark is not entitled to trademark rights in the mark where the owner has not made commercial trademark use of the mark. To succeed on a trademark infringement claim, a mark's owner must not only show that it used its mark in commerce, but also that it used the mark as a trademark. This means that the mark must be used to signify origin to customers and competitors. Here, there is no indication that Legends (P) ever made trademark use of the RUFFIAN mark, i.e., there was no bona fide use in commerce of RUFFIAN to signify the source of a product or service. Although Blum and Legends (P) took steps and actions to make a movie about Ruffian, and attempted to license the RUFFIAN mark to the Disney entities (D), in taking these actions Legends (P) did not use the RUFFIAN mark to identify the source of any service, but merely described it and claimed rights to the mark. One cannot acquire rights in a trademark by asserting one owns it. To acquire such rights, the party claiming ownership must have been the first to actually use the mark in the sale of goods or services—and Legends (P) failed to do that here. Legends' (P) attempt to license the mark for use on goods does not constitute such use, since the mark was never used—not in connection with goods, and certainly not with movie production. In short, Legends (P) and the other plaintiffs have not shown a genuine issue of material fact as to whether they acquired rights in the trademark RUFFIAN. Accordingly, their trademark infringement claims must be dismissed because they have not shown valid trademark rights. [Summary judgment is granted to the Disney entities (D).]

▶ **ANALYSIS**

It should be noted that the mere fact that Legends (P) succeeded in having the RUFFIAN mark registered did not by itself change the outcome of the case, since registration without actual use does not confer rights to a trademark,

Continued on next page.

and only use in the marketplace can establish a mark regardless of whether the mark is registered or unregistered. And although registration does create a presumption of validity, that presumption is easily rebuttable, since it merely shifts the burden of production to the alleged infringer.

■═■

Quicknotes

BONA FIDE In good faith.

ISSUE OF MATERIAL FACT A fact that is disputed between two or more parties to litigation that is essential to proving an element of the cause of action or a defense asserted, or which would otherwise affect the outcome of the proceeding.

SUMMARY JUDGMENT Judgment rendered by a court in response to a motion made by one of the parties, claiming that the lack of a question of material fact in respect to an issue warrants disposition of the issue without consideration by the jury.

TRADEMARK INFRINGEMENT The unauthorized use of another's trademark in such a manner as to cause a likelihood of confusion as to the source of the product or service in connection with which it is utilized.

■═■

Bell v. Streetwise Records, Ltd.

Singing group (P) v. Producer (D)

640 F. Supp. 575 (D. Mass. 1986).

NATURE OF CASE: Trademark ownership claim under the Lanham Act and state law.

FACT SUMMARY: A singing group and its producer both claimed ownership of the name, "New Edition." The group claimed it was their name; the producer claimed it was the name of the concept.

> 🏛 **RULE OF LAW**
> (1) A person acquires legal rights to a mark through prior use of the mark in intrastate commerce, even if another person had been the first to use the mark in interstate commerce.
> (2) A person owns a mark where the quality that the mark identifies is that person or his service.

FACTS: The members of the singing group "New Edition" (P) sought to establish the exclusive right to appear, perform, and record under the mark. They performed throughout the country, as well as overseas. The group (P) started in 1981, and their sixth engagement was at a talent show at the Strand Theatre. At the time, Maurice Starr, president of Boston International Music (BIM) (D), had developed a concept that was based on an updated version of the Jackson Five. Starr believed the members lacked talent, despite the fact that he decided to work with them. BIM (D) and Streetwise Records, Ltd. (Streetwise) (D) produced, recorded, and marketed the first New Edition album, along with singles from the album, and they claim they employed the five performers (P) to serve as a public front for a "concept" that they developed. BIM (D) and Streetwise (D) claimed that the mark "New Edition" identifies the recordings, not the group (P), and that they are therefore the rightful owners.

ISSUE:
(1) Does a person acquire legal rights to a mark through prior use of the mark in intrastate commerce, even if another person had been the first to use the mark in interstate commerce?
(2) Does a person own a mark where the quality that the mark identifies is that person or his service?

HOLDING AND DECISION: (Zobel, J.)
(1) Yes. A person acquires legal rights to a mark through prior use of the mark in intrastate commerce, even if another person had been the first to use the mark in interstate commerce. Ownership of a mark is established by priority of appropriation, and priority is established by usage. Usage must have been deliberate and continuous, not sporadic, casual, or transitory. As of the release of the first album, the first use in com-

merce, the group was calling itself New Edition and had publicly performed in the local entertainment market on 20 occasions. The group (P) therefore acquired legal rights to the mark through prior use. Even if BIM (D) and Streetwise (D) had been the first in interstate commerce, they used the name simultaneously in Massachusetts, where the group (P) had already appropriated.
(2) Yes. A person owns a mark where the quality that the mark identifies is that person or his service. Even assuming there was no prior appropriation, they own the mark under the controlling standard of the law. The party that controls or determines the nature and quality of the goods that have been marketed under the mark in question is the group (P), because the "goods are the entertainment services they provide." The public association of the mark is with the group (P). Personality, not marketing, led to the public's intimacy with the group (P).

▶ **ANALYSIS**

The court uses the terms "junior user" and "senior user" to signify who was first to use the trademark, not the strength of that use. Temporal matters are important in determining ownership with respect to the entertainment industry, particularly the music industry.

■■■

Quicknotes

LANHAM ACT Name of the Trademark Act of 1946 that governs federal law regarding trademarks.

TRADEMARK Any word, name, symbol, device or combination thereof that is either currently utilized, or which a person has a bona fide intent to utilize, in commerce in order to distinguish his goods from those of another.

■■■

ITC Ltd. v. Punchgini

Foreign restaurant owner (P) v. U.S. restaurant owner (D)

518 F.3d 159 (2d Cir. 2008).

NATURE OF CASE: Appeal from summary judgment for defendant in action for unfair competition based on deliberate copying of trademarks and trade dress.

FACT SUMMARY: ITC Ltd. (P), which operated and licensed high-end Indian restaurants internationally under the mark BUKHARA, contended that it was error to grant summary judgment to the owners of the Bukhara Grill (BG owners) (D), which operated in Manhattan, on ITC's (P) claim of unfair competition, asserting that the BG owners' (D) deliberate copying of the BUKHARA mark and trade dress was sufficient to establish secondary meaning, and that, in any event, it had adduced sufficient evidence of secondary meaning.

🏛 RULE OF LAW

Where a famous foreign mark or trade dress holder has established that the defendant has deliberately copied the mark or dress, to prevail on a state law unfair competition claim, the owner must also establish that the mark has obtained secondary meaning by showing that consumers in the relevant market associate the mark or dress with the owner.

FACTS: ITC Ltd. (P) operated and licensed high-end Indian restaurants internationally under the mark BUKHARA, but did not operate any restaurants in the United States. When a restaurant called the Bukhara Grill was opened in Manhattan, with décor, staff uniforms, and other trade dress that were very similar to those found in ITC's (P) Bukhara restaurants, ITC (P) sued Bukhara Grill's owners (BG owners) (D) for trademark infringement and unfair competition. The district court granted the BG owners (D) summary judgment, finding that even if the Lanham Act recognized a famous mark exception to the territoriality principle, ITC (P) had failed to prove sufficient fame. The court of appeals ruled that the Lanham Act did not provide such an exception, but noting that state law might, certified the issue to New York's highest court (the New York Court of Appeals), asking that court (1) whether New York permitted the owner of a famous foreign mark or trade dress to assert property rights therein by virtue of the owner's prior use of the mark or dress in a foreign country?; and (2) if so, how famous a foreign mark had to be to permit a foreign mark owner to bring a claim for unfair competition? The state high court answered the first question in the affirmative, but, in doing so, specifically stated that it did not recognize the famous marks doctrine as an independent theory of liability under state law. As to the second question, the court stated that protection from misappropriation of a famous foreign mark presupposes the existence of actual goodwill in New York, and that, at a minimum, consumers of the good or service provided under a certain mark by a defendant in New York must primarily associate the mark with the foreign plaintiff. Factors identified by the New York court as potentially relevant to the inquiry were: (1) evidence that the defendant intentionally associated goods with those of the foreign plaintiff in the minds of the public; (2) direct evidence, such as consumer surveys, indicating that consumers of defendant's goods or services believe them to be associated with the plaintiff; and (3) evidence of actual overlap between customers of the New York defendant and the foreign plaintiff. After receiving the state court's answers, the court of appeals reviewed the district court's ruling.

ISSUE: Where a famous foreign mark or trade dress holder has established that the defendant has deliberately copied the mark or dress, to prevail on a state law unfair competition claim, must the owner also establish that the mark has obtained secondary meaning by showing that consumers in the relevant market associate the mark or dress with the owner?

HOLDING AND DECISION: (Raggi, J.) Yes. Where a famous foreign mark or trade dress holder has established that the defendant has deliberately copied the mark or dress, to prevail on a state law unfair competition claim, the owner must also establish that the mark has obtained secondary meaning by showing that consumers in the relevant market associate the mark or dress with the owner. ITC (P) has clearly adduced sufficient evidence of deliberate copying, so the focus of the inquiry is on whether it has satisfied the secondary meaning element of its claim. ITC (P) has attempted to demonstrate that the BUKHARA mark, when used in New York, calls to mind for BG owners' (D) potential customers ITC's goodwill, or that the customers primarily associate the mark with ITC, through the use of foreign media reports and sources. However, ITC (P) failed to show that these reports or sources reach the relevant consumer market in New York. It made no attempt to prove its goodwill in the relevant market through consumer study evidence linking the Bukhara mark to itself, and it presented no research reports demonstrating strong brand name recognition for the BUKHARA mark anywhere in the United States. Further, ITC (P) failed to adduce any evidence of actual overlap between customers of the BG owners' (D) restaurant and ITC's (P) Bukhara. On the other hand, there was evidence

Continued on next page.

that numerous other Indian restaurants throughout the United States and the world have used the name Bukhara all without any affiliation or association with ITC (P). Even if, as ITC (P) claims, many of the BG owners' (D) customers are Indian or well-travelled, and know what authentic Indian food tastes like, this does not raise a triable issue of whether those customer primarily associate the name Bukhara with ITC (P). In addition, while there may be some circumstances in which intentional copying is sufficient to show secondary meaning, more than copying is necessary for a famous foreign mark holder to pursue a state law claim for unfair competition, and that foreign holder must further offer evidence that the defendant's potential customers primarily associate the mark with the foreign holder. Because ITC (P) cannot satisfy this burden here, the district court's grant of summary judgment to the BG owners (D) is affirmed. [Affirmed.]

▶ *ANALYSIS*

The relevant market in this case was potential customers for the BG owners' (D) Manhattan restaurant. The market was not limited to persons who had already eaten in the BG owners' (D) restaurants, nor was the relevant market expanded to encompass every New Yorker, whether or not he or she was inclined to eat in restaurants generally or Indian restaurants in particular. In any event, even if the relevant market had been expanded beyond potential customers for the Bukhara Grill, it seems that ITC (P) would not have been able to satisfy its burden of showing secondary meaning.

■══■

Quicknotes

SECONDARY MEANING A word or mark that becomes associated with a particular merchant or product as its source of origin.

SUMMARY JUDGMENT Judgment rendered by a court in response to a motion made by one of the parties, claiming that the lack of a question of material fact in respect to an issue warrants disposition of the issue without consideration by the jury.

TRADE DRESS The overall image of, or impression created by, a product that a court may enforce as a trademark if it determines that such image has acquired secondary meaning and that the public recognizes it as an indication of source.

UNFAIR COMPETITION Any dishonest or fraudulent rivalry in trade and commerce, particularly imitation and counterfeiting.

■══■

Aktieselskabet AF 21. November 2001 v. Fame Jeans, Inc.

Junior foreign trademark registrant/opposer (P) v. Senior U.S. trademark registrant (D)

525 F.3d 8 (D.C. Cir. 2008).

NATURE OF CASE: Appeal from affirmance of the Trademark Trial and Appeal Board's dismissal on summary judgment of opposition to trademark registration.

FACT SUMMARY: Aktieselskabet (Bestseller) (P), which had successfully sold jeans under the Jack & Jones label throughout the world except in the United States, opposed the registration by Fame Jeans, Inc. (Fame) (D), contending that Fame's (D) registration was likely to cause confusion with Bestseller's (P) Jack & Jones mark and interfere with Bestseller's (P) own application to register the mark—which application was junior to Fame's (D).

🏛 RULE OF LAW
An opposition to a trademark registration will survive summary judgment where the opposer has made enough analogous use to give the registrant fair notice of a claim to analogous use.

FACTS: Since the 1990s, Aktieselskabet (Bestseller) (P), a Danish company, successfully sold millions of jeans and other apparel items under the Jack & Jones label throughout the world, except in the United States, and it had trademark and domain name registrations for Jack & Jones in numerous countries. By the time Bestseller (P) was ready to enter the U.S. market, Fame Jeans, Inc. (Fame) (D) had already applied for trademark registration—on January 9, 2004; Bestseller (P) did not apply for registration until December 6, 2004. Both parties filed intent-to-use (ITU) applications, as neither party had actually sold any jeans under the Jack & Jones label in the United States. On December 15, 2004, Bestseller (P) filed an opposition to Fame's (D) application to register the mark, alleging that Fame's (D) registration was likely to cause confusion with Bestseller's (P) Jack & Jones mark and interfere with Bestseller's (P) application to register the mark. The Trademark Trial and Appeal Board (TTAB) granted summary judgment to Fame (D), concluding that foreign use alone did not give Bestseller (P) priority in the United States, so that its application was junior to Fame's (D). The district court affirmed and dismissed all claims. The court of appeals granted review.

ISSUE: Will an opposition to a trademark registration survive summary judgment where the opposer has made enough analogous use to give the registrant fair notice of a claim to analogous use?

HOLDING AND DECISION: (Brown, J.) Yes. An opposition to a trademark registration will survive summary judgment where the opposer has made enough

analogous use to give the registrant fair notice of a claim to analogous use. Bestseller (P) must establish either actual or constructive use prior to Fame's (D) filing date. Here, Bestseller (P) cannot establish constructive use under Lanham Act § 7(c), which grants priority, based on filing date, to a U.S. application or to a foreign application that was followed by a timely U.S. application under § 44(d). Bestseller (P) neither filed under § 44(d) nor complied with that section's timeliness requirements. Thus, to defeat Fame's (D) application, Bestseller (P) must sufficiently allege actual commercial use. One way it can do so is by showing that it made enough analogous use. That is because, in order to object to another's registration, it need not meet the statutory requirements to itself register the mark at issue. Under § 2(d), all that the opposer must show is use in the United States, and adoption of the mark by use analogous to strict trademark use suffices. Here, although Bestseller (P) has not alleged any sales in the United States, or to Americans abroad, it has alleged facts sufficient to give Fame (D) fair notice of a claim of analogous use. These allegations are that it conducted research and marketing for use of the mark within the United States, and, as a matter of reasonable inference, that this marketing was sufficiently extensive to create an awareness of the Jack & Jones brand among American consumers. That is all that is needed at this point in the proceedings to give Fame (D) fair notice of what it will have to contest. Although Bestseller (P) might have to supply substantial proof of public association with its mark, that will have to be done at trial. Accordingly, it was error to grant summary judgment to Fame (D) and to dismiss Bestseller's (P) opposition. [Reversed as to this issue.]

▶ ANALYSIS

To show analogous use, an opposer may rely on myriad forms of activity besides sales themselves, including, among others, regular business contacts, after-sales services, advertising of various forms, and marketing. Even marketing of a trademarked product before the product is ready for sale has the potential to defeat a rival's registration, although minimal marketing will not suffice. Analogous use must be of such a nature and extent as to create public identification of the target term with the opposer's product. Here, the court relies on Bestseller's (P) significant marketing efforts to conclude that Bestseller (P) has created a genuine issue of material fact as to

Continued on next page.

Bestseller's (P) analogous use, and, therefore, to conclude that dismissal on summary judgment was inappropriate.

■═■

Quicknotes

SUMMARY JUDGMENT   Judgment rendered by a court in response to a motion made by one of the parties, claiming that the lack of a question of material fact in respect to an issue warrants disposition of the issue without consideration by the jury.

TRADEMARK   Any word, name, symbol, device or combination thereof that is either currently utilized, or which a person has a bona fide intent to utilize, in commerce in order to distinguish his goods from those of another.

■═■

Blue Bell, Inc. v. Farah Manufacturing Co.

Clothing manufacturer (P) v. Competitor (D)

508 F.2d 1260 (5th Cir. 1975).

NATURE OF CASE: Appeal of order enjoining use of trademark.

FACT SUMMARY: Farah Manufacturing Co. (D) sought to use an internal shipment of clothing bearing a trademark as a basis for a claimed first use of the mark.

RULE OF LAW
An internal shipment of a product bearing a trademark may not form the basis of a first use of the mark.

FACTS: In 1973, Blue Bell, Inc. (P) and Farah Manufacturing Co. (Farah) (D) brought out a line of clothing under the name "Time Out." On July 3 of that year, Farah (D) shipped one pair of Time Out pants to each of its sales managers. On July 5, Blue Bell (P) shipped several hundred pairs in an intracompany transaction. Farah (D) started shipping to the public in September, and Blue Bell (P) began doing so in October. Blue Bell (P) brought a suit seeking to enjoin Farah (D) from using the label. Farah (D) counterclaimed for similar relief. A district court entered judgment for Farah (D), and Blue Bell (P) appealed, contending that Farah's (D) July 3 shipment to have been too small to be considered.

ISSUE: May an internal shipment of a product bearing a trademark form the basis of a first use of the mark?

HOLDING AND DECISION: (Gewin, J.) No. An internal shipment of a product bearing a trademark may not form the basis of a first use of the mark. The primary, perhaps singular purpose of a trademark is to provide a means for the consumer to separate or distinguish one manufacturer's goods from those of another. Personnel within a company can identify an item by its style number or other unique code. Trademarks are, therefore, relevant only in the context of the public's involvement with a product. Intracompany shipments of any size are not to be considered in determining when a trademark was first used. Here, not only was Farah's (D) July 3 shipment intracompany, but so was Blue Bell's (P) larger shipment. For these reasons, neither may be used as a basis for determining first use. Therefore, since Farah (D) first commenced sales to the general public, its use of the mark had priority. Affirmed.

ANALYSIS

Trademark law has both federal and state components. Federal trademark registration is afforded under the Lanham Act, codified at 15 U.S.C. § 1125. In this case, neither party had applied for federal registration, so state law applied. In this case, federal and state law regarding priority did not substantially differ.

Quicknotes

TRADEMARK Any word, name, symbol, device or combination thereof that is either currently utilized, or which a person has a bona fide intent to utilize, in commerce in order to distinguish his goods from those of another.

United Drug Co. v. Theodore Rectanus Co.

Massachusetts corporation (P) v. Kentucky corporation (D)

248 U.S. 90 (1918).

NATURE OF CASE: Appeal of denial of injunction.

FACT SUMMARY: [Parties not identified in casebook excerpt.] In 1877, a woman from Massachusetts began using the word "Rex" in connection with a medicinal product she sold through her store. Her business was acquired along with the rights to the word "Rex," by a Massachusetts corporation (P). The acquiring company began distributing the product in different states, with four stores in Louisville, Kentucky. Meanwhile, in 1883, Theodore Rectanus employed the word "Rex" as a trademark for a medicinal product. He sold his company to a Kentucky corporation (D), which continued using the word to a considerable extent in Louisville and vicinity.

RULE OF LAW
Where two parties independently use the same mark on goods of the same class, but in markets wholly separate from each other, there is no infringement if there is no evidence that the second adopter selected the mark to unfairly compete.

FACTS: [Parties not identified in casebook excerpt.] In 1877, Ellen M. Regis of Haverhill, Massachusetts, created and began selling a medicine that she called "Rex," which was derived from her surname. She recorded the mark in 1898 as a trademark in Massachusetts, and in 1900, registered in the U.S. Patent Office. The business was sold to Petitioner (P), a Massachusetts corporation, in 1911, along with the trademark right. Petitioner (P) operated retail drug stores known as "Rexall" stores. Meanwhile, in 1883, Theodore Rectanus, a druggist in Louisville who was known by friends and associates as "Rex," used the word Rex as a trademark for a "blood purifier." He used the mark in Louisville and its vicinity, and when he sold the business to Respondent (D), a Kentucky corporation, in 1906, he sold with it the trademark. The trial court found that use of the same mark on different drugs was carried on by the parties at the same time, but in different localities, in good faith, with neither side having any knowledge or notice of what the other was doing. Then, in April 1912, petitioner (P) first used the word "Rex" in connection with the sale of drugs in Louisville. There is no evidence that anyone in Kentucky had heard of the Regis drug, with or without the mark "Rex," or that the mark ever was associated with anything besides Rectanus and the "blood purifier." The court of appeals ruled in favor of the Respondent (D).

ISSUE: Where two parties independently use the same mark on goods of the same class, but in markets wholly separate from each other, is there trademark infringement if there is no evidence that the second adopter selected the mark to unfairly compete?

HOLDING AND DECISION: (Pitney, J.) No. Where two parties independently use the same mark on goods of the same class, but in markets wholly separate from each other, there is no infringement if there is no evidence that the second adopter selected the mark to unfairly compete. Ellen Regis and her company had done nothing to make her mark known outside New England states, and therefore her successor, the Petitioner (P), was estopped from asking for an injunction against the continued use of the mark in Louisville and vicinity by the Respondent (D). Affirmed.

ANALYSIS

This is the case that gave rise to the Tea Rose–Rectanus doctrine or remote, good-faith user doctrine, a common-law rule providing that a junior user of a mark that is geographically remote from the senior user of the mark may establish priority over a senior user's claim to the mark in the junior user's area. The constructive use and notice sections of the Lanham Act limited the applicability of this doctrine.

Quicknotes

GOOD FAITH An honest intention to abstain from taking advantage of another.

Thrifty Rent-a-Car System v. Thrift Cars, Inc.

Car rental company (P) v. Car rental company (D)

831 F.2d 1177 (1st Cir. 1987).

NATURE OF CASE: Appeal of trial court judgment.

FACT SUMMARY: Thrifty Rent-a-Car System, Inc. (Thrifty) (P) operated a large business renting cars nationwide. Thrifty (P) was formed in 1958 and registered its trademark in July 1964. Thrift Cars, Inc. (Thrift Cars) (D) operated a small business renting cars in Massachusetts. It was formed in 1962. Thrifty (P) brought a trademark infringement suit against Thrift Cars (D) after Thrift Cars (D) tried to expand its market. The district court enjoined Thrift Cars (D) from conducting business outside of East Taunton, Mass. under the "Thrift Cars" name and limited Thrift Cars' (D) advertising to those media it had used prior to July 1964. The court also prohibited Thrifty (P) from operating business in East Taunton, Mass., and from advertising in East Taunton.

> ⚖ **RULE OF LAW**
> Under the Lanham Act's limited area exception, a junior user has the right to continued use of an otherwise infringing mark in a remote geographical area if that use was established prior to the other party's federal registration, and the junior user used the mark continuously in that location and initially in good faith without notice of a registered mark.

FACTS: Thrifty Rent-a-Car System, Inc. (Thrifty) (P) operated a large business renting cars nationwide that was formed in 1958. Thrifty (P) registered its trademark in July 1964, and some time after, began opening outlets in Massachusetts. By the time of trial, it was the fifth largest car rental agency worldwide, and operated 23 locations in Massachusetts alone. Thrift Cars, Inc. (Thrift Cars) (D) operated a small business renting cars in Massachusetts that Peter A. Conlon began in 1962. It originated in East Taunton, Mass, and later expanded in limited measure to Cape Cod and Nantucket. The company advertised in these areas. It obtained a license to operate a car rental facility at the Nantucket airport in 1970, six years after Thrifty (P) obtained federal registration of its mark. Thrifty (P) brought a trademark infringement suit against Thrift Cars (D). The district court enjoined Thrift Cars (D) from conducting business outside of Taunton, Mass. under the "Thrift Cars" name and limited Thrift Cars' (D) advertising to those media it had used prior to July 1964. The court also prohibited Thrifty (P) from operating business in East Taunton, Mass., and from advertising in East Taunton. Both parties appealed.

ISSUE: Under the Lanham Act's limited area exception, does a junior user have the right to continued use of an otherwise infringing mark in a remote geographical area if that use was established prior to the other party's federal registration, and the junior user used the mark continuously in that location and initially in good faith without notice of a registered mark?

HOLDING AND DECISION: (Davis, J.) Yes. Under the Lanham Act's limited area exception, a junior user has the right to continued use of an otherwise infringing mark in a remote geographical area if that use was established prior to the other party's federal registration, and the junior user used the mark continuously in that location and initially in good faith without notice of a registered mark. The parties don't dispute that Thrift Cars (D) adopted its mark in good faith and without notice prior to Thrifty's (P) registration. As to whether Thrift Cars (D) had established a market presence in any locality, the mark had been in continuous use in East Taunton, but not outside. Thrift Car's (D) expansion into new market areas after the 1964 date of Thrifty's (P) federal registration does not fall within the protection of the exception, as the district court found. The company's advertising was limited, and only had sporadic rentals in Nantucket and in other areas around Cape Cod. The record shows that Thrift Cars (D) continually advertised in media directed to the East Taunton area, and had a general reputation in the area throughout the period involved. Thrift Cars' (D) business was not frozen by the injunction, either, because East Taunton and Nantucket are two separate market areas, not parts of a single southeastern Massachusetts market as Thrift Cars (D) argued. Finally, the district court did not abuse its discretion by allowing Thrift Cars (D) to advertise in those publications it had used prior to Thrifty's (P) registration, even though some of those publications were distributed beyond East Taunton. There may be some consumer confusion, but the Lanham Act doesn't require the complete elimination of confusion, and the confusion that will result will be minimal. Affirmed.

▶ **ANALYSIS**

This case illustrates the codification of the common-law rule set forth in *United Drug Co. v. Theodore Rectanus Co.,* 248 U.S. 90 (1918). In this age of the internet, however, the limited area exception's scope of protection shrinks; if one company operates a website from the company's start, it

Continued on next page.

could become more difficult for another company to show it did not have prior notice.

■≡■

Quicknotes

GOOD FAITH An honest intention to abstain from taking advantage of another.

LANHAM ACT Name of the Trademark Act of 1946 that governs federal law regarding trademarks.

TRADEMARK Any word, name, symbol, device or combination thereof that is either currently utilized, or which a person has a bona fide intent to utilize, in commerce in order to distinguish his goods from those of another.

TRADEMARK INFRINGEMENT The unauthorized use of another's trademark in such a manner as to cause a likelihood of confusion as to the source of the product or service in connection with which it is utilized.

■≡■

Registration of Trademarks

Quick Reference Rules of Law

CHAPTER 4

Larami Corp. v. Talk to Me Programs, Inc.

Trademark registration opposer (P) v. Trademark registration applicant (D)

36 U.S.P.Q.2d 1840 (T.T.A.B. 1995).

NATURE OF CASE: Motion for summary judgment, based on collateral estoppel, in trademark registration opposition proceeding.

FACT SUMMARY: Talk To Me Programs, Inc. (TTMP) (D), which filed an intent-to-use (ITU) application for registration of the mark "THE TOTALLY RAD SOAKER" for toy water guns, claimed in an opposition proceeding brought by Larami Corp. (P) that although the issues of descriptiveness and secondary meaning had been litigated and decided against it in a civil infringement action, collateral estoppel did not preclude relitigation of whether the mark had acquired secondary meaning as of the present date, since TTMP (D) was not required to show secondary meaning prior to use by Larami (P), but was instead entitled to the benefit of the constructive use provisions of Lanham Act § 7(c) to show that its mark had acquired distinctiveness as of the present date.

> 🏛 **RULE OF LAW**
> In an opposition proceeding before the Trademark Trial and Appeal Board (the TTAB), an intent-to-use applicant is entitled to rely on the priority provisions of § 7(c) of the Lanham Act, and, therefore, rely on its constructive use date based on its filing and assert priority based on such constructive use, to prove that its mark has acquired secondary meaning as of the present date.

FACTS: Talk To Me Programs, Inc. (TTMP) (D) filed an intent-to-use (ITU) application for registration of the mark "THE TOTALLY RAD SOAKER" for toy water guns. LaramiCorp. (P) opposed on the ground that it had used the mark "SUPER SOAKER" for toy water guns. TTMP (D) sued Larami (P) in a civil action for trademark infringement, and the opposition was suspended pending the termination of the civil action. In the civil action, the district court granted summary judgment to Larami (P), finding that the "THE TOTALLY RAD SOAKER" mark was merely descriptive and had not acquired the requisite secondary meaning to receive trademark protection. The court of appeals affirmed, and the Trademark Trial and Appeal Board (the TTAB) resumed the opposition. Larami (P) sought summary judgment, contending that collateral estoppel precluded the issues of descriptiveness and secondary meaning from being relitigated in the opposition. TTMP (D) argued that even if the mark at issue were merely descriptive, TTMP (D) was not required to show secondary meaning prior to use by Larami (P), but was instead entitled to the benefit of the constructive use provisions of Lanham Act § 7(c) and, therefore, needed only to

show the acquisition of secondary meaning as of the present date.

ISSUE: In an opposition proceeding before the TTAB, is an intent-to-use applicant entitled to rely on the priority provisions of § 7(c) of the Lanham Act, and, therefore, rely on its constructive use date based on its filing and assert priority based on such constructive use, to prove that its mark has acquired secondary meaning as of the present date?

HOLDING AND DECISION: (Board) Yes. In an opposition proceeding before the TTAB, an intent-to-use applicant is entitled to rely on the priority provisions of § 7(c) of the Lanham Act, and, therefore, rely on its constructive use date based on its filing and assert priority based on such constructive use, to prove that its mark has acquired secondary meaning as of the present date. For purposes of the infringement action, the district court held that TTMP (D) could not establish priority because (1) it could not base its claim of priority on the filing date of its application for registration and (2) under the circuit's law, a plaintiff charging infringement of a descriptive mark must establish that the mark had acquired secondary meaning prior to the first use by the alleged infringer—a burden TTMP (D) could not meet, since its first actual use of the mark in commerce was later than Larami's (P) first use. These rulings on priority are not binding on TTAB, which has held that in an ITU application proceeding the applicant is entitled to rely upon the filing date of its application in an opposition filed by a party alleging common-law rights based on use prior to any actual use that might be asserted by the applicant. To hold otherwise, would mean that an ITU applicant would never be able to defend its application in an opposition based on likelihood of confusion; to require registration of an applicant's mark prior to realization of its rights under § 7(c) would defeat the purpose of filing ITU applications. The district court's different interpretation of § 7(c) for purposes of an infringement action, that the priority rights conferred by § 7(c) are contingent upon registration of the mark, is thus not controlling in an opposition proceeding—and even the district court said as much. In an infringement action, it would not be equitable for an ITU applicant to be entitled to rely upon a constructive use date prior to registration of its mark, and thus potentially prior to any use whatsoever, to defeat the common-law rights of a first actual user of its mark. However, this equitable consideration is not triggered where the ITU applicant is attempting to register its

Continued on next page.

mark. Moreover, the legislative history supports the conclusion that Congress intended § 7(c) to operate differently in the district courts than it does in proceedings before the TTAB. Accordingly, TTMP (D) may rely on its constructive use date based on its filing, and may assert priority based on such constructive use. In addition, if TTMP (D) succeeds in showing that its mark obtained secondary meaning as of the present date, TTMP (D) may rely on its filing date to establish priority. In fact, a mark may be registered, and thus receive the benefits of constructive use under § 7(c), even where the claim of acquired distinctiveness was made after the filing date of the application, and even if the use on which the claim of distinctiveness was predicated was made mostly after the filing date of the application. For these reasons, Larami (P) has failed to show that there are no genuine issues of material fact respecting the distinctiveness of TTMP's (D) mark, and TTMP (D) must be allowed to show that its mark has acquired secondary meaning as of the present date. Summary judgment is granted as to the issue of descriptiveness, but is denied as to the issue of distinctiveness (secondary meaning).

▌ ANALYSIS

Although in this case the TTAB held that the applicant could rely defensively on the constructive use provisions of § 7(c), in proceedings before the TTAB the constructive use provisions of § 7(c) may be used both defensively and offensively. That is, not only may an applicant rely on these provisions to defeat an opposer's priority claim, but an opposer may, likewise, rely on the constructive use provisions of § 7(c) to establish its priority for purposes of § 2(d) where it owns a registration for the mark it is asserting under § 2(d) or where it has filed an application for registration of that mark. However, it should also be noted that any judgment entered in favor of a party relying on constructive use—whether that party is the plaintiff or defendant in the TTAB proceeding—is contingent on the ultimate issuance of a registration to that party.

■=■

Quicknotes

COLLATERAL ESTOPPEL A doctrine whereby issues litigated and determined in a prior proceeding are binding upon all subsequent litigation between the parties regarding that issue.

COMMON-LAW RIGHTS In trademark law, common-law rights arise from actual use of a mark and may allow the common-law user to successfully challenge a registration or application. These rights have been developed under a judicially created scheme of rights governed by state law, rather than being created by statute.

CONSTRUCTIVE USE Under the Lanham Act, § 7(c), 15 U.S.C. § 1057(c), filing an application for registration on the Principal Register, including an intent-to-use application, constitutes constructive use of the mark, provided the application matures into a registration. Once the mark is registered, filing affords the applicant nationwide priority over others, except: (1) parties who used the mark before the applicant's filing date; (2) parties who filed in the USPTO before the applicant; or (3) parties who are entitled to an earlier priority filing date based on the filing of a foreign application under 15 U.S.C. § 1126(d) or § 1141g.

DESCRIPTIVENESS A standard for trademark protection, whereby a descriptive mark has a dictionary meaning, or a meaning in common usage, that is used in connection with products or services directly related to, or suggestive of, that meaning. A descriptive mark is not entitled to trademark protection unless it has acquired distinctiveness over time.

DISTINCTIVENESS A standard for trademark protection, whereby the more distinctive a mark is, the greater its eligibility for protection. Distinctive marks typically consist of terms that are fanciful or coined, arbitrary, or suggestive. If a mark is descriptive, it is not entitled to trademark protection unless it has acquired distinctiveness through consumer association of goods or services with the mark (such acquired distinctiveness is also known as secondary meaning).

ISSUE OF MATERIAL FACT A fact that is disputed between two or more parties to litigation that is essential to proving an element of the cause of action or a defense asserted, or which would otherwise affect the outcome of the proceeding.

SECONDARY MEANING A word or mark that becomes associated with a particular merchant or product as its source of origin.

TRADEMARK INFRINGEMENT The unauthorized use of another's trademark in such a manner as to cause a likelihood of confusion as to the source of the product or service in connection with which it is utilized.

■=■

Compagnie Gervais Danone v. Precision Formulations, LLC

Trademark registration opposer (P) v. Trademark registration applicant (D)

89 U.S.P.Q.2d 1251 (T.T.A.B. 2009).

NATURE OF CASE: Motion for summary judgment, based on priority, in trademark registration opposition proceeding.

FACT SUMMARY: Compagnie Gervais Danone (P), which opposed the registration by Precision Formulations, LLC (Precision) (D) of the mark "FRUITOLOGY" as to certain international classes of goods, contended that it was entitled to summary judgment because it had priority based on an effective filing date that was earlier in time to Precision's (D) effective filing date.

> ## 🏛 RULE OF LAW
> In a trademark registration opposition proceeding, where the only issue is one of priority, the opposer is entitled to summary judgment where its effective filing date is earlier in time than the applicant's.

FACTS: Precision Formulations, LLC (Precision) (D) sought to register the mark "FRUITOLOGY" as to certain international classes of goods, including various nutritional goods and medicated skin creams in International Class 5 and various beverage goods in International Class 32. Precision (D) filed an intent-to-use (ITU) application on February 21, 2007. Compagnie Gervais Danone (Danone) (P) opposed Precision's (D) registration as to Class 5 and Class 32. The parties conceded that their respective marks were similar and that there was a likelihood of confusion. Danone (P) moved for summary judgment, claiming priority, based on a French application and registration, which Danone (P) claimed gave it an effective filing date of December 6, 2006 under §§ 66(b) and 67 of the Trademark Act. Danone (P) had applied for the French Registration on December 6, 2006, and the French Registration issued on May 11, 2007. Based on that registration, Danone (P) obtained an International Registration on May 22, 2007. The Trademark Trial and Appeal Board (the TTAB) considered Danone's (P) motion.

ISSUE: In a trademark registration opposition proceeding, where the only issue is one of priority, is the opposer entitled to summary judgment where its effective filing date is earlier in time than the applicant's?

HOLDING AND DECISION: (Board.) Yes. In a trademark registration opposition proceeding, where the only issue is one of priority, the opposer is entitled to summary judgment where its effective filing date is earlier in time than the applicant's. Here, the only issue is priority. Precision's effective filing date is February 21, 2007, since an ITU applicant may rely on the filing date of its applica-

tion to establish priority. As to Danone's (P) effective date, Danone (P) filed its application on May 22, 2007, pursuant to § 66 of the Trademark Act. Section 66 provides that an application under that section constitutes constructive use of the mark as of the earliest of the following: (1) the international registration date, if the request for extension of protection was filed in the international application; (2) the date of recordal of the request for extension of protection, if the request for extension of protection was made after the international registration date; and (3) the date of priority claimed pursuant to § 67. Section 67, in turn, provides that an applicant is entitled to claim a date of priority when it holds an international registration, makes a request for extension of protection (application) to the U.S., includes a claim of priority based on a right of priority under Article 4 of the Paris Convention for the Protection of Industrial Property, and the date of the international registration is within six months of the filing date of the application underlying the international registration. Here, Danone's (P) International Registration issued May 22, 2007, and that registration was based on the underlying French application, filed December 6, 2006, which issued on May 11, 2007. Danone (P) claimed priority based on the December 6, 2006, filing date of the French application. Thus, pursuant to §§ 66(b) and 67, Danone (P) is entitled to a December 6, 2006, priority date. Given that Danone's (P) effective filing date is earlier than Precision's (D) effective filing date, there is no genuine issue of material fact as to which party has priority. Summary judgment (contingent on Danone's (P) application maturing into a registration) is granted to Danone (P).

▶ ANALYSIS

Because § 66(b) of the Trademark Act confers the same rights as those specified in § 7(c), which provides that filing an application for registration on the Principal Register establishes constructive use and nationwide priority, contingent upon issuance of a registration, the TTAB issued a contingent judgment in this case to give effect to the requirements found in § 7(c). This demonstrates that applications made domestically and those made internationally under the Paris Convention for the Protection of Industrial Property are treated in the same manner as to constructive use and priority.

■═■

Continued on next page.

Quicknotes

CONSTRUCTIVE USE Under the Lanham Act, § 7(c), 15 U.S.C. § 1057(c), filing an application for registration on the Principal Register, including an intent-to-use application, constitutes constructive use of the mark, provided the application matures into a registration. Once the mark is registered, filing affords the applicant nationwide priority over others, except: (1) parties who used the mark before the applicant's filing date; (2) parties who filed in the USPTO before the applicant; or (3) parties who are entitled to an earlier priority filing date based on the filing of a foreign application under 15 U.S.C. § 1126(d) or § 1141g.

ISSUE OF MATERIAL FACT A fact that is disputed between two or more parties to litigation that is essential to proving an element of the cause of action or a defense asserted, or which would otherwise affect the outcome of the proceeding.

PRIORITY OF USE Trademark doctrine that confers trademark rights based on first use of a mark, whereby a prior user has superior rights to a subsequent user. Thus, for example, under the Lanham Act § 7(c), 15 U.S.C. § 1057(c), once the mark is registered, filing affords the applicant nationwide priority over others except, inter alia, parties who used the mark before the applicant's filing date.

■━━■

In re Fox

[Parties not identified.]

702 F.3d 633 (Fed. Cir. 2012).

NATURE OF CASE: Appeal from affirmance of decision denying trademark registration to a mark.

FACT SUMMARY: Fox (P) contended that her mark, "COCK SUCKER," as applied to rooster-shaped lollipops, was registrable, notwithstanding that one of the mark's possible meanings was vulgar, because she had presented sufficient evidence that the mark's nonvulgar definitions were more relevant to the product at issue.

> ## RULE OF LAW
> A mark that creates a double entendre that has a meaning that would be perceived as vulgar by a substantial composite of the public is unregistrable because the mark consists of "scandalous material."

FACTS: Fox (P) made and sold rooster-shaped lollipops, and sold them to fans of a couple of universities' sports teams that used gamecocks as their athletic mascots. She used a mark that used the words "COCK SUCKER" (with a space between the two words) and a design that featured a rooster. After over 20 years of using this mark, Fox (P) sought to register it. The examiner at the Patent and Trademark Office (PTO) rejected registration of the mark on the ground that it consisted of or comprised immoral or scandalous matter because one definition of "cocksucker" is someone who performs an act of fellatio. Fox (P) filed a response, noting that a "cock" is defined as a rooster, and a "sucker" as a lollipop." She asserted that these nonvulgar definitions, which matched both the product design and the design element of the mark, were "more relevant" than the vulgar definition. On reconsideration, the examiner noted that one definition of "cock" is penis, and that a definition of "sucker" is one who sucks, so that taking "cock" in context with "sucker," the primary meaning of this wording as a whole is "one who sucks a penis," and that "the strong and commonly known meaning of 'cocksucker' in the general public" ensures that the two component words, when used together, will "unequivocal[ly]" assume their vulgar meanings. The Trademark Trial and Appeal Board (the TTAB) affirmed, determining that the use of "COCK SUCKER" in connection with Fox's (P) products created a double entendre with one of the possible meanings being vulgar. The court of appeals granted review.

ISSUE: Is a mark that creates a double entendre that has a meaning that would be perceived as vulgar by a substantial composite of the public unregistrable because the mark consists of "scandalous material?"

HOLDING AND DECISION: (Dyk, J.) Yes. A mark that creates a double entendre that has a meaning that would be perceived as vulgar by a substantial composite of the public is unregistrable because the mark consists of "scandalous material." Fox's (P) argument, that there was no support for the examiner's conclusion that the mark is vulgar, is rejected. Even Fox (P) conceded that "cocksucker" has no nonvulgar definition. The space between the words in Fox's (P) mark does not make a difference in this regard, since the sound of a mark is central to its commercial impression. Also, the association of "COCK SUCKER" with a poultry-themed product does not diminish the vulgar meaning, but merely establishes an additional, nonvulgar meaning and a double entendre. Even Fox (P) concedes that the humor of the mark is derived from the mark's double entendre, with one meaning being vulgar and the other being nonvulgar. For these reasons, and especially because the mark's vulgar meaning is widely known, rather than being obscure, the examiner did not err in concluding that the mark was vulgar. Additionally, there is no requirement that a mark's vulgar meaning must be the only relevant meaning, or even the most relevant meaning. As long as a "substantial composite of the general public" perceives the mark, in context, to have a vulgar meaning, the mark as a whole "consists of or comprises . . . scandalous matter" under the Trademark Act. Thus, the PTO is not required to prove anything more than the existence of a vulgar meaning to a substantial composite of the general public to justify its refusal. Further, Fox's (P) contention, that precedent precludes barring marks that create double entendres, is incorrect, since the precedent she relies on dealt with ambiguous marks—not those in which the conceded effect of the mark is to invoke a "double meaning." In sum, merely because there is a humorous aspect to the mark does not preclude the mark having a meaning that a substantial composite of the public would find vulgar. Because there is sufficient evidence to establish that the mark consists or comprises "scandalous matter" within the meaning of 15 U.S.C. § 1052(a), the mark is not registrable. Affirmed.

> ## ANALYSIS
> The court in this case held that a mark that includes a double entendre is not exempt from the prohibition of 15 U.S.C. § 1052(a) when the mark would be seen by a substantial composite of the general public as having both a vulgar and a nonvulgar meaning. In so doing, the court upheld the statute's objective that scandalous marks not

Continued on next page.

occupy the time, services, and use of funds of the federal government. Because a refusal to register a mark has no bearing on the applicant's ability to use the mark, refusing to register the mark because the mark is vulgar does not implicate the First Amendment rights of trademark applicants—and here, Fox (P) may continue to sell her "COCK SUCKER" lollipops to the market that apparently has rewarded her for her humorous, albeit partly vulgar, use of the mark.

■≡■

Boston Red Sox Baseball Club Limited Partnership v. Sherman

Professional baseball organization/trademark opposer (P) v.

Apparel marketer/trademark applicant (D)

88 U.S.P.Q.2d 1581 (T.T.A.B. 2008).

NATURE OF CASE: Opposition proceeding in trademark registration action.

FACT SUMMARY: The Boston Red Sox Baseball Club Limited Partnership (the Red Sox) (P), in opposing Sherman's (D) intent-to-use application to register the mark "SEX ROD" in a stylized font used by the Red Sox (P) for their mark, "RED SOX," contended, that registration of Sherman's (D) mark should be denied, among other things, because it was vulgar and because it would disparage the Red Sox (P).

🏛 RULE OF LAW

(1) Where a mark submitted for registration is vulgar on its face, registration will be precluded because the mark is scandalous, notwithstanding that the mark may also be humorous and a vulgar parody.

(2) A mark is precluded from registration where it would be understood to refer to an opposer and where it would be considered offensive or objectionable by a reasonable person of ordinary sensibilities.

FACTS: Sherman (D) filed an intent-to-use application to register the mark "SEX ROD" in connection with numerous types of articles of clothing and accessories, both for adults and children. The Boston Red Sox Baseball Club Limited Partnership (the Red Sox) (P), which owns a national professional baseball team, and which had been in operation for 100 years, opposed the registration under Trademark Act § 2(a) on grounds that, among other things, Sherman's (D) mark was vulgar and would disparage the Red Sox (P) organization. The mark that Sherman (D) sought to register was in the same stylized font that the Red Sox (P) had used for 70 years in connection with baseball games and numerous types of goods. Sherman (D) conceded that the term "SEX ROD" possesses a sexual connotation," but also maintained that the term is only "sexually suggestive." Sherman (D) asserted that his mark was a parody of the "RED SOX" stylized mark, and that his mark was a clever, yet sophomoric type of humor prevalent in the market for his goods, i.e., ballparks, sports bars, and university campuses. The Trademark Trial and Appeal Board (the TTAB) considered the merits of the opposition.

ISSUE:

(1) Where a mark submitted for registration is vulgar on its face, will registration be precluded because the mark is

scandalous, notwithstanding that the mark may also be humorous and a vulgar parody?

(2) Is a mark precluded from registration where it would be understood to refer to an opposer and where it would be considered offensive or objectionable by a reasonable person of ordinary sensibilities?

HOLDING AND DECISION: (Holtzman, J.)

(1) Yes. Where a mark submitted for registration is vulgar on its face, registration will be precluded because the mark is scandalous, notwithstanding that the mark may also be humorous and a vulgar parody. One of the slang definitions of "rod" is a penis. Thus, when preceded by the word "sex,""rod" only denotes a penis, and the mark conveys not a sexually suggestive connotation but rather a sexually explicit message to the viewer. The use of the term on children's and infant clothing would make the term particularly lurid and offensive. For these reasons, Sherman's (D) mark is vulgar, and, therefore, precluded from registration as scandalous. Whether the mark is intended to be humorous, or whether some individuals would find the mark humorous, is irrelevant. Additionally, even if the mark were a parody, there is nothing in the parody itself that changes or detracts from the vulgar meaning inherent in the term. In other words, the parody, to the extent there is one, is itself vulgar, and the term would be perceived and understood as vulgar by a substantial portion of the purchasing public.

(2) Yes. A mark is precluded from registration where it would be understood to refer to an opposer and where it would be considered offensive or objectionable by a reasonable person of ordinary sensibilities. Here, the evidence is overwhelming that the "RED SOX" mark is associated with the Red Sox (P). There is no question that the name "Red Sox" is the identity of the baseball club, apart from being a trademark for the entertainment services the club provides and the goods it sells or licenses. In addition, the stylized mark "RED SOX" has come to be associated in the public's mind with the Red Sox (P) organization, not just its games or merchandise. In fact, Sherman (D) concedes that the design of his mark is intended to refer to, and to invoke, the Red Sox (P). Because "SEX ROD" would be perceived as a vulgar term by a substantial number of consumers, and because Sherman's (D) mark in the identical style and format would

Continued on next page.

be understood as a reference to the Red Sox (P), the mark would be viewed as a sexually vulgar version of the Red Sox (P) symbol and as making an offensive comment on or about the Red Sox (P). Sherman (D) argues that even though his mark is intended to refer to the Red Sox (P), it does not tarnish the organization's reputation. Sherman (P) points to the organization's referral to itself in the past as the "Idiots" to support his contention, and to the fact that the organization has itself used suggestive phrases such as "You Have RED SOX Envy" on its t-shirts. While the line between what is or is not offensive may not always be clear, in this case it is. The difference between the Red Sox's (P) expressions of subtle or good-natured ribbing and Sherman's (D) crude, overtly sexual mark is obvious. Because his mark is offensive, and because the public will associate the offensive message with the Red Sox (P), the mark may disparage the Red Sox (P), and, for this reason, registration of Sherman's (D) mark is precluded. [The TTAB also held that, given the disparaging nature of Sherman's (D) term, there was no likelihood of confusion or a false suggestion of connection with the Red Sox (P).] Registration is denied.

▶ *ANALYSIS*

Section 2(a) of the Trademark Act prohibits registration of a mark that "consists of or comprises . . . matter which may disparage . . . persons, living or dead, institutions, beliefs, or national symbols, or bring them into contempt, or disrepute." This provision embodies concepts of the right to privacy and publicity, i.e., the right to protect and to control the use of one's identity. In effect, this provision of Section 2(a) protects against appropriation of one's identity by another and subjecting it to contempt or ridicule, given that disparagement is essentially a violation of one's right of privacy—the right to be let alone from contempt or ridicule.

■≡■

In re Lebanese Arak Corp.

[Parties not identified.]

94 U.S.P.Q.2d 1215 (T.T.A.B. 2010).

NATURE OF CASE: Appeal from refusal to register a trademark on ground that it is disparaging to a religious group.

FACT SUMMARY: Lebanese Arak Corporation (Lebanese Arak) (P), which sought to register the mark "KHORAN" for wines, contended that, contrary to the examiner's conclusion that the mark disparaged the beliefs of Muslim Americans, the mark was not in fact disparaging, as it represented the Armenian word for "alter," and that, in any event, the proper test for determining whether a mark is disparaging is to consider the mark only from the standpoint of the public at large, rather than from the purportedly disparaged ethnic or religious group's standpoint.

🏛 RULE OF LAW
Where a mark is disparaging to an ethnic or religious group—whether intentionally or not—for purposes of registration the proper test is to determine whether the mark is disparaging from the purportedly disparaged group's standpoint, rather than from the standpoint of the public at large.

FACTS: Lebanese Arak Corporation (Lebanese Arak) (P) sought to register the mark "KHORAN" for alcoholic beverages and wines. The word "Khoran" in Armenian means "alter." The examiner denied registration, determining that the mark would disparage the beliefs of Muslim Americans, who believe that the Koran is the holiest text, and that the Koran prohibits the drinking of alcohol in any form. The examiner concluded that the mark "KHORAN" is the phonetic equivalent of "Koran," and pointed to evidence that one of the many transliterated spellings for the Koran is "Khoran." Further, there was no evidence that people other than those who speak and understand Armenian are likely to recognize "KHORAN" as the Armenian word for "altar," in particular, there was no evidence that Muslim Americans would be aware of the Armenian meaning of the word. Lebanese Arak (P) urged that there was no intent to disparage, and that the proper test for determining whether a mark is disparaging is to consider the mark only from the standpoint of the public at large, rather than from the purportedly disparaged ethnic or religious group's standpoint. The Trademark Trial and Appeal Board (the TTAB) granted review.

ISSUE: Where a mark is disparaging to an ethnic or religious group—whether intentionally or not—for purposes of registration is the proper test to determine whether the mark is disparaging from the purportedly

disparaged group's standpoint, rather than from the standpoint of the public at large?

HOLDING AND DECISION: (Seeherman, J.) Yes. Where a mark is disparaging to an ethnic or religious group—whether intentionally or not—for purposes of registration the proper test is to determine whether the mark is disparaging from the purportedly disparaged group's standpoint, rather than from the standpoint of the public at large. The determination whether a proposed mark is disparaging requires application of a two-part test: (1) what is the likely meaning of the matter in question, taking into account not only dictionary definitions, but also the relationship of the matter to the other elements in the mark, the nature of the goods or services, and the manner in which the mark is used in the marketplace in connection with the goods or services; and (2) if that meaning is found to refer to identifiable persons, institutions, beliefs or national symbols, whether that meaning may be disparaging to a substantial composite of the referenced group. Here, there is no real dispute as to the test's second prong, as there was sufficient evidence that most Americans would view "KHORAN" as the commercial equivalent of "Koran." Contrary to the dissent's argument, the mark should not be considered only from the standpoint of the public at large, since the prohibition against registration of disparaging marks encompasses marks that would be significant to a group, but would not be known or understood by the public at large. It is conceivable that there might be situations where a term that otherwise might be considered disparaging also has such a well-known alternative meaning that, as used in connection with particular goods or services, that alternative meaning would be found to be the applicable one, and registration would be permissible. That is not the case here, however, since the Armenian meaning of "KHORAN" would not be known to the vast majority of Americans, who would view "KHORAN" as the equivalent of "Koran." Even when considered in connection with particular goods, i.e., wine, consideration of the mark may not be limited to prospective purchasers of wine, because wine is a consumer product and is sold to the general public in retail establishments stocking many types of products, so that Muslim Americans potentially would be exposed to the mark even if they do not consume or purchase wine. Further, if the mark were to be registered, the applicant would not be required to provide indications that the product had nothing to do with the Koran. Moreover, the argument that because the term is so disparaging to Muslims and their beliefs, no one would

Continued on next page.

believe that the term could reference the Koran, is unavailing, since even if some people would not believe that a producer of wine would choose to use the name of the holy text of Islam in a disparaging manner, they still would understand "KHORAN" as "Koran," and the public would view "KHORAN" as "Koran" notwithstanding that they believed it to be disparaging. Finally, Lebanon Arak's (P) lack of intent to disparage is irrelevant if the mark does, in fact, disparage Muslim Americans and their beliefs.

DISSENT: (Mermelstein, J.) The majority misapplies the test for disparagement. Instead of considering how the referenced group would understand the mark, the inquiry must be of how the entire U.S. population would understand the mark in connection with the specific goods or services provided. Otherwise, by considering only the purported disparaged group in determining the likely meaning of a mark, the deck would be stacked for purposes of any disparagement test and would lead to cases where a proposed mark will be found disparaging despite the fact that most Americans attribute a different and inoffensive meaning to that mark. Here, when most Americans will encounter the "KHORAN" mark on wine, it is likely that they will not attribute any specific meaning to the mark. As to the argument that "KHORAN" is the phonetic equivalent of "Koran," precedent holds that there is no correct pronunciation of a trademark when the term is not a recognizable English word. In addition, there is nothing in the way Lebanon Arak (P) uses its mark that would suggest any connection to Islam or the Koran. Further, regarding the Koran's prohibition on the consumption of alcohol, it would be counterintuitive for persons familiar with that prohibition to associate "KHORAN" with the holy text prohibiting the goods being sold under the mark. When the "KHORAN" mark is heard or seen in connection with wine, it is more likely that the general public will not attach any particular meaning to the mark. Accordingly, the first part of the disparagement test has not been satisfied by the examiner. In any event, there is significant doubt as to whether or not the general public is even likely to equate "KHORAN," when considered in the context of wine, with the Koran, and this doubt should be resolved by allowing the mark to be published for opposition, thus enabling the parties to have an opportunity to fully develop an evidentiary record and argue the issue.

▶ ANALYSIS

This case illustrates that the disparagement bar to registration differs from the scandalousness provision, in that with the former there is a particular object of disparagement, i.e., a person, group, set of beliefs, or institution or symbol, and the statutory bar depends on the perspective of the object of disparagement. In contrast, the scandalousness provision protects the public as a whole and the effect of the trademark is judged from the perspective of the general public. In this case, the dissent strenuously disagrees with the majority's application of the first prong of the disparagement test, disputing the majority's contention that the determination of "what is the likely meaning of the matter in question" should be made from the perspective of the disparaged group. Instead, the dissent believes that the majority incorrectly conflated the two prongs and made both determinations from the standpoint of the purported disparaged group. Thus, it seems that the dissent would apply the test applicable to the scandalousness bar for the first prong of the test. On the other hand, the majority seems to hold that the proper ground for refusing marks that would offend the sensibilities of an ethnic or religious group is that the matter is disparaging to the members of that group, rather than that the matter is offensive or scandalous, so as to ensure that the group's beliefs and sensibilities are accounted for.

■=■

Bayer Aktiengesellschaft v. Stamatios Mouratidis

Opposer (P) v. Applicant for registration of mark (D)

2010 TTAB LEXIS 218 (T.T.A.B. May 21, 2010).

NATURE OF CASE: Opposition proceeding in trademark registration action.

FACT SUMMARY: Bayer Aktiengesellschaft (Bayer) (P) opposed the registration by Stamatios Mouratidis (D) of the mark "ORGANIC ASPIRIN" on the grounds that as applied to dietary supplements the mark was deceptive and deceptively misdescriptive.

🏛 RULE OF LAW
A mark will be denied trademark registration where it is both deceptively misdescriptive under § 2(e)(1) of the Trademark Act and deceptive under § 2(a) of the Act.

FACTS: Stamatios Mouratidis (Mouratidis) (D) sought to register the mark "ORGANIC ASPIRIN" for use with dietary supplements. Bayer Aktiengesellschaft (Bayer) (P) opposed the registration on the grounds that as applied to dietary supplements the mark was deceptive under § 2(a) of the Trademark Act and deceptively misdescriptive under § 2(e)(1). Aspirin is the generic term for acetylsalicylic acid, which Mouratidis (D) conceded his supplements did not contain. Acetylsalicylic acid is derived from salicylic acid, and is commonly used in tablet form to relieve pain and reduce fever and inflammation. It is also used as an antiplatelet agent. Although the supplements did not contain aspirin, Mouratidis's (D) website likened them to aspirin, as well as to a botanical predecessor of aspirin. The website also advertised that its dietary supplements were naturally occurring phytochemicals and salicylates, which form salicylic acid, and that they contained salicin from botanical forerunners of aspirin. The website also advertised that "ORGANIC ASPIRIN" provided anti-inflammatory and cardiovascular benefits without the gastrointestinal problems that aspirin can cause. "Organic" means produced without synthetic chemicals. Mouratidis (D) argued that the combination of the words "Organic" and "Aspirin" was incongruous, thus creating an inherently distinctive mark. This argument was based on the facts that there is no such thing as organically grown aspirin, that the term "ORGANIC ASPIRIN" is not synonymous with aspirin, and that "ORGANIC ASPIRIN" has no meaning. The Trademark Trial and Appeal Board (the TTAB) considered the opposition.

ISSUE: Will a mark be denied trademark registration where it is both deceptively misdescriptive under § 2(e)(1) of the Trademark Act and deceptive under § 2(a) of the Act?

HOLDING AND DECISION: (Bergsman, J.) Yes. A mark will be denied trademark registration where it is both deceptively misdescriptive under § 2(e)(1) of the Trademark Act and deceptive under § 2(a) of the Act. The test for whether a mark consists of or comprises deceptive matter consists of three questions. The first question asks whether the term is misdescriptive of the character, quality, function, composition, or use of the goods. If the first question is answered affirmatively, the second question asks whether prospective purchasers are likely to believe that the description actually describes the goods. Finally, if the first two questions are answered affirmatively, the third question asks whether the misdescription is likely to affect a significant portion of the relevant consumers' decision to purchase. If the first two questions are answered affirmatively, the mark is deceptively misdescriptive of the goods under § 2(e)(1). If the third question is also answered affirmatively, the mark is also deceptive under § 2(a). Here, the first question must be answered affirmatively. For a term to misdescribe goods, the term must be merely descriptive of a significant aspect of the goods that the goods could plausibly possess but in fact do not. It is plausible that dietary supplements could contain aspirin. However, Mouratidis's (D) products do not in fact contain aspirin. Therefore, the term "Aspirin" is misdescriptive of those products. The second question of the deceptiveness test, i.e., whether prospective purchasers are likely to believe "ORGANIC ASPIRIN" describes Mouratidis's (D) goods is also answered in the affirmative. Reasonably prudent consumers are likely to believe that "ORGANIC ASPIRIN" dietary supplements contain aspirin derived without synthetic chemicals, and Mouratidis's (D) advertising encourages such a belief by leading consumers to mistakenly believe that the supplements include a naturally occurring aspirin, thus leading consumers to believe there are two types of aspirin—synthetic and organic. Accordingly, the term "ORGANIC ASPIRIN" conveys the literal commercial impression that Mouratidis's (D) products are, or contain, a natural aspirin product. Furthermore, the argument made by Mouratidis (D), that the incongruous combination of the words "Organic" and "Aspirin" to form "ORGANIC ASPIRIN" reliably dissuades consumers from believing the goods are made of aspirin, is unpersuasive. The argument's premise, that all consumers know there is no such thing as organic aspirin, is undermined by the fact that Mouratidis (D) is leading consumers to mistakenly believe that his product is, or contains, aspirin derived from natural products. Thus, "ORGANIC ASPIRIN" mistakenly leads consumers to believe that Mouratidis's (D) dietary supplements contain

Continued on next page.

aspirin derived without the use of synthetic chemicals. For these reasons, the mark is deceptively misdescriptive. Finally, the third question of the deceptiveness test—i.e., whether the term "ORGANIC ASPIRIN" is likely to affect the purchasing decision—must also be answered affirmatively, rendering the mark deceptive as well. Consumers will purchase Mouratidis's (D) dietary supplements in the mistaken belief that the products contain aspirin and, thus, provide the health benefits of aspirin. They will want the benefits of aspirin from a natural source, as opposed to synthetic chemicals, without the problems that traditional aspirin may cause. Accordingly, the mark "ORGANIC ASPIRIN" for dietary supplements is both deceptively misdescriptive under § 2(e)(1) and deceptive under § 2(a). [Registration denied.]

▶ ANALYSIS

Whether a mark is merely "deceptively misdescriptive" or just "deceptive" may make a difference for registration purposes, as not all marks that contain an element of deception are both. A deceptive mark is absolutely barred from registration. However, a deceptively misdescriptive mark may be registrable if it is found to have become distinctive through a showing of secondary meaning.

■■■

Quicknotes

DECEPTIVE TRADEMARK A trademark is deceptive where the term is misdescriptive of the character, quality, function, composition or use of the goods; where prospective purchasers are likely to believe that the description actually describes the goods; and the misdescription is likely to affect a significant portion of the relevant consumers' decision to purchase. Alternatively, some courts hold that a deceptive trademark is one where its owner has the intent to actively deceive the purchasing public. A deceptive trademark is not eligible for trademark protection or registration.

DECEPTIVELY MISDESCRIPTIVE TRADEMARK A trademark is deceptively misdescriptive where the term is misdescriptive of the character, quality, function, composition or use of the goods, and where prospective purchasers are likely to believe that the description actually describes the goods. A deceptively misdescriptive trademark is not eligible for trademark protection or registration unless it has acquired secondary meaning.

DISTINCTIVENESS A standard for trademark protection, whereby the more distinctive a mark is, the greater its eligibility for protection. Distinctive marks typically consist of terms that are fanciful or coined, arbitrary, or suggestive. If a mark is descriptive, it is not entitled to trademark protection unless it has acquired distinctiveness through consumer association of goods or services with the mark (such acquired distinctiveness is also known as secondary meaning).

SECONDARY MEANING A word or mark that becomes associated with a particular merchant or product as its source of origin.

■■■

Hornby v. TJX Companies, Inc.

Celebrity (P) v. Clothing manufacturer (D)

87 U.S.P.Q.2d 1411 (T.T.A.B. 2008).

NATURE OF CASE: Proceeding to cancel a trademark registration.

FACT SUMMARY: Leslie Hornby (P), who in the late 1960s and early 1970s had gained celebrity status as the model known as "Twiggy," sought to cancel TJX Companies, Inc.'s (D) mark "TWIGGY" for use on children's clothing, on the ground, inter alia, that the mark created a false suggestion of a connection with her.

🏛 RULE OF LAW
A mark will be cancelled on the ground of false suggestion of a connection where the plaintiff shows that the plaintiff's name or identity is of sufficient fame or reputation that when the defendant's mark is used on its goods or services, a connection with the plaintiff would be presumed; that the mark points uniquely to the plaintiff; that the defendant's mark is the same as plaintiff's name or identity; that the mark would be recognized as such; and that the plaintiff is not connected with the activities performed by the defendant under the mark.

FACTS: Leslie Hornby (P) attained celebrity status in the late 1960s and early 1970s as the model known as "Twiggy." Although that period saw the pinnacle of her fame, she continued to appear before the public for decades afterward through various vehicles, including television shows, movies, Broadway shows, interviews, magazines, publicity tours, etc. In 2000, TJX Companies, Inc. (TJX) (D), registered the mark "TWIGGY" for children's clothing. Just prior to that, in 1999, the Franklin Mint asked Hornby (P) to license her name and likeness for a collectible doll that was one of several in a series of dolls of very famous people. Eventually, over a million "Twiggy" dolls were sold. Also, in 2000, *The American Heritage Dictionary* of the English Language listed "Twiggy" as an entry, as follows: "Originally Lesley Hornby. British model who epitomized the ultrathin look popular from 1966 to 1976." Hornby (P) petitioned to cancel TJX's (D) mark on the ground, inter alia, that as used on children's clothing, the mark created a false suggestion of a connection with Hornby (P). The Trademark Trial and Appeal Board (the TTAB) heard the petition.

ISSUE: Will a mark be cancelled on the ground of false suggestion of a connection where the plaintiff shows that the plaintiff's name or identity is of sufficient fame or reputation that when the defendant's mark is used on its goods or services, a connection with the plaintiff would be presumed; that the mark points uniquely to the plaintiff; that the defendant's mark is the same as plaintiff's name or identity; that the mark would be recognized as such; and that the plaintiff is not connected with the activities performed by the defendant under the mark?

HOLDING AND DECISION: (Seeherman, J.) Yes. A mark will be cancelled on the ground of false suggestion of a connection where the plaintiff shows that the plaintiff's name or identity is of sufficient fame or reputation that when the defendant's mark is used on its goods or services, a connection with the plaintiff would be presumed; that the mark points uniquely to the plaintiff; that the defendant's mark is the same as plaintiff's name or identity; that the mark would be recognized as such; and that the plaintiff is not connected with the activities performed by the defendant under the mark. To succeed on such a ground the plaintiff must demonstrate that the name or equivalent thereof claimed to be appropriated by another must be unmistakably associated with a particular personality or "persona" and must point uniquely to the plaintiff. Here, it is not disputed that Hornby (P) is known, both personally and professionally, as "Twiggy," and that TJX's (D) mark is identical to that name. It also is not disputed that she is not connected with TJX (D), and did not give TJX (D) permission to use her name as a trademark for its goods. One factor that is disputed is whether Hornby's (P) name or identity is of sufficient fame or reputation that consumers seeing it on children's clothing would presume a connection with her. Here, the evidence demonstrates that, as of the time of the registration of TJX's (D) mark in 2000, Hornby (P) continued to enjoy fame and reputation as a public figure, appearing before the public in numerous vehicles in the 30 years since the pinnacle of her fame. Her entertainment activities, and the promotional efforts surrounding them, successfully kept her name before the U.S. public, and built on the extraordinary initial reputation and celebrity that was created in the period from 1967–1970. The entry in *The American Heritage Dictionary*, and the enormous success of the sale of the Franklin Mint dolls bearing Hornby's (P) likeness, confirm that consumers would, at the time TJX (D) registered its mark, recognize her name, and that purchasers of children's clothing would, upon seeing the mark "TWIGGY" on such goods, presume an association with her. TJX (D) has argued that purchasers of children's clothing would not be aware of Hornby's (P) activities in 1967–1970, when she was a phenomenon, and that that purchasers who were too young to have been exposed to the "Twiggy phenomenon," or were born after 1970, would not necessarily be aware of her or her name through her various entertain-

Continued on next page.

ment activities subsequent to 1970. A close analysis of this argument reveals that it is unsupported. Although in 2000 some of the purchasers of children's clothing would come within the group pointed to by TJX (D) as not being aware of Hornby (D) *qua* Twiggy, there were men and women in 2000 who were familiar with Hornby (P) who would be purchasers of children's clothing, whether as parents, grandparents, or friends of people with children. Accordingly, Hornby (P) has established that her name is of sufficient fame or reputation that when the TJX's (D) mark is used on children's clothing, a connection with Hornby (P) would be presumed. Additionally, Hornby (P) must establish that TWIGGY, as used on children's clothes, would be recognized as pointing uniquely and unmistakably to "Twiggy" the model. She has done so here. Although "twiggy" has a few dictionary definitions (e.g., "resembling a twig"), the requirement that a defendant's mark point uniquely to the plaintiff does not mean that the term must be a unique term. Rather, in the context of the defendant's goods, it must be determined whether consumers would view the mark as pointing only to the plaintiff, or whether they would perceive it to have a different meaning. Here, there is no evidence that TJX's (D) mark has such a different meaning when used on its clothing. To the contrary, the connection between models and clothing supports the conclusion that the mark points uniquely to Hornby (P). Finally, use of the mark "TWIGGY" in connection with other goods by third parties, e.g., on bikes, and for entertainment services presenting a live squirrel water skiing behind a boat, are not for goods or services even remotely related to clothing, so they are of no value in showing that "TWIGGY" for children's clothing would have a meaning that does not point to Hornby (P). For all these reasons, Hornby (P) has proven that TJX's (D) mark falsely suggests a connection with her. [Registration cancelled].

▶ ANALYSIS

It is not necessary, in order to succeed on a § 2(a) false suggestion of a connection ground, that the plaintiff show that consumers would believe the defendant's goods emanate from the plaintiff. That is a requirement for a § 2(d) likelihood of confusion claim, but not a § 2(a) claim. Here, the court pointed to Hornby's (P) fame as a model not to show that consumers would expect her to be associated with the sale of clothing, but because consumers would likely associate clothing and models, and therefore view the mark "TWIGGY" as pointing to Hornby (P).

Coach Services, Inc. v. Triumph Learning LLC

Luxury leather goods purveyor/opposer (P) v. Test preparation company/registration applicant (D)

668 F.3d 1356 (Fed. Cir. 2012).

NATURE OF CASE: Appeal from dismissal of opposition to trademark registration.

FACT SUMMARY: Coach Services, Inc. (P), a luxury leather goods purveyor, opposed the registration by Triumph Learning, LLC (D) of the mark "COACH" for test preparation materials, and contended that the famousness of its registered mark should have outweighed other factors, including the similarity of the goods and the channels of trade, which weighed against a finding of likelihood of confusion.

🏛 RULE OF LAW
The famousness of an opposer's registered mark alone will not weigh in favor of a finding of likelihood of confusion with an identical mark where other factors, such as the similarity of the goods and the channels of trade, weigh against such a finding.

FACTS: Coach Services, Inc. (CSI) (P) made and sold luxury leather goods and accessories. It had registered the mark "COACH" for such products, and had used the mark for over half a century. It sold its products throughout the United States, through approximately 400 COACH retail stores and over 1000 third-party retailers. CSI (P) had annual sales of $3.5 billion; it advertised in numerous well-known magazines and newspapers, and it had received significant acclaim—so much so that its products were counterfeited. Triumph Learning, LLC (Triumph) (D), sought to register the mark "COACH" for test preparation educational materials, targeting educational professionals. The word mark was to be registered with a stylized "picture" of a tutor. CSI (P) opposed the registration of Triumph's (D) mark. The Trademark Trial and Appeal Board (the TTAB), however, weighing various factors of the test for likelihood of confusion, ruled against CSI (P) on its likelihood of confusion claim. CSI (P) appealed, contending that the famousness of its registered mark should have outweighed other factors, including the similarity of the goods, and the channels of trade, so that the TTAB erred in its determination. The Federal Circuit granted review.

ISSUE: Will the famousness of an opposer's registered mark alone weigh in favor of a finding of likelihood of confusion with an identical mark where other factors, such as the similarity of the goods and the channels of trade, weigh against such a finding?

HOLDING AND DECISION: (O'Malley, J.) No. The famousness of an opposer's registered mark alone will not weigh in favor of a finding of likelihood of confusion

with an identical mark where other factors, such as the similarity of the goods and the channels of trade, weigh against such a finding. The TTAB focused on some of the factors set forth in *In re E.I. DuPont de Nemours & Co., 476 F.2d 1357* (C.C.P.A. 1973), for determining likelihood of confusion: (1) the strength or fame of CSI's "COACH" marks; (2) the similarity of the goods; (3) the channels of trade; (4) the classes of consumers; and (5) the similarity of the marks in their entireties. Here, as CSI (P) asserts, the TTAB correctly determined that CSI's mark is famous based on factors such as length of use, advertising, sales, brand awareness, the variety of goods carrying the mark, and other factors indicating famousness. The TTAB also correctly found that although CSI's (P) mark and Triumph's (D) are identical, when viewed in their commercial contexts, together with the relevant designs and in connection with their respective goods, they convey entirely different commercial impressions. When applied to fashion accessories, CSI's (P) mark is either arbitrary or suggestive of carriage or travel accommodations, thereby engendering the commercial impression of a traveling bag. On the other hand, Triumph's (D) "COACH" marks call to mind a tutor who prepares a student for an examination. Thus, the TTAB correctly found that the two marks, although identical in sound and sight, are not similar. This is particularly true given that the word "coach" is a common English word that has many different definitions in different contexts. The TTAB also correctly found that the parties' goods were unrelated. CSI (P) contended there was overlap between the parties' goods because it had has used its mark in connection with books and audio and videotapes and in connection with tote bags, caps, and shirts. As to the books and tapes, there was no evidence presented of sales or advertising; regarding totes, caps, and shirts—which were used by Triumph's (D) sales agents to market Triumph's (D) test preparation materials—Triumph's (D) applications did not seek to register its "COACH" marks for those items. Finally, as to channels of trade and classes of customers, the TTAB correctly concluded that the channels of trade were distinct. Although there could be some overlap in the classes of purchasers for the parties' products, it was unlikely that, in the circumstances in which the products were sold, customers would associate CSI's "COACH" brand products with educational materials used to prepare students for standardized tests. There was also nothing in the record to suggest that a purchaser of test preparation materials who also purchased a luxury handbag would consider the

Continued on next page.

goods to emanate from the same source—especially given that Triumph (D) targets educational professionals, who are likely to exercise a high level of care in making purchasing decisions, which would minimize likelihood of confusion. In weighing these factors, the TTAB determined that the famousness of CSI's (P) mark and the potential overlap of consumers weighed in CSI's (P) favor. However, the TTAB also determined that because the goods of the parties were not similar or related, because the goods moved in different trade channels, because the marks used by the parties have different meanings and engender different commercial impressions, and because Triumph (D) markets to sophisticated purchasers, these latter factors outweigh the factors favoring CSI (P). CSI's (P) argument that the TTAB should have given more weigh to the famousness of its mark is rejected. It is well established that famousness alone cannot as a matter of law establish likelihood of confusion. Here, the unrelated nature of the parties' goods and their different channels of trade weigh heavily against CSI (P), and, accordingly, the TTAB did not err in holding there was no likelihood of confusion. [Affirmed as to this issue.] [The court also affirmed that there was no likelihood of dilution, but the court vacated and remanded on the question of whether Triumph's (D) mark was merely descriptive without secondary meaning.]

▶ ANALYSIS

The case *In re E.I. DuPont de Nemours & Co., 476 F.2d 1357* (C.C.P.A. 1973), set forth 13 nonexclusive factors that courts could use as proxies for likelihood of confusion. These factors are:(1) The similarity or dissimilarity of the marks in their entireties as to appearance, sound, connotation, and commercial impression. (2) The similarity or dissimilarity and nature of the goods or services as described in an application or registration or in connection with which a prior mark is in use. (3) The similarity or dissimilarity of established, likely-to-continue trade channels. (4) The conditions under which and buyers to whom sales are made, i.e., "impulse" vs. careful, sophisticated purchasing. (5) The fame of the prior mark (sales, advertising, length of use). (6) The number and nature of similar marks in use on similar goods. (7) The nature and extent of any actual confusion. (8) The length of time during and conditions under which there has been concurrent use without evidence of actual confusion. (9) The variety of goods on which a mark is or is not used (house mark, "family" mark, product mark). (10) The market interface between applicant and the owner of a prior mark. (11) The extent to which applicant has a right to exclude others from use of its mark on its goods. (12) The extent of potential confusion, i.e., whether de minimis or substantial. (13) Any other established fact probative of the effect of use.

Quicknotes

DE MINIMIS Insignificant; trivial; not of sufficient significance to require legal action.

PROBATIVE Tending to establish proof.

TRADEMARK DILUTION The diminishment of the capability of a trademark to identify and distinguish the particular good or service with which it is associated.

NutraSweet Co. v. K&S Foods, Inc.

Artificial sweetener manufacturer (P) v. Artificial seasoning manufacturer (D)

4 U.S.P.Q.2d 1964 (T.T.A.B. 1987).

NATURE OF CASE: Opposition to registration of mark.

FACT SUMMARY: K&S Foods, Inc. (K&S) (D) applied to register "NUTRA SALT" as a trademark for salt with trace minerals. The NutraSweet Company (P) opposed the application, claiming that K&S's (D) mark resembles NutraSweet's (P) mark to such a degree that it would cause consumers confusion.

🏛 RULE OF LAW
Use of the same or similar mark in connection with artificial sweeteners and artificial salt products likely would result in confusion as to source or sponsorship.

FACTS: K&S Foods, Inc. (K&S) (D) applied to register "NUTRA SALT" as a trademark for salt with trace minerals. The NutraSweet Company (P) opposed the application. The NutraSweet Company (P) owns the registered mark "NUTRASWEET" for an artificial sweetener that is used as an ingredient by food manufacturers. NUTRASWEET sweeteners are very well known, particularly as the main ingredient in EQUAL sweetener. The NutraSweet Company (P) claimed that K&S's (D) mark resembles its (P) mark to such a degree that it would cause consumers confusion. K&S (D) argued that no confusion will likely arise, because the marks are distinguishable, the goods are different, the market for the products are different, and many third parties use "NUTRA" as part of their trademarks for foods and additives for food.

ISSUE: Would use of the same or similar mark in connection with artificial sweeteners and artificial salt products likely result in confusion as to source or sponsorship?

HOLDING AND DECISION: (Krugman, Member) Yes. Use of the same or similar mark in connection with artificial sweeteners and artificial salt products likely would result in confusion as to source or sponsorship. In this case, the artificial sweetener and salt products are closely related, complementary products. Purchasers familiar with the NutraSweet product, either as an ingredient in Equal or as an ingredient in other food products, would be likely to believe that NUTRA SALT was a new product line put out by the same producer as the NUTRASWEET producer. K&G's (D) argument, that third-party uses of marks containing "NUTRA" is unsupported by the evidence. Finally, the fact that there have been no instances of actual confusion is not significant. The opposition is sustained.

▶ ANALYSIS

This case, like *In re White*, 80 U.S.P.Q.2d 1654 (T.T.A.B. 2006), is fact intensive. The Trademark Trial and Appeal Board's primary consideration is of the evidence supporting the opposition, and the possibility of confusion on the part of the consumer.

■━■

Quicknotes

TRADEMARK Any word, name, symbol, device or combination thereof that is either currently utilized, or which a person has a bona fide intent to utilize, in commerce in order to distinguish his goods from those of another.

■━■

In re Joint-Stock Company "Baik"

Foreign company (P) v. Patent and Trademark Office (D)

80 U.S.P.Q.2d 1305 (T.T.A.B. 2006).

NATURE OF CASE: Appeal to the Trademark Trial and Appeal Board of the Patent and Trademark Office's refusal to register a mark.

FACT SUMMARY: A Russian company, Joint-Stock Company "Baik" (P), sought to trademark the word "BAIKALSKAYA" for vodka it intended to sell. Registration was refused under the Trademark Act on the ground that the mark is primarily geographically descriptive of the company's goods.

RULE OF LAW
Under § 2(e)(2) of the Trademark Act, the test to determine whether a term is primarily geographically descriptive is whether (1) the term in the mark sought to be registered is the name of a place known generally to the public and (2) the public would make a goods/place association.

FACTS: A Russian company, Joint-Stock Company "Baik" (P), sought to trademark the word "BAIKALS-KAYA" for vodka it intended to sell. The Patent and Trademark Office (D) examining attorney found that translated from Russian, the term "BAIKALSKAYA" means "from Baikal," which is the name of a famous lake in Irkutsk, Russia, where Joint-Stock (P) is located, and that water from the lake was used to make the vodka. Registration was refused under the Trademark Act on the ground that the mark is primarily geographically descriptive of the company's goods.

ISSUE: Under § 2(e)(2) of the Trademark Act, is the test to determine whether a term is primarily geographically descriptive whether (1) the term in the mark sought to be registered is the name of a place known generally to the public and (2) the public would make a goods/place association?

HOLDING AND DECISION: (Kuhlke, J.) Yes. Under § 2(e)(2) of the Trademark Act, the test to determine whether a term is primarily geographically descriptive is whether (1) the term in the mark sought to be registered is the name of a place known generally to the public and (2) the public would make a goods/place association. Where the goods actually do come from the place named in the mark, the goods/place association can be presumed unless there is a genuine issue as to whether the place named in the mark is so obscure or remote that purchasers would fail to recognize the term as indicating the geographical source of the goods. Lake Baikal is well known because it is the world's deepest lake, and is the subject of numerous articles in U.S. publications. The fact that the term intended for registration—"Baikalskaya," which literally means "from Baikal"—is an adjective doesn't diminish its geographic significance. A significant number of consumers would conclude upon seeing a bottle of BAIKALSKAYA vodka that it is a place name, and that the vodka came from there. In addition, Baikal is not a remote or obscure place. The Examining Attorney submitted dictionary entries for Lake Baikal (the world's largest fresh water lake) and Irkutsk (an industrial center and major stop on the Trans-Siberian Railroad), Lexis/Nexis printouts, excerpts from travel web sites, and materials indicating the number of Russian speakers in this country. Joint-Stock's (P) argument that Americans have limited knowledge of world geography and that they "could not find the Atlantic Ocean on a globe" fails, since the company offered no evidence to support the contention, and the American public "as a whole" is not relevant. A subset of the Americans, those who purchase vodka, is what matters. Because one can infer that a significant portion of American vodka purchasers would conclude that "BAIKALSKAYA" refers to a place name, the first prong of the test is met. As to the second prong, a goods/place association is presumed, because Joint-Stock (P) is located near Lake Baikal, and the company has admitted that its vodka is made there, and by using waters from the lake. Affirmed.

ANALYSIS

Note that the court also ruled that Joint-Stock's (P) ownership of a now-cancelled registration did not help its cause. A cancelled registration is not entitled to any of the statutory presumptions of § 7(b) of the Trademark Act and prior decisions by examining attorneys are not binding on the Trademark Trial and Appeal Board.

■=■

Quicknotes

LANHAM ACT, § 43(a) Federal trademark infringement statute.

■=■

In re Miracle Tuesday, LLC

[Parties not identified.]

695 F.3d 1339 (Fed. Cir. 2012).

NATURE OF CASE: Appeal from affirmance of refusal to register a mark on the ground that it is geographically deceptively misdescriptive under § 2(e)(3) of the Lanham Act.

FACT SUMMARY: Miracle Tuesday LLC (P), which sought to register the mark "JPK PARIS 75" for use on fashion accessories, contended that registration should not have been denied on the ground that the mark was primarily geographically deceptively misdescriptive because, although the goods were neither designed nor manufactured in Paris, its principal, Jean-Pierre Klifa (JPK), who designed the accessories, was a French citizen who had lived in Paris before relocating to the United States, so that JPK's significant ties to Paris were sufficient to warrant the use of the term "Paris" in the mark.

🏛 RULE OF LAW

A mark is geographically deceptively misdescriptive under § 2(e)(3) of the Lanham Act, and therefore barred from registration, where the mark identifies a geographic location for goods that are associated with that location, but in fact the goods are neither designed nor produced at the location identified in the mark.

FACTS: Miracle Tuesday LLC (P) sought to register the mark "JPK PARIS 75" for use on fashion accessories. Miracle Tuesday's principal, Jean-Pierre Klifa (JPK), who designed the accessories, was a French citizen who had lived in Paris for over 20 years before relocating to the United States, where he had lived for over 26 years. The accessories were neither designed nor manufactured in Paris, and other than the connection to JPK, there was no connection of the goods to Paris. The examiner refused registration on the grounds that the mark was geographically deceptively misdescriptive under § 2(e)(3) of the Lanham Act, given that Paris is famous for fashion and fashion accessories, and that, therefore, consumers would likely associate the product with the geographic location in the mark. The Trademark Trial and Appeal Board (the TTAB) affirmed, finding that the monogram "JPK" was not the dominant portion of the mark, and that the designation "Paris" in the mark would serve to identify the geographic origin of the products, so that consumers would assume that Miracle Tuesday's (P) products had a connection with Paris either in their manufacture or their design. Miracle Tuesday (P) argued, inter alia, that the TTAB erred when it found that the goods identified did not originate in Paris even though JPK had significant ties to Paris, and erred by applying the wrong standard in

concluding that the use of the word "Paris" in the mark was deceptive. The court of appeals granted review.

ISSUE: Is a mark geographically deceptively misdescriptive under § 2(e)(3) of the Lanham Act, and therefore barred from registration, where the mark identifies a geographic location for goods that are associated with that location, but in fact the goods are neither designed nor produced at the location identified in the mark?

HOLDING AND DECISION: (O'Malley, J.) Yes. A mark is geographically deceptively misdescriptive under § 2(e)(3) of the Lanham Act, and therefore barred from registration, where the mark identifies a geographic location for goods that are associated with that location, but in fact the goods are neither designed nor produced at the location identified in the mark. A mark is primarily geographically deceptively misdescriptive if (1) the primary significance of the mark is a generally known geographic location; (2) the consuming public is likely to believe the place identified by the mark indicates the origin of the goods bearing the mark, when in fact the goods do not come from that place; and (3) the misrepresentation was a material factor in the consumer's decision to purchase the goods. Here, Miracle Tuesday (P) challenges the TTAB's findings as to the second and third elements of this test. Regarding the second element, there needs to be only a reasonable likelihood that consumers will believe the place identified by the mark indicates the origin of the goods bearing the mark. Such a showing can be based on the inference that the consumer associates the product with the geographic location in the mark because that place is known for producing the product. Because Paris is famous for fashion and fashion accessories, including the types of goods identified in the application, it is reasonably likely that relevant purchasers will think of Paris as a known source for fashion accessories, so that there is sufficient evidence of a goods/place association between Paris and the goods listed on Miracle Tuesday's (P) application. The second part of the second element asks whether the goods in fact originate in the place identified by the mark. Manufacture is an indication of origin, but other factors may also indicate origin. For example, the place of design can also designate origin, as can the inclusion in the goods of a main component or ingredient made in that place. Miracle Tuesday (P) argues that the fact that JPK lived and worked in Paris for 22 years is sufficient to justify the conclusion that the products originated in Paris, especially since fashion customers are more interested in the designer's origin

Continued on next page.

than the origin of the goods themselves. However, under the statute, the relevant inquiry is whether there is a connection between the goods and Paris—not between the designer and Paris. Here, there is no evidence of such a connection, as there is no evidence, for example, that JPK designed the goods while he was in Paris. Thus, the attempt to shift the inquiry to the historical origin of the designer fails. The TTAB's determinations as to the second element were thus correct and justified; simply put, there is no current connection between the goods listed in the application and Paris. As to the third element, there must be some indication that a substantial portion of the relevant consumers would be materially influenced in the decision to purchase the product or service by the geographic meaning of the mark. An inference of such materiality may be derived from evidence that the place is famous as a source of the goods at issue—and here it is undisputed that Paris is famous a source of fashion goods. Thus, the TTAB correctly inferred that a substantial portion of consumers who encountered Miracle Tuesday's (P) mark on its fashion goods would likely be deceived into believing that those products come from or were designed in Paris. Miracle Tuesday (P) unpersuasively argues that the TTAB applied the wrong standard and, instead, must have evidence that the geographic reference in the mark causes actual deception. According to Miracle Tuesday (P), because there is a substantial connection between JPK and Paris, the reference to Paris in the mark is a true statement that is not deceptive. The heightened standard Miracle Tuesday (P) would have the court apply is one that is used for services, not goods, but there is no authority for treating a mark for fashion goods as a service mark. Accordingly, the TTAB's inference of materiality was not erroneous. [Affirmed.]

▶ ANALYSIS

It should be noted that the standard under § 2(e)(3) is more difficult to satisfy for service marks than for marks on goods, since geographic marks in connection with services are less likely to mislead the public than geographic marks on goods. Given these differences, the evidence necessary to give rise to an inference of materiality for goods and that necessary to give rise to that same inference for services is not the same. Although for goods—as in this case—evidence that a place is famous as a source of those goods is sufficient to raise an inference of materiality, when dealing with service marks, there must be a heightened association between the services and geographic location. In other words, an inference of materiality arises in the event of a very strong services-place association. Without a particularly strong services-place association, an inference would not arise, leaving the Patent and Trademark Office to seek direct evidence of materiality.

Quicknotes

INTER ALIA Among other things.

MATERIALITY Importance; the degree of relevance or necessity to the particular matter.

In re Quadrillion Publishing Ltd.

Publisher (P) v. Patent and Trademark Office (D)

2000 WL 1195470, (2000 TTAB Lexis 562, Aug. 9, 2000).

NATURE OF CASE: Appeal to the Trademark Trial and Appeal Board of a Patent and Trademark Office refusal to register a mark.

FACT SUMMARY: The Patent and Trademark Office (D) refused to register the mark "BRAMLEY" for a variety of books, magazines, and stationery items intended for sale by Quadrillion Publishing Ltd. (P), on ground that the mark is primarily a surname.

🏛 RULE OF LAW
The test for determining whether a mark is primarily merely a surname is the primary significance of the mark to the purchasing public.

FACTS: The Patent and Trademark Office (D) refused to register the mark "BRAMLEY" for a variety of books, magazines, and stationery items intended for sale by Quadrillion Publishing Ltd. (P), on ground that the mark is primarily a surname. The examining attorney searched a database of 80 million names and found 433 "BRAMLEY" surname listings, and presented evidence that there was no listing of the word in the dictionary.

ISSUE: Is the test for determining whether a mark is primarily merely a surname the primary significance of the mark to the purchasing public?

HOLDING AND DECISION: (Bucher, J.) Yes. The test for determining whether a mark is primarily merely a surname is the primary significance of the mark to the purchasing public. Factors in making a surname determination include: (1) the degree of surname rareness, (2) whether anyone connected with the applicant has the surname, (3) whether the term has any recognized meaning other than that of a surname, and (4) the structure and pronunciation or "look and sound" of the surname. The burden is on the examining attorney to show a prima facie case that a mark is primarily merely a surname. The record shows that the examining attorney in this case met that burden. With respect to the first factor, telephone directories and address books from across the country were consulted, and while "BRAMLEY" is not as common as some other surnames, it is not rare. As to the second factor, no one connected to Quadrillion Publishing (P) has been shown to have the "BRAMLEY" name, but the fact that this is true does not compel the conclusion that consumers will perceive the name as a nonsurname. Third, while the term does have meanings other than the surname—it is the name of a tiny rural English village and is the name of a variety of apple—they are remote or obscure meanings that would not be recognized by a significant number of people.

Finally, with respect to the fourth factor, "BRAMLEY" has the structure and pronunciation of a surname, not of an arbitrary designation. The refusal to register is affirmed.

▶ ANALYSIS

Surnames that are now distinctive under § 2(f)—for example, surnames that have a secondary meaning—are registrable. That registration gives the registrant exclusive use, but the Trademark Trial and Appeal Board supports exclusive use rarely.

∎═∎

Quicknotes

PRIMA FACIE CASE An action where the plaintiff introduces sufficient evidence to submit the issue to the judge or jury for determination.

∎═∎

In re Becton, Dickinson and Co.

[Parties not identified.]

675 F.3d 1368 (Fed. Cir. 2012).

NATURE OF CASE: Appeal from affirmance of refusal to register a design on the ground that the design is functional.

FACT SUMMARY: Gibson Becton, Dickinson and Co. (BD) (P), which sought to register a design of a closure cap for blood collection tubes as a trademark, contended that registration should not have been refused on the grounds that the design as a whole was functional and that the design's nonfunctional elements served to remove the mark as a whole from the realm of functionality.

🏛 RULE OF LAW
In determining whether a design mark, taken as a whole, is functional, and therefore not trademark registrable, the functional and nonfunctional features of the mark may be weighed against each other.

FACTS: Gibson Becton, Dickinson and Co. (BD) (P) sought to register a design of a closure cap for blood collection tubes as a trademark. The design had several elements, including vertically elongated ribs set out in combination sets of numerous slim ribs bordered by fatter ribs around most of the cap circumference, where a smooth area separated sets of ribs. The slim ribs tapered at their top to form triangular shapes that intersected and blended together at a point where a smooth surface area ringed the top of the cap above the ribs, thus extending the cap's vertical profile. At the bottom, a flanged lip ringed the cap and protruded from the sides in two circumferential segments with the bottom-most segment having a slightly curved contour. BD (P) had filed a utility patent (the '446 patent) that disclosed the utilitarian advantages of the design sought to be registered, and BD (P) had also filed several design patents for the design. BD's (P) advertising had extoled the utilitarian advantages of several design features of the proposed mark, including (1) the ridges on the side of the cap that allow for a more secure grip, (2) the flanged lip at the bottom that inhibits the handler's ability to roll their thumb to pop off the cap, thereby reducing the risk of splattering, and (3) the hooded feature of the cap whereby the bottom of the cap extends over the top of the tube and thus prevents the user's gloves from getting pinched between the stopper and tube when closing the tube. No evidence was presented as to whether the design resulted from a comparatively simple or inexpensive method of manufacture. The examiner refused registration on the ground that the design, as a whole, was functional, and the Trademark Trial and Appeal Board (the TTAB) affirmed, applying a four-part test. The TTAB weighed the mark's functional aspects against its nonfunctional aspects and determined that the mark as a whole was functional. BD (P) appealed, contending that the TTAB had committed legal error and that the design's nonfunctional elements served to remove the mark as a whole from the realm of functionality. The court of appeals granted review.

ISSUE: In determining whether a design mark, taken as a whole, is functional, and therefore not trademark registrable, may the functional and nonfunctional features of the mark be weighed against each other?

HOLDING AND DECISION: (Clevenger, J.) Yes. In determining whether a design mark, taken as a whole, is functional, and therefore not trademark registrable, the functional and nonfunctional features of the mark may be weighed against each other. The established, four-part test for determining de jure functionality comes from *In re Morton-Norwich Prods., Inc.,* 671 F.2d 1332 (CCPA 1982): (1) the existence of a utility patent disclosing the utilitarian advantages of the design; (2) advertising materials in which the originator of the design touts the design's utilitarian advantages; (3) the availability to competitors of functionally equivalent designs; and (4) facts indicating that the design results in a comparatively simple or cheap method of manufacturing the product. The TTAB gave weight in favor of a finding of functionality to the existence of the '446 patent, and to BD's (P) advertising that touted the advantages of the cap design. Regarding the availability of alternative designs, the TTAB found that the record did not establish that there were alternative designs for collection tube closure caps, which weighed in favor of functionality, and, finding no evidence as to whether the cap design resulted from a comparatively simple or inexpensive method of manufacture, the TTAB determined that it would not give weight to this factor. Weighing these factors, the TTAB concluded that the cap design, as a whole, was functional. BD (P) asserted that the elongated shape of the closure cap, the spacing of the ribs and their particular shapes, as well as the design relationship of those features to the whole of the closure cap were the design embraced by the mark, and that the TTAB should have concluded that these nonfunctional features saved the design from being functional as a whole. When, as here, there are both functional and nonfunctional elements of a design, the key inquiry is the degree of utility present in the overall design of the mark. In determining the degree of utility, de facto functionality, which simply means that a design has a function, is irrelevant to the inquiry. Instead, the focus is on de jure

Continued on next page.

functionality, which means that a product is in its particular shape because it works better in this shape. Whether an overall design is functional is based on the superiority of the design as a whole, rather than on whether each design feature has utility. Accordingly, the TTAB committed no legal error by weighing the functional and nonfunctional features of BD's (P) mark against each other in determining whether BD's (P) mark in its entirety was overall de jure functional. Here, the TTAB did not err in concluding that the '446 patent revealed the utilitarian nature of two prominent features of BD's (P) mark, and that this factor favored a finding of functionality. The TTAB also did not err in discounting the existence of several design patents for the cap, since there was no identity between the designs in the patents and the design submitted for trademark registration. Similarly, the TTAB was correct in determining that BD's (P) advertising favored a finding of functionality, since such advertising touted the utilitarian advantages of the prominent features of the mark, and since the designs shown in the advertisements, although not exactly the same as the proposed mark's design, were sufficiently similar to the features of the claimed mark to show an identity of functionality between the articles shown in the advertising and the proposed mark's prominent features. As to the third factor, if functionality is found based on other considerations, it is not necessary to consider the availability of alternative designs, because the feature cannot be given trade dress protection merely because there are alternative designs available. Thus, the TTAB, having found functionality based on other factors, was not required to consider this factor. Nevertheless, the TTAB did consider this factor, and in doing so determined that one of three third-party designs was irrelevant and the other two could not be characterized as alternative designs because they shared the same utilitarian features of BD's (P) design. The TTAB did not err in determining that this factor also weighed in favor of a finding of functionality. Finally, the TTAB did not err in refusing to give any weight to the fourth factor, as to which no evidence was available. The evidence showed that BD's (P) competitors used the same key design features on their caps, and from this the TTAB concluded that there were no meaningful alternative designs. For all these reasons, the TTAB's conclusion was supported by substantial evidence, and the TTAB committed no legal error. Affirmed.

DISSENT: (Linn, J.) Although the majority is correct that the focus of the inquiry must be on the degree of de jure functionality, the majority errs in approving the weighing of the elements of a mark against one another to develop an understanding of whether the mark as a whole is essentially functional and thus nonregistrable. The proper inquiry is to examine the degree to which the mark as a whole is dictated by utilitarian concerns or is arbitrary. The degree of design utility must be analyzed for the whole mark, not the mark's dissociated functional elements. The TTAB and the majority placed principal focus on the function served by certain features of the mark, including the top's opening (to allow for the insertion of a needle), the ribs on the side of the cap (to allow for increased grip), and the bottom's flanged lip (to allow for a safer opening). These considerations relate to the de facto functionality of individual product features and not the de jure functionality of the overall design. Even considering each design element—which it is not proper to do—there was no evidence that any of those elements had to be the way they were as presented in the application. Additionally, the '446 patent failed to shed light on functionality, since it claimed none of the features of BD's design mark, so that the majority and the TTAB were incorrect in relying on this utility patent for proof of functionality. Also, BD's (P) ads supported a finding of nonfunctionality because they demonstrated that there were alternative designs available that were nonetheless functionally identical (thus supporting the third *Morton-Norwich* factor). Moreover, the TTAB and the majority improperly discounted the most probative evidence submitted in the case—the design patents and evidence of alternative designs—which suggested that the design at issue was not "made in the form it must be made if it is to accomplish its purpose." In fact, precedence has held that the presence of a design patent, even when a utility patent exists, presumptively indicates a design is de jure nonfunctional. Although the majority was correct in noting that there is no need to consider alternative designs when functionality has been established, that does not mean that the availability of alternative designs cannot be a legitimate source of evidence to determine whether a feature is functional in the first place. Here, the TTAB and the majority improperly discounted the evidence of alternative designs because those designs shared the same utilitarian features as those of BD's (P) cap; such disregard is unsupported by law. To the contrary, this evidence strongly suggests that BD's (P) design is not functional because BD (P) faces competition from products with similar functionality, yet differing designs. Finally, some evidence was presented on the fourth *Morton-Norwich* factor, and the TTAB was obligated to consider it, regardless of its quantity. For all these reasons, the TTAB committed legal error in failing to analyze the functionality of BD's (P) mark as a whole and lacked substantial evidence for its finding.

ANALYSIS

De jure functionality is directed to the appearance of the design (not the thing itself) and is concerned with whether the design is made in the form it must be made if it is to accomplish its purpose. In other words, the inquiry is whether the appearance is dictated by function. Nevertheless, evidentiary concerns allow the Patent and Trademark Office to establish a prima facie case of functionality by

Continued on next page.

analyzing de facto functional features of a design, but the applicant may rebut the prima facie case of functionality by presenting evidence of a lack of de jure functionality. Here, the majority concluded that there was substantial evidence that BD's (P) design was dictated by function, whereas the dissent concluded that the evidence failed to prove that the overall design, rather than the functionality of the disparate design elements, was the best design or one of a few superior designs available, so that the design was arbitrary and not dictated by function.

■━━■

Quicknotes

DE JURE FUNCTIONALITY Functionality of a product that is essential to the use or purpose of the article or that affects the cost or quality of the article, so that exclusive use of the feature through the grant of trade dress protection would put competitors at a significant non-reputation-related disadvantage. De jure functionality is distinguished from de facto functionality, which simply means that the product or packaging performs the function that it was intended to perform.

■━━■

In re Vertex Group LLC

[Parties not identified.]

89 U.S.P.Q.2d 1694 (T.T.A.B. 2009).

NATURE OF CASE: Appeal from refusal to register as a trademark a sound mark on the ground that the mark is functional.

FACT SUMMARY: Vertex Group LLC (P) sought to register as a trademark a loud pulsing "alarm" sound for use with bracelets to prevent child abduction; registration was refused on the ground that the mark was functional.

🏛 RULE OF LAW
A mark is functional, and therefore barred from trademark registration, where its use is essential to the use or purpose of applicant's products, and where factors used for determining functionality weigh in favor of a finding of functionality.

FACTS: Vertex Group LLC (Vertex) (P) sought to register as a trademark a pulsing "alarm" sound for use with bracelets to prevent child abduction. The application specified that its sound pulses would be between 1,500 Hz and 2,300 Hz. The description of the sound was not limited to any particular loudness. However, the specimen of use showed that the loudness of the sound was an essential feature of the product. Vertex (P) also had a utility patent for a digital wristwatch with a "loud alarm" as an exemplary embodiment for the product, and its advertising extolled the loudness of the alarm sound. The sound of Vertex's (P) product had no bearing on the cost or ease of manufacture of its alarms. The examiner refused registration on the ground that the mark was functional. The Trademark Trial and Appeal Board (the TTAB) heard the appeal.

ISSUE: Is a mark functional, and therefore barred from trademark registration, where its use is essential to the use or purpose of applicant's products, and where factors used for determining functionality weigh in favor of a finding of functionality?

HOLDING AND DECISION: (Rogers, J.) Yes. A mark is functional, and therefore barred from trademark registration, where its use is essential to the use or purpose of applicant's products, and where factors used for determining functionality weigh in favor of a finding of functionality. There are two possible bases upon which a finding of functionality may be made. First, if the product feature is essential to the use or purpose of the article it may be found functional. Second, if the product feature affects the cost or quality of the article, so that exclusive right to use it would put a competitor at a disadvantage, this, too, may support a conclusion that the product feature is functional. In addition, a four-part test for functionality, derived from *In re Morton-Norwich Prods., Inc.*, 671 F.2d 1332 (CCPA 1982), may also be used to determine functionality. This test looks at: (1) the existence of a utility patent disclosing the utilitarian advantages of the design; (2) advertising materials in which the originator of the design touts the design's utilitarian advantages; (3) the availability to competitors of functionally equivalent designs; and (4) facts indicating that the design results in a comparatively simple or cheap method of manufacturing the product. Here, Vertex's (P) mark is functional under any of these tests. The use of a loud, pulsating sound is essential to the use or purpose of Vertex's (P) products, and it has been shown that such a sound is predominantly used for alarms. Although Vertex (P) is not seeking to register a sound of any particular loudness, its application effectively encompasses all reasonable degrees of loudness for an alarm sound. Based on the specimen of use, it is clear that the alarm emits a loud sound and that the loudness of the sound is an essential feature of the product. For this reason alone, the functionality refusal must be affirmed. However, consideration of the *Morton-Norwich* factors leads to the same conclusion. First, Vertex's (P) utility patent focuses on a loud alarm. Even if Vertex (P) is correct in its argument that the existence of its patent application for its product is not relevant to a *Morton-Norwich* analysis regarding the registrability of its sound, the absence of a patent for the sound would merely render this factor neutral for the functionality analysis. Second, the focus of Vertex's (P) advertising on the loudness of its alarm favors a finding of functionality. Third, the inquiry of whether competitors would have functionally equivalent sounds available to them if Vertex (P) were accorded the exclusive rights attendant to registration also supports a functionality finding. Although there are thousands of specific frequencies within the range that is most suitable for use in alarms—between 1,000 and 3,000 Hz—and although Vertex's (P) description of its mark only specifies that its sound pulses will be between 1,500 Hz and 2,300 Hz, based on this description, Vertex (P) would be free to combine sound pulses for any of the frequencies within this range, which constitutes a large swath of the optimal range for alarms. This would potentially deprive competitors of many of those options. Accordingly, this factor weighs in favor of a functionality finding. Finally, because the sound of Vertex's (P) product has no bearing on the cost or ease of manufacture of its alarms, the final *Morton-Norwich* factor is neutral. Weighing these factor leads to the conclu-

Continued on next page.

sion that the mark is functional and, therefore, not registrable. [Affirmed.]

▶ *ANALYSIS*

Where, as here, the design is determined to be functional
because the product feature to be registered is essential to
the use or purpose of the article, there is no need to
proceed further to consider if there is a competitive necessity for the feature. In this case, although it did not have to
consider this competitive necessity factor—having already
determined that Vertex's (P) sound was functional—the
TTAB nevertheless undertook an analysis of this factor in
its assessment of the third *Morton-Norwich* factor, concluding that this factor weighed in favor a finding of
functionality.

■══■

Quicknotes

FUNCTIONALITY Doctrine that protection will only be
afforded to the elements of a product's trade dress,
such as shape or color, as long as the elements are not
essential to the use or purpose of the product, and
competition would not be impaired if exclusive rights
were granted therein.

■══■

CHAPTER 5

Loss of Trademark Rights

Quick Reference Rules of Law

Bayer Co. v. United Drug Co.

Drug company (P) v. Competitor (D)

272 F. 505 (S.D.N.Y. 1921).

NATURE OF CASE: Common-law trademark infringement lawsuit.

FACT SUMMARY: Bayer Co. (P) owned a patent for the term "Aspirin." After the patent expired and the term passed into the public domain, United Drug Co. (D) began to use the term for its medicine. Bayer (P) sought to enjoin United Drug (D) from using the term, on the grounds that it constituted trademark infringement.

RULE OF LAW
Where the only reasonable inference that can be drawn from the evidence is that the consumer understands a term as nothing more than a kind of drug, without association with a particular source, the term is generic, and therefore not subject to trademark protection.

FACTS: Bayer Co. (P) owned a patent for the term "Aspirin." After the patent expired and the term passed into the public domain, United Drug Co. (D), a competitor of Bayer's (P), began to use the term for its medicine. Bayer (P) filed a common-law trademark infringement suit, seeking to enjoin United Drug (D) from using the term. United Drug (D) argued that "Aspirin" had become commonly recognized name for the drug, and that when the patent expired, anyone could manufacture the drug and use the term to describe it.

ISSUE: Where the only reasonable inference that can be drawn from the evidence is that the consumer understands a term as nothing more than a kind of drug, without association with a particular source, is the term generic, and therefore not subject to trademark protection?

HOLDING AND DECISION: (Hand, J.) Yes. Where the only reasonable inference that can be drawn from the evidence is that the consumer understands a term as nothing more than a kind of drug, without association with a particular source, the term is generic, and therefore not subject to trademark protection. Initially, when the drug was sold by prescription, it was sold as a powder, and it was not labeled as a Bayer (P) product. At that time, people who worked in the trade—physicians, pharmacists, and so on—understood the term "Aspirin" as a description of medication produced by Bayer (P). In 1904, chemists began to make tablets and by 1915, the consumer had become accustomed to purchasing the drug himself. The bottles of tablets they bought during this time were labeled as "Aspirin," along with some indication of the maker, but none of Bayer (P). So by this time, United Drug (D) seems to have rebutted any presumption

that the term might have been connected to Bayer (P). By the time Bayer (P) began marketing its name with its use of the word "Aspirin" in 1915, it was too late to reclaim the word, which had already passed into the public domain. Consumers understand the term only as a kind of goods, and it makes no difference how hard Bayer (P) tries to make them understand a connection with Bayer (P) at this point. In this situation, where the consumer already understands the word as a kind of medication, United Drug (D), by using the term, is not taking away customers who wanted to deal with Bayer (P).

ANALYSIS

It was Bayer's (P) failure to appropriate the term in any way between 1904, when tablets became generally available, and 1915, when it began selling the tablets in bottles that included the name of the company, that allowed the court to conclude that the word "Aspirin" was a generic term in the minds of consumers. Had the term been used in conjunction with use of the company name, the outcome may have been different.

■=■

Quicknotes

COMMON-LAW RIGHTS In trademark law, common-law rights arise from actual use of a mark and may allow the common-law user to successfully challenge a registration or application. These rights have been developed under a judicially created scheme of rights governed by state law, rather than being created by statute.

GENERIC MEANING A term that encompasses a class of related products and lacks the requisite distinctiveness for federal trademark protection.

TRADEMARK INFRINGEMENT The unauthorized use of another's trademark in such a manner as to cause a likelihood of confusion as to the source of the product or service in connection with which it is utilized.

■=■

E.I. DuPont de Nemours & Co. v. Yoshida International, Inc.

Trademark owner (P) v. Infringer (D)

393 F. Supp. 502 (E.D.N.Y. 1975).

NATURE OF CASE: Trademark infringement action.

FACT SUMMARY: E.I. DuPont de Nemours & Co. (DuPont) (P) owned the "teflon" trademark for nonstick cookware coating. DuPont (P) brought a trademark infringement action against Yoshida International, Inc. (YKK) (D), which manufactured the "eflon" easy-glidezipper. YKK (D) argued that "teflon" was a generic term, and produced two surveys of the public in support of its assertion. DuPont (P) introduced surveys indicating the opposite conclusion.

🏛 RULE OF LAW

(1) A survey that specifically asks respondents whether they think a term is a trademark or a generic term carries more weight than one that does not make that distinction.

(2) If the trademark owner presents evidence of sufficient policing activity to prevent unauthorized use of the mark by others, any skepticism should be resolved in the trademark owner's favor.

FACTS: E.I. DuPont de Nemours & Co. (DuPont) (P) owned the "teflon" trademark for nonstick cookware coating. DuPont (P) brought a trademark infringement action against Yoshida International, Inc. (YKK) (D), which manufactured the "eflon" easy-glide zipper. YKK (D) argued that "teflon" was a generic term, and produced two surveys of the public in support of its assertion. DuPont (P) introduced two surveys indicating the opposite conclusion. YKK's (D) surveys asked about "kitchen pots and pans that have their surfaces coated by chemical substances" and "substances that are applied to surfaces of certain products to prevent sticking, and a majority of the respondents indicated awareness of the tools and processes. A majority named "teflon" as the surface or process. DuPont's (P) surveys were asked whether they knew of a brand name or trademark for such a coating, and most of them named "teflon" as a trade name for such a coating.

ISSUE:

(1) Does a survey that specifically asks respondents whether they think a term is a trademark or a generic term carry more weight than one that does not make that distinction?

(2) If the trademark owner presents evidence of sufficient policing activity to prevent unauthorized use of the mark by others, should any skepticism be resolved in the trademark owner's favor?

HOLDING AND DECISION: (Neaher, J.)

(1) Yes. A survey that specifically asks respondents whether they think a term is a trademark or a generic term carries more weight than one that does not make that distinction. DuPont's (P) surveys asked essentially the same question as YKK's (D), but used the expression "brand name or trademark." Specifically, one of DuPont's (P) surveys asks whether "teflon" is a brand name, and that is the crux of the matter. A majority indicated that it is, and that is unrebutted evidence that a substantial majority of the public continues to believe that "teflon" is a brand name.

(2) Yes. If the trademark owner presents evidence of sufficient policing activity to prevent unauthorized use of the mark by others, any skepticism should be resolved in the trademark owner's favor. In this case, there is no evidence that DuPont (P) has been less than diligent in its effort to protect the trademark significance of "teflon." YKK (D) was required to make a clear and convincing showing that the principal significance of the word "teflon" to the public is a term for nonstick coatings and finishes rather than its trademark significance. It has not met its burden.

▶ ANALYSIS

The casebook excerpt does not explain in detail the second holding, but it is significant, because it suggests that the court will consider evidence of the trademark owner's efforts to protect its connection with the mark when deciding whether the mark is generic.

Quicknotes

GENERIC MEANING A term that encompasses a class of related products and lacks the requisite distinctiveness for federal trademark protection.

TRADEMARK Any word, name, symbol, device or combination thereof that is either currently utilized, or which a person has a bona fide intent to utilize, in commerce in order to distinguish his goods from those of another.

America Online, Inc. v. AT&T Corp.

Internet service provider (P) v. Infringer (D)

243 F.3d 812 (4th Cir. 2001).

NATURE OF CASE: Trademark infringement lawsuit.

FACT SUMMARY: America Online, Inc. (AOL) (P) filed a trademark infringement lawsuit against AT&T Corporation (D) after AT&T (D) began using the words "You Have Mail," "You've Got Mail," "Buddy List," and "IM." The federal district court granted summary judgment for AT&T (D), and AOL (P) appealed.

RULE OF LAW
A generic term cannot be converted into a trademark through de facto secondary meaning.

FACTS: Both America Online, Inc. (AOL) (P) and AT&T Corporation (D) provide Internet access, including e-mail services, to their customers. AOL (P) has been using, for varying lengths of time, the words "You Have Mail," "Buddy List," and "IM" (for "Instant Messenger"). When AT&T (D) began using these same words in connection with its e-mail service, AOL (P) filed suit in federal court alleging trademark infringement and unfair trade competition. The federal district court granted summary judgment for AT&T (D), holding that all three of the claimed marks were generic and therefore functioning as trademarks. The district court used as support for its decision Internet dictionaries, published users' guides to both the Internet and to AOL services, use of the marks by competitors, and use by AOL of the marks. AOL (P) introduced evidence in the form of surveys that suggested that many consumers understood the terms to be trademarks owned by AOL, but the district court considered the survey evidence irrelevant because generic words cannot become trademarks by association. AOL (P) appealed, arguing that "Buddy List" is a suggestive mark because it was registered with the Patent and Trademark Office (PTO), that the district court erred in disregarding survey evidence suggesting that "You Have Mail" is associated with AOL, and that "IM" is a trademark associated with AOL.

ISSUE: Can a generic term be converted into a trademark through de facto secondary meaning?

HOLDING AND DECISION: (Niemeyer, J.) No. A generic term cannot be converted into a trademark through de facto secondary meaning. First, in deciding whether "Buddy List" was generic, the district court should have received the certification of the PTO registration for "Buddy List" into evidence and treated that certificate as prima facie evidence of the validity of the mark, and as prima facie evidence that it was suggestive. Because the validity of "Buddy List" cannot be determined on summary judgment, the issue is remanded. But AOL's (P) use of the phrase "You Have Mail" was generic and not enforceable, and AOL's use of the initials "IM" to denote its instant messaging service was not enforceable. AOL's (P) argument that there is no evidence that "You Have Mail" is primarily perceived by consumers as a generic, common phrase, and that the district court erred in disregarding survey evidence suggesting that "You Have Mail" is associated with AOL is rejected. The phrase was not registered with the PTO, and AOL (P) therefore had to carry the burden of establishing the validity and ownership of the mark as part of a larger burden in a trademark infringement action. The record shows that "You Have Mail" has been used to inform computer users since the 1970s, which is 10 years before AOL came into existence. In addition, other companies providing e-mail services have used "You Have Mail" or derivations of it to notify subscribers of the arrival of e-mail. And AOL's (P) own use of "You Have Mail" has been inconsistent with its claim that the phrase is a trademark, in that it does not describe a service that AOL (P) offers, but simply notifies the subscriber that there is mail in the electronic mailbox. Its use is functional, and is consistent with a public perception of the phrase as describing whether or not mail is in the mailbox. When words are used in a context that suggests only their common meaning, they are generic and may not be appropriated as exclusive property. The farther an alleged mark falls from the heartland of this common meaning, the more "distinctive" the alleged mark can become. In this case, AOL's (P) usage of the alleged mark falls within the common meaning and usage and therefore, AOL (P) may not exclude others from using the same words in connection with their e-mail service. Even assuming a portion of the public associates "You Have Mail" with AOL (P), this fact does not necessarily show that the primary significance of the phrase "You Have Mail" is not the functional, heartland usage of the phrase. Such secondary meaning does not entitle AOL (P) to exclude others from a functional use of the words. With respect to "IM," AOL (P) argued that the media has frequently associated "IM" with AOL (P) and no other online Internet service provider. But AOL (P) offered no support for that conclusion, and its alleged trademark in the initials cannot be enforced.

There is a genuine issue of material fact as to whether AOL's (P) use of "Buddy List" constituted a valid service mark and that part of district court's decision that granted summary judgment to AT&T (D) on AOL's (P) claim of infringement of the "Buddy List" trademark is reversed and

Continued on next page.

remanded. In all other respects, the district court's grant of summary judgment for AT&T (D) is affirmed.

▶ *ANALYSIS*

Part of the rationale for never allowing generic or functional terms to be granted exclusive rights—even where the alleged owner has done everything possible to preserve rights in the mark and secondary meaning has accrued through usage, policing, or advertising campaign—is a strong public interest in allowing competitors to use words that inform the public about the nature of their goods. Doing so would be nearly impossible if exclusive rights are granted in the words necessary to describe a product. Thus, the doctrine of de facto secondary meaning precludes the granting of monopoly powers available.

■■■■

Quicknotes

GENERIC MEANING A term that encompasses a class of related products and lacks the requisite distinctiveness for federal trademark protection.

TRADEMARK Any word, name, symbol, device or combination thereof that is either currently utilized, or which a person has a bona fide intent to utilize, in commerce in order to distinguish his goods from those of another.

TRADEMARK INFRINGEMENT The unauthorized use of another's trademark in such a manner as to cause a likelihood of confusion as to the source of the product or service in connection with which it is utilized.

■■■■

Silverman v. CBS, Inc.

Broadway producer (P) v. Media company (D)

870 F.2d 40 (2d Cir.), *cert. denied*, 492 U.S. 907 (1989).

NATURE OF CASE: Appeal of judgment in trademark infringement trial.

FACT SUMMARY: Stephen M. Silverman (Silverman) (P) wrote a script for a musical based on characters that originally appeared on the CBS, Inc. (D) radio program, "Amos 'n' Andy." CBS (D) alleged that Silverman's (P) script violated CBS's (D) copyrights and the Lanham Act by infringing various trademarks. The trial court ruled that CBS (D) had trademarks in scripts for post-1948 radio programs and that Silverman (P) had infringed these trademarks.

> ## 🏛 RULE OF LAW
> Under the Lanham Act a trademark shall be deemed to be "abandoned" when its use has been discontinued with intent not to resume.

FACTS: Stephen M. Silverman (Silverman) (P) wrote a script for a musical based on characters that originally appeared on the CBS, Inc. (D) radio program, "Amos 'n' Andy." Silverman (P) asked CBS (D) for permission to produce the musical, but the company declined. Silverman (P) then filed a lawsuit seeking a declaration that the radio programs broadcast before 1948 were in the public domain. CBS (D) counterclaimed, alleging that Silverman's (P) script violated CBS's (D) copyrights and the Lanham Act by infringing various trademarks. The trial court ruled that although pre-1948 radio programs were in the public domain, CBS (D) had trademarks in scripts for post-1948 radio programs and that Silverman (P) had infringed these trademarks.

ISSUE: Under the Lanham Act shall a trademark be deemed to be "abandoned" when its use has been discontinued with intent not to resume?

HOLDING AND DECISION: (Newman, J.) Yes. Under the Lanham Act a trademark shall be deemed to be "abandoned" when its use has been discontinued with intent not to resume. There are two elements for abandonment: (1) non-use and (2) intent not to resume use. The second element, "intent not to resume," means intent not to resume use within the reasonably foreseeable future, and it may be inferred from circumstances. As to the first element, two years of non-use creates a rebuttable presumption of abandonment. A trademark proprietor that temporarily suspends use of a mark can rebut the presumption of abandonment by showing reasonable grounds for the suspension and plans to resume use in the reasonably foreseeable future when the conditions requiring suspension abate. In this case, CBS (D) discontinued use of the mark for more than 20 years and no plans to use or permit its use in the reasonably foreseeable future. The company's bare assertion of possible future use is not enough. In addition, the fact that Silverman's (P) use is connected to artistic expression is relevant and helpful to his case. Trademark rights must be balanced against competing interests, and where artistic expression is involved, those competing interests implicate the First Amendment and its values. Trademark protection is not lost simply because the allegedly infringing use is artistic in nature, but in determining the outer limits of trademark protection, the fact that the allegedly infringing use is in connection with a work of artistic expression may tip the scales against trademark protection. Reversed.

▶ ANALYSIS

CBS (D) had hoped to avoid a finding of abandonment of its "Amos 'n' Andy" trademarks as a result of 20 years of nonuse by arguing that it intended to use the marks at some point, and that such prolonged nonuse has been the result of "social changes beyond its control." Be that as it may, the company could have avoided a finding of abandonment if it had a specific plan to use the mark in the foreseeable future—a future point that would not be determined by the winds of societal mores.

■■■

Quicknotes

ABANDONMENT The surrender of rights in a trademark with the intent to abandon the mark and to permanently relinquish its use; course of conduct of a trademark owner that causes the mark to become generic in association with goods or services, or to diminish in its significance.

■■■

Clark & Freeman Corp. v. Heartland Co. Ltd.

Trademark assignee (P) v. Competitor (D)

811 F. Supp. 137 (S.D.N.Y. 1993).

NATURE OF CASE: Trademark infringement action.

FACT SUMMARY: Clark & Freeman Corp. (P) and Heartland Co. Ltd. (D) claimed the exclusive right to use the name "Heartland" in connection with their business operations. Heartland (D) began using the name in 1985, and Clark & Freeman (P) began using it in 1986, but Clark & Freeman (P) claimed priority because it obtained an assignment of the name from a third party, Sears, Roebuck & Co., which had used the name since 1983.

RULE OF LAW

An assignment of a trademark entitles the assignee to "step into the shoes" of the assignor, thereby gaining whatever priority the assignor might have had in the mark, only where the mark is assigned along with its accompanying goodwill.

FACTS: Clark & Freeman Corp. (P), which sells men's shoes and boots, and Heartland Co. Ltd. (D), which sells shirts, sweaters, pants, and jackets, claimed the exclusive right to use the name "Heartland" in connection with their business operations. The dispute arose when Clark & Freeman (P) decided to launch a clothing line under the "Heartland" name. Heartland (D) began using the name in 1985, and Clark & Freeman (P) began using it in 1986, but Clark & Freeman (P) claimed priority because it obtained an assignment of the name from a third party, Sears, Roebuck & Co., which had used the name since 1983 in connection with its line of women's boots. After obtaining the assignment, Clark & Freeman (P) registered the mark with the Patent and Trademark Office.

ISSUE: Does an assignment of a trademark entitle the assignee to "step into the shoes" of the assignor, thereby gaining whatever priority the assignor might have had in the mark, only where the mark is assigned along with its accompanying goodwill?

HOLDING AND DECISION: (Martin, J.) Yes. An assignment of a trademark entitles the assignee to "step into the shoes" of the assignor, thereby gaining whatever priority the assignor might have had in the mark, only where the mark is assigned along with its accompanying goodwill. An assignment of a trademark "in gross," without the accompanying goodwill, is invalid, and the assignee must rely upon his or her own use to establish priority. Use of the mark by the assignee with a different goodwill and different product would likely defraud the consumer, which might assume that the mark signifies the same thing. Clark & Freeman (P) argued that goodwill was also assigned because (1) Sears immediately stopped manufacture and marketing of its "Heartland" boots upon assigning the mark, thereby assigning goodwill ipso facto, and (2) the mark was applied to "substantially similar" goods, but the arguments fail. First, there is no precedent holding that forbearance by the assignor operates to transfer goodwill ipso facto. Second, while assignments can be upheld where the assignee is producing a product or performing a service substantially similar to that of the assignor, so that there is no danger that the consumer might be deceived, the products sold by Clark & Freeman (P) are not substantially similar to Sears's products. Case law is sparse on the subject, but "substantial similarity" is not a matter only of equal quality; the products must be similar in other ways as well. In this case, the facts tend to show that the products are not substantially similar, because Sears sold only women's boots under the "Heartland" mark, whereas Clark & Freeman (P) applied it only to men's shoes and boots. The markets are substantially distinct. And Clark & Freeman (P) was using the "Heartland" mark before the assignment, which tends to show that the company only sought to gain from Sears the ability to use the name "Heartland," rather than the goodwill associated with it. The assignment is therefore an assignment in gross, and Heartland (D) has priority in the use of the name.

ANALYSIS

Many courts have interpreted the assignment of underlying goodwill as a requirement that the assignor sell its related underlying assets connected to the mark. Doing so will ensure that the substantial similarity test is met as well.

━▅■

Quicknotes

ASSIGNEE A party to whom another party assigns his interest or rights.

ASSIGNMENT A transaction in which a party conveys his or her entire interest in property to another.

ASSIGNOR A party who assigns his interest or rights to another.

GOODWILL An intangible asset reflecting a corporation's favor with the public and expectation of continued patronage.

IPSO FACTO By the fact itself.

━▅■

Eva's Bridal Ltd. v. Halanick Enterprises, Inc.

Former trademark licensor (P) v. Former trademark licensee (D)

639 F.3d 788 (7th Cir. 2011).

NATURE OF CASE: Appeal from dismissal of trademark action on the ground of abandonment through naked licensing.

FACT SUMMARY: Eva's Bridal Ltd. (P), which had licensed the "Eva's Bridal" name and mark to Halanick Enterprises, Inc. (Halanick) (D), contended that it had not abandoned its mark through naked licensing, because Halanick (D) had high standards and needed no supervision.

🏛 RULE OF LAW
A licensor of a trademark abandons the mark through naked licensing by exercising no control or decision-making authority over the quality of the licensee's products and business.

FACTS: Eva's Bridal Ltd. (P) licensed the "Eva's Bridal" name and mark to Halanick Enterprises, Inc. (Halanick) (D). The license agreement neither provided for any supervision by Eva's Bridal (P) of Halanick's (D) inventory or business practices, nor for Halanick (D) to operate its business in any particular way, and Eva's Bridal (P) in fact exercised no control or decision-making authority over the quality of Halanick's (D) products and business. The agreement provided that Halanick (D) would pay $75,000 a year for the right to use the "Eva's Bridal" name and marks. Five years after the license expired, Eva's Bridal (P) brought a trademark action on the grounds that Halanick (D) continued to use the "Eva's Bridal" name and mark without paying a royalty, and without a license agreement. The district court dismissed the suit, on the ground that Eva's Bridal (P) had abandoned the "Eva's Bridal" mark by engaging in naked licensing—i.e., by allowing others to use the mark without exercising reasonable control over the nature and quality of the goods, services, or business on which the mark is used by the licensee. The court of appeals granted review.

ISSUE: Does a licensor of a trademark abandon the mark through naked licensing by exercising no control or decision-making authority over the quality of the licensee's products and business?

HOLDING AND DECISION: (Easterbrook, C.J.) Yes. A licensor of a trademark abandons the mark through naked licensing by exercising no control or decision-making authority over the quality of the licensee's products and business. Eva's Bridal's (P) argument that what was required was that Halanick (D) have "high quality" products, so that, given that Halanick (D) had high standards and carried the same inventory that other Eva's

Bridal (P) stores carried, meant that Eva's Bridal (P) did not have to actively supervise Halanick (D), is unavailing. Eva's Bridal's (P) argument misunderstands the legal requirement that the licensor ensure "quality." What is required is supervision that produces consistent quality, so that consumers know what to expect from the mark's source, and so that the mark distinguishes the licensor's products and/or services from those of its competitors. The degree of control necessary varies from business to business. Here, however, Eva's Bridal (P) failed to retain any control—not via the license agreement, not via course of performance. Such an extreme failure to supervise is the paradigm of naked licensing. Affirmed.

▶ ANALYSIS

This decision rejects the argument that licensors may relinquish all control of licensees that operate "high quality" businesses, and the decision seems to suggest that licensors may not rely on the reputations of their licensees without exercising some type of "quality" control. As the court indicates, the degree of such control varies from business to business and depends on the circumstances of the type of business at issue, but the decision's clear message is that some retained quality control—perhaps even minimal in some circumstances—is necessary to avoid abandonment of the licensor's mark through naked licensing.

■▬■

Quicknotes

LICENSE A right that is granted to a person allowing him or her to conduct an activity that without such permission he or she could not lawfully do, and which is unassignable and revocable at the will of the licensor.

LICENSEE Person known to an owner or occupier of land, who comes onto the premises voluntarily and for a specific purpose although not necessarily with the consent of the owner.

LICENSOR A party that grants another a right allowing him or her to conduct an activity that without such permission he or she could not lawfully do, and which is unassignable and revocable at the will of the granting party.

NAKED LICENSE A license in which the licensee is allowed to use a trademark on any goods and services the licensee chooses.

■▬■

Infringement

Quick Reference Rules of Law

Naked Cowboy v. CBS

Street performer/service mark holder (P) v. Media company (D)

844 F. Supp. 2d 510 (S.D.N.Y. 2010).

NATURE OF CASE: Trademark infringement action.

FACT SUMMARY: The street performer known as the Naked Cowboy (P), who had registered the service mark "Naked Cowboy," contended that CBS (D), the television network, infringed his trademark by posting online a clip of a performer dressed like the Naked Cowboy (P), and by purchasing from YouTube the adwords "naked cowboy." CBS (D) moved to dismiss.

🏛 RULE OF LAW
A plaintiff cannot prevail on a trademark infringement claim if the defendant has not made use of the plaintiff's mark in commerce.

FACTS: The Naked Cowboy is a street performer in New York City who when performing wears only briefs, cowboy boots, a cowboy hat, and a guitar. The words "Naked Cowboy" are displayed across the back of his briefs, on his hat, and on his guitar. The word "Tips" or the symbol "$" is painted on his boots. Wearing this costume, he interacts with the public and has been doing so since 1997. He has also appeared throughout the country and in movies, radio, magazines, newspapers, and television appearances. He also had several endorsement agreements. According to the New York State tourism department, the Naked Cowboy (P) is "more recognizable than The Statue of Liberty." He registered the mark "Naked Cowboy," sold licensed merchandise, and had several corporate sponsorships. CBS (D), a television network, broadcasts "The Bold and the Beautiful," a 30-minute daytime television series. During one episode of this show, a character named Oliver appeared for a few seconds only in his briefs, cowboy boots, and a cowboy hat, while singing and playing the guitar. None of the marks used by the Naked Cowboy (P) were displayed or spoken in connection with this performance. Over 3 million viewers saw the episode, and CBS (D) profited from paid commercial advertisements. CBS (D) posted a clip of the episode on its YouTube channel, titling the clip "The Bold and the Beautiful—Naked Cowboy," and it began selling advertising with that video immediately. CBS's (D) "Eye" logos were displayed prominently on the YouTube page, as well as at the end of the clip, and the caption "Oliver has a surprise for Amber" appeared beneath the clip. A couple of the keyword tags used to help viewers find the content for which they were searching were "naked" and "cowboy." CBS (D) also purchased adword advertising from YouTube for the specific search term "naked cowboy," which gave the clips top page visibility as a "Featured Video" on

YouTube. The Naked Cowboy (P) sued CBS (D), asserting several trademark claims, including a claim for trademark infringement. CBS (D) moved to dismiss for failure to state a claim.

ISSUE: Can a plaintiff prevail on a trademark infringement claim if the defendant has not made use of the plaintiff's mark in commerce?

HOLDING AND DECISION: [Judge not identified in casebook extract.] No. A plaintiff cannot prevail on a trademark infringement claim if the defendant has not made use of the plaintiff's mark in commerce. The Lanham Act prohibits the "use in commerce [of] any reproduction, counterfeit, copy, or colorable imitation of a registered mark in connection with the sale, offering for sale, distribution, or advertising of any goods or services on or in connection with which such use is likely to cause confusion, or to cause mistake, or to deceive." Thus, a key element of a trademark infringement claim is the defendant's use in commerce of the plaintiff's registered mark. A mark is used in commerce for trademark infringement purposes when, inter alia, it is placed in any manner on the goods or the displays associated therewith or on the tags or labels affixed thereto, and the goods are sold or transported in commerce. Here, there was no use in commerce in the episode itself, since none of the contents of the episode contained the word mark "Naked Cowboy." Similarly, inclusion of "naked" and "cowboy" as separate tags associated with the YouTube video clips was not use of the word mark "Naked Cowboy." Further, the purchase from YouTube of adword advertising for the term "naked cowboy" likewise did not constitute "use in commerce" because the "naked cowboy" mark was not placed on any goods or containers or displays or associated documents, and the mark was not used in any way to indicate source or sponsorship. [Although CBS's (D) use of the term "Naked Cowboy" in the title of its YouTube video clip is a use in commerce, that use is not actionable for other reasons.]

▶ ANALYSIS

As the court's holding regarding use in commerce of the title of its YouTube video suggests, not every unauthorized use of a protected mark is actionable. Use of protected marks is permitted in descriptive ways, as long as the marks are not used to identify the defendant's own product. Here, CBS's (D) use of the challenged phrase "Naked Cowboy" as a title is an example of such nontrademark use, since it is clear that CBS (D) used the phrase in an

Continued on next page.

effort to describe the contents of the video clip, rather than as a mark to identify the source of the video clips.

■■■

Quicknotes

INTER ALIA Among other things.

TRADEMARK INFRINGEMENT The unauthorized use of another's trademark in such a manner as to cause a likelihood of confusion as to the source of the product or service in connection with which it is utilized.

■■■

Steele v. Bulova Watch Co.

U.S. citizen (D) v. Trademark owner (P)

344 U.S. 280 (1952).

NATURE OF CASE: Appeal from reversal of dismissal of trademark infringement and unfair competition action for lack of jurisdiction.

FACT SUMMARY: Steele (D), a U.S. citizen and resident, contended that the Lanham Act did not confer jurisdiction on federal courts to hear claims against him for trademark infringement and unfair competition brought by Bulova Watch Co. (P), a U.S. company, where his allegedly infringing acts occurred outside the United States.

🏛 RULE OF LAW
A district court has jurisdiction to award relief to a United States corporation against acts of trademark infringement and unfair competition consummated in a foreign country by a citizen and resident of the United States.

FACTS: Steele (D), a U.S. citizen and resident, conducted a watch business in Mexico and stamped the name "Bulova" on the watches he assembled and sold there after registering that mark in Mexico. Bulova Watch Co. (Bulova) (P), a U.S. watch company, owns the U.S. trademark "Bulova." It brought suit for trademark infringement and unfair competition against Steele (D), since he had not obtained permission to use its trademark. Steele (D) purchased component parts in the United States, and some of the watches he sold made their way into the United States. Eventually, the Supreme Court of Mexico nullified Steele's (D) Mexican registration of the mark. Steele (D) claimed that the district court did not have subject matter jurisdiction under the Lanham Act to hear the case. The district court agreed, finding Steele (D) had committed no wrongs in the United States, and dismissed the case "with prejudice." The court of appeals reversed, and the United States Supreme Court granted certiorari.

ISSUE: Does a district court have jurisdiction to award relief to a United States corporation against acts of trademark infringement and unfair competition consummated in a foreign country by a citizen and resident of the United States?

HOLDING AND DECISION: (Clark, J.) Yes. A district court has jurisdiction to award relief to a United States corporation against acts of trademark infringement and unfair competition consummated in a foreign country by a citizen and resident of the United States. Congress in prescribing standards of conduct for U.S. citizens may project the impact of its laws beyond the territorial boundaries of the United States. The issue, therefore, is whether Congress intended the Lanham Act to so extend congressional power. The Lanham Act confers broad jurisdictional powers upon the courts of the United States. On the facts presented, Steele's (D) conduct falls within the jurisdictional scope of the Act. The United States is not barred from governing its citizens' conduct abroad where doing so does not infringe on foreign nations' rights. In such instances, international law is not implicated. Instead, the issue is one of domestic law, which establishes the duty of the citizen in relation to his own government. Regardless of whether the government or a private party brings suit to enforce the statute at issue, the public policy served is the same in each instance. Here, Steele's (D) watches could reflect adversely on Bulova (P) both in the United States and in foreign markets where it advertises. Given the Lanham Act's broad jurisdictional grant to reach "all commerce which may lawfully be regulated by Congress," the steps Steele (D) took, though separately not illegal, became part of an unlawful commercial scheme that was consummated abroad and that came within the Act's scope. Affirmed.

▶ ANALYSIS

This is the seminal case establishing the now well-settled principle that the Lanham Act can, in appropriate cases, be applied extraterritorially. However, because the Court concluded that the facts of the case fell within the limits of congressional power, the case did not define the outer limits of such power. The circuit courts have thus had to make this determination on a case-by-case basis and have developed various frameworks for determining when the extraterritorial application of the Lanham Act is appropriate.

■■■

Quicknotes

JURISDICTION The authority of a court to hear and declare judgment in respect to a particular matter.

LANHAM ACT Name of the Trademark Act of 1946 that governs federal law regarding trademarks.

■■■

McBee v. Delica

U.S. jazz musician (P) v. Japanese clothing company (D)

417 F.3d 107 (1st Cir. 2005).

NATURE OF CASE: Appeal from dismissal of action for false endorsement and dilution for lack of subject matter jurisdiction.

FACT SUMMARY: Cecil McBee (McBee) (P), a U.S. jazz musician who had toured in Japan, brought suit under the Lanham Act for false endorsement and dilution against Delica Co. Ltd. (Delica) (D), a Japanese clothing company, for using his name on a line of clothing marketed to teenage girls in Japan.

🏛 RULE OF LAW
A federal court does not have subject matter jurisdiction over a case brought under the Lanham Act to reach foreign activities of a foreign defendant where they do not have a substantial effect on U.S. commerce.

FACTS: Cecil McBee (McBee) (P) is a well-known U.S. jazz musician and citizen, living in the United States. He has toured Japan several times and contributed to hundreds of albums, but he has never licensed or authorized the use of his name to anyone, other than in direct connection with his musical performances. Delica Co. Ltd. (Delica) (D) is a Japanese clothing company that adopted McBee's (P) name for a line of clothing marketed to teenage girls in Japan. Delica (D) holds a Japanese trademark for "Cecil McBee," in both Japanese and Roman or English characters, for a variety of product types. Delica (D) owns and operates retail shops throughout Japan under the brand name "Cecil McBee"; these are the only stores where "Cecil McBee" products are sold. There are no "Cecil McBee" retail shops outside of Japan. Delica (D) has experienced steady growth in sales, which have reached $112 million annually. Delica (D) has never shipped "Cecil McBee" goods outside Japan and refuses orders from the U.S. for this merchandise. Delica's (D) website for its "Cecil McBee" apparel is primarily in Japanese, and is hosted in Japan. However, online purchases are not permitted. After McBee (P) became aware that Delica (D) was using his name without authorization, he initiated litigation in Japan. The outcome was that the mark, which was initially invalidated by the Japanese Patent Office, was reinstated. McBee (P) brought suit in U.S. district court under the Lanham Act for false endorsement and dilution, seeking to enjoin access in the United States to Delica's (D) website, and seeking damages for harm to McBee (P) arising from Delica's (D) sales in Japan. In his suit, McBee (P) presented virtually no evidence that "Cecil McBee" clothing entered the United States after being sold in Japan, only that certain individuals had spotted his name on clothes or merchandise in various U.S. cities, either being worn or carried by a young girl. The district court dismissed for lack of subject matter jurisdiction, and the First Circuit Court of Appeals granted review.

ISSUE: Does a federal court have subject matter jurisdiction over a case brought under the Lanham Act to reach foreign activities of a foreign defendant where they do not have a substantial effect on U.S. commerce?

HOLDING AND DECISION: (Lynch, J.) No. A federal court does not have subject matter jurisdiction over a case brought under the Lanham Act to reach foreign activities of a foreign defendant where they do not have a substantial effect on U.S. commerce. This case raises as a matter of first impression in this circuit the appropriate framework for deciding when extraterritorial use of the Lanham Act is proper. In the case where a plaintiff is attempting to reach the foreign activities of a foreign defendant, as here, the appropriate test is whether the complained-of activities have a substantial effect on U.S. commerce. Here, McBee (P) has made no showing that Delica's (D) activities had a substantial effect on U.S. commerce, and, accordingly, the district court correctly ruled that it did not have subject matter jurisdiction over the case. This conclusion is supported by the United States Supreme Court's decision in *Steele v. Bulova Watch Co.*, 344 U.S. 280 (1952), where the Court's decision explicitly and implicitly relied on congressional power. First, it explicitly relied on the power of Congress to regulate "the conduct of its own citizens," even extraterritorial conduct, since that does not raise international concerns. Second, it seemed to also implicitly rely on congressional power over foreign commerce. Thus, when the purported infringer is not a U.S. citizen, and the alleged illegal activities occur abroad, the analysis appears to rest solely on Congress's foreign commerce power. In this context, the Supreme Court's antitrust decisions provide useful guidance. The Court has found jurisdiction where extraterritorial antitrust activities threaten to harm American commerce. Harms aimed at by the Lanham Act, such as false endorsements, passing off, product disparagement, or confusion over sponsorship, could be created extraterritorially and could affect American commerce and cause loss of American sales—as with global piracy of American goods, which causes $200 billion in annual losses for American companies. In both the antitrust and the Lanham Act areas, there is a risk that, absent a certain degree of extraterritorial enforcement, violators will either take advantage of international coordination problems or hide in countries

Continued on next page.

without efficacious antitrust or trademark laws, thereby avoiding legal authority. McBee's (P) argument, that his claim to enjoin Delica's (D) website (so that U.S. consumers will not be able to see it), does not call for an extraterritorial application of the Lanham Act must be rejected. McBee (P) claims harm from the website by its mere existence, whereby U.S. consumers can view the site and become confused about his relationship with Delica (D), and because the website often comes up on Internet search results lists ahead of fan sites about his career. The site is not, however, connected with sales of "Cecil McBee" products in the United States or online sales anywhere, and it is not a targeted advertising in the United States, especially given that it is almost entirely in Japanese. To hold that any website in a foreign language, wherever hosted, is automatically reachable under the Lanham Act so long as it is visible in the United States would be senseless. The conclusion that McBee's (P) injunction claim calls for an extraterritorial application of the Lanham Act is supported by case law relating to personal jurisdiction and websites, which holds that the mere existence of a website that is visible in a forum and that gives information about a company and its products is not enough, by itself, to subject a defendant to personal jurisdiction in that forum: something more than mere existence of the website is necessary; something which actively directs consumers to the website's sponsor. Given the omnipresence of websites, allowing personal jurisdiction to be premised on mere presence alone would "eviscerate" the limits on a state's jurisdiction over out-of-state or foreign defendants. Similarly, allowing subject matter jurisdiction under the Lanham Act to automatically attach whenever a website is visible in the United States would eviscerate the territorial curbs on judicial authority that are presumed in this area. On the other hand, if the website had a substantial effect on U.S. commerce, subject matter jurisdiction would be proper, as where the website had interactive features that enabled the successful online ordering of the offered products for sale in the United States. Delica's (D) website had no such substantial effect, being written almost entirely in Japanese and not permitting online ordering anywhere. American consumers thus would not be confused about McBee's (P) connection with Delica (D), and would likely ignore search results that precede those for McBee's (P) fan sites, which usually immediately follow those for Delica's (P) products. Finally, McBee (P) has adduced no evidence of actual confusion. Affirmed.

▶ ANALYSIS

While based on formulations adopted by other circuits, the framework adopted here by the First Circuit is different from those in the other circuits. The best-known test, the Vanity Fair test, asks (1) whether the defendant is an American citizen, (2) whether the defendant's actions have a substantial effect on United States commerce, and (3) whether relief would create a conflict with foreign law,

Vanity Fair Mills v. T. Eaton Co., 234 F.2d 633, 642-43 (2d Cir. 1956). These three prongs are given an uncertain weight. The court here disaggregated the three prongs of the Vanity Fair test, identified the different types of "extraterritorial" application questions, and isolated the factors pertinent to subject matter jurisdiction. The First Circuit's framework first asks whether the defendant is a U.S. citizen. That inquiry is different because a separate constitutional basis for jurisdiction exists for control of activities, even foreign activities, of an U.S. citizen. Further, when the Lanham Act plaintiff seeks to enjoin sales in the United States, there is no question of extraterritorial application; the court has subject matter jurisdiction. However, the Circuit rejects the notion that a comity analysis is part of subject matter jurisdiction, reasoning that comity considerations, including potential conflicts with foreign trademark law, are properly treated as questions of whether a court should, in its discretion, decline to exercise subject matter jurisdiction that it already possesses. A determination of whether the foreign activities have a substantial effect on U.S. commerce resolves the issue without the need to conduct a comity analysis.

Quicknotes

COMITY A rule pursuant to which courts in one state give deference to the statutes and judicial decisions of the court of another state.

TRADEMARK DILUTION The diminishment of the capability of a trademark to identify and distinguish the particular good or service with which it is associated.

E. & J. Gallo Winery v. Consorzio del Gallo Nero

U.S. winery (trademark owner) (P) v. Italian wine association (alleged infringer) (D)

782 F. Supp. 457 (N.D. Cal. 1991).

NATURE OF CASE: Action for trademark infringement and dilution.

FACT SUMMARY: E. & J. Gallo Winery (Gallo) (P), the largest U.S. winery, alleged that Consorzio del Gallo Nero (Gallo Nero) (D), an Italian wine trade association, infringed Gallo's (P) trademark in the name "Gallo."

🏛 RULE OF LAW
Summary judgment will be granted to a trademark holder on a trademark infringement claim where the trademark is exceptionally strong and use of the allegedly infringing mark will lead to a likelihood of consumer confusion with trademarked products.

FACTS: E. & J. Gallo Winery (Gallo) (P), the largest U.S. winery, produces and sells a variety of wines featuring the "Gallo" trademark and is the owner of several federal registrations of the "Gallo" mark. Gallo (P) has spent about $500 million promoting its "Gallo" brand of wines. Consorzio del Gallo Nero (Gallo Nero) (D), an Italian wine trade association, promotes one type of wine from Italy, and is a successor to a similar trade association that had used the symbol of the black rooster, or "gallonero," to represent its wines. This symbol has been used on the neck seal of bottles of wine produced by its members for a period longer than Gallo (P) has used its "Gallo" trademark. Gallo (P) brought an action for trademark infringement and dilution against Gallo Nero (D), and sought summary judgment on its infringement claim.

ISSUE: Will summary judgment be granted to a trademark holder on a trademark infringement claim where the trademark is exceptionally strong and use of the allegedly infringing mark will lead to a likelihood of consumer confusion with trademarked products?

HOLDING AND DECISION: (Jensen, J.) Yes. Summary judgment will be granted to a trademark holder on a trademark infringement claim where the trademark is exceptionally strong and use of the allegedly infringing mark will lead to a likelihood of consumer confusion with trademarked products. In determining whether there has been infringement, various trademark infringement factors must be assessed. The first is the strength of the trademark. A registered mark, such as the "Gallo" mark, is presumed valid and distinctive. Thus, Gallo (P) has the exclusive right to use the mark in promoting and selling its wines in the United States. The mark has also been recognized by other courts as having achieved universal recognition as a trademark for wine. It is an extremely strong mark. While it is true, as Gallo Nero (D) points out, that there are numerous third-party uses of the "Gallo" name, those other uses are neither connected with wine, nor have they achieved significant consumer recognition. Therefore, evidence of such uses is irrelevant to the strength of the "Gallo" mark. Also, although "Gallo" is a common Italian surname and word, a family name is entitled to protection as a mark if it has achieved secondary meaning through use, advertising, and public recognition. The "Gallo" mark has achieved such secondary meaning. The second factor is the similarity of the marks used. Gallo (P) asserts that the two marks share total identity of the substantive term "Gallo," while Gallo Nero (D) argues that the use of surrounding terms, "Nero" and "Consorzio del Gallo Nero" renders the uses dissimilar. Gallo (P), however, has valid trademark registrations of the "Gallo" mark used in conjunction with other words, so that consumers are used to seeing the "Gallo" mark in conjunction with other words. The distinctive term in each instance is "Gallo." Even though the presentation of the terms on Gallo Nero's (D) bottles differs from the presentation of the mark on Gallo's (P) bottles, this is not dispositive as to whether consumer confusion would likely be caused, since the consuming public finds the single term "Gallo" to be wholly and uniquely distinctive when used in conjunction with wine. Thus, the two terms are significantly similar for purposes of finding a likelihood of confusion between the two uses. The third factor is the similarity of the goods sold. Wines of all types constitute a single class of goods, so even though Gallo Nero (D) produces only one kind of wine (chianti) and Gallo (P) produces numerous types of wine other than chianti, the wines compete in the marketplace and the products are substantially similar for purposes of establishing a likelihood of confusion. The fourth factor is the similarity of the marketing channels used. The evidence clearly shows that both parties use similar marketing channels to distribute their wines. The fifth factor is the degree of care exercised by purchasers. Confusion between marks is generally more likely where the goods at issue involve relatively inexpensive, "impulse" products to which the average, "unsophisticated" consumer does not devote a great deal of care and consideration in purchasing. Wine is considered an "impulse" product, especially with regard to average consumers, and Gallo Nero (D) has failed to adduce evidence to controvert that the U.S. wine-buying public are generally unsophisticated "impulse" buyers who are an easy mark for a trademark infringer. Thus, the lack of consumer sophistication significantly enhances the likelihood of consumer confusion

Continued on next page.

between the two products. The sixth factor is evidence of actual confusion. This is only one of several factors as to likelihood of confusion, so even if actual confusion is not shown, if the other factors tend to show a likelihood of confusion the absence of actual confusion will not defeat the claim. Here, Gallo Nero (D) presented evidence of a side-by-side survey that showed little consumer confusion. However, such surveys have been held legally irrelevant by numerous courts as to whether a consumer, familiar with one party's mark, would likely be confused when confronted with the other party's goods alone. Gallo (P) also presented a survey, which showed that consumers would be confused when presented only with the Gallo Nero (D) name. That survey would thus be both relevant and dispositive in those courts. Other courts hold that the proper survey evidence is that which attempts to most closely replicate the marketplace setting in which consumers will typically encounter the competing marks. Under such a view, the Gallo Nero (D) survey would be relevant. Because both surveys present some evidence of a likelihood of confusion, even if slight, this factor supports a finding of infringement. The seventh and final factor is the alleged infringer's intent in adopting the allegedly infringing mark. Just as with actual confusion, a showing of intent is not necessary to support a finding of a likelihood of confusion. The record shows that Gallo Nero (D) was aware of the "Gallo" mark prior to marketing its wines in the United States and that foreign trademark offices found a likelihood of confusion. The issue is not Gallo Nero's (D) continued use of its distinctive black rooster symbol, but whether, when entering the U.S. wine market, it was aware that its use of "Gallo Nero" would likely cause confusion. The record shows that it was. On balance, the factors establish as a matter of law that Gallo (P) is entitled to summary judgment on its infringement claim. Summary judgment for Gallo (P).

▎ *ANALYSIS*

Trademark infringement under the Lanham Act is established when the infringer's use of the plaintiff's trademark creates a "likelihood of confusion," 15 U.S.C. § 1114(1). Each of the circuits has adopted its own list of factors to use in determining such "likelihood of confusion," and the factors vary to some degree among the circuits. This list of factors is not exhaustive, and other factors may be considered depending on the particular facts of the case, e.g., where the mark may have been abandoned.

Quicknotes

SECONDARY MEANING A word or mark that becomes associated with a particular merchant or product as its source of origin.

TRADEMARK DILUTION The diminishment of the capability of a trademark to identify and distinguish the particular good or service with which it is associated.

Banfi Products Corp. v. Kendall-Jackson Winery, Ltd.

Wine importer and producer (P) v. Winery (D)

74 F. Supp. 2d 188 (E.D.N.Y. 1999).

NATURE OF CASE: Action seeking declaratory judgment of noninfringement, and counterclaim for false designation of origin, as well as other claims.

FACT SUMMARY: Banfi Products Corp. (Banfi) (P), the country's largest importer of Italian wine, asserted that a wine it imported, COL-DI-SASSO, did not infringe on the "COLLINE DI SASSI" mark owned by Kendall-Jackson Winery, Ltd. (Kendall-Jackson) (D).

🏛 RULE OF LAW
There is not a likelihood of confusion between two marks, and, therefore, trademark infringement, where the allegedly infringed mark is relatively weak, the marks are dissimilar, the products do not compete directly, there is little indication that the owner of the allegedly infringed mark plans to enter the alleged infringer's market, there is no actual confusion, the alleged infringer adopted its mark in good faith, the allegedly infringing product is not inferior to that of the claimant, and consumers are sophisticated.

FACTS: Banfi Products Corp. (Banfi) (P), the country's largest importer of Italian wine, started importing and selling COL-DI-SASSO wine in late 1991 and, in 1992, was granted a trademark registration in the name "COL-DI-SASSO." The name is an Italian term meaning "hill of stone." Sales of this wine increased in 1993 and by 1998, U.S. sales had exceeded $1.3 million. Banfi (P) has invested hundreds of thousands of dollars in advertising and promoting this wine, which has received generally favorable reviews. The wine's trade dress is very distinctive. The wine sells for between $8 and $10 per bottle in stores and between $16 and $23 per bottle in restaurants. In 1994, Kendall-Jackson Winery, Ltd. (Kendall-Jackson) (D) acquired the Pepi winery, which produces "COLLINE DI SASSI" wine in California. When the label for this wine was approved by the Bureau of Alcohol, Tobacco and Firearms (BAFT) in 1990, "ROBERT PEPI" was listed as the brand name, and "COLLINE DI SASSI" as the fanciful name. Distribution of this wine was relatively limited, as were advertising and promotional expenditures for it. It is marketed as a high-end, limited edition wine and is sold in higher-end wine shops and restaurants, usually for $20 to $25 per bottle in stores and $35 to $45 or more in restaurants. When Banfi (P) learned of the "COLLINE DI SASSI" wine in 1994, it demanded that Pepi cease using that name because of the risk of consumer confusion and because it was inappropriate for a California wine to be given the name of an Italian geographical location. Pepi responded by asserting that its rights in its mark were superior to

Banfi's (P) because of the BATF approval it had received in 1990, and requested that Banfi (P) cease using the "COL-DI-SASSO" name and withdraw its trademark registration. After investigating sales figures and other information, Banfi (P) concluded that there was no likelihood of confusion between the two marks and accordingly declined to cease using the "COL-DI-SASSO" mark. To ensure no confusion, it started placing the word "Banfi" on its labels. After Kendall-Jackson (D) purchased Pepi, it continued demanding that Banfi (P) cease using the "COL-DI-SASSO" mark. Before the dispute, the wines had co-existed for around four years without actual consumer confusion, or confusion by retailers, critics, distributors, or anyone else. Banfi (P) commenced an action under the Lanham Act seeking a judgment that its mark did not infringe Kendall-Jackson's (D) mark. Kendall-Jackson (D) counterclaimed, arguing that it had priority, the marks were confusing, and Banfi (P) should be enjoined from using the "COL-DI-SASSO" mark. The parties stipulated that there was no actual confusion between the two wines. There was also evidence that there was widespread third-party use in the wine industry of names similar to the marks at issue. There was evidence that stores segregate wines according to geographic origin, and that restaurants give wines similar treatment. Other evidence was that wine consumers tend to be older, wealthier, and better educated than the average population. In reaching its decision, the district court evaluated eight factors (the *Polaroid* factors, *Polaroid Corp. v. Polarad Electronics Corp.*, 287 F.2d 492 (2d Cir. 1961)) to determine trademark infringement.

ISSUE: Is there a likelihood of confusion between two marks, and, therefore, trademark infringement, where the allegedly infringed mark is relatively weak, the marks are dissimilar, the products do not compete directly, there is little indication that the owner of the allegedly infringed mark plans to enter the alleged infringer's market, there is no actual confusion, the alleged infringer adopted its mark in good faith, the allegedly infringing product is not inferior to that of the claimant, and consumers are sophisticated?

HOLDING AND DECISION: (Platt, J.) No. There is not a likelihood of confusion between two marks, and, therefore, trademark infringement, where the allegedly infringed mark is relatively weak, the marks are dissimilar, the products do not compete directly, there is little indication that the owner of the allegedly infringed mark plans to enter the alleged infringer's market, there is no actual confusion, the alleged infringer adopted its mark

Continued on next page.

in good faith, the allegedly infringing product is not inferior to that of the claimant, and consumers are sophisticated. The first *Polaroid* factor looks at the strength of the allegedly infringed mark. Here, while the "ROBERT PEPI COLLINE DI SASSI" mark is an arbitrary mark, it is not particularly distinctive in the marketplace, since advertising for it, and its distribution, has been limited. Also, numerous vintners have used variations of the words "Colline" and "Sassi" in their respective marks. Therefore, this factor weighs in favor of Banfi (P). The second factor looks at the degree of similarity between the two marks. Here, the marks are dissimilar. Banfi's (P) mark is composed of three words, separated by hyphens, whereas Kendall-Jackson's (D) is composed of five words with no hyphens. There are also phonetic differences between the two marks, and their meanings are different. The products' labels are different, Banfi's (P) name appears on the cork of its wine, and one wine indicates it is a product of Italy whereas the other indicates it is a product of California. This factor favors Banfi (P). The third factor looks at whether the two products compete with each other in the same marketplace. The wines are of different types—one is a 50–50 Sangiovese-Cabernet blend, the other is marketed as solely Sangiovese. Additionally, the pricing for the respective wines is different, they are marketed accordingly—one as affordable, the other as high-end—and one is sold by the glass whereas the other is not. This factor favors Banfi (P). The fourth factor considers the likelihood that the party alleging infringement will "bridge the gap," meaning whether Kendall-Jackson (D) will enter Banfi's (P) market. No evidence has been presented that this will happen. Accordingly, this factor favors Banfi (P). The fifth factor is whether there has been actual confusion. This factor is easily disposed of since the parties have stipulated there has been no actual confusion. Accordingly, this factor favors Banfi (P). The sixth factor considers the alleged infringer's good faith in adopting its mark, and whether it did so to capitalize on the opposing party's reputation and goodwill. Here, the marks were conceived at approximately the same time. Banfi's (P) mark was adopted without knowledge of the Kendall-Jackson (D) mark and was based on a kind of rock in Tuscany. The Pepi mark was adopted at a family meal and was unrelated to geographical formations. Furthermore, Banfi (P) showed its continuing good faith by initiating this instant action, seeking resolution of both party's rights to the marks at issue. Accordingly, this factor weighs against a finding of likelihood of confusion. The seventh factor looks at the quality of the alleged infringer's product to see if the senior user's reputation could be jeopardized by the junior user's product of an inferior quality. Here there was no evidence that Banfi's (P) wine was of a lesser quality than that of Kendall-Jackson (D). Therefore, this factor favors Banfi (P). Finally, the last factor considers the sophistication of the buyers. Based on the evidence that wine consumers in the United States tend to be older, more affluent, and more educated, this factor also favors Banfi (P). Because all the *Polaroid*

factors favor Banfi (P), there is little likelihood that consumers will confuse Banfi's (P) wine with that of Kendall-Jackson (D). Moreover, the parties' remaining claims are meritless. Judgment of noninfringement is granted to Banfi (P).

▶ *ANALYSIS*

As this case demonstrates, the outcomes of trademark infringement cases usually turn on the facts and evidence established during the course of the case and on the factors—such as the Second Circuit's *Polaroid* factors— that the court applies to those facts and evidence. In the U.S. wine industry, for example, which is growing, there exists a greater likelihood that a newcomer's name, label, or bottling may be similar to that of a senior user. Accordingly, there is likelihood that the number of trademark disputes will increase with the industry's continued growth.

■==■

Quicknotes

TRADEMARK INFRINGEMENT The unauthorized use of another's trademark in such a manner as to cause a likelihood of confusion as to the source of the product or service in connection with which it is utilized.

■==■

Maker's Mark Distillery, Inc. v. Diageo North America, Inc.

Bourbon distiller (P) v. Tequila distiller (D)

679 F.3d 410 (6th Cir. 2012).

NATURE OF CASE: Appeal from finding of trademark infringement and permanent injunction prohibiting the use of a mark.

FACT SUMMARY: Maker's Mark Distillery, Inc. (Maker's Mark) (P), which produces bourbon, and which uses a dripping red wax seal on its bottles, which it had registered as a trademark, sought, inter alia, to enjoin Jose Cuervo (D) and its affiliates, including Diageo North America, Inc. (collectively, "Cuervo" (D)), which produce tequila, from using a similar seal on their premium tequila bottles. The district court, finding trademark infringement, granted the injunction. Cuervo (D) appealed, contending that the district court's findings were erroneous as to the strength of Maker's Mark's (P) trademark, the similarity of the parties' marks, and actual confusion.

🏛 RULE OF LAW

A finding of trademark infringement is justified where the balance of factors used to determine likelihood of confusion weighs in favor of a finding of such confusion, and the defendant has used the plaintiff's valid trademark without permission.

FACTS: Maker's Mark Distillery, Inc. (Maker's Mark) (P), which produces and markets bourbon whiskey, trademarked as part of its trade dress a dripping red wax seal for use on its bottles, which go for around $24 per bottle. Maker's Mark (P) has used this seal for over 50 years. Jose Cuervo (D), which along with its affiliates, including Diageo North America, Inc. (collectively, "Cuervo" (D)) produce tequila, began producing a premium tequila, "Reserva de la Familia," (Reserva) in 1995, which sold for around $100 per bottle. The tequila bottle had a wax seal that was straight-edged and did not initially feature drips. By 2001, Cuervo (D) had begun selling this tequila in the United States in bottles with a red dripping wax seal that was similar to the Maker's Mark red dripping wax seal. In 2003, Maker's Mark (P) filed suit against Cuervo (D), alleging state and federal trademark infringement and federal trademark dilution; sometime thereafter, Cuervo (D) discontinued use of the red dripping wax seal and reverted to a red straight-edged wax seal. Maker's Mark (P) sought damages, injunctions against dilution and infringement, and costs. Cuervo (D) counterclaimed for cancellation of the Maker's Mark (P) trademark. The district court found that Maker's Mark's (P) red dripping wax seal is a valid trademark, and that Cuervo (D) had infringed, but not diluted, that trademark, and accordingly, the court permanently enjoined Cuervo (D) from using that mark. Cuervo (D) appealed, contending that the district court's findings

were erroneous as to the strength of Maker's Mark's (P) trademark, the similarity of the parties' marks, and actual confusion. As to these factors, the district court had found that Maker's Mark's (P) mark was very strong and distinctive, and enjoyed great customer recognition, based on extensive advertising and media attention. The district court also found that as to similarity, this factor weighed slightly in favor of Maker's Mark (P), because although consumers likely would not buy one product believing it was the other, the marks were facially similar so that consumers might believe there was an association between the two producers. As to actual confusion, on which there was no evidence presented, the district court concluded that the lack of evidence rendered this factor "neutral." The court of appeals granted review, and reviewed the district court's findings de novo.

ISSUE: Is a finding of trademark infringement justified where the balance of factors used to determine likelihood of confusion weighs in favor of a finding of such confusion, and the defendant has used the plaintiff's valid trademark without permission?

HOLDING AND DECISION: (Martin, J.) Yes. A finding of trademark infringement is justified where the balance of factors used to determine likelihood of confusion weighs in favor of a finding of such confusion, and the defendant has used the plaintiff's valid trademark without permission. Eight factors are considered in determining likelihood of confusion: 1. strength of the plaintiff's mark; 2. relatedness of the goods; 3. similarity of the marks; 4. evidence of actual confusion; 5. marketing channels used; 6. likely degree of purchaser care; 7. Defendant's intent in selecting the mark; and 8. likelihood of expansion of the product lines. Here, Cuervo (D) challenges the district court's findings as to the first, third, and fourth factors. As to the first factor, the strength of Maker's Mark's (P) trademark, the district court did not clearly err in determining that the mark is extremely strong. The strength inquiry is comprised of two elements: the distinctiveness, or conceptual strength, of the mark, as well its recognition among the public. The district court appropriately evaluated both components of the strength factor, finding that the red dripping wax seal is inherently distinctive based on its uniqueness and its potential to "draw in the customer" in an unusual manner, and finding that the seal acquired secondary meaning and commercial strength through over 50 years of use, extensive advertising, and consumer recognition. Cuervo (D) argues that the district court erred in its evaluation of

Continued on next page.

the strength of the mark by (1) disregarding third-party use of red dripping wax seals; (2) failing to give proper weight to the lack of a survey regarding recognition of the red dripping wax seal; (3) relying in its analysis on Maker's Mark's (P) advertisements without evidence of their dates or circulation; and (4) relying on evidence of the strength of the mark in the overbroad group of distilled spirits drinkers instead of prospective Reserva purchasers. Although extensive third-party uses of a trademark may substantially weaken the strength of a mark, the district court here did consider such use, but concluded that the market in which those uses occurred (the entire distilled spirits market) was too broad, and did not apply to the "relevant market." The district court did not err in this respect. Also, while survey evidence is the best evidence of secondary meaning, such evidence is not indispensable to the broader question of commercial recognition. Given the abundance of other evidence demonstrating strong market recognition, the district court did not err in overlooking the lack of survey evidence, since that evidence was not determinative of the strength of the mark. As to advertising evidence, the district court did not err in relying on this, as the advertisements considered were recent, relevant, and strong enough to convince the media that the dripping wax seal was one of the most recognizable branding symbols in the world. Finally, as to the evidence of the mark's strength within the broader group of distilled spirits drinkers, as opposed to Reserva drinkers, the district court considered, but did not rest its holding on, this evidence. For these reasons, the district court did not err in finding "that the Maker's Mark red dripping wax seal is an extremely strong mark due to its unique design and the company's singular marketing efforts." As to the third factor of the eight-factor test, in assessing similarity, courts must determine whether a given mark would confuse the public when viewed alone. The district court determined that this factor weighed slightly in Maker's Mark's (P) favor, since the marks were facially similar, and could suggest an association between the producers. Cuervo (D) argues that the presence of labels on the respective producers' bottles identifying the name of the manufacturer (house labels) significantly diminished the likelihood of confusion. While in some instances the presence of a house label may diminish the likelihood of confusion, the district court did not err in concluding that this consideration is not as important in an association case, when the two products are related enough that one might associate with or sponsor the other and still use their own house mark. The diminished importance of the house marks in this case was supported by evidence that many consumers are unaware of the affiliations between brands of distilled spirits and that some companies produce multiple types of distilled spirits. Finally, as to the fourth factor of the eight-factor test, the district court did not place weight on the fact that Maker's Mark (P) did not furnish meaningful evidence of actual confusion, given that Cuervo (P) sold Reserva for a limited time and in limited quantities. While evidence of actual confusion is the best evidence of likelihood of confu-sion, a lack of such evidence is rarely significant, and the district court did not err in finding the lack of actual confusion evidence nondeterminative. Thus, the district court's factual findings were not clearly erroneous. Weighing the eight factors for likelihood of confusion based on the district court's factual findings leads to the conclusion that there was likelihood of confusion. Factor one, as to the mark's strength—which here is very strong—is weighted very heavily. The second factor, as to the products' relatedness, in this case is accorded little weight, because the respective producers' goods were only somewhat related in the broader distilled spirits but not competitive (i.e., Cuervo's (D) $100 bottle vs. Maker's Mark's (P) $24 bottle). The third factor, similarity, is accorded considerable weight. The Reserva product was sold for a short time and in limited quantities. Under such circumstances, the fourth factor, actual confusion, is accorded little weight. As to the fifth factor, the marketing channels used by the parties, the district court determined that the channels were similar in some ways and dissimilar in others. Based on this finding, this factor is given very little weight. The sixth factor is the likely degree of purchaser care. The district court found this factor favored Cuervo (D) because of the degree of care potential tequila customers would exercise in purchasing a $100 bottle of Reserva, and because knowledgeable bourbon customers would also exercise similar care and, further, know that Maker's Mark (P) sells only one kind of liquor. This factor, though strongly favoring Cuervo (D), is not dispositive, since confusingly similar marks may lead a purchaser who is extremely careful and knowledgeable to assume nonetheless that the seller is affiliated with or identical to the other party. This factor is given substantial weight. Although, with respect to the seventh factor of intent, Cuervo (D) did not intend to infringe, resolution of this issue may benefit only the cause of the senior user, not of an alleged infringer; hence, this factor is accorded no weight. As to the eighth and final factor (product line expansion), this factor is neutral where neither party puts forth evidence of significant expansion plans. This factor does not weight against Maker's Mark (P) and is given no weight. Weighing the eight factors compels a finding of infringement. Excluding the neutral factors, the majority of the factors—strength, relatedness of the goods, similarity, and marketing channels—favor Maker's Mark (P). The one factor favoring Cuervo (D)—degree of purchaser care—which is given substantial weight, cannot overcome the factors favoring Maker's Mark (P). Accordingly, there is a likelihood of confusion between the products, and Cuervo (D) has infringed. [Affirmed.]

▶ ANALYSIS

In determining the strength of Maker's Mark's (P) mark, the district court considered the extent to which the mark had obtained secondary meaning. In light of its finding that

Continued on next page.

the mark was inherently distinctive, the court did not need to consider secondary meaning, since an identifying mark is distinctive and capable of being protected if it either (1) is inherently distinctive or (2) has acquired distinctiveness through secondary meaning. However, the district court's findings on secondary meaning were nonetheless relevant to the broader questions of commercial recognition and overall strength, and not just to whether the mark was deserving of protection. This illustrates the importance of distinguishing between the analyses used to determine secondary meaning and strength.

■═■

Quicknotes

INTER ALIA Among other things.

SECONDARY MEANING A word or mark that becomes associated with a particular merchant or product as its source of origin.

TRADE DRESS The overall image of, or impression created by, a product that a court may enforce as a trademark if it determines that such image has acquired secondary meaning and that the public recognizes it as an indication of source.

TRADEMARK DILUTION The diminishment of the capability of a trademark to identify and distinguish the particular good or service with which it is associated.

TRADEMARK INFRINGEMENT The unauthorized use of another's trademark in such a manner as to cause a likelihood of confusion as to the source of the product or service in connection with which it is utilized.

■═■

Mobil Oil Corp. v. Pegasus Petroleum Corp.

Petroleum products company (P) v. Oil trading company (D)

818 F.2d 254 (2d Cir. 1987).

NATURE OF CASE: Appeal from judgment of trademark infringement, unfair competition, and other claims under the Lanham Act.

FACT SUMMARY: Mobil Oil Corp. (Mobil) (P) claimed that Pegasus Petroleum Corp. (D) infringed Mobil's (P) pictorial "flying horse" symbol through the use of the word "Pegasus."

RULE OF LAW

Trademark infringement of a senior user's pictorial mark by a junior user's word mark occurs where the senior user's mark is exceptionally strong, the two marks are nearly synonymous, there is competitive proximity between the two marks, there is an inference of the junior user's bad faith in adopting its mark, there is evidence of actual confusion between the two marks, and even though consumers are sophisticated, there is nonetheless a likelihood of initial confusion.

FACTS: Mobil Oil Corp. (Mobil) (P), a petroleum products company since 1931 has made extensive use of its well-known "flying horse" symbol—representing Pegasus, the winged horse of Greek mythology—in connection with various aspects of its petroleum business. One aspect of its business in connection with which Mobil (P) does not use its flying horse symbol is its oil trading business, which is made up of highly sophisticated, professional buyers and brokers. Pegasus Petroleum Corp. (D) in 1981 started using the "Pegasus" mark in connection with oil trading—its only business activity. Pegasus Petroleum's (D) founder knew of Mobil's (P) flying horse symbol, but claimed he did not know that symbol represented Pegasus. Pegasus Petroleum (D) also sent a letter to the oil trading market indicating that Pegasus Petroleum (D) was part of the "Callimanopulos group of companies," and used an interlocking double P as a letterhead. Pegasus Petroleum (D) never used a flying horse symbol and sells no products with the name "Pegasus" on them. After attempts to reach agreement failed, Mobil (P) brought suit for trademark infringement, unfair competition, and other claims under the Lanham Act, and Pegasus Petroleum (D) counterclaimed. The district court, after applying the Polaroid factors, held for Mobil (P) on all its claims and enjoined Pegasus Petroleum's (D) further use of the mark "Pegasus" in connection with the oil industry. The Second Circuit Court of Appeals granted review.

ISSUE: Does trademark infringement of a senior user's pictorial mark by a junior user's word mark occur where the senior user's mark is exceptionally strong, the two

marks are nearly synonymous, there is competitive proximity between the two marks, there is an inference of the junior user's bad faith in adopting its mark, there is evidence of actual confusion between the two marks, and even though consumers are sophisticated, there is nonetheless a likelihood of initial confusion?

HOLDING AND DECISION: (Lumbard, J.) Yes. Trademark infringement of a senior user's pictorial mark by a junior user's word mark occurs where the senior user's mark is exceptionally strong, the two marks are nearly synonymous, there is competitive proximity between the two marks, there is an inference of the junior user's bad faith in adopting its mark, there is evidence of actual confusion between the two marks, and even though consumers are sophisticated, there is nonetheless a likelihood of initial confusion. There is no question that Mobil's (P) mark is exceptionally strong, and, as an arbitrary mark, deserves the most protection available under the Lanham Act. A strong point of contention is whether the two marks are similar. Pegasus Petroleum (D) argues that the district court erred by blindly equating the word "Pegasus" with its pictorial representation. While words and their pictorial representations should not be equated as a matter of law, a district court may make such a determination as a factual matter. As to competitive proximity, while it is true that Mobil (P) does not use the flying horse symbol in connection with its oil trading business, direct competition between products is not a prerequisite to relief, as confusion, or the likelihood of confusion, not competition, is the true test of trademark infringement. Moreover, this factor must be measured with reference to the first two Polaroid factors: The exceptional strength of Mobil's (P) mark requires that it be given broad protection. Mobil's (P) ubiquitous presence throughout the petroleum industry further increases the likelihood that a consumer will confuse Pegasus Petroleum (D) with Mobil (P). Finally, the great similarity between the two marks entitles Mobil's (P) mark to protection over a broader range of related products. These three factors support a finding of likelihood of confusion. In addition, the fourth factor, as to the alleged infringer's good faith, supports such a finding. The district court determined that Pegasus was intentionally chosen by Pegasus Petroleum's (D) founder to create confusion. Pegasus Petroleum's (D) letter to the oil trading market identifying its affiliation, while relevant, falls far short of establishing Pegasus Petroleum's (D) good faith, since actual or constructive knowledge of the senior user's mark may give rise to an inference of bad faith and the attempt

Continued on next page.

to get a free ride on the senior user's reputation. The record supports such an inference here. Also, as to the fifth Polaroid factor, there is evidence, based on surveys, that there was some actual confusion between the two marks. The district court's conclusion to that effect was therefore not clearly erroneous. Its conclusion that Pegasus Petroleum (D) would gain an advantage in the early stages of an oil trade, by gaining crucial credibility by potentially being associated with Mobil (P), was also not erroneous, so that the absence of misdirected mail or telephone calls was not indicative of a lack of actual confusion. The district court did not consider the sixth *Polaroid* factor—whether Mobil (P) would "bridge the gap" by extending its use of the flying horse symbol to its oil trading business—but likelihood of confusion may be established in the absence of this factor. The seventh factor, the quality of the junior user's product, also was not addressed by the district court. Even if, as Pegasus Petroleum (D) contends, its oil is the same quality as that of Mobil (P), a senior user may sue to protect its reputation even where the infringer's goods are of top quality. Finally, as to the eighth and final factor—the sophistication of purchasers—notwithstanding that professionals in the oil trading business are sophisticated, the district court did not err in finding that there was a likelihood of confusion, since that confusion would occur with potential purchasers who might be misled into an initial interest in Pegasus Petroleum (D). Such initial confusion works a sufficient trademark injury, and there was evidence that supported the conclusion that such confusion could occur, given that Pegasus Petroleum (D) would solicit business through telephone cold calls. Affirmed.

▶ *ANALYSIS*

As this case demonstrates, the law today rewards a famous or well known mark with a larger cloak of protection than in the case of a lesser known mark because of the tendency of the consuming public to associate a relatively unknown mark with one to which they have long been exposed if the relatively unknown mark bears any resemblance thereto. In addition, diversification makes it more likely that a potential customer would associate the non-diversified company's services with the diversified company, even though the two companies do not actually compete.

■■■

Quicknotes

BAD FAITH Conduct that is intentionally misleading or deceptive.

GOOD FAITH An honest intention to abstain from taking advantage of another.

■■■

Network Automation, Inc. v. Advanced Systems Concepts, Inc.

Job management software company (P) v. Job management software company (D)

638 F.3d 1137 (9th Cir. 2011).

NATURE OF CASE: Appeal from preliminary injunction in an action seeking a declaratory judgment of noninfringement, and counterclaim for trademark infringement.

FACT SUMMARY: Network Automation, Inc. (P) contended that its use as a search engine keyword of the mark "ActiveBatch"—which belonged to its direct competitor Advanced Systems Concepts, Inc. (D)—did not constitute trademark infringement.

🏛 RULE OF LAW
When determining whether there has been trademark infringement on the Internet, a flexible, case-by-case approach must be used, rather than rigidly applying a predetermined set of factors.

FACTS: Both Network Automation, Inc. (Network) (P) and Advanced Systems Concepts, Inc. (Systems) (D) produce and sell job management software, and both advertise their respective products on the Internet. Network (P) sells its software under the mark "Auto-Mate," while Systems (D) sells its product under the registered trademark "ActiveBatch." Network (P) decided to purchase "ActiveBatch" as a keyword for search engines so that when an Internet user entered the keyword, the results page would display a "sponsored link" for Network's (P) page. This link would appear above or alongside a link to Systems (D) page. As a result, consumers searching for business software who entered "ActiveBatch" as a search term would locate a results page where the top objective results were links to Systems' (D) own website and various articles about the product, and in the "Sponsored Links" or "Sponsored Sites" section of the page, above or to the right of the regular results, users would see Network's (P) advertisement, either alone or alongside Systems' (D) own sponsored link. Network's (P) ads began with phrases such as "Job Scheduler," "Intuitive Job Scheduler," or "Batch Job Scheduling." Systems (D) demanded that Network (P) cease and desist from using "ActiveBatch" as a search term. Believing its action to be noninfringing, Network (P) filed an action seeking a judgment of noninfringement, and Systems (D) counterclaimed for trademark infringement. The district court, finding that Network (P) had used the mark in commerce, and finding a likelihood of initial interest confusion, issued a preliminary injunction against Network's (P) use of the "ActiveBatch" mark. In reaching its conclusion, the district court focused on three factors of an eight-factor test which had previously been used in assessing trademark infringement involving domain names on the Internet: (1) the similarity of the marks, (2) the relatedness of the goods

or services, and (3) the simultaneous use of the Web as a marketing channel. The district court indicated this troika of factors had to be present for any case addressing trademark infringement on the Internet. The court of appeals granted review.

ISSUE: When determining whether there has been trademark infringement on the Internet, must a flexible, case-by-case approach be used, rather than rigidly applying a predetermined set of factors?

HOLDING AND DECISION: (Wardlaw, J.) Yes. When determining whether there has been trademark infringement on the Internet, a flexible, case-by-case approach must be used, rather than rigidly applying a predetermined set of factors. Given the multifaceted and evolving nature of the Internet and the ever-expanding ways in which this technology is used, it makes no sense to prioritize—as the district court did—the same three factors for every type of potential online commercial activity. In fact, the three factors used by the district court are a particularly poor fit for the circumstances presented here. Instead, when determining the appropriate factors to apply, it should be kept in mind that the eight factors used for determining trademark infringement are nonexhaustive and should be applied flexibly, particularly in the context of Internet commerce. Moreover, where, as here, initial interest confusion is at issue, the owner of the mark must demonstrate likely confusion, not mere diversion. As to the first factor—strength of the mark—this factor weighs heavily here. A user searching for a distinctive term like "ActiveBatch" is more likely to be looking for a particular product, and therefore could be more susceptible to confusion when sponsored links appear that advertise a similar product from a different source. However, if the ordinary consumers of this particular product are particularly sophisticated and knowledgeable, they might also be aware that Systems (D) is the source of ActiveBatch software and not be confused at all. Thus, the sophistication of consumers must be addressed as a component of the inquiry into the mark's strength. The second factor is the proximity of the goods to each other. Generally, related goods are more likely than unrelated goods to confuse the public as to the producers of the goods. In this case, where the goods are virtually interchangeable, however, this factor may be helpful, but it must be considered in conjunction with the labeling and appearance of the advertisements and the degree of care exercised by the consumers of ActiveBatch software. In

Continued on next page.

other words, this factor should not have been considered in isolation by the district court. The third factor is the similarity of the marks. Here, the consumer does not confront two distinct trademarks. Nonetheless, this factor may be of help in determining initial interest confusion, but it must be considered in conjunction with the labeling and appearance of the advertisement, including whether it identifies Network's (P) own mark, and the degree of care and sophistication of the consumer. Regarding this factor, the district court erred in treating "ActiveBatch," the keyword purchased by Network (P), as conceptually separate from "ActiveBatch" the trademark owned by Systems (D). This is an artificial distinction that does not reflect what consumers "encountered in the marketplace." As to the fourth factor, actual confusion, the district court correctly gave this factor little weight, since its importance is diminished at the preliminary injunction stage of the proceedings where little evidence has been presented on this factor. Nonetheless, this is a relevant factor for determining the likelihood of confusion in keyword advertising cases. Generally, as to the fifth factor—marketing channels—convergent marketing channels increase the likelihood of confusion. However, here, the district court erred in weighting this factor in favor of Systems (D), because today most retailers advertise online, so that the shared use of a ubiquitous marketing channel does not shed much light on the likelihood of consumer confusion. The sixth factor, the nature of the goods and the type of consumer, is highly relevant to determining the likelihood of confusion in the keyword advertising context. A sophisticated consumer of business software exercising a high degree of care is more likely to understand the mechanics of Internet search engines and the nature of sponsored links, whereas an un-savvy consumer exercising less care is more likely to be confused. The district court determined that this factor weighed in Systems' (D) favor because "there is generally a low degree of care exercised by Internet consumers." However, the degree of care analysis cannot begin and end at the marketing channel. In addition, the nature and cost of the goods, and whether the products being sold are marketed primarily to expert buyers, must also be analyzed. Moreover, the default degree of consumer care is becoming more heightened as the novelty of the Internet evaporates and online commerce becomes commonplace, and consumers searching for expensive products online tend to be even more sophisticated. Given these new realities, the district erred in weighting this factor in favor of Systems (D) based on the outdated conclusion that Internet users on the whole exercise a low degree of care. Similarly, the seventh factor—intent—cannot be considered in isolation, as it was by the district court. The defendant's intent may be relevant, but only insofar as it bolsters a finding that the use of the trademark serves to mislead consumers rather than truthfully inform them of their choice of products. The district court thus incorrectly concluded that this factor weighed in Systems' (D) favor without first determining

that Network (P) intended to deceive consumers rather than compare its product to ActiveBatch. Where two companies are direct competitors, as in this case, the eighth factor—product line expansion—is unimportant. Therefore, the district court correctly declined to consider the likelihood of expansion. These eight factors are not exhaustive. In the keyword advertising context, another factor that should be considered is the appearance of the advertisements and their surrounding context on the user's screen. Thus, even if Network (P) did not clearly identify itself in the text of its ads, the search engines partitioned their search results pages so that the advertisements appeared in separately labeled sections for "sponsored" links. The labeling and appearance of the advertisements as they appear on the results page includes more than the text of the advertisement, and must be considered as a whole. In sum, in a keyword advertising case, the most relevant factors to the analysis of the likelihood of confusion are: (1) the strength of the mark; (2) the evidence of actual confusion; (3) the type of goods and degree of care likely to be exercised by the purchaser; and (4) the labeling and appearance of the advertisements and the surrounding context on the screen displaying the results page. Because the district court failed to appropriately consider and weigh these factors to fit the particular facts and circumstances of this case, the district court abused its discretion, and the case must be remanded for reconsideration in light of the factors that should have been considered. Reversed, vacated and remanded.

▶ *ANALYSIS*

This decision endorses the principle that it would be wrong to expand the initial interest confusion theory of infringement beyond the realm of misleading and deceptive to the context of legitimate comparative and contextual advertising. For example, the experience of browsing clearly labeled keyword advertisements has been analogized to shopping at Macy's, where if a shopper en route to the Calvin Klein section is diverted by a prominently displayed Charter Club (Macy's own brand) collection and never reaches the Calvin Klein collection, it could not be said that Macy's had infringed on Calvin Klein's trademark by diverting the customer from it with a clearly labeled, but more prominent display. *Playboy Enters. v. Netscape Communs. Corp.,* 354 F.3d 1020 at 1035 (Berzon, J., concurring). The factors the court places an emphasis on in this case are intended to prevent a finding of initial interest confusion when a consumer is never confused as to source or affiliation, but instead knows, or should know, from the outset that a product or web link is not related to that of the trademark holder because the list produced by the search engine so informs him.

▰▱▰

Continued on next page.

Quicknotes

TRADEMARK INFRINGEMENT The unauthorized use of another's trademark in such a manner as to cause a likelihood of confusion as to the source of the product or service in connection with which it is utilized.

■━━■

Mastercrafters Clock & Radio Co. v. Vacheron & Constantin-Le Coultre Watches, Inc.

U.S. electric clock manufacturer (P) v. Importer and distributor of Swiss watches (D)

221 F.2d 464 (2d Cir. 1955).

NATURE OF CASE: Appeal from declaratory judgment of no unfair competition.

FACT SUMMARY: Vacheron & Constantin-Le Coultre Watches, Inc. (Vacheron) (D) contended that Mastercrafters Clock & Radio Co.'s (Mastercrafters) (P) Model 308 electric clock unfairly competed with the Atmos clock that Vacheron (D) distributed, arguing that the Atmos clock's unique appearance had obtained a secondary meaning and that the Model 308 was likely to injure the reputation of the Atmos's Swiss manufacturer.

🏛 RULE OF LAW
An unfair competition claim is made out regardless of whether a product has multiple distributors and sources where the product's appearance has gained secondary meaning, an allegedly infringing product has copied that appearance for the purpose of profiting therefrom, and there is a likelihood of consumer confusion resulting from such copying.

FACTS: Mastercrafters Clock & Radio Co. (Mastercrafters) (P) is a U.S. electric clock manufacturer that produced and distributed the Model 308 clock. This clock sold for between $30 and $40 and had an electric cord as well as Mastercrafters' (P) name on it. Vacheron & Constantin-Le Coultre Watches, Inc. (Vacheron) (D), a U.S. importer and distributor of Swiss watches and clocks, upon learning of the Model 308 clock, informed Mastercrafters (P) and its customers-distributors that Model 308 was a counterfeit of the distinctive appearance and configuration of the Atmos clock, which Vacheron (D) distributed for a Swiss manufacturer. The Atmos clock sold for $175 and did not have an electric cord. Vacheron (D) brought suit in several state courts against Mastercrafters' (P) distributors, and Mastercrafters (P) responded by filing a claim seeking a declaratory judgment that its Model 308 clock did not unfairly compete with the Atmos, damages from the suits, and an injunction restraining Vacheron (D) from prosecuting further suits. Vacheron (D) counterclaimed for damages due to unfair competition and an injunction restraining the manufacture and distribution of the Model 308 clock. The district court found that before Mastercrafters (P) began production of its Model 308, the Atmos clock "was readily distinguishable from all other clocks then on the market by virtue of its appearance"; that Mastercrafters' (P) Model 308 copied that appearance; that Mastercrafters "undoubtedly intended to, and did, avail itself of an eye-catching design and hoped to cater

to the price-conscious purchaser who desires to own a copy of a luxury design clock regardless of mechanism or source." Nevertheless, the district court dismissed Vacheron's (D) counterclaims and ruled for Mastercrafters (P) on the grounds that there was no unfair competition, concluding that there was more than one distributor of the Atmos clock; the public did not care what was the ultimate source of the Atmos; and that the Model 308 was clearly marked and advertised as being made by Mastercrafters (P).

ISSUE: Is an unfair competition claim made out regardless of whether a product has multiple distributors and sources where the product's appearance has gained secondary meaning, an allegedly infringing product has copied that appearance for the purpose of profiting therefrom, and there is a likelihood of consumer confusion resulting from such copying?

HOLDING AND DECISION: (Frank, J.) Yes. An unfair competition claim is made out regardless of whether a product has multiple distributors and sources where the product's appearance has gained secondary meaning, an allegedly infringing product has copied that appearance for the purpose of profiting therefrom, and there is a likelihood of consumer confusion resulting from such copying. The existence of a secondary meaning, attaching to the unique appearance of the Atmos clock, is not precluded by the mere fact that more than one person distributed that clock in the same area. The actionable harm in a secondary-meaning case may result either from the likelihood (a) of loss of customers or (b) of loss of reputation, or (c) of both. Such loss can result from the consumer's belief that the source of the competing article is the same source for the original article, and it does not matter whether the consumer knows its exact source. Although purchasers of the Model 308 would see the electric cord and Mastercrafters' (P) name on it, some purchasers would buy this clock for the purpose of obtaining a "luxury design" for cheap. When this clock would be displayed by those purchasers, others would be duped into thinking it was a prestigious article, i.e., an Atmos clock. Therefore, the likelihood of such confusion is sufficient to render Mastercrafters' (P) conduct actionable. Because it is clear that Mastercrafters (P) intended to reap financial benefits from poaching on the reputation of the Atmos clock, and a likelihood of confusion (by some purchasers' guests or friends) has been shown, Mastercrafters' (P) intent gives rise to a strong inference that confusion is likely, so that Mastercrafters (P) bears the burden of showing the absence

Continued on next page.

of such a likelihood. Because Mastercrafters (P) failed to satisfy this burden, the district court erred in holding there was no unfair competition. The case must be remanded to dismiss Mastercrafters' (P) claim and to grant the injunction requested by Vacheron (D). On remand, the district court will have to determine whether Vacheron's (D) damages equal Mastercrafters' (P) profits from the sale of the Model 308 clock. Reversed and remanded.

▶ *ANALYSIS*

The court in this case bases its finding of likelihood of confusion on comparisons of the post-sale products, i.e., where the confusion occurs after the products have been sold. The courts that have decided the question have split as to whether pre-sale products or post-sale product provide the proper basis for analysis. If the court had based its analysis on the pre-sale product, the outcome likely would have been different since the court acknowledged that purchasers themselves would not be confused before making their purchases, given that they would see the electric cord and Mastercrafters' (P) name on the clock and therefore know that it was not an "atmospheric" Atmos clock. Instead, the confusion is on the part of others viewing the clock after it has been purchased, since those viewers—at least according to the court—will not see the electric cord or pay attention to the name on the clock. Thus, supposedly, the loss of sales to Vacheron (D) arises from those purchasers who wish to dupe others by buying a knock-off. Arguably, however, those who view the Model 308 after it has been purchased and believe it is an Atmos would be encouraged to buy an Atmos for its prestige value.

■■■

Quicknotes

SECONDARY MEANING A word or mark that becomes associated with a particular merchant or product as its source of origin.

■■■

Munsingwear, Inc. v. Jockey International

Clothing manufacturer (P) v. Clothing manufacturer (D)

31 U.S.P.Q.2d 1146 (D. Minn.), *aff'd*, 39 F.3d 1184 (8th Cir. 1994).

NATURE OF CASE: Motions for preliminary injunction and summary judgment in action for trademark infringement and other trademark-related claims.

FACT SUMMARY: Munsingwear, Inc. (P), which had trademark rights in a horizontal-fly ("H-FLY") mark for underwear, contended that Jockey International (Jockey) (D) infringed its trademark by producing and selling a line of horizontal-fly briefs under the "Jockey Pouch" ("Pouch") name. Jockey (D) claimed there was no likelihood of confusion as a matter of law between the two manufacturers' underwear.

> ## 🏛 RULE OF LAW
> (1) A likelihood of confusion analysis should be undertaken on a pre-sale product where the evidence indicates that any likely consumer confusion will occur prior to sale, if at all.
> (2) There is not a likelihood of confusion and, therefore, trademark infringement, where the two products at issue are dissimilar, there is no intent to pass off by the alleged infringer, there is no actual confusion, and the products are relatively cheap and the consumers relatively unsophisticated.

FACTS: Munsingwear, Inc. (P) had trademark rights in a horizontal-fly ("H-FLY") mark for underwear, although it did not have actual federal registration of the mark. It used the "H-FLY" mark and design since 1946, and spent millions of dollars advertising it. In 1992, Jockey International (Jockey) (D) introduced a line of horizontal-fly briefs under the "Jockey Pouch" ("Pouch") name. The "JOCKEY" trademark was woven into the waistband. The packaging for the "Pouch" underwear consisted of standard cellophane wrapped around the brief with the "JOCKEY" trademark and Jockey Design trademark on both the front and back of the packaging. Munsingwear (P) brought suit against Jockey (D) under § 43(a) of the Lanham Act for trademark infringement, as well as for common-law trademark infringement, and deceptive practices. Munsingwear (P) moved for a preliminary injunction, and Jockey (D) moved for summary judgment claiming that there was no likelihood of confusion between the two manufacturers' underwear as a matter of law.

ISSUE:

(1) Should a likelihood of confusion analysis be undertaken on a pre-sale product where the evidence indicates that any likely consumer confusion will occur prior to sale, if at all?

(2) Is there a likelihood of confusion and, therefore, trademark infringement, where the two products at issue are dissimilar, there is no intent to pass off by the alleged infringer, there is no actual confusion, and the products are relatively cheap and the consumers relatively unsophisticated?

HOLDING AND DECISION: (Doty, J.)

(1) Yes. A likelihood of confusion analysis should be undertaken on a pre-sale product where the evidence indicates that any likely consumer confusion will occur prior to sale, if at all. Here, the pre-sale product consists of the underwear as packaged and sold to the consuming public. The post-sale product consists of the actual individual briefs themselves. Determination of whether to use the former or the latter depends on how consumers will encounter the products in the marketplace. Jockey (D) urges that the pre-sale product should be the basis of comparison because consumers purchase underwear in single or multi-unit cellophane wrapped packages that indicate sources and style information. Muningswear (P), on the other hand, advocates using the post-sale product for the analysis, arguing that consumers make their decisions based on the quality and style of the underwear, as well as exposure to the product while it is on mannequins. Courts that have decided the issue have split as to whether pre-sale or post-sale products provide the proper basis for analysis, and the court of appeals in this circuit has not addressed the issue. Here, the argument for pre-sale exposure is stronger because any relevant consumer confusion will likely occur prior to sale, if at all. As customarily worn, underwear is concealed by other articles of clothing. The general public does not ordinarily see underwear in the same manner and to the extent that it views outerwear. Thus, the potential for customer confusion is not as great as it could be for other articles of clothing, and underwear's inherently concealed nature diminishes the concern for post-sale confusion. Therefore, the likelihood of confusion analysis will be conducted on the pre-sale product.

(2) No. There is not a likelihood of confusion and, therefore, trademark infringement, where the two products at issue are dissimilar, there is no intent to pass off by the alleged infringer, there is no actual confusion, and the products are relatively cheap and the consumers relatively unsophisticated. The first factor in the likelihood of confusion analysis is the similarity of the two products. Here, comparing the pre-sale products, the

Continued on next page.

Jockey (D) packages have a cardboard insert, the "JOCKEY POUCH" label and the "JOCKEY" and Jockey logo trademarks. The Munsingwear (P) packaging has a "band and medallion" through the middle, a kangaroo design, "MUNSINGWEAR KANGAROO BRIEF," and the Munsingwear trademark. There is thus no substantial similarity between the two products. The second factor is competitive proximity. Both products are sold in men's departments of stores, and sometimes are sold side-by-side. There is a high likelihood that the two products will be sold in relatively close proximity, but this is a function of market decisions made by the stores, rather than by the parties. The third factor is intent to pass-off by the alleged infringer. Munsingwear (P) argues that Jockey (D) intended to pass-off its "Pouch" underwear as Munsingwear's (P) "H-FLY" underwear. Jockey (D) contends that the existing strength of its trademark and the amount spent in advertising indicate it did not have such an intent, and that its marketing of "Pouch" underwear is a form of competition for market share rather than an attempt to pass-off its underwear as that of Munsingwear (P). Viewing the two packages together, it is evidence there was no intent to pass-off by Jockey (D). The fourth factor is actual confusion, and there was no evidence of such confusion. The fifth factor is survey evidence, but no surveys were submitted. The final factor is the cost of the product and conditions of purchase. The cost of both products is relatively inexpensive, and purchasers are therefore deemed to exercise less purchasing care and to not give much thought to their purchasing decision. Accordingly, the consumer is deemed unsophisticated. Balancing all these factors leads to the conclusion that, as a matter of law, there is no likelihood of confusion between the two products. Summary judgment is granted to Jockey (D).

▶ ANALYSIS

This case could be analyzed from two different perspectives, either as a trademark infringement action or a trade dress infringement action. A trademark is a distinctive mark of authenticity, through which the products of particular manufacturers or the commodities of particular merchants may be distinguished from those of others. Trade dress consists of the product's packaging and image, broadly construed, not the words and symbols that a manufacturer uses on its goods. While the Lanham Act (the Act) fails to specify either trade dress or trademark in its text, protection of both trade dress and trademarks serves the Act's purpose to secure to the owner of the mark the goodwill of the business and to protect the ability of consumers to distinguish among competing producers. A seller's adoption of a trademark or trade dress that is confusingly similar to a competitor's constitutes unfair competition and is actionable under § 43(a) of the Lanham Act. While the scope of trade dress has been said to exceed that of a trademark, the analysis for trade dress and an unregistered trademark under § 43(a) is very similar. In fact, courts look to trademark cases for guidance on trade dress and vice versa.

Quicknotes

LANHAM ACT, § 43(a) Federal trademark infringement statute.

SUMMARY JUDGMENT Judgment rendered by a court in response to a motion made by one of the parties, claiming that the lack of a question of material fact in respect to an issue warrants disposition of the issue without consideration by the jury.

TRADE DRESS The overall image of, or impression created by, a product that a court may enforce as a trademark if it determines that such image has acquired secondary meaning and that the public recognizes it as an indication of source.

TRADEMARK Any word, name, symbol, device or combination thereof that is either currently utilized, or which a person has a bona fide intent to utilize, in commerce in order to distinguish his goods from those of another.

Anheuser-Busch, Inc. v. Balducci Publications

Beer brewer (P) v. Humor magazine publisher (D)

28 F.3d 769 (8th Cir. 1994).

NATURE OF CASE: Appeal from dismissal of trademark action asserting claims for trademark infringement, trademark dilution, and unfair competition.

FACT SUMMARY: Anheuser-Busch, Inc. (P), a beer brewer that produces the Michelob family of beers, contended that Balduccci Publications (Balducci) (D) infringed and diluted its "Michelob" trademarks by using several Anheuser-Busch marks in a fictitious ad for "Michelob Oily" in a humor magazine that Balducci (D) published, purportedly in an effort to parody the impacts of environmental pollution.

RULE OF LAW
A parody that uses another's trademarks without alteration or permission infringes and dilutes the other's marks where such use creates a likelihood of confusion and is not otherwise protected by the First Amendment.

FACTS: Anheuser-Busch, Inc. (P) is a beer brewer that operates a brewery in St. Louis, and that produces the Michelob family of beers. It owns several federally-registered and state-registered trademarks, including: "Michelob"; "Michelob Dry"; "A & Eagle Design"; and the phrase "ONE TASTE AND YOU'LL DRINK IT DRY." Balducci Publications (Balducci) (D) published *Snicker*, a humor magazine, and in one of the issues it published a mock advertisement on the back of the magazine for the fictitious product "Michelob Oily." The advertisement stated in bold type, "ONE TASTE AND YOU'LL DRINK IT OILY" immediately above "MICHELOB OILY (R)." The accompanying graphics include a partially obscured can of Michelob Dry pouring oil onto a fish, an oil-soaked rendition of the A & Eagle design (with the eagle exclaiming "Yuck!") below a Shell Oil symbol, and various "Michelob Oily" products bearing a striking resemblance to Anheuser-Busch's (P) Michelob family. In smaller text the ad opined, "At the rate it's being dumped into our oceans, lakes and rivers, you'll drink it oily sooner or later, anyway." In extremely small text, the ad included the disclaimer: "Snicker Magazine Editorial by Rich Balducci. Art by Eugene Ruble. Thank goodness someone still cares about quality (of life)." Anheuser-Busch (P) asserted federal and state trademark infringement, trademark dilution, and unfair competition claims against Balducci (D) based on the Michelob Oily ad. Balducci (D) claimed that it used the parody to comment on: (1) the effects of environmental pollution, including a specific reference to the then-recent Shell oil spill in the Gasconade River—a source of Anheuser-Busch's (P) water

supply; (2) Anheuser-Busch's (P) subsequent decision to temporarily close its St. Louis brewery; and (3) the proliferation of Anheuser-Busch (P) beer brands and advertisements. The primary evidence offered by Anheuser-Busch (P) was a study conducted in St. Louis shopping malls, involving 301 beer drinkers or purchasers who claimed to periodically review magazines or newspapers. Many of those interviewed for the study expressed an impression of Anheuser-Busch's (P) role in the ad's creation. The district court dismissed the claims, finding that in the context of an editorial, the mock ad did not create a likelihood of confusion in the marketplace, and that First Amendment considerations supported dismissal. The court of appeals granted review.

ISSUE: Does a parody that uses another's trademarks without alteration or permission infringe and dilute the other's marks where such use creates a likelihood of confusion and is not otherwise protected by the First Amendment?

HOLDING AND DECISION: (Gibson, Sr. J.) Yes. A parody that uses another's trademarks without alteration or permission infringes and dilutes the other's marks where such use creates a likelihood of confusion and is not otherwise protected by the First Amendment. Here, the district court gave too much weight to First Amendment concerns initially. Instead, the court should have determined if there was likelihood of confusion, and only then addressed the First Amendment concerns. The test for likelihood of confusion is expansive. Here, Anheuser-Busch's (P) marks that Balducci (D) displayed virtually unaltered in the ad parody are very strong, and this weighs heavily in favor of Anheuser-Busch (P). Although Balducci (D) does not directly compete with Anheuser-Busch (P), confusion may exist in the absence of direct competition, and, here, Balducci (D) published the parody on the back cover of a magazine—a location frequently devoted to real ads, even in *Snicker*—which could confuse consumers accustomed to seeing advertisements on the back cover of magazines. As to intent, the evidence suggests that Balducci (D) at least had an indifference to the possibility that some consumers might be misled by the parody. For example, no significant steps were taken to remind readers that they were viewing a parody, since Balducci (D) carefully designed the fictitious ad to appear as authentic as possible and several of Anheuser-Busch's (P) marks were used with little or no alteration. The disclaimer was virtually undetectable. Balducci (D) even included a "®" symbol after the words "Michelob Oily." These facts weigh against Balducci

Continued on next page.

(D). The evidence raises a significant doubt as to whether many consumers would develop the understanding that Balducci's (D) true purpose was to create a parody, especially since the back cover of magazines is frequently used for advertisements and cannot be expected to command the thoughtful deliberation of all or even most of the viewing public. The survey evidence also weighs in favor of Anheuser-Busch (P), since over half of those surveyed thought Balducci (D) needed Anheuser-Busch's (P) approval to publish the ad, and six percent thought that the parody was an actual Anheuser-Busch (P) advertisement. For these reasons, the court erred in finding no likelihood of confusion. Once likelihood of confusion has been established, the next step in the analysis is to determine whether the First Amendment protects the parody. In doing so, the public interest in protecting Balducci's (D) expression must be balanced against the public interest in avoiding consumer confusion. Here, the First Amendment does not bar trademark protection for Anheuser-Busch (P) because Balducci's (D) parody was likely to confuse consumers as to its origin, sponsorship or approval, and such was wholly unnecessary to Balducci's (D) stated purpose. By using an obvious disclaimer, positioning the parody in a less-confusing location, altering the protected marks in a meaningful way, or doing some collection of the above, Balducci (D) could have conveyed its message with substantially less risk of consumer confusion. [Reversed.]

▶ ANALYSIS

This decision highlights not only the tension between trademark protection and the First Amendment, but also highlights how different courts have approached this issue; here, the district court's approach is ruled erroneous by the court of appeals, but other courts, applying the district court's approach, have reached similar conclusions as the district court did here. Given that decisions involving parodies that use others' trademarks are highly fact-sensitive, and that various courts have arrived at different results under similar circumstances, it seems that there is currently no clear guidance for a parodist as to what will and will not constitute a parody. Given the disparate court decisions and outcomes as to this issue, a parodist cannot know until it is too late whether he or she made too much use of the targeted work. Thus, although the absence of a bright-line test in this area ensures some flexibility in determining fair use, it may also chill the very speech the fair use doctrine was intended to protect.

Quicknotes

TRADEMARK DILUTION The diminishment of the capability of a trademark to identify and distinguish the particular good or service with which it is associated.

TRADEMARK INFRINGEMENT The unauthorized use of another's trademark in such a manner as to cause a likelihood of confusion as to the source of the product or service in connection with which it is utilized.

UNFAIR COMPETITION Any dishonest or fraudulent rivalry in trade and commerce, particularly imitation and counterfeiting.

Inwood Labs., Inc. v. Ives Labs., Inc.

Generic drug manufacturer (D) v. Original drug manufacturer (P)

456 U.S. 844 (1982).

NATURE OF CASE: Appeal from reversal of dismissal of claim brought under § 32 of the Trademark Act of 1946 (Lanham Act) for inducing a trademark violation by another.

FACT SUMMARY: Ives Laboratories, Inc. (Ives) (P), which originally held a patent on the prescription drug cyclandelate, claimed that generic drug manufacturers (D) were liable for violations of §§ 32 and 43(a) of the Trademark Act of 1946 (Lanham Act) by inducing pharmacists to mislabel generic drugs as "CYCLOSPASMOL," Ives's (P) trademarked name for the drug, through the use of similarly shaped and colored capsules as used by Ives (P). The district court dismissed these claims, but, without finding that the district court had clearly erred, the court of appeals reversed.

🏛 RULE OF LAW
As to claims of vicarious liability brought under the Lanham Act, where the district court finds that the defendant has not intentionally induced trademark violations by another, either directly or indirectly, to set aside the district court's findings and reverse the district court's judgment, the court of appeals must determine that the district court's findings are clearly erroneous.

FACTS: Ives Laboratories, Inc. (Ives) (P) manufactured and marketed the patented prescription drug cyclandelate to wholesalers, retail pharmacists, and hospitals in colored capsules under the registered trademark "CYCLOSPASMOL." After Ives's (P) patent expired, several generic drug manufacturers, including Inwood Laboratories, Inc. (collectively "the generic manufacturers" (D)), began marketing the drug, intentionally copying the appearance of the "CYCLOSPASMOL" capsules. Ives (P) then brought an action against the generic drug manufacturers (D) in district court under, inter alia, §§ 32 and 43(a) of the Trademark Act of 1946 (Lanham Act), alleging that some pharmacists had dispensed generic drugs mislabeled as "CYCLOSPASMOL" and that the generic drug manufacturers' (D) use of look-alike capsules and catalog entries comparing prices and revealing the colors of generic capsules contributed to the pharmacists' mislabeling. Ives (P) sought injunctive relief and damages. The district court entered judgment for the generic drug manufacturers (D), finding that although the pharmacists had violated § 32, Ives (P) had not made the necessary factual showing that the generic drug manufacturers (D) had intentionally induced the pharmacists to mislabel generic drugs or continued to supply cyclandelate to pharmacists who the

generic drug manufacturers (D) knew or should have known were mislabeling generic drugs. The district court also found that Ives (P) failed to establish its claim based upon § 43(a), finding that the capsule colors were functional to patients and physicians, and that because the colors failed to indicate the drugs origin, the colors had not acquired a secondary meaning. The court of appeals reversed, rejecting the district court's findings even though it did not find them to be clearly erroneous, and held that the generic drug manufacturers (D) violated § 32. The United States Supreme Court granted certiorari.

ISSUE: As to claims of vicarious liability brought under the Lanham Act, where the district court finds that the defendant has not intentionally induced trademark violations by another, either directly or indirectly, to set aside the district court's findings and reverse the district court's judgment, must the court of appeals determine that the district court's findings are clearly erroneous?

HOLDING AND DECISION: (O'Connor, J.) As to claims of vicarious liability brought under the Lanham Act, where the district court finds that the defendant has not intentionally induced trademark violations by another, either directly or indirectly, to set aside the district court's findings and reverse the district court's judgment, the court of appeals must determine that the district court's findings are clearly erroneous. If a manufacturer or distributor intentionally induces another to infringe a trademark, or if it continues to supply its product to one whom it knows or has reason to know is engaging in trademark infringement, the manufacturer or distributor is contributorially responsible for any harm done as a result of the deceit. Those pharmacists who mislabeled generic drugs with Ives's (P) registered trademark violated § 32, so the issue becomes whether the generic drug manufacturers (D) were liable for those infringing acts. The determination of such liability depends on whether the generic drug manufacturers (D) intentionally induced the pharmacists to mislabel generic drugs or, in fact, continued to supply cyclandelate to pharmacists whom they knew were mislabeling generic drugs. The district court concluded, as a finding of fact, that Ives (P) made neither of those factual showings. In reviewing the district court's factual findings, the court of appeals was bound by the clearly erroneous standard of review found in Rule 52(a) of the Federal Rules of Civil Procedure. By rejecting the findings simply because it would have given more weight to evidence of mislabeling than did the trial court, the court of appeals clearly erred. Determining the weight and credibility of the evidence is

Continued on next page.

the special province of the trier of fact. Because the district court's findings concerning the significance of the instances of mislabeling were not clearly erroneous, they should not have been disturbed. Moreover, each of the conclusions that the court of appeals made in holding that the evidence established a § 32 violation was contrary to the district court's findings. An appellate court cannot substitute its interpretation of the evidence for that of the trial court simply because the reviewing court "might give the facts another construction, resolve the ambiguities differently, and find a more sinister cast to actions which the district court apparently deemed innocent." Accordingly, the court of appeals' holding is reversed as to the § 32 claim. Because the court of appeals did not address the other claims, the district court's decision dismissing those claims must be independently reviewed. Therefore, those claims are remanded to the court of appeals for consideration.

▌ANALYSIS

The Restatement (Third) of Unfair Competition, § 26 imposes liability for contributory trademark infringement when "...(a) the actor intentionally induces the third person to engage in the infringing conduct; or (b) the actor fails to take reasonable precautions against the oc-currence of the third person's infringing conduct in circumstances in which the infringing conduct can be reasonably anticipated."

Quicknotes

FED. R. CIV. P. 52(a) Requires that findings of fact not be set aside unless clearly erroneous.

INTER ALIA Among other things.

VICARIOUS LIABILITY The imputed liability of one party for the unlawful acts of another.

Tiffany Inc. v. eBay, Inc.

Trademark holder (P) v. Alleged infringer (D)

600 F.3d 93 (2d Cir. 2010).

NATURE OF CASE: Appeal from finding of no infringement in trademark case.

FACT SUMMARY: Tiffany (NJ) Inc. (P) and Tiffany and Company (P) (Tiffany) sold high-end jewelry in retail stores, catalogues, and online but not through second-hand vendors or third-party online retailers. eBay Inc. (D) sells goods online by connecting third-party sellers and buyers and without ever taking possession of the goods. Tiffany (P) accused eBay (D) of knowingly permitting the sale of counterfeit Tiffany goods in violation of Tiffany's (P) trademark.

RULE OF LAW
Service provider liability for contributory trademark infringement requires a showing of intentional inducement to infringe or "knows or should have known" of the direct infringement and a continued providing of the service to the infringer.

FACTS: eBay (D) is an Internet marketplace that permits registered sellers to sell various items to registered buyers without eBay ever taking possession of the item. eBay, an extremely successful company, makes its money by charging sellers to list goods and charging a percentage of the final sale price. eBay also makes money through its ownership of PayPal, which charges a percentage and small flat fee for eBay users to process purchases. Tiffany (P) is a world-famous jeweler. It sells its merchandise exclusively through its own retail stores, catalogue, and website. It does not sell overstock, discontinued, or discount merchandise. Tiffany (P) learned of counterfeit Tiffany sales on eBay (D) and alerted eBay (D) to the problem. eBay initiated a variety of anti-counterfeit sales measures, including a fraud engine, a notice-and-takedown system so rights holders could complete a Notice of Claimed Infringement Form and request the takedown of a particular seller's allegedly counterfeit goods, and cancellation of seller accounts of repeat offenders. Tiffany (P) also put a buyers' notice on the eBay (D) site informing buyers of the potential danger in purchasing Tiffany products on the second-hand market. Tiffany (P) filed suit against eBay (D), claiming inter alia, eBay's (D) conduct constituted direct and contributory trademark infringement, trademark dilution, and false advertising. The district court found for eBay (D) on all counts. Tiffany (P) appealed.

ISSUE: Does service provider liability for contributory trademark infringement require a showing of intentional inducement to infringe or "knows or should have known" of the direct infringement and a continued providing of the service to the infringer?

HOLDING AND DECISION: (Sack, J.) Yes. Service provider liability for contributory trademark infringement requires a showing of intentional inducement to infringe or "knows or should have known" of the direct infringement and a continued providing of the service to the infringer. The district court correctly found eBay's (D) use of Tiffany's (P) mark to be nominative fair use and did not suggest Tiffany (P) endorsed or partnered with eBay (D). Tiffany's (P) argument that eBay (D) knew or should have known of the counterfeit sales and thus directly infringed upon its mark for failing to identify and remove the illegitimate goods fails. It would unduly limit the resale of legitimate second-hand Tiffany goods to impose liability on eBay (D) for an inability to guarantee the genuineness of all purported Tiffany products. Next, Tiffany (P) argues eBay's conduct constitutes contributory trademark infringement, which is a more difficult argument. This is a judicially created doctrine most recently addressed by the United States Supreme Court in *Inwood Laboratories, Inc. v. Ives Laboratories, Inc.*, 456 U.S. 844 (1982). *Inwood*, applies on its face to manufacturers and distributors of goods but has been extended to providers of services. This Court's precedent in related decisions does not provide great insight and this is the first case in which *Inwood* is applied to an online marketplace. *Inwood* assesses liability for contributory infringement on service providers if the provider: (1) intentionally induces the infringement; or (2) knows or has reason to know of infringement and continues to supply its service to the offending party. Tiffany (P) argues the second factor applies to eBay (D). Tiffany (P) does not challenge the district court's finding that eBay (D) was not liable for those sales it terminated upon receipt of notice from Tiffany (P) about allegedly offending products. Tiffany (P) does challenge the district court's finding eBay (D) had insufficient knowledge about infringement of other, nonterminated listings because its generalized knowledge of counterfeit products on its site did not translate into sufficient knowledge under *Inwood*. It is a high burden to prove "knowledge" of contributory infringement. Tiffany (P) argues here that generalized knowledge and specific knowledge of particular sellers is the same under *Inwood* and creates liability. This court does not read *Inwood* to be so broad and does not find *Inwood* established the parameters of "knows or has reason to know" when it only applied the inducement prong of the test. Another United States Supreme Court case held *Inwood* had a narrow standard and interpreted *Inwood*'s second prong to require knowledge of identified individuals. *Sony Corp. of America v. Universal City Studios, Inc.* 464 U.S. 417 (1984). eBay (D)

Continued on next page.

had no such knowledge here. Tiffany (P) argues "willful blindness" cannot be permitted to overcome liability. If eBay (D) deliberately shielded itself from knowledge of offending sales, it could become liable under the *Inwood* second prong. That is not the case, however, as eBay (D) had only general knowledge and did not ignore the issue. Finally, Tiffany's (P) dilution claims fail because eBay (D) did not use the Tiffany mark to associate it with its own products but to identify Tiffany products on its site. [False advertising analysis is omitted from the casebook excerpt.] Affirmed as to trademark infringement and dilution; remanded as to false advertising.

▶ *ANALYSIS*

Consumer advocates worried a victory for Tiffany (P) would require online merchants to prohibit even lawful uses of trademarks on their sites because of the fear of liability for contributory trademark infringement. eBay's (D) existing safeguards and rapid response to notifications of counterfeit products gave it a significant advantage in this case, but not many online retailers are so responsive. Trademark infringement is rampant online and rights holders must be vigilant about policing the use of their marks. This case did not offer the hoped-for protection for trademark holders.

■■■

Quicknotes

TRADEMARK DILUTION The diminishment of the capability of a trademark to identify and distinguish the particular good or service with which it is associated.

TRADEMARK INFRINGEMENT The unauthorized use of another's trademark in such a manner as to cause a likelihood of confusion as to the source of the product or service in connection with which it is utilized.

■■■

Section 43(A)(1)(A) of the Lanham Act

Quick Reference Rules of Law

DC Comics v. Powers

Comic book publisher (P) v. Newspaper publisher (D)

465 F. Supp. 843 (S.D.N.Y. 1978).

NATURE OF CASE: Cross motions for preliminary injunction in action for trademark dilution and unfair competition.

FACT SUMMARY: Both DC Comics (P) and Powers (D) claimed the exclusive rights to use the name the "Daily Planet" under common-law trademark principles, since neither party held a trademark in the name. Each party sought to preliminarily enjoin the other from using the name.

🏛 RULE OF LAW

(1) Where each of two users of a mark, to which neither user holds a registration, seeks exclusive use of the mark under § 43(a) of the Lanham Act, the prevailing party must show an association of such duration and association with its use of the mark sufficient to establish a common-law trademark therein.

(2) A holder of a common-law trademark may obtain the same relief under § 43(a) of the Lanham Act as a holder of a registered trademark by showing that an alleged infringer's use of the mark is likely to either confuse or deceive purchasers as to the source of items bearing the mark.

FACTS: In 1938, DC Comics (P) created the fictional character Superman and called the newspaper where he worked, as a reporter as Superman's alter ego, The Daily Planet. DC Comics (P) has used the name Daily Planet since 1940 in comic books and comic strips, and on television and radio, and the Daily Planet has been an integral part of the Superman story and Superman's development. The Daily Planet is also the title of a promotional news column appearing periodically within Superman comic books. DC Comics (P) licenses the Superman character in connection with myriad products, and the Superman story is licensed as a package, with the Daily Planet being part of that story. Thus, a typical licensing agreement permits use of all the Superman characters. The Daily Planet has been prominently featured on many products emanating from these licensing agreements. DC Comics (P) does not hold a registered trademark for the term the "Daily Planet." Powers (D) published an underground newspaper called the "Daily Planet," which appeared between 1969 and 1973. Although Powers (D) registered "Daily Planet" in 1970, and incorporated his company under the name Daily Planet, Inc., he permitted the trademark registration to lapse, and it was cancelled. Throughout its brief history, the paper was primarily a local paper in the Miami, Florida,

area. There were numerous references in the paper not only to Superman, but also to the Superman story, including drawings of Superman, use of a masthead that copied the Daily Planet insignia from the comic books, etc. After the paper's demise, Powers (D) attempted to create another paper called "Superstar." DC Comics (P) brought suit under § 43(a) of the Lanham Act, claiming that Powers's (D) use of the name Daily Planet constituted unfair competition and diluted its common-law trademark in the name. In response, Powers (D) moved for a preliminary injunction to preclude DC Comics (P) from any use of the name Daily Planet, including the advertisement, promotion, distribution or sale of any products in connection with a multi-million dollar cinema production of "Superman" that was scheduled to be released within weeks. DC Comics (P) cross-moved for injunctive relief to preclude Powers (D) from any use of the Daily Planet.

ISSUE:

(1) Where each of two users of a mark, to which neither user holds a registration, seeks exclusive use of the mark under § 43(a) of the Lanham Act, must the prevailing party show an association of such duration and association with its use of the mark sufficient to establish a common-law trademark therein?

(2) May a holder of a common-law trademark obtain the same relief under § 43(a) of the Lanham Act as a holder of a registered trademark by showing that an alleged infringer's use of the mark is likely to either confuse or deceive purchasers as to the source of items bearing the mark?

HOLDING AND DECISION: (Duffy, J.)

(1) Yes. Where each of two users of a mark, to which neither user holds a registration, seeks exclusive use of the mark under § 43(a) of the Lanham Act, the prevailing party must show an association of such duration and association with its use of the mark sufficient to establish a common-law trademark therein. Each party claims that as a result of prior appropriation and use of the name Daily Planet, it possesses exclusive rights to its use. Because neither presently holds a registered trademark in that name, any rights to the exclusive use thereof are to be determined solely under the common law of trademarks. Based on the evidence presented, only DC Comics (P) has demonstrated an association of such duration and consistency with the Daily Planet sufficient to establish a common-law trademark therein, as the Daily Planet has become

Continued on next page.

inextricably woven into the fabric of the Superman story over the years. Powers (D), to the contrary, abandoned the mark and began publishing a paper with a different name.

(2) Yes. A holder of a common-law trademark may obtain the same relief under § 43(a) of the Lanham Act as a holder of a registered trademark by showing that an alleged infringer's use of the mark is likely to either confuse or deceive purchasers as to the source of items bearing the mark. It is not a prerequisite for remedial relief that the mark in issue be registered; a plaintiff who holds a common-law trademark is entitled to relief if the alleged infringer has affixed the plaintiff's mark to his goods in a manner that misrepresents to the public the source of the goods. Thus, here, DC Comics (P) must prove that Powers's (D) use of the Daily Planet is likely to either confuse or deceive purchasers as to the source of items bearing the mark, and liability will attach even if the two parties are not in direct competition. Here, the evidence demonstrates that Powers's (D) use of the Daily Planet name was merely an attempt to cash in on the Superman story, as indicated by the numerous references to the Superman character and Superman story in the paper. Thus, in adopting the Daily Planet as the paper's title, it is clear that Powers (D) intended to at least confuse, if not to deceive the public as to the publication's origin. Even though DC Comics (P) was less than diligent in policing its mark, given the local and limited distribution of Powers's (D) paper, such lack of diligence was not so great as to warrant a loss of its trademark. Because Powers's (D) continued use of the Daily Planet is likely to cause irreparable harm to DC Comics' (P) reputation, goodwill, and trademark, Powers's (D) requested injunction is denied and DC Comics' (P) motion for a preliminary injunction is granted.

▶ ANALYSIS

A common-law trademark, paralleling its statutory counterpart, includes any word, name or symbol adopted and used by a manufacturer or merchant to identify his goods and to distinguish them from those manufactured or sold by others. To claim ownership of a common-law mark, a party must demonstrate that his use of the mark has been of such a quality and for such a duration that it has come to identify goods bearing it as originating from that party. That is, the mark must have developed a secondary meaning. Thus, by determining here that DC Comics' (P) use of the Daily Planet was of great duration and consistency, the court essentially determines that DC Comics' (P) use had obtained secondary meaning sufficient to establish a trademark.

Quicknotes

INJUNCTIVE RELIEF A court order issued as a remedy, requiring a person to do, or prohibiting that person from doing, a specific act.

TRADEMARK DILUTION The diminishment of the capability of a trademark to identify and distinguish the particular good or service with which it is associated.

■■■■

Two Pesos, Inc. v. Taco Cabana, Inc.

Restaurant (D) v. Restaurant chain (P)

505 US. 763 (1992).

NATURE OF CASE: Appeal from award of damages in trade dress infringement case.

FACT SUMMARY: Taco Cabana, Inc. (P) had a chain of Mexican restaurants in Texas in a "day-glo" colorful style that it claimed was copied by Two Pesos, Inc. (D).

🏛 RULE OF LAW
If the trade dress of a restaurant can be shown to be inherently distinctive, no proof of secondary meaning is required for protection under § 43(a) of the Lanham Act.

FACTS: In 1978, Taco Cabana, Inc. (P) began its Mexican restaurant empire in San Antonio, adopting as its motif an atmosphere of gaudy interior and exterior seating with colorful murals and ersatz artifacts. In 1985, a Two Pesos (D) restaurant in Houston put forth an appearance that was suspiciously similar. In 1986, Taco Cabana (P) made a push into the Houston market, saw Two Pesos' (D) setup, and sued Two Pesos (D) for trade dress infringement under § 43(a) of the Lanham Act and theft of trade secrets under Texas common law. Responding to five questions from the judge, a jury concluded that Taco Cabana (P) had a trade dress that was nonfunctional and inherently distinctive, that the trade dress had not acquired secondary meaning in Texas, and that the alleged infringement created a likelihood of confusion in the public as to the source or association of the two restaurant chains. The Fifth Circuit affirmed, holding the evidence was sufficient for the jury's findings and rejecting Two Pesos' (D) contention that secondary meaning must be shown to protect unregistered trade dress. Their position was supported by the rulings of the Second Circuit (alone). The United States Supreme Court granted certiorari to resolve the split among the circuits.

ISSUE: If the trade dress of a restaurant can be shown to be inherently distinctive, is proof of secondary meaning required for protection under § 43(a) of the Lanham Act?

HOLDING AND DECISION: (White, J.) No. If the trade dress of a restaurant can be shown to be inherently distinctive, no proof of secondary meaning is required for protection under § 43(a) of the Lanham Act. Section 43(a) of the Lanham Act protects qualifying unregistered trademarks, and the general principles of § 2 qualification determine if an unregistered mark is protectable under § 43(a). Although the decision here is limited to trade dress, there is no distinction from trademark. Basic to trademark protection is that demonstration of secondary meaning is required only when the claimed trademark is not sufficiently inherently distinctive to identify the producer. Distinctiveness can be acquired either way and entitles the mark to protection. In addition, the mark must be, as always, nonfunctional. The Court does not address these contentions here, despite Two Pesos' (D) briefing on the subject. Our decision, deals only with the requirement of secondary meaning before protection attaches under § 43(a). The Second Circuit held that unregistered marks do not have the presumptive source association enjoyed by registered marks and thus, even if distinctive and thus ordinarily entitled to registration and protection, were not protectable under § 43(a). Their decision fails to recognize the potential for fraud on new businesses that are unregistered and have yet to acquire secondary meaning—competitors are free to pirate any aspect of distinctive design with impunity. Since § 2 requires secondary meaning only with descriptive marks, this gap dividing registered protected distinctive marks and unregistered unprotected distinctive marks is unacceptable and nonsensical. The deception and unfair competition that trademark law is designed to circumvent would go unchecked here. Even if unregistered, a distinctive mark is able to distinguish the users of the mark, and the copier of the mark can still falsely designate its origins injuriously. There are no differences between § 2 and § 43(a) that justify the Second Circuit's interpretation. Affirmed.

CONCURRENCE: (Stevens, J.) Section 43(a) has evolved in the circuit courts from a narrow prohibition of false advertising and common-law "passing off" to the congressionally approved federal infringement action protecting unregistered marks to the same degree as registered ones. Originally intended to reach false designations of origin and false representations, the terms "origin" and "representation" have expanded to a point where § 43(a) is a vigorous national unfair competition statute. State law protections have varied, and the need for a uniform statute has been filled by § 43(a).

▶ ANALYSIS

The Second Circuit's insistence on treating unregistered marks as second-class citizens is unsurprising; it seems natural that if someone wants the protection, he or she should register the mark. But trademark is not designed as

Continued on next page.

a merit system; it is meant to protect businesses from unfair competition and the public from confusion.

■━■

Quicknotes

SECONDARY MEANING A word or mark that becomes associated with a particular merchant or product as its source of origin.

TRADE DRESS The overall image of, or impression created by, a product that a court may enforce as a trademark if it determines that such image has acquired secondary meaning and that the public recognizes it as an indication of source.

■━■

Louis Vuitton Malletier v. Dooney & Bourke, Inc.

Luxury handbags manufacturer (P) v. Luxury handbags manufacturer (D)

454 F.3d 108 (2d Cir. 2006).

NATURE OF CASE: Appeal from denial of preliminary injunction in trademark infringement action.

FACT SUMMARY: Louis Vuitton Malletier (Vuitton) (P), a designer and manufacturer of, inter alia, luxury handbags, contended that Dooney & Bourke, Inc. (D), also a designer and manufacturer of luxury handbags, had infringed Vuitton's (P) Multicolore mark, consisting of one of its monograms, featuring entwined "LV" initials, printed in 33 bright colors on a white or black background, by selling handbags that featured the Dooney & Bourke (D) "DB" monogram in an array of bright colors set against white and black backgrounds. Vuitton (P) also contended that the district court erred in denying it a preliminary injunction against Dooney & Bourke (D) based primarily on a side-by-side comparison instead of viewing the parties' marks sequentially in the context of the marketplace.

🏛 RULE OF LAW
For purposes of determining whether trademark infringement has occurred, in assessing the similarity of marks, the mark's overall impression on a consumer must be assessed, considering the context in which the marks are displayed and the totality of factors that could cause confusion among prospective purchasers, instead of relying overwhelmingly on just a side-by-side comparison of the marks.

FACTS: For over a century, Louis Vuitton Malletier (Vuitton) (P), a designer and manufacturer of, inter alia, luxury handbags, has used as registered trademark the Toile Monogram, featuring entwined "LV" initials with three motifs: a curved diamond with a four-point star inset, its negative, and a circle with a four-leafed flower inset. In late 2002, Vuitton (P) introduced a new line of handbags (Murakami handbags) featuring an update on the Toile marks, which it called the Louis Vuitton Monogram Multicolore pattern (Multicolore mark). The design included a modified version of the Toile marks, printed in 33 bright colors on a white or black background. The mark was unregistered. Vuitton (P) spent over $4 million in 2003–2004 advertising and promoting the Multicolore mark and associated handbags, which garnered significant media and celebrity attention. In 2003, Dooney & Bourke, Inc. (D), also a designer and manufacturer of luxury handbags, introduced its "It-Bag" collection, which featured the Dooney & Bourke (D) "DB" monogram in an array of bright colors set against white and black backgrounds. The intertwined initials, with the "D" and the "B" displayed in contrasting colors, were printed forward and backward in

repeating diagonal rows. There were no geometric shapes, unlike the Toile design. The handbags also sported a multicolor zipper, with fabric similar to that used by Vuitton (P), and a small pink enamel heart bearing the legend "Dooney & Bourke" on a tag hanging from the handle. Eventually, additional background colors were added to the It-Bag collection. Vuitton (P) brought a trademark action against Dooney & Bourke (D), claiming trademark infringement under §§ 32 and 43(a) of the Lanham Act, and sought a preliminary injunction to enjoin Dooney & Bourke (D) from using the It-Bag design. The district court denied the injunction. Although the district court concluded that Vuitton's (P) Multicolore mark was protectable both because it was inherently distinctive and because it had acquired secondary meaning, and although it found that the It-Bag design was similar to the Multicolore mark, the district court nevertheless concluded—primarily on the basis of a side-by-side comparison—that there was no likelihood of confusion. The court of appeals granted review.

ISSUE: For purposes of determining whether trademark infringement has occurred, in assessing the similarity of marks, must the mark's overall impression on a consumer be assessed, considering the context in which the marks are displayed and the totality of factors that could cause confusion among prospective purchasers, instead of relying overwhelmingly on just a side-by-side comparison of the marks?

HOLDING AND DECISION: (Cardamone, J.) Yes. For purposes of determining whether trademark infringement has occurred, in assessing the similarity of marks, the mark's overall impression on a consumer must be assessed, considering the context in which the marks are displayed and the totality of factors that could cause confusion among prospective purchasers, instead of relying overwhelmingly on just a side-by-side comparison of the marks. The analysis is the same under both §§ 32 and 43(a) of the Lanham Act. Here, the district court erred in focusing on the similarity of the marks in a side-by-side comparison instead of viewing them sequentially in the context of the marketplace. The district court emphasized that a consumer seeing the respective parties' trademarks printed on their bags, either up close or at a distance, was not likely to be confused, since the Vuitton (P) bags have the initials "LV" and the Dooney & Bourke (D) bags use

Continued on next page.

the initials "D" and "B," and since Vuitton (P) incorporates geometric shapes into its mark whereas Dooney & Bourke (D) does not. The district court also found that the colors used by Dooney & Bourke (D) were toned down as compared to the Multicolore colors. While such a side-by-side comparison can be helpful in investigating similarities and differences in respective designs, the focus must be on the ultimate issue of the likelihood of consumer confusion, since the law requires only confusing similarity, not identity. Further, where, as here, the plaintiff claims initial-interest and post-sale confusion, market conditions must be examined closely to see whether the differences between the marks are likely to be memorable enough to dispel confusion on serial viewing. Therefore, the case must be remanded for review in accordance with these principles so the district court can assess whether, under market conditions and when viewed sequentially, Vuitton (P) can prove likelihood of confusion between its Multicolore mark and the pattern of Dooney & Bourke's (D) It-Bag. [Affirmed in part, vacated, and remanded.]

▶ ANALYSIS

It should be noted that Vuitton (P) was not seeking to protect the overall look of its handbags, that is, its trade dress, but rather the narrower trademark it had established in its colored pattern. It did not claim a separate trademark in the colors alone. If it had claimed such a trademark, it would have been required to show that the multicolors, set on a white or black background, created a separate and distinct commercial impression, apart from the monogram motif design, and that the colors alone served to indicate Vuitton (P) as the source. Instead, Vuitton (P) maintained that the polychromatic display was an essential part of its trademarked design, and that other handbag manufacturers were free to create their own brightly colored handbags so long as they did not do so in a manner confusingly similar to the Vuitton (P) combination of color and defined design. It was this trademark plus color scheme that the court here indicated required more than a side-by-side comparison to determine confusing similarity.

Quicknotes

DISTINCTIVENESS A standard for trademark protection, whereby the more distinctive a mark is, the greater its eligibility for protection. Distinctive marks typically consist of terms that are fanciful or coined, arbitrary, or suggestive. If a mark is descriptive, it is not entitled to trademark protection unless it has acquired distinctiveness through consumer association of goods or services with the mark (such acquired distinctiveness is also known as secondary meaning).

INTER ALIA Among other things.

SECONDARY MEANING A word or mark that becomes associated with a particular merchant or product as its source of origin.

Conopco, Inc. v. May Dept. Stores, Co.

National-brand manufacturer (P) v. Retailer (D)

46 F.3d 1556 (Fed. Cir. 1994).

NATURE OF CASE: Appeal from judgment of infringement, treble damages, attorneys' fees and costs, prejudgment interest, a recall order and an injunction in action for trademark and trade dress infringement.

FACT SUMMARY: Some retailers and makers of private-label hand lotions and containers (collectively, "Venture") (D) contended that they did not infringe trademarks and trade dress held by Conopco, Inc. (P) in the relaunched version of its national brand Vaseline Intensive Care Lotion (VICL) product.

🏛 RULE OF LAW
(1) A showing of actual consumer confusion, which is necessary to support a trade dress infringement action that seeks monetary damages, is not made on the basis of isolated instances of actual confusion and a presumption of actual confusion based on an intent to deceive.
(2) Where competing products are clearly labeled and differentiated, a showing of a likelihood of consumer confusion is not made where no proof is presented that real consumers have real confusion or likelihood of it as to the origin of the products involved.

FACTS: Conopco, Inc. (P) relaunched its Vaseline Intensive Care Lotion (VICL), a national-brand hand lotion product, with a new, less greasy, lotion formula and revised bottle shape and label. Conopco (P) aggressively marketed the new VICL. When a private label hand lotion manufacturer became aware of Conopco's (P) relaunch plans, it developed a private label product to compete with VICL. Together with a container company, it developed a container for the product, and together with a retailer, it developed the labeling for the container. (These companies, collectively, will be referred to as "Venture" (D).) The product was then marketed through several retailers soon after VICL was relaunched. The private-label product and VICL were sold side-by-side and in direct competition by the retailers for over 10 years (in both prior incarnations and as relaunched). Conopco (P) informed Venture (D) it believed Venture (D) was infringing various propriety rights held by Conopco (P) in VICL. Venture (D) denied those claims, and Conopco (P) sued for trademark and trade dress infringement. The district court, finding the case was exceptional, ruled that Venture (D) had willfully infringed Conopco's (P) proprietary rights and that enhanced damages were warranted. The court awarded Conopco (P) treble damages, attorneys' fees and costs,

prejudgment interest, a recall order and an injunction, as well as imposing joint and several liability on all defendants. The court of appeals granted review.

ISSUE:
(1) Is a showing of actual consumer confusion, which is necessary to support a trade dress infringement action that seeks monetary damages, made on the basis of isolated instances of actual confusion and a presumption of actual confusion based on intent to deceive?
(2) Where competing products are clearly labeled and differentiated, is a showing of a likelihood of consumer confusion made where no proof is presented that real consumers have real confusion or likelihood of it as to the origin of the products involved?

HOLDING AND DECISION: (Plager, J.)
(1) No. A showing of actual consumer confusion, which is necessary to support a trade dress infringement action that seeks monetary damages, is not made on the basis of isolated instances of actual confusion and a presumption of actual confusion based on an intent to deceive. To establish entitlement to monetary relief, a plaintiff must show actual confusion. Here, Conopco (P) failed to make such a showing. The district court based its finding of actual confusion on the testimony of a consumer, Sickles, and on a presumption of actual confusion arising from the court's determination that Venture (D) intended to deceive and confuse the public. Sickles stated that she purchased a private label brand of VICL thinking it to have originated from Conopco (P). The problem with the testimony is that Sickles's confusion arose at least in part from her assumption, erroneous as applied to this case, that national brand manufacturers secretly market private label brands. First, there is no evidence that this assumption is widely held by the relevant consumers. Second, where, as here, the national brand is being sold side-by-side with the private label brand, the assumption is at best counter-intuitive because it assumes that a national brand manufacturer would embark on a scheme to deliberately erode its sales of the national brand. Sickles's experience was atypical and an isolated incident. Such isolated incidents of actual confusion do not support an award of monetary relief. Therefore, Sickles's testimony was legally insufficient to sustain such an award. Actual confusion should be proven through testimony of the buying public and consumer surveys, not based on a presumption of actual confusion arising from intent to deceive. Here, the retailer's

Continued on next page.

product was packaged in a way to indicate it was similar to the national brand and intended for the same purpose, but was also clearly marked with its private logo. The retailer also invited the consumer to compare the private-label product with the named national product. This form of competition has become commonplace and well-known in the marketplace. Therefore, where, as here, the private-label product is clearly labeled and differentiated, a rule that would make such competition presumptively unlawful is rejected. Accordingly, the district court erred in presuming actual confusion from Venture's (D) intent to copy the overall package design. Consequently, there is a complete absence of proof of actual confusion. The district court's award of monetary relief is thus not sustainable. Reversed as to this issue.

(2) No. Where competing products are clearly labeled and differentiated, a showing of a likelihood of consumer confusion is not made where no proof is presented that real consumers have real confusion or likelihood of it as to the origin of the products involved. A showing of likelihood of confusion is necessary for injunctive relief. The district court concluded that such a likelihood of confusion was established on the basis of various factors, including that Conopco's (P) marks are strong; the trade dress of the two products is "extremely similar;" the two products are "directly competitive;" Venture (D) "acted with deliberate intent to imitate and infringe the revised VICL trade dress;" a presumption of likelihood of confusion arising from Venture's (D) intent to deceive and copy; and the presence of actual confusion. As previously held, the district court erred as to actual confusion. Even if the district court's finding on the other factors were not erroneous, they are nonetheless merely inferentially or presumptively relevant as to whether there was a likelihood of confusion, since a more probative factor, which the district court failed to address, was the significance of Venture's (D) logo that was prominently displayed on its private-label product. Based on Venture's (D) annual sales (around $1.3 billion) and the fact that its logo was on everything associated with its stores and its advertising, it is reasonable to expect that consumers identify the logo with Venture (D) rather than Conopco (P), and that the use of that logo succeeds in distinguishing between the two brands. That Venture (D) and other retailers compete in this manner is all that the evidence establishes, and this evidence is therefore insufficient to amount to proof that real consumers have real confusion or likelihood of it regarding the origin of the product involved. No such evidence was presented. Therefore, the district court erred in concluding that a likelihood of confusion had been established. For these reasons, the judgment of trade dress infringement, injunctive relief, attorneys' fees and costs, and prejudgment interest are reversed, as is the district court's finding of willfulness, the determination that the case is exceptional, and the determi-

nation that enhanced damages are warranted. Reversed as to this issue. Injunction and recall order are vacated.

▶ ANALYSIS

Judge Mayer, concurring in part and dissenting in part, faulted the majority for reaching its conclusion on likelihood of confusion by impermissibly reweighing the evidence that was before the district court. Judge Mayer indicated that this is not only beyond the appellate court's competence but intrudes on the fact finding role of the district court and encourages litigants to ignore the outcome of the trial and retry the case on appeal. Sometimes, like here, such a strategy works. Noting that a district court's findings are entitled to considerable deference and cannot be reversed unless clearly erroneous, Judge Mayer concluded that the district court's findings were comprehensive, amply supported by the evidence in the record, not clearly erroneous, and provided a sufficient basis for the determination that a likelihood of confusion existed. Other courts, faced with similar look-alike private-label cases have also declined—as Judge Mayer would— to find dispositive the fact that the private-label product carries the private-label logo on it and invites consumers to compare the products. These courts have found that if the private-label company truly wanted to distinguish its product from the national brand, it would have made its packages as distinct as possible from that of the national brand, and that by copying the national brand's dress, it was deliberately attempting to confuse consumers. See, e.g., *McNeil-PPC, Inc. v. Guardian Drug Co.*, 984 F. Supp. 1066 (E.D. Mich. 1997).

■=■

Quicknotes

JOINT AND SEVERAL LIABILITY Liability amongst tortfeasors allowing the injured party to bring suit against any of the defendants, individually or collectively, and to recover from each up to the total amount of damages awarded.

TRADE DRESS The overall image of, or impression created by, a product that a court may enforce as a trademark if it determines that such image has acquired secondary meaning and that the public recognizes it as an indication of source.

TRADEMARK Any word, name, symbol, device or combination thereof that is either currently utilized, or which a person has a bona fide intent to utilize, in commerce in order to distinguish his goods from those of another.

■=■

Jeffrey Milstein, Inc. v. Greger, Lawlor, Roth, Inc.

Greeting card manufacturer (P) v. Greeting card manufacturer (D)

58 F.3d 27 (2d Cir. 1995).

NATURE OF CASE: Appeal from denial of preliminary injunction in trade dress infringement action under § 43(a) of the Lanham Act.

FACT SUMMARY: Jeffrey Milstein, Inc., d/b/a Paper House Productions (Paper House) (P), a greeting cards company, contended that its competitor, Greger, Lawlor, Roth, Inc., d/b/a/ Triangle Enterprises (Triangle) (D), infringed its unregistered trade dress, which comprised photographs die cut to the shapes of the objects depicted on the cards.

🏛 RULE OF LAW
Trade dress protection is unavailable to protect a generalized idea or concept, which renders the trade dress features generic, and, thus inherently nondistinctive.

FACTS: Jeffrey Milstein, Inc., d/b/a Paper House Productions (Paper House) (P), a greeting cards company, used as unregistered trade dress for its cards photographs die cut to the shapes of the objects depicted on the cards. With this die-cutting technique, the photograph completely filled the front panel of the card; the inside panels and the back panel of the card were usually blank. Paper House (P) packaged the cards in clear cellophane bags. Greger, Lawlor, Roth, Inc., d/b/a/ Triangle Enterprises (Triangle) (D), which used this die-cutting technique on other types of products, started to use this technique on greeting cards. However, unlike Paper House's (P) greeting cards, which depicted the photographic image only on the front face, Triangle's (D) cards depicted the die-cut image on the front of all three panels of each card. Like Paper House's (P) cards, Triangle's (D) cards had blank interiors and were packaged in clear cellophane wrapping. Paper House (P) brought suit against Triangle (D) asserting infringement of its die-cut trade dress under § 43(a) of the Lanham Act, asserting that it was the first company to produce a line of greeting cards that applied the die-cutting process to photographs, and seeking to enjoin Triangle (D) from using the die-cutting technique on Triangle's (D) cards. The district court concluded that Paper House's (P) trade dress was "generic," consisting solely of common and functional elements such as die-cutting, photographs, and blank white interiors. The district court also determined that the trade dress had not obtained secondary meaning, and that Paper House (P) had shown neither distinctiveness of its trade dress nor likelihood of consumer confusion. Accordingly, the district court denied the injunction requested by Paper House (P). The court of appeals granted review.

ISSUE: Is trade dress protection unavailable to protect a generalized idea or concept, which renders the trade dress features generic, and, thus inherently nondistinctive?

HOLDING AND DECISION: (Newman, C.J.) No. Trade dress protection is unavailable to protect a generalized idea or concept, which renders the trade dress features generic, and, thus inherently nondistinctive. To prevail in an action for trade dress infringement under § 43(a) of the Lanham Act, a plaintiff must prove (1) that its dress is distinctive and (2) that a likelihood of confusion exists between its product and the defendant's product. To determine whether a trade dress is distinctive, the combination of its elements is assessed, not each element separately. However, where a trade dress is composed exclusively of commonly used or functional elements the dress should be regarded as unprotectable or "generic." Additionally, in evaluating claims to distinctive trade dresses, it must be kept in mind that trade dress protection should not be overextended to the point where such protection undermines the restrictions of copyright and patent law designed to prevent the monopolization of products and ideas. Thus, trade dress law does not protect an idea, a concept, or a generalized type of appearance. In drawing the line between an idea (nonprotectable) and its concrete expression (protectable), the level of generality at which a trade dress is described, as well as the fact that a similar trade dress is already being used by manufacturers of other kinds of products, may indicate that that dress is no more than a concept or idea to be applied to particular products. Here, Paper House's (P) trade dress cannot qualify for trade dress protection because Paper House (P) is effectively seeking protection for an idea or concept—die-cut photographic greeting cards. Moreover, since the features of Paper House's (P) trade are generic, even a showing of secondary meaning could not make that dress distinctive. Therefore, the district court did not err in concluding that Paper House's (P) trade dress failed the distinctiveness test for trade dress protection. Having correctly reached this conclusion, the district court did not have to consider whether Paper House (P) had demonstrated a likelihood of confusion, but the court nevertheless considered this part of the trade dress protection test. In doing so, the district court correctly determined that, here, there was no likelihood of confusion. In weighing the weakness of Paper House's (P) dress, the similarity of Paper House's (P) and Triangle's (D) greeting card designs, the competi-

Continued on next page.

tive proximity of the two brands of greeting cards, the issue of bridging the gap (which adds no weight here, since Paper House (P) and Triangle (D) are selling similar products in the same market, and there is no gap to bridge), the lack of evidence of actual confusion or bad faith copying on Triangle's (D) part, the comparable quality of Paper House's (P) and Triangle's (D) cards, and the relative lack of sophistication of consumers, the balance favors Triangle (D). Affirmed.

▶ *ANALYSIS*

At one time, trade dress referred only to the manner in which a product was "dressed up" to go to market with a label, package, display card, and similar packaging elements. However, trade dress has taken on a more expansive meaning and includes the design and appearance of the product as well as that of the container and all elements making up the total visual image by which the product is presented to customers. Thus, trade dress is essentially a product's total image and overall appearance, as defined by its overall composition and design, including size, shape, color, texture, and graphics. As this decision demonstrates, generic dresses—those that refer to the genus of which the particular product is a species—are never protectable, whereas suggestive and arbitrary or fanciful trade dresses are considered to be inherently distinctive. If a dress is descriptive, however, the plaintiff must establish that it has acquired secondary meaning in order to become distinctive.

■▬■

Quicknotes

DISTINCTIVENESS A standard for trademark protection, whereby the more distinctive a mark is, the greater its eligibility for protection. Distinctive marks typically consist of terms that are fanciful or coined, arbitrary, or suggestive. If a mark is descriptive, it is not entitled to trademark protection unless it has acquired distinctiveness through consumer association of goods or services with the mark (such acquired distinctiveness is also known as secondary meaning).

SECONDARY MEANING A word or mark that becomes associated with a particular merchant or product as its source of origin.

TRADE DRESS The overall image of, or impression created by, a product that a court may enforce as a trademark if it determines that such image has acquired secondary meaning and that the public recognizes it as an indication of source.

■▬■

Best Cellars Inc. v. Grape Finds at Dupont, Inc.

Wine store operator (P) v. Wine store operator (D)

90 F. Supp. 2d 431 (S.D.N.Y. 2000).

NATURE OF CASE: Trade dress infringement action.

FACT SUMMARY: Best Cellars Inc. (P), which operated retail wine stores that had a novel and unique design, contended that Grape Finds at Dupont, Inc. (D) infringed its trade dress in the design and elements of its stores.

🏛 RULE OF LAW

Trade dress is infringed where the dress is arbitrary and, therefore, inherently distinctive, and where there is a substantial likelihood of confusion between the dress and allegedly infringing dress.

FACTS: Best Cellars Inc. (P) owned and operated four wine stores, including its flagship store on the Upper East Side of Manhattan, which pursued the novel marketing strategy of organizing wines by taste category rather than by grape type or country of origin. The flagship store had a clean, crisp, modern decor that demonstrated that the owners invested energy and capital in the design of the store as well as in the development of the marketing theme. Best Cellars (P) opened its flagship store in 1996. The store's genesis dated from some time earlier when Wesson, a wine expert and author, began developing the idea of a totally new kind of retail store for wine intended to simplify the wine shopping experience for the novice wine consumer. In 1995, Wesson joined forces with other industry professionals, including Green, the managing director of a New York wine store, and Marmet, a corporate lawyer affiliated with "Food and Wine" magazine. After developing the concept of a store that retails wine by eight primary taste categories (such as light, medium or heavy-bodied white or red wines, sparkling and dessert wines), the three men selected an architectural firm and graphic design firm to create the interior decor for the store. The interior design included wine racks built into a wall, which consisted of translucent Plexiglas tubes to hold bottles of wine horizontally, creating the appearance of a grid of steel rimmed holes in a light wood-paneled wall. The bottles were backlit and looked like they were glowing. Below each display bottle and its shelf-talker, nine additional bottles of the same wine were stored in a vertically arrayed racking system. The entire racking system was patented. The graphic design elements included computer-generated icons and brightly colored signs associated with each taste category. The combination of the visual elements—color-coded, iconographic wall signs identifying taste categories, single display bottles on stainless-steel wire pedestals along the store perimeter, identical color-coded textually formatted square shelf talkers below the display bottles, vertical arrays of nine glowing bottles stacked horizontally, and a strip of cabinets or drawers between the wine racks and the floor—dominated the overall look of the Best Cellars (P) stores. Many of these design elements were not found in any other retail wine store. As a result of the unique marketing concept and design, Best Cellars (P) stores received extensive press coverage locally, nationally, and internationally and were highlighted on local and national television programs. Mazur (D), who had visited the Best Cellars (P) New York store on many occasions, sought to capitalize on Best Cellars (P) innovations. In 1999, he opened a store in Washington, DC, owned by Grape Finds at Dupont, Inc. (Grape Finds) (D), which had many of the design elements found in the Best Cellars (P) stores. Similarly, displays were organized according to eight taste categories; each taste category was identified with a corresponding color and icon-identifier; each display wine was placed in a racking system almost identical to the Best Cellar's (P) racking system, with backlit, glowing bottles; etc. In sum, most of the visual elements unique to the Best Cellars (P) stores were also found in the Grape Finds (D) store. There were also some differences. Grape Finds (D) had a vaulted ceiling, a cork floor, and mobile boxes that could be used for seating or display. Stainless steel was more prominent in the Grape Finds (D) design. Best Cellars (P) sued Grape Finds (D) for trade dress infringement. The court found that although Mazur (D) testified that he had not intended to copy the Best Cellars (P) trade dress, he was not a credible witness.

ISSUE: Is trade dress infringed where the dress is arbitrary and, therefore, inherently distinctive, and where there is a substantial likelihood of confusion between the dress and allegedly infringing dress?

HOLDING AND DECISION: (Sweet, J.) Yes. Trade dress is infringed where the dress is arbitrary and, therefore, inherently distinctive, and where there is a substantial likelihood of confusion between the dress and allegedly infringing dress. To establish a claim of trade dress infringement under § 43(a) of the Lanham Act, a plaintiff must demonstrate (1) "that its trade dress is either inherently distinctive or that it has acquired distinctiveness through a secondary meaning," (2) "that there is a likelihood of confusion between defendant's trade dress and plaintiff's," and (3) where, as here, the dress has not been registered, that the design is nonfunctional. The inherent distinctiveness of trade dress is evaluated against a spec-

Continued on next page.

trum of increasing distinctiveness, from generic, to descriptive, to suggestive, to arbitrary/fanciful. The combination of elements is the focus of the evaluation, not each individual element. By contrast, "an idea, a concept, or a generalized type of appearance" cannot be protected under trade dress law, but the concrete expression of an idea in a trade dress can. When deciding if what is sought to be protected is merely an idea or protectable trade dress, the purpose of trade dress law must be kept in mind: to protect an owner of a dress in informing the public of the source of its products, without permitting the owner to exclude competition from functionally similar products. Here, Best Cellars (P) has met its burden of showing its trade dress is inherently distinctive because it has demonstrated that its trade dress—the total visual image that a customer encounters—is arbitrary. This conclusion is supported by numerous articles that have concluded that the look of the Best Cellars (P) stores is distinctive and not like that of any other wine store. As such, the trade dress is not suggestive of wine, let alone descriptive or generic. Best Cellars (P) listed fourteen specific elements that it believed constituted the uniqueness of its trade dress. The essence of the look, however, is the "wall of wine," i.e., the color-coded, iconographic wall signs identifying eight taste categories above single display bottles on stainless-steel wire pedestals which run along the store perimeter, above identical color-coded textually formatted square shelf-talkers, above vertical arrays of nine glowing bottles stacked horizontally, above a strip of cabinets or drawers which extend to the floor. Moreover, contrary to Grape Finds's (D) argument, Best Cellars' (P) trade dress is not functional—it is not essential to the use or purpose of the article or affect the cost or quality of the article. Also, the exclusive use of the design would not put competitors at a significant nonreputation-related disadvantage. First, there is nothing inherently functional about a vertical array of identical bottles. Also, many of Best Cellars' (P) trade dress, while containing functional components, contain equally non-functional components. All that Best Cellars (P) needs to show is that at least some of the elements are nonfunctional, and it has done that. Because the design is inherently distinctive, Best Cellars (P) does not need to demonstrate that its trade dress has developed secondary meaning. As to whether there is a substantial likelihood of confusion between the trade dresses of Best Cellars (P) and Grape Finds (D), the courts apply an eight-factor test based on the Polaroid factors. *Polaroid Corp. v. Polarad Electronics Corp.*, 287 F.2d 492 (2d Cir. 1961). The first factor is the strength of the trade dress. Arbitrary trade dress is by definition distinctive and strong. Therefore, Best Cellars' (P) trade dress is quite strong. There is also evidence that no similar dress is used in connection with the sale of wine and that the dress has acquired secondary meaning. The dress has received extensive media coverage, and there is evidence that Grape Finds (D) deliberately attempted to copy it. The second factor is similarity between the dresses. No difference in the Grape Finds (D) store significantly

modifies the overall visual effect of the "wall of wine," which is the dominant visual element of the Best Cellars (P) stores. Thus, the evidence demonstrates a significant probability that numerous prudent consumers in the Grape Finds (D) store would be confused as to whether they were, in fact, in a Best Cellars (P) store. The third factor is proximity of the products. Here, the products are very similar, being value-priced bottles of wine aimed at a similar market. There is great proximity between the products. The fourth factor is bridging the gap, but here there is no bridge to gap: both parties sell the same products in the same field. The fifth factor is evidence of actual confusion. Some evidence of such confusion has been presented, but is based on anecdotal accounts. Nonetheless, it is unnecessary to show actual confusion to prevail under the Lanham Act. This factor weights slightly in favor of Best Cellars (P). The sixth factor is bad faith. Here, there was "overwhelming" evidence of intentional copying of a great many aspects of Best Cellars' (P) business. Thus, it strains credulity to think that the reproduction of the trade dress was not meant to capitalize on the reputation, goodwill, and any confusion between Grape Finds (D) and Best Cellars (P). The seventh factor is the quality of the products. Here, the quality is comparable, so this factor weighs in favor of Grape Finds (D). The eighth and final confusion factor is the sophistication of purchasers. Here, both businesses target unsophisticated consumers. Therefore, this factor favors Best Cellars (P). Because Best Cellars (P) has demonstrated a substantial likelihood that its trade dress is distinctive, and that there is a likelihood of confusion between its trade dress and the trade dress of Grape Finds (D), it has demonstrated that it is likely to prevail on the merits of its trade dress claim. Therefore, irreparable harm is assumed, and Best Cellars (P) has met the requirements for a preliminary injunction. This injunction will enjoin Grape Finds (D) from continuing to display its wine using a "wall of wine" that is similar to that of Best Cellars (P). By finding a different way to display its wines, Grape Finds (D) will eliminate confusion between the two stores. The other elements claimed by Best Cellars (P) as protectable trade dress do not need to be changed, i.e., the use of eight words, colors, and images to describe eight categories of wine, of light wood and stainless steel, of open flooring, of wall signs above the display bottles and wine racks, and of a limited selection of value-priced wines.

▶ ANALYSIS

As this case demonstrates, it is well settled that an idea, concept, or generalized type of appearance will not be protected by trade dress law. Here the court's decision supports this standard by essentially finding that the idea of marketing wine by taste, however innovative it may be, is not protected by trade dress law, and that Best Cellars

Continued on next page.

(P) cannot invoke the Lanham Act to preserve a monopoly on operating retail stores that categorize wines by taste. That is why the court only enjoins Grape Finds (D) from continuing to use the wall of wine—which the court has determined is the essential visual element of Best Cellars' (P) trade dress—but does not enjoin the other elements of the store design. "Uniqueness of an idea and not the trade dress itself is not a proper basis upon which a court can base a finding that a trade dress is capable of being a source identifier. The connection must be between the trade dress and the product, not the idea and the product."

■══■

Quicknotes

DISTINCTIVENESS A standard for trademark protection, whereby the more distinctive a mark is, the greater its eligibility for protection. Distinctive marks typically consist of terms that are fanciful or coined, arbitrary, or suggestive. If a mark is descriptive, it is not entitled to trademark protection unless it has acquired distinctiveness through consumer association of goods or services with the mark (such acquired distinctiveness is also known as secondary meaning).

SECONDARY MEANING A word or mark that becomes associated with a particular merchant or product as its source of origin.

TRADE DRESS The overall image of, or impression created by, a product that a court may enforce as a trademark if it determines that such image has acquired secondary meaning and that the public recognizes it as an indication of source.

■══■

Allen v. National Video, Inc.

Celebrity (P) v. Video rental chain (D)

610 F. Supp. 612 (S.D.N.Y. 1985).

NATURE OF CASE: Motion for summary judgment in action for violations of the right to privacy, the right to publicity, and the Lanham Act's prohibition on misleading advertising.

FACT SUMMARY: Woody Allen (P), the celebrity, claimed that ads by National Video, Inc. (National) (D) that used a photograph of an Allen (P) look-alike, Boroff, to promote National's (D) nationally franchised video rental chain, violated Allen's (P) statutory right to privacy, right to publicity, and constituted misleading advertisement under the Lanham Act § 43(a) because they were likely to result in consumer confusion as to Allen's (P) endorsement of National's (D) services.

RULE OF LAW
The Lanham Act's § 43(a) prohibition on misleading advertising prohibits the use of a celebrity look-alike in an ad where such use is likely to mislead the public as to the celebrity's endorsement of or association with the advertised product or service.

FACTS: Woody Allen (P) is a celebrity film director, writer, actor, and comedian; his name and his face are familiar to millions of people. National Video, Inc. (National) (D) used a photograph of an Allen (P) lookalike, Boroff, to promote National's (D) nationally franchised video rental chain. The photo pictures Boroff in typical Allen (P) dress and pose in a National (D) store, leaning on a counter, and videos of films associated with Allen (P) are also on the counter. Boroff is holding up a National (D) card, which provides the holder favorable terms on movie rentals, and the woman behind the counter is smiling at the customer and appears to be gasping in exaggerated excitement at the presence of a celebrity. The headline on the advertisement reads "Become a V.I.P. at National Video. We'll Make You Feel Like a Star." The copy goes on to explain that holders of the V.I.P. card receive "hassle-free movie renting" and "special savings" and concludes that "you don't need a famous face to be treated to some pretty famous service." Some versions of the ad had a disclaimer about the "celebrity double," whereas others did not. Allen (P) brought suit for state statutory right to publicity and right to privacy violations, and for violation of the Lanham Act's § 43(a) prohibition on misleading advertising. He sought summary judgment on each claim. As to the Lanham Act claim, he asserted that the use of Boroff's picture in the ads was materially misleading and likely to result in consumer confusion as to his endorsement of National's (D) services. National (D) claimed that summary judgment

was inappropriate because the idea of the ads was that even people who are not stars are treated like stars, and that the ads depict an Allen (P) fan, who is so dedicated that he has adopted his idol's appearance and mannerisms, and is able to live out his fantasy by receiving star treatment at National (D). The knowing viewer is supposed to be amused that the counter person actually believes that the customer is Allen (P). Thus, National (D) argued that if Boroff was merely appearing as someone who looks like Allen (P), but not as Allen (P) himself, then Allen's (P) rights were not violated. The district court declined to grant Allen (P) summary judgment on his right to privacy and right to publicity claims because when a look-alike portrays a celebrity, a reasonable trier of fact could conclude that the ad did not display Allen's (P) likeness, but that of Boroff. The district court then addressed Allen's (P) claim under § 43(a).

ISSUE: Does the Lanham Act's § 43(a) prohibition on misleading advertising prohibit the use of a celebrity look-alike in an ad where such use is likely to mislead the public as to the celebrity's endorsement of or association with the advertised product or service?

HOLDING AND DECISION: (Motley, C.J.) Yes. The Lanham Act's § 43(a) prohibition on misleading advertising prohibits the use of a celebrity look-alike in an ad where such use is likely to mislead the public as to the celebrity's endorsement of or association with the advertised product or service. The Act applies to situations that are not trademark infringement per se, but that involve potential deception that threatens economic interests analogous to those protected by trademark law, such as the interest of the public to be free from harmful deception and the "trademark" holder's interest in the value of his distinctive mark. Because a celebrity has a commercial investment in the "drawing power" of his or her name and face in endorsing products and services, which depends on the public's goodwill, the underlying purposes of the Act are implicated in cases of misrepresentation of the endorsement of goods and services. False representations in this regard are actionable whether they are express (literally false) or implied, and the plaintiff is only required to show a likelihood of confusion, rather than actual consumer deception. Additionally, the Act extends to misrepresentations in labeling, and no trademark need be involved. Prior precedent also suggests that the unauthorized use of a person's name or photograph in a manner that creates the false impression that the party has endorsed

Continued on next page.

a product or service in interstate commerce violates the Lanham Act. Even though only a look-alike's photo is involved here, rather than a photo of Allen (P) himself, the Lanham Act nevertheless does not require a finding that Boroff's photo is, as a matter of law, a "portrait or picture" of Allen (P). Instead, the key issue is whether the challenged ad creates the likelihood of consumer confusion over whether Allen (P) endorsed or was otherwise involved with National's (D) goods and services. In this endeavor, traditional trademark analysis, which looks at several factors, is useful. The first factor, the strength of the plaintiff's "mark," weighs in Allen's (P) favor because his "mark," i.e., his unique, positive public image, is a strong one, and his name and likeness are well-known to the public. The second factor, the similarity of the "marks," i.e., Boroff's similarity to Allen (P), is also strong and not disputed. Under the third factor, proximity of the products, while Allen (P) does not own a video rental chain, he is involved in producing and distributing his own movies and he is associated in the public's mind with movies. The market for National's (D) ad was therefore the same as Allen's (P) market—movie watchers. As to the fourth factor, actual confusion, no reliable evidence of actual confusion has been presented. The fifth factor measures the sophistication of the intended market. While the audience for the ad is comparatively sophisticated as to movies, and many among this group might realize that Allen (P) was not actually in the ad, given the close resemblance between Boroff and Allen (P), there is no reason to believe that the audience's relative sophistication eliminates all likelihood of confusion. At a cursory glance, many consumers are likely to be confused. The final factor addresses the defendant's good faith. Although National (D) did not intentionally set out to fool people, it admitted that the ad was designed to make an association with Allen (P). They must therefore at least have been aware of the risk of consumer confusion, which militates against a finding that their motives were completely innocent, as does the lack of a disclaimer on all but one of the uses of the photograph. Taking all the factors together leads to the inescapable conclusion that the ads created a likelihood of confusion over Allen's (P) endorsement of or involvement with National's (D) goods and services. This conclusion also illustrates why Allen's (P) case is more appropriately resolved under the Lanham Act rather than under the statutory privacy provisions. First, the likelihood of confusion standard is broader than the strict "portrait or picture" standard under the statutory privacy provisions. Mere evocation of a person's likeness or persona can be sufficient to create a likelihood of confusion, whereas it is insufficient to make out a privacy rights violation. Similarly, even if the public does not believe that a plaintiff actually appears in a photograph, it nonetheless may be led to believe by the intentional reference to the plaintiff that he or she is somehow involved in or approves of the defendant's products or services. Second, the broader likelihood of confusion standard is easier to satisfy in this case. National's (D) explanation that the picture was of a

fan can defeat a "portrait or picture" requirement, but it cannot defeat a likelihood of confusion requirement. Even the use of a disclaimer that a celebrity double was in the photo by itself would not dispel the likelihood of confusion. To be effective, the disclaimer would have to expressly state that the celebrity does not endorse, and is not involved with, the defendant's products or services. Finally, national injunctive relief is appropriate under the Lanham Act, given Allen's (P) national reputation and National's (D) national presence and scope of advertising. The injunction as to Boroff must prevent him from passing himself off as Allen (P) and from appearing in ads that are likely to confuse the public as to whether he is Allen (P) or that Allen (P) approved of his appearance. To satisfy the injunction, Boroff must either cease to work as an Allen (P) double, or to cease working with advertisers who "recklessly skirt the edges of misrepresentation." He may still work as an Allen (P) look-alike under circumstances where it is made completely clear that he is a look-alike and that Allen (P) has nothing to do with the project. Summary judgment is granted to Allen (P) on his Lanham Act claim.

▶ ANALYSIS

Although the question of identifiability under the state statutory privacy rights provisions is generally one of fact for the jury, the likelihood-of-confusion standard may be applied by the court. While confusing similarity is technically a question of fact, it has sometimes been regarded as "one for the court to decide through its own analysis, comparison, and judgment." That is why the court here was able to render summary judgment on an issue that largely is one of fact. While some cases have emphasized the role of summary judgment in this area only in disposing of meritless cases, the court, at a minimum, arguably has the analogous responsibility to grant summary judgment when no reasonable jury could fail to find a likelihood of confusion.

■■■

Quicknotes

RIGHT OF PUBLICITY The right of a person to control the commercial exploitation of his name or likeness.

SUMMARY JUDGMENT Judgment rendered by a court in response to a motion made by one of the parties, claiming that the lack of a question of material fact in respect to an issue warrants disposition of the issue without consideration by the jury.

■■■

Tom Waits v. Frito-Lay, Inc.

Performer (P) v. Food products company (D)

978 F.2d 1093 (9th Cir. 1992).

NATURE OF CASE: Appeal from jury verdict for plaintiff in action for, inter alia, false endorsement under § 43(a) of the Lanham Act.

FACT SUMMARY: For one of its commercials, Frito-Lay, Inc. (D) imitated a song by, and the voice of, Tom Waits (P), a well-known performer with a distinctive gravelly voice. Frito-Lay (D) contended that false endorsement claims, including those premised on the unauthorized imitation of an entertainer's distinctive voice, are not cognizable under § 43(a) of the Lanham Act, and that even if such claims are cognizable, Waits (P) could not prevail on such a claim because the commercial did not represent that Waits (P) sponsored or endorsed their product.

RULE OF LAW

(1) False endorsement claims, including those premised on the unauthorized imitation of an entertainer's distinctive voice, are cognizable under § 43(a) of the Lanham Act.
(2) A plaintiff can prevail on a false endorsement claim under § 43(a) of the Lanham Act by showing that ordinary consumers would be confused as to whether the plaintiff endorsed or sponsored the defendant's product, notwithstanding that the defendant did not expressly represent that the plaintiff endorsed or sponsored the defendant's product.

FACTS: Frito-Lay, Inc. (D), a food products company, wanted to advertise its new product, SalsaRio Doritos. It looked to its ad agency, Tracy-Locke, Inc. (D), to develop the ad campaign. Tracy-Locke (D) believed a parody of a Tom Waits (P) song, "Step Right Up," would be suitable. Tom Waits (P) is a well-known and well-regarded singer, songwriter, and actor with a distinctive gravelly, raspy voice. One of Waits's (P) longstanding policies was not to do commercials, and he let this policy be known publicly, expressing his philosophy in interviews that musical artists should not do commercials because it detracts from their artistic integrity. Tracy-Locke (D) wanted not only to capture the feel of the Waits (P) song, but also wanted someone who sounded like Waits (P). Tracy-Locke picked a performer who had consciously perfected an imitation of Waits's (P) voice. The ad was broadcast on over 250 radio stations located in 61 markets nationwide. When Waits (P) heard it, he realized that anyone who knew his voice and heard the ad would believe that he had agreed to endorse Frito-Lay's (D) product. He sued Frito-Lay (D) and Tracy-Locke (D), alleging claims for voice misappropriation

under state law and false endorsement under the Lanham Act. A jury, after listening to recordings of Waits (P) singing and to the commercial, found in Waits' (P) favor, awarding him $375,000 compensatory damages and $2 million punitive damages for voice misappropriation, and $100,000 damages for violation of the Lanham Act. The court awarded Waits (P) attorneys' fees under the Lanham Act. Frito-Lay (D) and Tracy-Locke (D) appealed, arguing, inter alia, that false endorsement claims, including those premised on the unauthorized imitation of an entertainer's distinctive voice, are not cognizable under § 43(a) of the Lanham Act, and that even if such claims are cognizable, Waits (P) could not prevail on such a claim because the commercial did not represent that Waits (P) sponsored or endorsed their product. The court of appeals granted review.

ISSUE:

(1) Are false endorsement claims, including those premised on the unauthorized imitation of an entertainer's distinctive voice, cognizable under § 43(a) of the Lanham Act?
(2) Can a plaintiff prevail on a false endorsement claim under § 43(a) of the Lanham Act by showing that ordinary consumers would be confused as to whether the plaintiff endorsed or sponsored the defendant's product, notwithstanding that the defendant did not expressly represent that the plaintiff endorsed or sponsored the defendant's product?

HOLDING AND DECISION: (Boochever, J.)

(1) Yes. False endorsement claims, including those premised on the unauthorized imitation of an entertainer's distinctive voice, are cognizable under § 43(a) of the Lanham Act. Courts have recognized that § 43(a), as written when the Doritos commercial aired, authorizes false endorsement claims brought by plaintiffs, including celebrities, for the unauthorized imitation of their distinctive attributes, where those attributes amount to an unregistered commercial "trademark." This conclusion is supported by the legislative history, which, in the 1988 Lanham Act amendments, intended to codify the case law in this area. Although the 1988 amendments became effective in 1989, about a year after the commercial aired, the amended language codified case law interpreting § 43(a) to encompass false endorsement claims. Section 43(a) now expressly prohibits, inter alia, the use of any "symbol or device" which is likely to deceive consumers as to the association, sponsorship,

Continued on next page.

or approval of goods or services by another person; the amendments approved the broad judicial interpretation of these terms to include distinctive sounds and physical appearance. For these reasons, Waits's (P) claim is cognizable. Affirmed as to this issue.

(2) Yes. A plaintiff can prevail on a false endorsement claim under § 43(a) of the Lanham Act by showing that ordinary consumers would be confused as to whether the plaintiff endorsed or sponsored the defendant's product, notwithstanding that the defendant did not expressly represent that the plaintiff endorsed or sponsored the defendant's product. The district court correctly instructed the jury that in considering Waits's (P) claim, it had to determine whether ordinary consumers would be confused as to whether Waits (P) sang on the commercial and whether he sponsored or endorsed SalsaRio Doritos. The jury was correctly told that in making this determination, it should consider the totality of the evidence, including the distinctiveness of Waits's (P) voice and style, the evidence of actual confusion as to whether Waits (P) actually sang on the commercial, and the defendants' intent to imitate Waits's (P) voice. As there was ample evidence of actual consumer confusion as to whether Waits (P) was singing on the commercial, the evidence was sufficient to support the jury's finding that consumers were likely to be misled by the commercial into believing that Waits (P) endorsed SalsaRio Doritos. Affirmed as to this issue.

ANALYSIS

A false endorsement claim based on the unauthorized use of a celebrity's identity is a type of false association claim, as it essentially alleges the misuse of a trademark, i.e., a symbol or device such as a visual likeness, vocal imitation, or other uniquely distinguishing characteristic, which is likely to confuse consumers as to the plaintiff's sponsorship or approval of the product. Standing to bring such a claim, therefore, does not require "actual competition" in the traditional sense that it is required for most trademark cases. Instead, standing extends to a purported endorser who has an economic interest akin to that of a trademark holder in controlling the commercial exploitation of his or her identity. Moreover, the wrongful appropriator is in a sense a competitor of the celebrity, even when the celebrity has chosen to disassociate himself or herself from advertising products, as Waits (P) did in this case. The thinking is that the appropriator and the celebrity compete with respect to the use of the celebrity's name or identity, and that both utilize or market that personal property for commercial purposes.

Quicknotes

DISTINCTIVENESS A standard for trademark protection, whereby the more distinctive a mark is, the greater its eligibility for protection. Distinctive marks typically consist of terms that are fanciful or coined, arbitrary, or suggestive. If a mark is descriptive, it is not entitled to trademark protection unless it has acquired distinctiveness through consumer association of goods or services with the mark (such acquired distinctiveness is also known as secondary meaning).

INTER ALIA Among other things.

White v. Samsung Electronics America, Inc.

TV star (P) v. Electronics manufacturer (D)

971 F.2d 1395 (9th Cir.), *reh. and reh. en banc denied*, 989 F.2d 1512 (9th Cir. 1992).

cert. denied, 508 U.S. 951 (1993).

NATURE OF CASE: Appeal from dismissal of action seeking damages for commercial misappropriation.

FACT SUMMARY: White (P), a well-known television personality, contended that an advertisement by Samsung Electronics America, Inc. (D) had usurped her right of publicity, even though her likeness had not been incorporated in the advertisement.

> 🏛 **RULE OF LAW**
> A person's right of publicity may be usurped even if the offending use did not incorporate that person's likeness.

FACTS: Samsung Electronics America, Inc. (Samsung) (D) ran an advertisement which clearly indicated that Vanna White (P) of the television game show "Wheel of Fortune" had been the basis for the images. However, White's (P) likeness was not used in the advertisement. White (P) sued, alleging violations of state statutory and common-law right to publicity and the federal Lanham Act. The district court dismissed, and White (D) appealed.

ISSUE: May a person's right to publicity, be usurped even if the offending use did not incorporate that person's likeness?

HOLDING AND DECISION: (Goodwin, J.) Yes. A person's right to publicity may be usurped even if the offending use did not incorporate that person's likeness. The state statute at issue, California Civil Code § 3344, requires appropriation of a person's likeness for actionability, so White (P) did not have a cause of action under this law. However, the state common-law right of publicity is not so specific. The right of publicity relates to one's "identity," not just his likeness. While White's (P) image was not being used here, there is no question but that her identity was being appropriated. The facts as alleged here do state a cause of action. Also, under the Lanham Act, which deals with consumer confusion, it is possible that the advertisement could mislead the public into thinking that White (P) endorsed Samsung's (D) product. This would be actionable under the Lanham Act. Affirmed in part, reversed in part and remanded. District court erred and the claim must be submitted to the jury.

PETITION FOR REHEARING: The petition for rehearing is denied and the suggestion for rehearing en banc is rejected.

DISSENT FROM DENIAL OF REHEARING: (Kozinski, J.): The panel has created a rule of overbroad protection that will stifle creativity. Under the majority's opinion, it is a tort for advertisers to merely remind the public of a celebrity, rather than using a celebrity's name, voice, signature or likeness or implying the celebrity endorses a product. This is an "Orwellian notion" that "withdraws far more from the public domain than prudence and common sense allow." The panel majority holds that the right of publicity extends beyond name and likeness to any "appropriation" of a celebrity's "identity" through the use of anything that "evokes" that celebrity's personality. However, in the context of intellectual property rights, what the majority does is not prevent the "evisceration" of White's existing rights, but creates a new and much broader property right. White is invoked because the robot is standing next to the Wheel of Fortune. If the Wheel of Fortune were removed, no one would associate the robot with White. Thus, the majority is giving a celebrity an exclusive right not in what she looks like or who she is, but in what she does for a living. Such a sweeping right places the balance between the public's interests and those of the celebrity in the wrong place. The balance deprives the public of too much, and is contrary to the approach taken in intellectual property law of carefully balancing between what's set aside for the owner and what's left in the public domain. This rule potentially will prevent parody and criticism, and comes at the expense of future creators and of the public at large.

▶ *ANALYSIS*

A similar and better-known case was *Midler v. Ford Motor Co.*, 849 F.2d 460 (9th Cir. 1988). There, Ford had unsuccessfully attempted to hire entertainer Bette Midler to release the rights to her version of the song "Do You Want to Dance" to be used in an advertisement. Ford then hired a "sound-alike" of Midler to record the song, which Ford incorporated into an advertisement. Midler (P) successfully argued that her right of publicity had been violated.

■=■

Quicknotes

LANHAM ACT § 43(a) Persons who use a false description or representation are liable to those damaged.

Continued on next page.

RIGHT OF PUBLICITY The right of a person to control the commercial exploitation of his name or likeness.

■≡■

America Online v. LCGM, Inc.

Internet service provider (P) v. Unauthorized spammer (D)

46 F. Supp. 2d 444 (E.D. Va. 1988).

NATURE OF CASE: Motion for summary judgment in action for false designation under the Lanham Act.

FACT SUMMARY: America Online (AOL) (P), an Internet service provider, contended that LCGM, Inc. (D), which operated and transacted business from Internet domains offering pornographic websites, sent unauthorized and unsolicited bulk email advertisements (spam) to AOL (P) customers, and, in so doing, violated the Lanham Act's prohibition on false designation.

🏛 RULE OF LAW
A plaintiff establishes a false designation claim under the Lanham Act where the plaintiff proves that the defendant used a designation in interstate commerce in connection with goods and services, which designation was likely to cause confusion, mistake or deception as to origin, sponsorship, or approval of the defendant's goods or services, and that plaintiff was, or was likely to be, damaged by these acts.

FACTS: America Online (AOL) (P) is an Internet service provider that has registered the mark "AOL" and the domain name "aol.com." LCGM, Inc. (D) operated and transacted business from Internet domains offering pornographic websites. AOL (P) brought suit against LCGM (D) for violating the Lanham Act's prohibition on false designation, alleging that LCGM (D) sent around 92 million unauthorized and unsolicited bulk email advertisements (spam) to AOL (P) customers in violation of its terms of service and email policies. LCGM (D) admitted that it maintained AOL (P) memberships to harvest or collect the email addresses of other AOL (P) members, and it admitted that it forged the domain information "aol .com" in the "from" line of email messages sent to AOL (P) members. AOL (P) alleged that as a result of LCGM's (D) actions, many AOL (P) members expressed confusion about whether AOL (P) endorsed LCGM's (D) pornographic websites or their bulk emailing practices. LCGM (D) also admitted to sending email messages from its computers through its network via email software to AOL (P), which then relayed the messages to AOL (P) members. AOL (P) asserted significant damages that resulted from LCGM's (D) conduct.

ISSUE: Does a plaintiff establish a false designation claim under the Lanham Act where the plaintiff proves that the defendant used a designation in interstate commerce in connection with goods and services, which designation was likely to cause confusion, mistake or deception as to origin, sponsorship, or approval of the defendant's goods or services, and that plaintiff was, or was likely to be, damaged by these acts?

HOLDING AND DECISION: (Lee, J.) Yes. A plaintiff establishes a false designation claim under the Lanham Act where the plaintiff proves that the defendant used a designation in interstate commerce in connection with goods and services, which designation was likely to cause confusion, mistake or deception as to origin, sponsorship, or approval of the defendant's goods or services, and that plaintiff was, or was likely to be, damaged by these acts. Here, each of the false designation elements has been satisfied. First, LCGM (D) clearly used the "aol.com" designation, incorporating the registered trademark and service mark "AOL" in their email headers. Second, LCGM's (D) activities involved interstate commerce because all emails sent to AOL (P) members were routed from its computers in Michigan through AOL's (P) computers in Virginia. Third, the use of AOL's (P) designation was in connection with goods and services, given that LCGM's (D) emails advertised its commercial websites. Fourth, the use of "aol.com" in LCGM's (D) emails was likely to cause confusion as to the origin and sponsorship of LCGM's (D) goods and services, since any recipient of those emails could logically conclude that a message containing "aol.com" in the header would originate from AOL's (P) registered Internet domain, which incorporates the registered mark "AOL," and that the message had been sent by an AOL (P) member or AOL (P) itself. In fact, AOL (P) alleged that this is what happened, and that the false designation did cause such confusion among—and complaints and protests from—many AOL (P) members, who believed that AOL (P) sponsored and authorized LCGM's (D) bulk emailing practices and pornographic websites. Finally, AOL (P) asserted that these acts damaged AOL's (P) technical capabilities and its goodwill. Because AOL (P) has satisfied all elements of a false designation claim, and because there is no genuine issue of material fact regarding AOL's (P) claim, AOL (P) is entitled to summary judgment.

▶ ANALYSIS

In addition to prevailing on its false designation claim, AOL (P) prevailed on its trademark dilution claim under the Federal Trademark Dilution Act of 1995, which provides relief to an owner of a mark whose mark or trade name is used by another person in commerce "if such use begins after the mark has become famous and causes dilution of

Continued on next page.

the distinctive quality of the mark." The legislative history of the Act indicates that it was intended to address Internet domain name issues. Here, AOL (P) was able to satisfy the two elements necessary to establish a dilution claim: (1) the ownership of a distinctive mark, and (2) a likelihood of dilution. Finally, AOL (P) also prevailed on claims under federal and state computer fraud and crimes acts, as well as common-law trespass claims.

■━■

Quicknotes

DISTINCTIVENESS A standard for trademark protection, whereby the more distinctive a mark is, the greater its eligibility for protection. Distinctive marks typically consist of terms that are fanciful or coined, arbitrary, or suggestive. If a mark is descriptive, it is not entitled to trademark protection unless it has acquired distinctiveness through consumer association of goods or services with the mark (such acquired distinctiveness is also known as secondary meaning).

TRADEMARK DILUTION The diminishment of the capability of a trademark to identify and distinguish the particular good or service with which it is associated.

■━■

Dastar Corporation v. Twentieth Century Fox Film Corporation

Video producer (D) v. Owner of book rights (P)

539 U.S. 23 (2003).

NATURE OF CASE: Appeal from affirmance of summary judgment in action for violation of § 43(a) of the Lanham Act.

FACT SUMMARY: Twentieth Century Fox Film Corporation (Fox) (P), owner of rights in a book entitled *Crusade in Europe*, sued Dastar Corp. (Dastar) (D), a producer of a video copy of a television series in the public domain which was based on the book. Fox (P) alleged that Dastar (D) marketed the video as its own product without giving credit to the original television series, and, therefore, falsely designated the origin of the video in violation of § 43(a) of the Lanham Act, codified at 15 U.S.C. § 1125(a).

🏛 **RULE OF LAW**
Section 43(a) of the Lanham Act does not prevent the unaccredited copying of an uncopyrighted work.

FACTS: General Dwight D. Eisenhower's World War II book, *Crusade in Europe*, was published by Doubleday, which registered the work's copyright and granted exclusive television rights to an affiliate of Twentieth Century Fox Film Corporation (Fox) (P). Fox (P), in turn, arranged for Time, Inc., to produce a *Crusade in Europe* television series based on the book, and Time assigned its copyright in the series to Fox. The series was first broadcast in 1949. In 1975, Doubleday renewed the book's copyright, but Fox (P) never renewed the copyright on the television series, which expired in 1977, leaving the series in the public domain. In 1988, Fox (P) reacquired the television rights in the book, including the exclusive right to distribute the *Crusade* television series on video and to sublicense others to do so. SFM Entertainment (P) and New Line Home Video, Inc. (P) acquired from Fox (P) the exclusive rights to manufacture and distribute *Crusade* on video. In 1995, Dastar Corporation (Dastar) (D) released a video set, *World War II Campaigns in Europe*, which it made from tapes of the original version of the *Crusade* television series and sold as its own product for substantially less than New Line's (P) video set. Fox (P), SFM (P), and New Line (P) brought an action alleging, inter alia, that Dastar's (D) sale of *Campaigns* without proper credit to the Crusade television series constituted "reverse passing off" in violation of § 43(a) of the Lanham Act. The district court granted summary judgment to Fox (P) and the other plaintiffs. The court of appeals affirmed in relevant part, holding, among other things, that because Dastar (D) copied substantially the entire *Crusade* series, labeled the resulting product with a different name, and marketed it without

attribution to Fox (P), Dastar (D) had committed a "bodily appropriation" of Fox's (P) series, which was sufficient to establish the reverse passing off (the remedy for which was twice Dastar's (D) profits). The United States Supreme Court granted certiorari.

ISSUE: Does § 43(a) of the Lanham Act, prevent the unaccredited copying of an uncopyrighted work?

HOLDING AND DECISION: (Scalia, J.) No. Section 43(a) of the Lanham Act does not prevent the unaccredited copying of an uncopyrighted work. Section 43(a) created a federal remedy against a person who used in commerce "a false designation of origin" of goods or services. The key issue thus depends on what the statute means by "origin." Fox's (P) claim would undoubtedly be sustained if Dastar (D) had bought some of New Line's (P) *Crusade* videotapes and merely repackaged them as its own. However, Dastar (D) has instead taken a creative work in the public domain, copied it, made modifications (arguably minor), and produced its very own series of videotapes. If "origin" refers only to the manufacturer or producer of the physical "good" that is made available to the public (here, the videotapes), Dastar (D) was the origin. If, however, "origin" includes the creator of the underlying work that Dastar (D) copied, then someone else, perhaps Fox (P), was the origin of Dastar's (D) product. Because Dastar (D) was the "origin" of the physical products it sold as its own, Fox (P) cannot prevail on its Lanham Act claim. As dictionary definitions affirm, the most natural understanding of the "origin" of "goods"—the source of wares—is the producer of the tangible product sold in the marketplace, here Dastar's (D) *Campaigns* videotape. The phrase "origin of goods" in the Lanham Act is incapable of connoting the person or entity that originated the ideas that "goods" embody or contain. The consumer typically does not care about such origination, and § 43(a) should not be stretched to cover matters that are of no consequence to purchasers. Although purchasers do care about ideas or communications contained or embodied in a communicative product such as a video, giving the Lanham Act special application to such products would cause it to conflict with copyright law, which is precisely directed to that subject and which grants the public the right to copy without attribution once a copyright has expired. Recognizing a § 43(a) cause of action here would render superfluous the provisions of the Visual Artists Rights Act that grant an artistic work's author "the right ... to claim authorship of that work," 17 U.S.C. § 106A(a)(1)(A), but carefully limit

Continued on next page.

and focus that right. It would also pose serious practical problems. Without a copyrighted work as the basepoint, the word "origin" has no discernable limits. Another practical difficulty of adopting a special definition of "origin" for communicative products is that it places the manufacturers of those products, in a difficult position. On the one hand, they would face Lanham Act liability for failing to credit the creator of a work on which their lawful copies are based; and on the other hand they could face Lanham Act liability for crediting the creator if that should be regarded as implying the creator's "sponsorship or approval" of the copy, 15 U.S.C. § 1125(a)(1)(A). In sum, "origin" refers to the producer of the tangible goods that are offered for sale, and not to the author of any idea, concept, or communication embodied in those goods. To hold otherwise would be akin to finding that § 43(a) created a species of perpetual patent and copyright, which Congress may not do. For merely saying it is the producer of the video, no Lanham Act liability attaches to Dastar (D). Reversed.

▶ ANALYSIS

The Berne Convention for the Protection of Literary and Artistic Works requires member states to recognize the right of paternity. Such a right of attribution of authorship has been a feature of numerous legal systems (not including the United States) for many years and has not posed the kinds of problems postulated by Justice Scalia. It is arguable that requiring identification of a work's author once the work enters the public domain would not in any way interfere with the right to copy that work, and that, therefore, the kinds of "serious practical problems" anticipated by the Court would, in fact, never materialize. Nonetheless, as the Court points out, if Congress wishes to create such a right, it should do so as an addition to the law of copyright, not through the ambiguous use of "origin" in the Lanham Act.

■≡■

Quicknotes

LANHAM ACT § 43(a) Federal trademark infringement statute.

LANHAM ACT § 1125 Imposes civil liability on any person who uses any trademark, false designation of origin, or false or misleading description of fact, that is likely to cause confusion or mistake or misrepresents the nature or origin of his or another's goods or service, to anyone likely to be damaged by that act.

■≡■

Bretford Manufacturing, Inc. v. Smith System Manufacturing Corporation

Computer table manufacturer (P) v. Computer table manufacturer (D)

419 F.3d 576 (7th Cir. 2005).

NATURE OF CASE: Appeal from judgment for defendant in action for trade dress infringement and reverse passing off.

FACT SUMMARY: Bretford Manufacturing, Inc. (Bretford) (P), which manufactured computer tables with a special V-shaped height adjustment system, claimed that Smith System Manufacturing Corporation (Smith System) (D) infringed trade dress in the V shape design and engaged in reverse passing off when Smith System (D) incorporated Bretford (P) hardware in a sample table used to solicit a purchase order.

> ## 🏛 RULE OF LAW
> (1) A manufacturer does not have trade dress rights in a design element of a product that does not serve as a source identifier.
> (2) A manufacturer does not engage in reverse passing off by incorporating another's hardware into its product where there is no resulting consumer confusion as to the origin of the product.

FACTS: Bretford Manufacturing, Inc. (Bretford) (P) manufactured computer tables with a special V-shaped height adjustment system, and for eight years was the only seller of such V-Design tables. Smith System Manufacturing Corporation (Smith System) (D) decided to copy the V design system for its own line of computer tables. Smith System (D) subcontracted the leg assemblies to another company, whose initial efforts were unsatisfactory. Therefore, at the time, when a major metropolitan school system asked Smith System (D) to see one of its tables, Smith System (D) used the leg assembly from a Bretford (P) table, which it attached to its own table top. The school system ordered the tables from Smith System (D), and all tables delivered to the school system were made by Smith System's (D) subcontractor. Invoking § 43(a) of the Lanham Act, Bretford (P) brought suit against Smith System (D) for trade dress infringement and reverse passing off. Bretford (P) claimed that the V-shaped design was its table's trade dress, and that it was wrongful for Smith System (D) to use its hardware in the sample it used to solicit the purchase order from the school system. The district court ruled in favor of Smith System (D), finding that V-shaped legs did not signal Bretford (P) as a source, and that no actual confusion had resulted from Smith System's (D) use of that design. The district court also ruled that Smith System (D) had not engaged in

reverse passing off. The Seventh Circuit Court of Appeals granted review.

ISSUE:
(1) Does a manufacturer have trade dress rights in a design element of a product that does not serve as a source identifier?
(2) Does a manufacturer engage in reverse passing off by incorporating another's hardware into its product where there is no resulting consumer confusion as to the origin of the product?

HOLDING AND DECISION: (Easterbrook, J.)
(1) No. A manufacturer does not have trade dress rights in a design element of a product that does not serve as a source identifier. The record supports the conclusion that the V-shape leg design did not signal "Bretford" in consumers' minds. Instead, both Bretford (P) and Smith System (D) sell through distributors and field representatives to sophisticated buyers who know exactly where their goods are coming from. The fact that many buyers ask for tables with V-shaped legs implies that the leg design is functional and shows that buyers are seeking a certain function and do not care who makes the table. Merely because Bretford (P) was the only manufacturer of such tables for eight years and spent $4 million to promote sales is insufficient to protect it from the type of competition presented by Smith System (D). Otherwise, competition would be stifled, since new entrants would be curtailed unduly by the risk and expense of trademark litigation where a prior innovator had introduced a new design. "Consumers should not be deprived of the benefits of competition with regard to the utilitarian and esthetic purposes that product design ordinarily serves by a rule of law that facilitates plausible threats of suit against new entrants based on alleged inherent distinctiveness." Affirmed as to this issue.
(2) No. A manufacturer does not engage in reverse passing off by incorporating another's hardware into its product where there is no resulting consumer confusion as to the origin of the product. Passing off or palming off occurs when an entity puts someone else's trademark on its own (usually inferior) goods; reverse passing off or misappropriation is selling someone else's goods under your own mark. Reverse passing off is actionable when a misdescription of goods' origin causes commercial injury in the nature of a trademark loss, meaning

Continued on next page.

that it must arise from the misrepresentation of the goods' origin. Most, if not all, products are made with components supplied by others. If, however, there is no confusion as to who is the finished product's originator, regardless of whether the components constitute a significant part or a minor part of the finished product, the Lanham Act is not violated. The portion of § 43(a) that addresses reverse passing off is the one that condemns false designations of origin. "Origin" means "the producer of the tangible product sold in the marketplace." Thus, here, as far as the school system was concerned, the table's "origin" was Smith System (D), no matter who made any component or subassembly. While such an outcome may be "unfair," it is not prohibited by federal statute. To the contrary, federal law encourages competition and wholesale copying to drive down prices, since it is the consumer, not the producer, who is the object of the law's solicitude. Affirmed as to this issue.

▶ *ANALYSIS*

Originators such as Bretford (P) may receive protection via design patents, and strictly aesthetic features of products may be copyrighted. The availability of these and other protections greatly reduces any harm to the producer that might ensue from limiting trademark protection to features that have acquired secondary meaning. Here, Bretford (P) did not obtain patent or copyright protection, so it cannot block Smith System's (D) copy-cat tables. Even if the record had evidence of secondary meaning, Bretford (P) likely would lose because the leg design appeared to be functional in the first place.

■≡■

Quicknotes

TRADE DRESS The overall image of, or impression created by, a product that a court may enforce as a trademark if it determines that such image has acquired secondary meaning and that the public recognizes it as an indication of source.

■≡■

Defenses to Infringement

Quick Reference Rules of Law

Park 'N Fly, Inc. v. Dollar Park and Fly, Inc.

Holder of incontestable mark (P) v. Long-term airport parking provider (D)

469 U.S. 189 (1985).

NATURE OF CASE: Appeal of reversal of injunction against trademark infringement.

FACT SUMMARY: Park 'N Fly, Inc. (P) attempted to use incontestability status of its name as a basis for enjoining Dollar Park and Fly, Inc. (D) from using its name.

🏛 **RULE OF LAW**
An action to enjoin the infringement of an incontestable trademark may not be defended on the basis that the mark is merely descriptive.

FACTS: Park & Fly, Inc. (P) registered its name as a trademark, giving it incontestable status. Park 'N Fly (P) brought a trademark infringement action against Dollar Park and Fly, Inc. (D), seeking to enjoin the latter's use of the name. The district court granted the injunction. The court of appeals reversed, holding that incontestability could not be used as an offensive weapon, and that the name "Park 'N Fly" was merely descriptive, and not entitled to trademark protection. Park 'N Fly (P) appealed.

ISSUE: May an action to enjoin the infringement of an incontestable trademark be defended on the basis that the mark is merely descriptive?

HOLDING AND DECISION: (O'Connor, J.) No. An action to enjoin the infringement of an incontestable trademark may not be defended on the basis that the mark is merely descriptive. The 1946 Lanham Act created a registration system for trademarks, and one so registered gains an incontestability status. Per statute, an incontestable mark may be challenged as void if the term becomes generic, is abandoned, or is used as a basis for fraud. The fact that a mark is descriptive is insufficient to void an incontestable mark. The court of appeals held that incontestability could be a factor only in an action to nullify a mark, not to enforce it. There is no statutory or decisional basis for this. This being so, the court of appeals' use of descriptiveness alone as a basis for overturning the injunction was improper. Reversed and remanded.

a meaning in common usage, that is used in connection with products or services directly related to, or suggestive of, that meaning. A descriptive mark is not entitled to trademark protection unless it has acquired distinctiveness over time.

TRADEMARK INFRINGEMENT The unauthorized use of another's trademark in such a manner as to cause a likelihood of confusion as to the source of the product or service in connection with which it is utilized.

◼️═◼️

▶ *ANALYSIS*

The 1946 Lanham Act was a major development in trademark law. It represented the first major federal intrusion into the area. Prior to 1946, federal trademark statutes had largely left the field to state common law.

◼️═◼️

Quicknotes

DESCRIPTIVEVENESS A standard for trademark protection, whereby a descriptive mark has a dictionary meaning, or

In re Bose Corp.

[Parties not identified.]

580 F.3d 1240 (Fed. Cir. 2009).

NATURE OF CASE: Appeal from order cancelling a trademark registration on the grounds of fraud in the registration's renewal.

FACT SUMMARY: Bose Corp. (P) contended that because it had not intended to deceive the Patent and Trademark Office when it renewed its "WAVE" mark for certain goods, the mark should not have been cancelled on the grounds of fraud, notwithstanding that it made a material misrepresentation in its renewal.

> ## 🏛 RULE OF LAW
> A trademark applicant does not commit fraud in procuring a registration when it makes material representations of fact in its declaration that it knows to be false, but does so without an intent to deceive.

FACTS: Bose Corp. (P) had registered and renewed the mark "WAVE" for various goods, including audio tape recorders and players. In an opposition proceeding initiated by Bose (P) against Hexawave, Inc., Hexawave counterclaimed for cancellation of Bose's (P) "WAVE" mark, on the grounds that Bose committed fraud in its registration renewal application when it claimed use on all goods in the registration while knowing that it had stopped manufacturing and selling certain goods. In Bose's (P) combined Section 8 affidavit of continued use and Section 9 renewal application, filed in 2001, Bose's (P) counsel, Mr. Sullivan, had attested that the "WAVE" mark was still in use in commerce on various goods, including audio tape recorders and players. The Trademark Trial and Appeal Board (the Board) found that Bose (P) had stopped manufacturing and selling audio tape recorders and players sometime between 1996 and 1997, and that Sullivan knew this when he signed the Section 8/9 renewal. At the time Sullivan signed the Section 8/9 renewal, Bose (P) continued to repair previously sold audio tape recorders and players, some of which were still under warranty. Sullivan testified that in his belief, the "WAVE" mark was used in commerce because "in the process of repairs, the product was being transported back to customers." The Board concluded that the repairing and shipping back did not constitute sufficient use to maintain a trademark registration for goods, and further found Sullivan's belief that transporting repaired goods constituted use was not reasonable. Finally, the Board found that the use statement in the Section 8/9 renewal was material. Thus, the Board ruled that Bose (P) committed fraud on the Patent and Trademark Office (PTO) in maintaining the "WAVE" mark registration and ordered the cancellation of Bose's (P) "WAVE" mark reg-

istration in its entirety. The court of appeals granted review.

ISSUE: Does a trademark applicant commit fraud in procuring a registration when it makes material representations of fact in its declaration that it knows to be false, but does so without an intent to deceive?

HOLDING AND DECISION: (Michel, J.) No. A trademark applicant does not commit fraud in procuring a registration when it makes material representations of fact in its declaration that it knows to be false, but does so without an intent to deceive. There is a material legal distinction between a "false" representation and a "fraudulent" one, the latter involving an intent to deceive, whereas the former may be occasioned by a misunderstanding, an inadvertence, a mere negligent omission, or the like. To determine intent to deceive, the Board has erroneously adopted the standard that an applicant commits fraud when the applicant makes material representations of fact that it knows or should know are false or misleading. This standard impermissibly equates "should have known" with subjective intent to deceive, and thereby lowers the fraud standard to a simple negligence standard. However, mere negligence is insufficient to raise an inference of fraud or dishonesty. The correct standard—supported by precedent, including the Board's precedents—is that a trademark is obtained fraudulently under the Lanham Act only if the applicant or registrant knowingly makes a false, material representation with the intent to deceive the PTO. Under this standard, the evidence of intent to deceive must be clear and convincing, and inferences drawn from lesser evidence cannot satisfy the deceptive intent requirement. Applying this standard here, while Sullivan's statement in the renewal was false and material, it was not made with an intent to deceive. Sullivan attested to his belief that Bose's (P) repairing of damaged, previously sold WAVE audio tape recorders and players and returning the repaired goods to the customers met the "use in commerce" requirement for the renewal of the trademark. Whether this belief was reasonable is not part of the intent-to-deceive analysis, since there is no fraud if a false misrepresentation is occasioned by an honest misunderstanding or inadvertence without a willful intent to deceive. Here, Sullivan testified that he believed his statement was true when he made it; in the absence of clear and convincing evidence to the contrary, Bose (P) did not commit fraud in renewing its "WAVE" mark, and the Board erred in canceling the mark in its entirety. However, because the "WAVE" mark

Continued on next page.

is no longer in use on audio tape recorders and players, the case needs to be remanded so the registration can be restricted to reflect commercial reality. Reversed and remanded.

▶ *ANALYSIS*

The Patent and Trademark Office (PTO) in this case argued that making a submission to the PTO with reckless disregard of its truth or falsity satisfies the intent to deceive requirement. The court left this issue open, reasoning that before Sullivan submitted his declaration in 2001, neither the PTO nor any court had interpreted "use in commerce" to exclude the repairing and shipping of repaired goods, so that even if it was assumed that reckless disregard satisfied the intent to deceive requirement, there was no basis for finding Sullivan's conduct reckless. The court did emphasize, however, that even a finding that particular conduct amounts to gross negligence does not of itself justify an inference of intent to deceive.

■══■

Quicknotes

FRAUD A false representation of facts with the intent that another will rely on the misrepresentation to his detriment.

■══■

United States Shoe Corp. v. Brown Group, Inc.

Shoe company (P) v. Shoe company (D)

740 F. Supp. 196 (S.D.N.Y.), *aff'd*, 923 F.2d 844 (2d Cir. 1990).

NATURE OF CASE: Trademark infringement and unfair competition action.

FACT SUMMARY: United States Shoe Corp. (P), which used the slogan "Looks Like a Pump, Feels Like a Sneaker" in connection with certain of its women's dress shoes, claimed that its competitor, Brown Group, Inc. (D), engaged in trademark violation and unfair competition by describing the defendant's comparable shoes by using the phrase "feels like a sneaker."

🏛 RULE OF LAW
An alleged trademark infringer's good faith use of a phrase in a slogan to describe its goods is a fair use of the phrase.

FACTS: United States Shoe Corp. (P), a shoe manufacturer, began selling a line of comfortable women's dress pumps, and its ads and catalogs for those shoes used the slogan or tag line "Looks Like a Pump, Feels Like a Sneaker," and an associated musical jingle in television ads. Plaintiff spent $9 million advertising its pumps. Brown Group, Inc. (D), plaintiff's competitor, also introduced a similar line of shoes. Its slogan for those shoes was "Think of It as a Sneaker with No Strings Attached." The text of the ad included the phrase, "And when we say it feels like a sneaker, we're not just stringing you along." Other elements of the ad clearly indicated that the shoes were those of defendant. United States Show Corp. (P) brought suit claiming trademark violation and unfair competition, contending that defendant's use of the phrase "And when we say it feels like a sneaker" was intended to mislead consumers into believing Brown Shoe Group's (D) pumps were those advertised by United States Show Corp. (P).

ISSUE: Is an alleged trademark infringer's good faith use of a phrase in a slogan to describe its goods a fair use of the phrase?

HOLDING AND DECISION: (Leval, J.) Yes. An alleged trademark infringer's good faith use of a phrase in a slogan to describe its goods is a fair use of the phrase. The fair use doctrine provide an alleged infringer a statutory defense where that party uses the allegedly infringing name, term, or device in good faith to describe its goods or services, or their geographic origin. If the holder's mark has descriptive qualities, the fair use doctrine thus recognizes that the holder cannot exclude some kinds of competing uses. The limited monopoly created by trademark law, which is relatively cost-free to society, depends on the exclusivity of the monopoly being practiced only over identifiers that are not needed by others for trade communication. Otherwise society would be impoverished to the degree that it would not be able to obtain useful information about competing products. Thus, while trademark law presumptively forbids rights in descriptive marks, an exception arise where those marks have developed secondary meaning, since it would be unfair to permit competitors to piggyback on the reputation earned by a merchant that had over time developed such secondary meaning (customer recognition) in its mark. Although a user of a descriptive word may acquire the exclusive right to use that word as an identifier of its product, this does not justify barring others from using the words in good faith for descriptive purposes associated with their products. Here, defendant uses the phrase "feels like a sneaker" in a descriptive sense, i.e., that its pumps feel like athletic shoes. Moreover, defendant does not use the phrase as an identifier or trademark to indicate origin or source; the other logos, slogans, and marks on its ads serve that purpose. The use is not prominent as a caption or slogan, but is merely a fragment of a sentence in small print. In other words, defendant satisfies the requirement of the statute because it uses the words "otherwise than as a trade or service mark, . . . fairly and in good faith only to describe to users the goods" marketed by defendant. Additionally, plaintiff has not demonstrated a likelihood of consumer confusion as to source. Descriptive advertising claiming a product's virtues is likely to be understood as such rather than as an identifier of source, and that is the case here. Even assuming that plaintiff has built up consumer recognition in its slogan and associated musical jingle, there is no reason to believe that consumers will assume that any manufacturer that claims its shoes feel like a sneaker is the plaintiff. Therefore, plaintiff has failed to meet its burden of demonstrating that defendant's ad is likely to confuse consumers as to the sources of the defendant's products. Judgment for defendant.

▶ ANALYSIS

To prove infringement, a trademark owner must demonstrate that the alleged infringer's use of the mark is likely to cause confusion or mistake as to the origin of the two products. When a mark is made of descriptive terms, the alleged infringer may defend his use of the terms by demonstrating that he used them in good faith in their descriptive sense and not as a trademark, thus making "fair use" of descriptive terms, as codified in § 33 (b)(4) of the Lanham Act. Here, it seems the court concludes that

Continued on next page.

defendant's use of the phrase at issue does not create a sufficient likelihood of consumer confusion in the first place, but that even if it did, the use falls within the fair use doctrine. Thus, arguably, the court did not need to engage in a fair use analysis, given its apparent conclusion that there was no trademark violation to begin with.

■■■■

Quicknotes

DESCRIPTIVEVENESS A standard for trademark protection, whereby a descriptive mark has a dictionary meaning, or a meaning in common usage, that is used in connection with products or services directly related to, or suggestive of, that meaning. A descriptive mark is not entitled to trademark protection unless it has acquired distinctiveness over time.

FAIR USE An affirmative defense to a claim of copyright infringement providing an exception from the copyright owner's exclusive rights in a work, for the purposes of criticism, comment, news reporting, teaching, scholarship, or research.

SECONDARY MEANING A word or mark that becomes associated with a particular merchant or product as its source of origin.

■■■■

Car-Freshner Corp. v. S.C. Johnson & Son, Inc.

Car freshener manufacturer (P) v. Home freshener manufacturer (D)

70 F.3d 267 (2d Cir. 1995).

NATURE OF CASE: Appeal from grant of summary judgment to defendant, on grounds of dissimilarity, and cross-appeal from grant of summary judgment to plaintiff, on grounds of lack of fair use, in trademark infringement action.

FACT SUMMARY: Car-Freshner Corp. (P), which makes air fresheners for cars in the shape of a pine tree, contended that S.C. Johnson & Son, Inc. (Johnson) (D) infringed its trademark by making a plug-in air freshener for home use during the Christmas holiday season that was also pine-tree-shaped. Johnson (D) defended by claiming fair use and lack of confusion.

> ## 🏛 RULE OF LAW
> The use of imagery for descriptive purposes is a fair use that defeats the claims of a trademark owner to exclusivity, even where the owner's mark is not descriptive.

FACTS: Car-Freshner Corp. (P) makes air fresheners for cars in the shape of a pine tree, and has trademarked the name "Little Tree." These come in a variety of colors and odors. S.C. Johnson & Son, Inc. (Johnson) (D) makes a line of "Glade" plug-in air fresheners that emit a scent when plugged into an electrical outlet. During the Christmas holiday season, Johnson (D) made a plug-in freshener that was pine-tree-shaped called "Holiday Pine Potpourri." Car-Freshner (P) brought suit claiming that Johnson's (D) plug-in pine tree infringed its Little Tree trademark and design, and Johnson (D) defended by claiming fair use and lack of confusion. The district court granted summary judgment on the issue of fair use to Car-Freshner (P), finding that the fair use defense is available only when the plaintiff's mark is descriptive, and that here Car-Freshner's (P) mark was suggestive. The district court nonetheless granted summary judgment to Johnson (D) on the grounds that the two products were sufficiently dissimilar that there was no likelihood of consumer confusion. Accordingly, the district court granted judgment for Johnson (D). Car-Freshner (P) appealed, and Johnson (D) cross-appealed, contending that the district court erred in its fair use determination. The Second Circuit Court of Appeals granted review.

ISSUE: Is the use of imagery for descriptive purposes a fair use that defeats the claims of a trademark owner to exclusivity, even where the owner's mark is not descriptive?

HOLDING AND DECISION: (Leval, J.) Yes. The use of imagery for descriptive purposes is a fair use that defeats the claims of a trademark owner to exclusivity, even where the owner's mark is not descriptive. The district

court's notion—that a fair use defense is only available where an allegedly infringed product is suggestive—is misguided. It makes no difference whether the plaintiff's mark is descriptive or suggestive, since the relevant inquiry is whether the defendant is using the protected word or image descriptively, and not as a mark. Whether a mark is descriptive, and therefore ineligible for trademark protection without having obtained secondary meaning, depends on the relationship between the mark and the product described. In sum, § 1115(b)(4) does not require that a mark be descriptive for the defendant to have a fair use defense; under the statute, fair use permits others to use a protected mark to describe aspects of their own goods, provided the use is in good faith and not as a mark. And that is how Johnson (D) used the pine-tree shape here. The shape referred to the pine scent of the plug-in, and also referred to the Christmas season, since a Christmas tree is traditionally a pine tree. Therefore, Johnson's (D) use of the shape is descriptive, not as a mark. The plug-ins and their packaging clearly indicate that they are made by Johnson (D). Furthermore, merely because Johnson (D) was aware of Car-Freshner's (P) mark but failed to consult counsel is not indicative of bad faith, since Johnson (D) had the right to use the shape descriptively. Summary judgment for Car-Freshner (P) is reversed on the fair use issue and granted to Johnson (D). Dismissal of Car-Freshner's (P) complaint is affirmed.

▶ ANALYSIS

The Restatement (Third) of Unfair Competition § 28, comment, provides that trademark rights extend only to the source significance that has been acquired by a descriptive mark, not to their original descriptive meanings. Thus, as this case holds, regardless whether the protected mark is descriptive, suggestive, arbitrary, or fanciful as used in connection with the product or service covered by the mark, the public's right to use descriptive words or images in good faith in their ordinary descriptive sense must prevail over the exclusivity claims of the trademark owner. In such cases, if any confusion results to the detriment of the mark holder, that is a risk the holder assumed when selecting a mark with descriptive attributes.

■━■

Quicknotes

DESCRIPTIVENESS A standard for trademark protection, whereby a descriptive mark has a dictionary meaning, or

Continued on next page.

a meaning in common usage, that is used in connection with products or services directly related to, or suggestive of, that meaning. A descriptive mark is not entitled to trademark protection unless it has acquired distinctiveness over time.

FAIR USE An affirmative defense to a claim of copyright infringement providing an exception from the copyright owner's exclusive rights in a work for the purposes of criticism, comment, news reporting, teaching, scholarship or research.

■≡■

KP Permanent Make-Up, Inc. v. Lasting Impression I, Inc.

Permanent makeup manufacturer (P) v. Permanent makeup manufacturer (D)

543 U.S. 111 (2004).

NATURE OF CASE: Appeal from reversal of summary judgment for plaintiff on its fair use defense on a trademark infringement counterclaim in declaratory action seeking judgment of no infringement.

FACT SUMMARY: KP Permanent Make-Up, Inc. (KP) (P) claimed that its use of "microcolor" to describe its permanent makeup was a fair use that defeated Lasting Impression I, Inc.'s (D) claim that KP (P) had infringed its trademark in "Micro Colors," which it had obtained after KP's (P) first use of the term.

🏛 RULE OF LAW
A party raising the statutory affirmative defense of fair use to a claim of trademark infringement does not have a burden to negate any likelihood that the practice complained of will confuse consumers about the origin of the goods or services affected.

FACTS: KP Permanent Make-Up, Inc. (KP) (P) and Lasting Impression I, Inc. (Lasting) (D) both use the term "micro color" (as one word or two, singular or plural) in marketing permanent cosmetic makeup. KP (P) used the single-word version since 1990 or 1991. In 1992, Lasting (D) registered a trademark that included the words "Micro Colors," and, in 1999, the registration became incontestable. When Lasting (D) demanded KP (P) stop using the word "microcolor," KP (P) sued for declaratory relief. Lasting (D) counterclaimed, alleging, inter alia, that KP (P) had infringed Lasting's (D) trademark. KP (P) responded by asserting the statutory affirmative defense of fair use under 15 U.S.C. § 1115(b)(4). Finding that Lasting (D) conceded that KP (P) used "microcolor" only to describe its goods and not as a mark, the district court held that KP (P) was acting fairly and in good faith because KP (P) undisputedly had employed the term continuously from before Lasting (D) adopted its mark. Without inquiring whether the practice was likely to cause consumer confusion, the court concluded that KP (P) had made out its affirmative defense under § 1115(b)(4) and entered summary judgment for KP (P) on Lasting's infringement claim (D). Reversing, the court of appeals ruled that the district court erred in addressing the fair use defense without delving into the matter of possible consumer confusion about the origin of KP's (P) goods. The court did not pointedly address the burden of proof, but appears to have placed it on KP (P) to show the absence of such confusion. The United States Supreme Court granted certiorari.

ISSUE: Does a party raising the statutory affirmative defense of fair use to a claim of trademark infringement have a burden to negate any likelihood that the practice complained of will confuse consumers about the origin of the goods or services affected?

HOLDING AND DECISION: (Souter, J.) No. A party raising the statutory affirmative defense of fair use to a claim of trademark infringement does not have a burden to negate any likelihood that the practice complained of will confuse consumers about the origin of the goods or services affected. Although § 1115(b) makes an incontestable registration "conclusive evidence . . . of the registrant's exclusive right to use the . . . mark," it also subjects a plaintiff's success to "proof of infringement as defined in section 1114." Section 1114(1) in turn requires a showing that the defendant's actual practice is "likely to cause confusion, or to cause mistake, or to deceive" consumers about the origin of the goods or services in question. Thus, a plaintiff claiming infringement of an incontestable mark must show likelihood of consumer confusion as part of the prima facie case. This plaintiff's burden must be kept in mind when reading § 1115(b)(4), which provides the fair use defense to a party whose "use of the . . . term . . . charged to be an infringement is a use, otherwise than as a mark, . . . of a term . . . which is descriptive of and used fairly and in good faith only to describe the goods or services." It is evident that § 1115(b) places a burden of proving likelihood of confusion (that is, infringement) on the party charging infringement even when relying on an incontestable registration, and that Congress said nothing about likelihood of confusion in setting out the elements of the fair use defense in § 1115(b)(4). It therefore takes a long stretch to claim that a fair use defense entails any burden to negate confusion. It is not plausible that Congress would have used § 1114's phrase "likely to cause confusion, or to cause mistake, or to deceive" to describe the requirement that a mark holder show likelihood of consumer confusion, but would have relied on § 1115(b)(4)'s phrase "used fairly" to give a defendant the burden to negate confusion. Lasting (D) argues unpersuasively that "used fairly" in § 1115(b)(4) is an oblique incorporation of a likelihood-of-confusion test developed in the common law of unfair competition. While some cases are consistent with taking account of the likelihood of consumer confusion as one consideration in deciding whether a use is fair, they cannot be read to make an assessment of confusion alone dispositive or provide that the defense has a burden to negate it entirely. Finally, a look at the typical course of litigation in an infringement action, points out the incoherence of placing a burden to show nonconfusion on a defendant. If a plaintiff succeeds in

Continued on next page.

making out a prima facie case, including the element of likelihood of confusion, the defendant may offer rebutting evidence to undercut the force of the plaintiff's evidence on this element, or raise an affirmative defense to bar relief even if the prima facie case is sound, or do both. It would make no sense to give the defendant a defense of showing affirmatively that the plaintiff cannot succeed in proving some element (like confusion); all the defendant needs to do is leave the fact finder unpersuaded that the plaintiff has carried its own burden on that point. Nor would it make sense to provide an affirmative defense of no confusion plus good faith, when merely rebutting the plaintiff's case on confusion would entitle the defendant to judgment, good faith or not. Since the burden of proving likelihood of confusion rests with the plaintiff, and the fair-use defendant has no freestanding need to show confusion unlikely, it follows that some possibility of consumer confusion is compatible with fair use. While this holding does not rule out the pertinence of the degree of consumer confusion under the fair use defense, it also does not pass upon the position that § 1115(b)(4)'s "used fairly" requirement demands only that the descriptive term describe the goods accurately. The court of appeals therefore erroneously required KP (P) to shoulder a burden on the confusion issue. Vacated and remanded.

▶ ANALYSIS

The Court in this case indicated that accuracy has to be a consideration in assessing fair use, and because the proceedings below had not given it the occasion to evaluate other concerns that courts might pick as relevant—e.g., commercial justification and the strength of the plaintiff's mark—the Court also indicated that "the door is not closed" as to such concerns. The Court also stated that its holding did not foreclose the relevance of the extent of likely consumer confusion to a determination of whether a defendant's use is objectively fair. Based on these statements, on remand, the Ninth Circuit reversed summary judgment for KP (P), finding that the degree of customer confusion "remains a factor in evaluating fair use," and that, therefore, summary judgment on this issue was inappropriate as there were genuine issues of material fact as to such confusion, the strength of the trademark, the descriptive nature of the term in relation to KP's (P) products, the availability of alternative descriptive terms, the extent of the use of the term prior to registration of Lasting's (D) mark, and any differences among the times and contexts in which KP (P) had used the term.

■■■

Quicknotes

AFFIRMATIVE DEFENSE A manner of defending oneself against a claim not by denying the truth of the charge, but by the introduction of some evidence challenging the plaintiff's right to bring the claim.

FAIR USE An affirmative defense to a claim of copyright infringement providing an exception from the copyright owner's exclusive rights in a work for the purposes of criticism, comment, news reporting, teaching, scholarship or research.

■■■

Jay Franco & Sons, Inc. v. Franek

Distributor of bath, bedding, and beach accessories (P) v. Circular beach towel seller (D)

615 F.3d 855 (7th Cir. 2010).

NATURE OF CASE: Appeal from summary judgment invalidating a trademark.

FACT SUMMARY: Franek (D) contended that his incontestable circular beach towel trademark should not have been invalidated on the grounds that it was functional, arguing that the towel's circular shape was not essential to the use or purpose of the device.

🏛 RULE OF LAW
An incontestable registered trademark may be invalidated if it is found to be functional.

FACTS: Franek (D) obtained a trademark for his circular bath towel in 1988. Franek (D) had advertised the towel as a fashion statement, as well as a boon for heliotropic sunbathers—tanners who swivel their bodies in unison with the sun's apparent motion in order to maintain an even tan—by enabling them to remain on their towels as they rotate rather than exert the energy to stand up and reposition their towels every so often, as conventional rectangular towels require. In 2006, Franek (D) discovered that that Jay Franco & Sons (Jay Franco) (P), a distributor of bath, bedding, and beach accessories, was selling round beach towels. After Franek (D) sued Jay Franco's (P) clients for trademark infringement, Jay Franco (P) sued Franek (D) to invalidate his mark. A utility patent (the '029 patent) introduced into evidence had claimed a round towel for its ability to help heliotropic sunbathers not have to move their towels. The district court granted summary judgment to Jay Franco (P), and the court of appeals granted review.

ISSUE: May an incontestable registered trademark be invalidated if it is found to be functional?

HOLDING AND DECISION: (Easterbrook, C.J.) Yes. An incontestable registered trademark may be invalidated if it is found to be functional. Franek's (D) mark is incontestable, because it has been in use continuously since its 1988 registration. Because it is incontestable, it is presumed to be distinctive, and it cannot be invalidated on the grounds that it lacks distinctiveness. Nevertheless, Franek's (D) incontestable mark may nonetheless be invalidated if it is functional. A design is functional when it is essential to the use or purpose of the device or when it affects the cost or quality of the device, so that a design that produces a benefit other than source identification is functional. Here, the '029 claims an aspect of a circular towel that Franek (D) advertised, i.e., its ability to be of help to lazy sunbathers. Even if Franek (D) did not infringe the patent, the patent is strong evidence of the circular towel's utility. While proving patent infringement can be sufficient to show that a

trademarked design is useful, as it means that the infringing design is quite similar to a useful invention, such proof is not necessary, since functionality is determined by a feature's usefulness, not its patentability or its infringement of a patent. Franek (D) correctly argues that any towel can satisfy a heliotropic tanner if it has enough surface area. That is true, and it is enough to keep the roundness of his towel from being functional under the first prong of the definition of functional ("essential to the use or purpose of the device") but not the second. For heliotropic sunbathers, a circle surpasses other shapes because it provides the most rotational space without waste. Any noncircle polygon will either limit full rotations or not use all the surface area. Also, compared to other shapes that permit full rotations, the round towel requires less material, which makes it easier to fold and carry. That's evidence that the towel's circularity "affects the . . . quality of the device." Even if, as Franek (D) argues, the heliotropic assistance qualities of the circular towel are not what set it apart from towels of other shapes, the towel is still functional because it would put competitors at a significant nonreputation-related disadvantage. Granting Franek (D) the exclusive use of a basic element of design (here, a circle) would impoverish other designers' palettes. A circle is the kind of basic design that a producer like Jay Franco (P) adopts because alternatives are scarce and some consumers want the shape regardless of who manufactures it. There are only so many geometric shapes; few are both attractive and simple enough to fabricate cheaply. To put things another way, a trademark holder cannot block innovation by appropriating designs that undergird further improvements. Patent holders can do this, but a patent's life is short; trademarks can last forever, so granting trademark holders this power could permanently stifle product development. Accordingly, Franek (D) cannot be permitted to keep the indefinite competitive advantage in producing circular beach towels his trademark creates, and the mark must be invalidated. Affirmed.

▶ ANALYSIS

The court here also notes that even fashion items may be functional, so that Franek's (D) circular towels may be functional even if they are fashionable. In this regard, the court observes that fashion is a form of function and that a design's aesthetic appeal can be as functional as its tangible characteristics. The chief difficulty is distinguishing between designs that are fashionable enough to be functional and those that are merely pleasing; it is only the

Continued on next page.

latter group that can be protected, since only the latter group serves only as a source identifier. Otherwise, fashionable designs can be freely copied unless protected by patent law. As the court remarked, if Franek (D) was worried that consumers would confuse Jay Franco's (P) round beach towels with his, he could imprint a distinctive verbal or pictorial mark on his towels, which would enable him to reap the benefits of his brand while still permitting healthy competition in the beach towel market.

■■■■

Christian Louboutin, S.A. v. Yves St. Laurent America Holding, Inc.

High-fashion designer (P) v. High-fashion designer (D)

696 F.3d 206 (2d Cir. 2012).

NATURE OF CASE: Appeal from judgment denying injunctive relief and enforcement of a trademark.

FACT SUMMARY: Christian Louboutin, S.A. (Louboutin) (P) contended that Yves Saint Laurent America Holding, Inc. (YSL) (D) violated Louboutin's (P) trademark in a red glossy lacquered outsole for its high-heeled shoes by placing a red outsole on YSL's (D) monochrome red high-heeled shoes, arguing that a single color may serve as a legally protected trademark in the fashion industry. Louboutin (P) sought to enjoin YSL (D) from placing a red outsole on YSL's (D) shoes.

RULE OF LAW

Under the aesthetic functionality test, a single color can serve as a legally protected trademark in the fashion industry where the use of the color is such that it does not significantly hinder competition.

FACTS: Christian Louboutin, S.A. (Louboutin) (P) is a high-fashion designer who registered as a trademark a red glossy lacquered outsole for its high-heeled shoes. The red outsole became closely associated with Louboutin (P) in high-fashion circles. A few years after Louboutin (P) registered the mark, Yves Saint Laurent America Holding, Inc. (YSL) (D), also a high-fashion designer, prepared to market a line of "monochrome" shoes in purple, green, yellow, and red. YSL (D) shoes in the monochrome style—which YSL (D) had used previously—feature the same color on the entire shoe, so that the red version is all red, including a red insole, heel, upper, and outsole. Louboutin (P) brought suit against YSL (D) to enforce Louboutin's (P) trademark and to preliminarily enjoin YSL (D) from using a red outsole on YSL's (D) footwear. The district court, ruling that a single color can never be protected by trademark in the fashion industry, reasoned that Louboutin's (P) trademark likely was unenforceable, and declined to issue the requested injunction. The court of appeals granted review.

ISSUE: Under the aesthetic functionality test, can a single color serve as a legally protected trademark in the fashion industry where the use of the color is such that it does not significantly hinder competition?

HOLDING AND DECISION: (Cabranes, J.) Yes. Under the aesthetic functionality test, a single color can serve as a legally protected trademark in the fashion industry where the use of the color is such that it does not significantly hinder competition. Under the aesthetic functionality test, if a design feature is considered "essential to the use or purpose" of the article, or to affect its cost or quality, then the design feature is functional and that ends

the inquiry. If, however, the design feature is not "functional" from this traditional perspective, and is shown not to have a significant effect on competition, it may receive trademark protection. The inquiry into whether the design significantly impacts competition is fact-intensive and asks whether configurations of ornamental features would significantly limit the range of competitive designs available. Thus, the aesthetic functionality doctrine bars protection of a mark that is necessary to compete in the relevant market, but does not bar trademark protection where distinctive and arbitrary arrangements of predominantly ornamental features do not hinder potential competitors from entering the same market with differently dressed versions of the product. In making this determination, courts must carefully weigh the competitive benefits of protecting the source-identifying aspects of a mark against the competitive costs of precluding competitors from using the feature. Additionally, courts must ensure that a mark's very success in denoting and promoting its source does not itself defeat the mark holder's right to protect that mark. In *Qualitex Co. v. Jacobson Products Co.*, 514 U.S. 159 (1995), the United States Supreme Court specifically forbade the implementation of a per se rule that would deny protection for the use of a single color as a trademark in a particular industrial context. Instead, *Qualitex* requires an individualized, fact-based inquiry into the nature of the trademark. Here, the district court created precisely the kind of per se rule that the Supreme Court forbade, and, accordingly, the district court erred in doing so. It must be remembered that the functionality defense is designed to prevent a mark holder from monopolizing a functional design, but it does not guarantee a competitor the greatest range for the competitor's creative outlet, but only the ability to fairly compete within a given market. Thus, by focusing upon hindrances to legitimate competition, the aesthetic functionality test, carefully applied, can accommodate consumers' somewhat conflicting interests in being assured enough product differentiation to avoid confusion as to source and in being afforded the benefits of competition among producers. Here, Louboutin's (P) trademark is limited to uses in which the red outsole contrasts with the remainder of the shoe (known as the "upper"). The trademark, as thus modified, is entitled to trademark protection. However, the monochrome design employed by YSL (D) is not a use of Louboutin's (P) modified trademark. Accordingly, although the district court erred in announcing a per se rule against protecting the use of a single color in the fashion industry, the district court correctly denied the

Continued on next page.

preliminary injunction sought by Louboutin (P). [Affirmed in part, reversed in part, and remanded.]

▶ *ANALYSIS*

It is arguable that, in the particular circumstances of this case, the more appropriate vehicle for the protection of Louboutin's (P) red sole mark would have been copyright rather than trademark. In this regard, the case serves to demonstrate the sharp contrast between the trademark system and the copyright system. Copyright, unlike trademark, rewards creativity and originality even if they interfere with the rights of an existing copyright holder. In the copyright system, there is a defense to infringement known as "independent creation": if a writer or musician, through the creative process, independently arrives at an arrangement of words or notes that is the subject of a copyright, she may market the result of her creativity despite the existing copyright. The trademark system, unlike the copyright system, aims to prevent consumer confusion even at the expense of a manufacturer's creativity: in trademark, if a branding specialist produces a mark that is identical to one already trademarked by another individual or corporation, she must "go back to the drawing board."

Quicknotes

PER SE An activity that is so inherently obvious that it is unnecessary to examine its underlying validity.

Pro-Football, Inc. v. Harjo

Professional football team owner (P) v. Native American (D)

565 F.3d 880 (D.C. Cir. 2009).

NATURE OF CASE: Appeal from dismissal of trademark disparagement action on grounds of laches.

FACT SUMMARY: Seven Native Americans (D) contended that the owner of the Washington Redskins professional football team, Pro-Football, Inc. (P), failed to demonstrate sufficient trial or economic prejudice from their nearly eight-year delay in bringing their trademark disparagement action.

🏛 RULE OF LAW
Laches will bar the cancellation of a trademark where the delay of the party seeking cancellation in bringing the cancellation action harms the mark holder through trial and economic prejudice.

FACTS: Pro-Football, Inc. (P), the owner of the Washington Redskins professional football team, registered six "Redskins" trademarks starting in 1967. At the time, Redskins' president Williams met with Native American leaders to discuss their views. In 1992, seven Native Americans (D) filed suit seeking to have the "Redskins" marks cancelled on the grounds that they were disparaging to members of their ethnic group. Pro-Football (P) defended before the Trademark Trial and Appeal Board (the TTAB) by arguing that its long-standing use of the "Redskins" name, combined with the Native Americans' (D) delay in bringing the case, called for application of the defense of laches, which applies where there is (1) lack of diligence by the party against whom the defense is asserted, and (2) prejudice to the party asserting the defense. The TTAB rejected the defense, and, finding the marks disparaging, cancelled them. Pro-Football (P) then brought a civil action in district court challenging the TTAB's decision. The district court agreed with Pro-Football (P) that laches was applicable, finding that the 25-year delay between the mark's first registration in 1967 and the TTAB filing in 1992 required dismissal. The court of appeals reversed, holding that the period of unjustifiable delay necessary to support a laches defense cannot start before a plaintiff reaches the age of majority, and since the youngest plaintiff, Romero, was only a year old in 1967, the delay and the consequent prejudice to Pro-Football (P) had to be considered only from when he turned 18 in 1984. On remand, the district court held that the nearly eight-year "Romero Delay Period" evinced a lack of diligence on Romero's part, and harmed Pro-Football (P) through both trial and economic prejudice. In reaching this conclusion, the district court relied on the fact that Williams died during the "Romero Delay Period," causing the unavailability of his testimony regarding the Native American view expressed to

him in 1967 (since disparagement is measured as of the time of registration). The district court also relied on the delay period's general contribution to the time lapse from the date of registration. The court of appeals granted review.

ISSUE: Will laches bar the cancellation of a trademark where the delay of the party seeking cancellation in bringing the cancellation action harms the mark holder through trial and economic prejudice?

HOLDING AND DECISION: (Tatel, J.) Yes. Laches will bar the cancellation of a trademark where the delay of the party seeking cancellation in bringing the cancellation action harms the mark holder through trial and economic prejudice. The narrow question presented here is whether the district court properly found trial and economic prejudice sufficient to support a laches defense. The district court concluded that Romero's delay limited Pro-Football's (P) ability to marshal evidence supporting its mark, since Williams's death resulted in the loss of contemporaneous evidence of public attitudes towards the mark. The lost evidence of contemporaneous public opinion was not entirely irrelevant, and weighing the prejudice resulting from its loss fell well within the zone of the district court's discretion. Thus, even if, as Romero argues, Williams's testimony would have had minimal value, since it would have reflected only a narrow set of views on the disparaging nature of the "Redskins" marks, the district court did not abuse its discretion, since it cannot be assumed that legally relevant evidence possibly available in an earlier action would have lacked persuasive content. Thus, the district court did not abuse its discretion in finding trial prejudice to Pro-Football (P) from the "Romero Delay Period." Similarly, the district court did not abuse its discretion in finding that Romero's delay also caused economic prejudice to Pro-Football (P), which during this period made a sizeable investment in its marks and merchandising efforts. The district court did not abuse its discretion in rejecting Romero's argument that Pro-Football (P), in addition to showing it invested in its mark, had to show that it would have acted differently, e.g., by changing the "Redskins" name, if Romero had sued earlier. Economic prejudice arises from investment in and development of a trademark, and the continued commercial use and economic promotion of a mark over a prolonged period adds weight to the evidence of prejudice. In other words, laches requires only general evidence of prejudice, which may arise from mere proof of continued investment

Continued on next page.

in the late-attacked mark alone. Accordingly, the lost value of Pro-Football's (P) investments was sufficient evidence of prejudice for the district court to exercise its discretion to apply laches, even absent specific evidence that more productive investments would in fact have resulted from an earlier suit. In so holding, it should be kept in mind that laches is an equitable defense, which requires the weighing of the length of the delay against the amount of prejudice inflicted. This equitable weighing leaves the district court very broad discretion to take account of the particular facts of particular cases. Under the particular facts of this case, it cannot be said that the district court abused its relatively broad discretion. Affirmed.

▶ ANALYSIS

In contrast to the defense of estoppel, which requires evidence of specific reliance on a particular plaintiff's silence, laches requires only general evidence of prejudice, which, as this case emphasizes, may arise from mere proof of continued investment in the attacked mark alone. Thus, when there has been an unreasonable period of delay by a plaintiff, economic prejudice to the defendant may ensue whether or not the plaintiff overtly lulled the defendant into believing that the plaintiff would not act, or whether or not the defendant believed that the plaintiff would have grounds for action.

■=■

Quicknotes

ESTOPPEL An equitable doctrine precluding a party from asserting a right to the detriment of another who justifiably relied on the conduct.

LACHES An equitable defense against the enforcement of rights that have been neglected for a long period of time.

■=■

New Kids on the Block v. News America Publishing

Singing group (P) v. Publisher (D)

971 F.2d 302 (9th Cir. 1992).

NATURE OF CASE: Appeal of a defense summary judgment in trademark infringement and Lanham Act suit.

FACT SUMMARY: New Kids on the Block (P), a popular singing group, brought suit on a wide variety of trademark and unfair competition claims against News America Publishing (D) for running a series of newspaper articles geared to a fan poll as to who was the most popular member of the group.

RULE OF LAW

The conducting of an unauthorized poll using a person's name does not necessarily imply that such person is sponsoring the poll so as to violate trademark, false advertising, or unfair competition laws.

FACTS: News America Publishing (D) ran a series of newspaper articles consisting of a public opinion poll by which fans of the popular singing group New Kids on the Block (NKOTB) (P), could phone in (for a fee) and state which member of the group was the most popular and sexiest. NKOTB (P) brought a ten-count "shotgun" complaint against News America Publishing (D) for running the poll, based on trademark infringement, Lanham Act false advertising, unfair competition, misappropriation, and intentional interference with prospective economic advantage. The federal district court rendered summary judgment for News America Publishing (D), and NKOTB (P) appealed.

ISSUE: Does the conducting of an unauthorized poll using a person's name necessarily imply that such person is sponsoring the polls so as to violate trademark, false advertising, or unfair competition laws?

HOLDING AND DECISION: (Kozinski, J.) No. NKOTB (P) did not claim there was anything false or misleading about the newspaper's (D) use of its mark. Rather, most of the allegations focused on their argument that the newspaper's public poll (as to which member of the group was sexiest) somehow implied that NKOTB (P) was sponsoring the poll, yet it was clear this was not the case. Trademark protection does not extend to rendering newspaper articles, conversations, polls, and comparative advertising impossible. The newspaper's reference to NKOTB (P) was only to the extent necessary to identify its members as the subject of the polls; the newspaper did not use group's distinctive logo or anything else that was not needed to make the announcements intelligible to readers. Finally, nothing in the announcements suggested any joint sponsorship or endorsement by NKOTB (P).

While the group members have a limited property right in their name, that right does not entitle them to control their fans' use of their own money. Affirmed.

▶ ANALYSIS

The court noted that, as to the claim for intentional interference with prospective economic advantage, "all's fair in love, war, and the free market" and that it is no tort to beat a business rival to prospective customers.

■■■

Quicknotes

TRADEMARK Any word, name, symbol, device or combination thereof that is either currently utilized, or which a person has a bona fide intent to utilize, in commerce in order to distinguish his goods from those of another.

UNFAIR COMPETITION Any dishonest or fraudulent rivalry in trade and commerce, particularly imitation and counterfeiting.

■■■

WCVB-TV v. Boston Athletic Association

Television station (D) v. Marathon sponsor (P)

926 F.2d 42 (1st Cir. 1991).

NATURE OF CASE: Appeal from denial of injunction in action for trademark infringement.

FACT SUMMARY: The Boston Athletic Association (BAA) (P), which owned the trade and service mark "Boston Marathon," contended that WCVB-TV (Channel 5) (D), a television station, infringed the trademark by broadcasting the words "Boston Marathon" before, during, and after its unlicensed broadcast of a prior BAA (P) marathon event, and would do so again, thus necessitating an injunction to prevent Channel 5 (D) from again infringing BAA's (P) trademark.

🏛 **RULE OF LAW**
There is no trademark infringement where the use of a mark is descriptive and not likely to cause confusion.

FACTS: The Boston Athletic Association (BAA) (P) has spent a lot of money promoting the annual Boston Marathon and has a registered trade and service mark in the term "Boston Marathon." For a fee, it licensed a television station (Channel 4) to broadcast the event. WCVB-TV (Channel 5) (D), a different television station, was not licensed to broadcast the event or use the trademark, but nevertheless broadcast the prior year's event and broadcast the words "Boston Marathon" before, during and after its broadcast of the event; Channel 5 (D) intended to do so again during the current year's upcoming event. Channel 5 (D) offered to broadcast whatever disclaimers the BAA (P) might want, at BAA's (P) specified time intervals—from every 30 seconds to every 10 minutes—to ensure the public was not led to believe that Channel 5 (D) had any special broadcasting status. Notwithstanding this offer, BAA (P) brought suit to enjoin Channel 5's (D) use of the words "Boston Marathon," but the district court refused to issue the requested preliminary injunction. The First Circuit Court of Appeals granted review.

ISSUE: Is there trademark infringement where the use of a mark is descriptive and not likely to cause confusion?

HOLDING AND DECISION: (Breyer, J.) No. There is no trademark infringement where the use of a mark is descriptive and not likely to cause confusion. The dispositive legal issue is whether there was a likelihood of consumer confusion arising from Channel 5's (D) use of the words "Boston Marathon." Although this is not a classic case of trademark use by a head-to-head competitor—after all, Channel 5 (D) is not sponsoring its own marathon on the same day that BAA (P) is sponsoring its marathon—there is the possibility that Channel 5's (D) use

of the mark could confuse the public into believing that it has BAA's (P) official imprimatur. However, the evidence does not support such likelihood. Moreover, there is no rebuttable presumption of confusion here because there was no demonstrable intent to use the words "Boston Marathon" to suggest official sponsorship of Channel 5's (D) broadcasts, or to profit from any confusion that might so arise. To the contrary, it is not unreasonable to believe that television viewers merely wish to see the event and do not particularly care about the relation of the station to the event-promoter. Finally, and critically, Channel 5's (D) use of the words "Boston Marathon" was descriptive of the event Channel 5 (D) was broadcasting and thus would not confuse the typical viewer. Such a descriptive use is a fair use permitted under trademark law. Channel 5's (D) use of the mark was thus not deceptive and was not being used primarily as an "attention-getting symbol." For all these reasons, BAA (P) has not shown a real likelihood of relevant confusion. Affirmed.

▶ **ANALYSIS**

In reaching its decision, the court in this case distinguished an earlier case, also involving BAA (P), *Boston Athletic Assn. v. Sullivan*, 867 F.2d 22 (1st Cir. 1989), where it had held that use of BAA's (P) service marks on shirts sold to fans created a rebuttable presumption of confusion as to sponsorship where the (1) defendant intentionally referred to the Boston Marathon on its shirts, and (2) purchasers were likely to buy the shirts precisely because of that reference. The court in this case interpreted *Sullivan* to mean that the rebuttable presumption of confusion will arise where the alleged infringer intends to suggest official sponsorship and to profit from this deception. Here, the court found no such intent to deceive, or even the ability to profit from any confusion that might result, and hence rejected the availability of the rebuttable presumption. The court also emphasized that *Sullivan*, taken as a whole, did not intend to depart from the bedrock trademark law principle that a likelihood of confusion is necessary to a finding of a trademark violation.

▃▀▃

Quicknotes

INJUNCTION A court order requiring a person to do, or prohibiting that person from doing, a specific act.

TRADEMARK INFRINGEMENT The unauthorized use of another's trademark in such a manner as to cause a

Continued on next page.

likelihood of confusion as to the source of the product or service in connection with which it is utilized.

■■■

Smith v. Chanel

Perfume duplicator (D) v. Original perfume manufacturer (P)

402 F.2d 562 (9th Cir. 1968).

NATURE OF CASE: Appeal from preliminary injunction enjoining use of trademark in advertising.

FACT SUMMARY: Smith d/b/a Ta'Ron, Inc. (D), which advertised a fragrance claimed to duplicate Chanel, Inc.'s (P) "Chanel No. 5" perfume and referred to "Chanel No. 5" in the advertising, contended that it did not violate Chanel's (P) trademarks.

🏛 RULE OF LAW
One who has copied an unpatented product sold under a trademark may use the trademark in his advertising to identify the product he has copied provided such use does not create a likelihood of confusion and is not misleading.

FACTS: Smith d/b/a Ta'Ron, Inc. (D) created a line of perfumes, called "The Ta'Ron Line of Perfumes," that duplicated the exact scents of the world's finest and most expensive perfumes and colognes. Smith advertised this line of perfumes. In particular, one advertisement suggested that a blindfold test would make it impossible to detect any difference between Ta'Ron's (D) "Second Chance" perfume and Chanel, Inc.'s (P) "Chanel No. 5" perfume, which sold for over three times as much as Second Chance. An order form also paired Second Chance with Chanel No. 5. Chanel (P) sought and obtained a preliminary injunction prohibiting any reference to "Chanel No. 5" in the promotion or sale of Smith's (D) product. Chanel (P) conceded at trial that Smith (D) had the right to copy and duplicate Chanel No. 5, which was unpatented, and that Second Chance had the exact same scent as Chanel No. 5. Chanel (P) also did not claim that the packaging or labeling of Second Chance was misleading or confusing. The Ninth Circuit Court of Appeals granted review.

ISSUE: May one who has copied an unpatented product sold under a trademark use the trademark in his advertising to identify the product he has copied provided such use does not create a likelihood of confusion and is not misleading?

HOLDING AND DECISION: (Browning, J.) Yes. One who has copied an unpatented product sold under a trademark may use the trademark in his advertising to identify the product he has copied provided such use does not create a likelihood of confusion and is not misleading. This rule is supported by precedent, which has held that articles may be reproduced if not patented and may be sold with the representation that the articles are identical, so long as the seller does not claim they are the originator's. Thus, where there is no evidence of deception

or confusion as to origin or sponsorship, a trademark violation does not occur, whether under the Lanham Act or common law. This result stems from the traditionally accepted premise that the only legally relevant function of a trademark is to impart information as to source or sponsorship, which in turn promotes effective competition in a complex, impersonal marketplace. An additional consideration is that the copying of unpatented goods serves the public interest by fostering competition and the unimpeded availability of substantially equivalent units that permits the normal operation of supply and demand to yield the fair price society must pay for a given commodity. This benefit could be lost if imitators were prohibited from telling potential purchasers that their product is equivalent to that of an originator—and cheaper. A contrary result would in effect give the originator a perpetual monopoly on its product. While it is true that the originator has expended effort, skill, ability and money in building up goodwill in its product, a large expenditure of these does not in itself create legally protectable rights. The copyist's opportunism is supported in deference to the greater public good, since the public is served by having comparable goods at lower prices. And, if it turns out the copyist's product is inferior to the originator's, the copyist will bear the burden of consumer disapproval since the copyist has made it known to consumers that the product is the copyist's. Finally, the argument that the originator's trademark is diluted must be rejected. The uniqueness and distinctiveness of the originator's mark is not threatened because the copyist does not use the mark as a generic term. Instead, it is only used to identify the originator's product, not that of the copyist. Here, for example, Smith's (D) use of "Chanel No. 5" does not challenge the distinctiveness of that mark, or of Chanel's (P) exclusive right to use that mark to indicate source or sponsorship. Reversed.

▶ ANALYSIS

It has been suggested that protection of trademark values other than source identification, as urged in this case by Chanel (P), would create serious anti-competitive consequences with little compensating public benefit. To the extent that a trademark were endowed with sales appeal independent of the quality or price of the product to which it was attached, economically irrational elements could be introduced into consumer choices and the trademark owner could be insulated from the normal pressures of price and quality competition. Consequently, the competi-

Continued on next page.

tive system might fail to perform its function of allocating available resources efficiently.

∎══∎

Quicknotes

DISTINCTIVENESS A standard for trademark protection, whereby the more distinctive a mark is, the greater its eligibility for protection. Distinctive marks typically consist of terms that are fanciful or coined, arbitrary, or suggestive. If a mark is descriptive, it is not entitled to trademark protection unless it has acquired distinctiveness through consumer association of goods or services with the mark (such acquired distinctiveness is also known as secondary meaning).

GENERIC MEANING A term that encompasses a class of related products and lacks the requisite distinctiveness for federal trademark protection.

TRADEMARK DILUTION The diminishment of the capability of a trademark to identify and distinguish the particular good or service with which it is associated.

TRADEMARK INFRINGEMENT The unauthorized use of another's trademark in such a manner as to cause a likelihood of confusion as to the source of the product or service in connection with which it is utilized.

∎══∎

College Savings Bank v. Florida Prepaid Postsecondary Education Expense Board

Bank (P) v. State agency (D)

527 U.S. 666 (1999).

NATURE OF CASE: Appeal from affirmance of dismissal of action under the Trademark Remedy Clarification Act for false and misleading advertising.

FACT SUMMARY: College Savings Bank (P), which helped students finance their education, brought suit under the Trademark Remedy Clarification Act against the Florida Prepaid Postsecondary Education Expense Board (Florida Prepaid) (D), a state agency, claiming that Florida Prepaid (D) made misstatements about its tuition savings plans. Florida Prepaid (D), claiming sovereign immunity, sought dismissal of the action.

🏛 RULE OF LAW
The federal courts do not have jurisdiction to entertain a suit against a state agency under the Trademark Remedy Clarification Act (TRCA) for false and misleading advertising where the state's sovereign immunity is neither validly abrogated by the TRCA nor voluntarily waived.

FACTS: College Savings Bank (College Savings) (P), which helped students finance their education, brought suit under the Trademark Remedy Clarification Act (TRCA) against the Florida Prepaid Postsecondary Education Expense Board (Florida Prepaid) (D), a state agency, claiming that Florida Prepaid (D) made misstatements about its tuition savings plans. The TCRA subjects the states to suits brought under § 43(a) of the Lanham Act for false and misleading advertising and provides that state entities are not immune, under the Eleventh Amendment or any other doctrine of sovereign immunity, from suit. Florida Prepaid (D), claiming sovereign immunity, sought dismissal of the action. The district court granted the motion to dismiss, and the court of appeals affirmed. The United States Supreme Court granted certiorari.

ISSUE: Do the federal courts have jurisdiction to entertain a suit against a state agency under the Trademark Remedy Clarification Act (TRCA) for false and misleading advertising where the state's sovereign immunity is neither validly abrogated by the TRCA nor voluntarily waived?

HOLDING AND DECISION: (Scalia, J.) No. The federal courts do not have jurisdiction to entertain a suit against a state agency under the Trademark Remedy Clarification Act (TRCA) for false and misleading advertising where the state's sovereign immunity is neither validly abrogated by the TRCA nor voluntarily waived. There are only two circumstances where an individual may sue a

state. First, an individual may sue a state where Congress has validly authorized such a suit in the exercise of its power to enforce the Fourteenth Amendment, and second, where the state has waived its sovereign immunity by consenting to suit. Here, neither of those circumstances is present. The state's sovereign immunity was not validly abrogated by the TRCA. Congress may legislate under § 5 of the Fourteenth Amendment to enforce the Amendment's other provisions, but the object of such legislation must be the remediation or prevention of constitutional violations. College Savings' (P) argument that Congress enacted the TRCA to remedy and prevent state deprivations of two property interests without due process is rejected, for neither a right to be free from a business competitor's false advertising about its own product nor a right to be secure in one's business interests qualifies as a protected property right. As to the first, the hallmark of a constitutionally protected property interest is the right to exclude others. The Lanham Act's false-advertising provisions bear no relationship to any right to exclude, and Florida Prepaid's (D) alleged misrepresentation concerning its own products intruded upon no interest over which College Savings (P) had exclusive dominion. Also, the state's sovereign immunity was not voluntarily waived by its activities in interstate commerce. Generally, waiver occurs when a state voluntarily invokes, or clearly declares that it intends to submit itself to, the jurisdiction of the federal courts. College Savings (P) maintains that an implied or constructive waiver is possible when Congress provides unambiguously that a state will be subject to private suit if it engages in certain federally regulated conduct and the state voluntarily elects to engage in that conduct. The precedent relied on by College Savings (P) for this position, *Parden v. Terminal R. Co. of Ala. Docks Dept.*, 377 U.S. 184 (1964), has been limited by subsequent cases, and its discussion of congressional intent to negate Eleventh Amendment immunity has been overruled. In any event, *Parden*'s experiment with constructive waiver was ill-conceived and is now expressly overruled. Even when supplemented by a requirement of unambiguous statement of congressional intent to subject the states to suit, *Parden* cannot be squared with this Court's cases requiring that a state's express waiver of sovereign immunity be unequivocal. Recognizing constructive waivers of sovereign immunity would permit Congress to circumvent this Court's antiabrogation cases, and it is irrelevant that the asserted basis for constructive waiver is conduct by the state that is undertaken for profit, that is traditionally

Continued on next page.

performed by private entities, and that otherwise resembles the behavior of market participants. Since sovereign immunity itself was not traditionally limited by these factors, and since they have no bearing upon the voluntariness of the waiver, there is no principled reason why they should enter a waiver analysis. Affirmed.

DISSENT: (Stevens, J.) The majority's assumptions are wrong. First, it is doubtful that Florida Prepaid (D) should be assumed to be an arm of the state for purposes of the TRCA because, unlike state agents in the 18th century, it plays an active role in the commercial marketplace. Second, the majority assumes there has not been a deprivation of College Savings' (P) property. Neither of these assumptions is relevant to the core issue, which is whether Congress had the constitutional power to authorize suits against states for Lanham Act violations. The Constitution grants Congress ample power to do so in § 5 of the Fourteenth Amendment, which authorizes Congress to enact appropriate legislation to prevent deprivations of property without due process. Here, even if Florida Prepaid's (D) false advertising did not violate the Constitution, it deprived College Savings (P) of property in the form of good will and its business; a "state's deliberate destruction of a going business is surely a deprivation of property within the meaning of the Due Process Clause."

▶ *ANALYSIS*

Contrary to the dissent's opinion, the majority stated that as to the second asserted property interest—the right to be secure in one's business interests—while a business's assets are property, and any state taking of those assets is a "deprivation," business in the sense of the activity of doing business or of making a profit is not property at all—and it is only that which is impinged upon by a competitor's false advertising about its own product.

Quicknotes

SOVEREIGN IMMUNITY Immunity of government from suit without its consent.

Rogers v. Grimaldi

Celebrity (P) v. Film producer (D)

875 F.2d 994 (2d Cir. 1989).

NATURE OF CASE: Appeal from summary judgment dismissing common-law rights of publicity and privacy claims and a claim for false advertising under § 43(a) of the Lanham Act.

FACT SUMMARY: The celebrity Ginger Rogers (P) contended that producers (D) and distributors (D) of the motion picture "Ginger and Fred" violated § 43(a) of the Lanham Act and infringed her common-law rights of publicity and privacy because the fictional movie only obliquely related to her and her famous dance and film partner, Fred Astaire.

🏛 RULE OF LAW
(1) A movie title that references a celebrity's name does not violate § 43(a) of the Lanham Act where it has minimal artistic relevance to the movie's content and is at most ambiguous or implicitly misleading.
(2) A state right of publicity claim for use of a celebrity's name in a title of a fictional work, which is related to the content of the work and not a disguised ad for a good or service, is barred where the state interprets its free speech clause broadly.

FACTS: Ginger Rogers (P) and Fred Astaire are among the most famous show business duos in history, appearing in numerous shows and movies together as dance and acting partners for over 40 years. Their names are internationally recognized, especially when paired together, and even the pairing of their first names calls to mind their identities. Rogers's (P) name alone had enormous drawing power in the entertainment world, and she used her name in connection with a commercial enterprise. Without consulting with Rogers (P), a resident of Oregon, producers (D) and distributors (D) titled a movie "Ginger and Fred." The movie, created and directed by the famous Italian director, Federico Fellini, told the story of two fictional Italian cabaret performers who imitated Rogers (P) and Astaire and became known in Italy as "Ginger and Fred." The film focused on a television reunion of these performers many years after their retirement. Rogers (P) brought suit, seeking permanent injunctive relief and money damages, claiming that the producers (D) and distributors (D) violated § 43(a) of the Lanham Act by creating the false impression that the film was about her or that she sponsored, endorsed, or was otherwise affiliated with the film, and that they infringed her common-law rights of publicity and privacy as codified by New York statute. Rogers (P) presented evidence of actual consumer confusion through survey and other evi-

dence. The district court granted summary judgment to the producers (D) and distributors (D), finding that the use of Rogers's (P) first name in the title of the movie was an exercise of artistic expression entitled to First Amendment protection. Because the use was not commercial, the court ruled that the Lanham Act was inapplicable. The court also held that the First Amendment concerns barred the state law rights of publicity and privacy claims. The court ruled that where a motion picture title is within the realm of artistic expression and relates to the film's content, it does not violate the Lanham Act. The Second Circuit Court of Appeals granted review.

ISSUE:
(1) Does a movie title that references a celebrity's name violate § 43(a) of the Lanham Act where it has minimal artistic relevance to the movie's content and is at most ambiguous or implicitly misleading?
(2) Is a state right of publicity claim for use of a celebrity's name in a title of a fictional work, which is related to the content of the work and not a disguised ad for a good or service, barred where the state interprets its free speech clause broadly?

HOLDING AND DECISION: (Newman, J.) (1) No. A movie title that references a celebrity's name does not violate § 43(a) of the Lanham Act where it has minimal artistic relevance to the movie's content and is at most ambiguous or implicitly misleading. In deciding this issue, a balance must be struck between First Amendment concerns and the celebrity's rights and protection of the public. Movies and other creative works are indisputably works of artistic expression deserving of First Amendment protection, but they are also commercial products, making the danger of consumer deception a legitimate concern. Thus, where a title of a creative work has acquired secondary meaning, the holder of the rights thereto may prevent the use of the same or confusingly similar titles by other authors. Because titles may be both an integral part of the work as well as a significant means of marketing the work, consumers of artistic works also have an interest in not being misled by a title, and also have an interest in enjoying the results of the author's freedom of expression. Therefore, the expressive element of titles requires more protection than the labeling of ordinary commercial products. Because the Lanham Act must be construed narrowly so as not to impinge on First Amendment rights, the argument propounded by Rogers (P), that First Amendment concerns are only implicated where a title is so intimately related to the work's subject matter that the

Continued on next page.

author has no alternative means of expressing what the work is about, must be rejected. Such a "no alternative" standard provides insufficient leeway for literary expression and the public's interest in such expression. The district court's standard—that the Lanham Act does not apply to any titles that can be considered artistic expression—goes too far in the other direction by insufficiently protecting the public from flagrant deception. Thus, in the context of allegedly misleading titles using a celebrity's name, the Act will normally not apply unless the title has no artistic relevance to the underlying work whatsoever, or, if it has some artistic relevance, unless the title explicitly misleads as to the source or the content of the work. Where a title is misleading and has no artistic relevance, it cannot be justified by a freedom of expression interest. Even titles that have minimal artistic relevance may include explicit statements about the work's content that are seriously misleading. Such titles also are not justified by First Amendment concerns. However, as in this case, many titles with a celebrity's name may make no explicit statement that the work is about the celebrity in any direct sense, and the reference will only be oblique and may become clear only after viewing or reading the work. As to such titles, the consumer interest in avoiding deception is too slight to warrant application of the Lanham Act. This, in part, is because most consumers of artistic works know that they cannot judge the contents of the work based solely on the title. Accordingly, where a title with some artistic relevance to the work is not explicitly misleading, it is not false advertising under the Act. Applying this standard to Rogers' (P) claim, it is undisputed that the title at issue has minimal artistic relevance to the movie's content. The nicknames of the cabaret performers have genuine relevance to the film's story. The title also does not contain any explicit indication that Rogers (P) endorsed the film or had a role in producing it. Even assuming that Rogers's (P) survey evidence of actual consumer confusion is valid, the risk that some members of the public will draw the incorrect inference that Rogers (P) is involved with the movie is outweighed by the interests in artistic expression, so application of the Lanham Act is precluded. Rogers's (P) claim that consumers will be misled that the movie is about her and Astaire also fails. Even though there is no doubt that, based on the title some consumers will believe the movie is biographical, the title is also truthful as it relates to the film's content. The title also is ironic, in that, according to Fellini, Rogers and Astaire were to him "a glamorous and care-free symbol of what American cinema represented during the harsh times which Italy experienced in the 1930s and 1940s." In the film, he contrasts this elegance and class to the gaudiness and banality of contemporary television, which he satirizes. Therefore, the title is not misleading, but instead is an integral element of the film and the filmmaker's artistic expressions. Any confusion engendered by the title is outweighed by the danger that artistic expression will be suppressed. Affirmed as to this issue.

(2) Yes. A state right of publicity claim for use of a celebrity's name in a title of a fictional work, which is related to the content of the work and not a disguised ad for a good or service, is barred where the state interprets its free speech clause broadly. The district court did not reach the issue of which state's right of publicity law would apply to Rogers's (P) state law claims as a matter of constitutional law. The correct approach is to decide the choice of law issue first and then determine if there is a triable claim under the applicable substantive law before reaching constitutional issues. This suit was brought in New York, and, therefore, the federal courts must apply the choice of law rules of New York. Those rules require application of the plaintiff's domicile, which here is Oregon. Oregon courts have not determined the scope of the right of publicity. However, New York courts would determine as best they can what the other state's courts would do. Here, New York courts would likely find that Oregon would bar the claims, given that the Oregon Supreme Court has interpreted that state's free speech clause as providing broader protections that those in the federal Constitution. Other courts, interpreting New York law, have also refused to extend the right of publicity to bar the use of a celebrity's name in the title and text of a fictional or semi-fictional movie or book where the use of the name is neither "wholly unrelated" to the individual nor used to promote or endorse a collateral commercial product. Thus, because "Ginger and Fred" is clearly related to the content of the movie and is not a disguised ad for the sale of goods and services or a collateral commercial product, under Oregon law the right of publicity would not provide relief for Rogers's (P) claim. Affirmed as to this issue.

▶ *ANALYSIS*

Rogers has hitherto been the seminal case on conflicts between trademark rights and First Amendment concerns. Arguably, as new technologies and types of entertainment expand, it is likely that what makes a title or creative element "artistically relevant" and "explicitly misleading" will have to evolve to accommodate the new entertainment environment. For example, in *E.S.S. Entertainment 2000, Inc. v. Rock Star Videos, Inc.*, 2008 WL 4791705 (9th Cir. 2008), involving the altered portrayal in a video game of a Los Angeles strip club, the Ninth Circuit expanded Rogers by holding that with creative works, the First Amendment balancing test set forth in Rogers extends beyond use of a mark or name to reach use of the mark, name, or trade dress within a work's content. In doing so, the court indicated that the first prong of the Rogers test, whether the title is artistically relevant to the work, is satisfied where the relevance is "above zero," thus providing a very low threshold for authors to meet in rebuffing Lanham Act challenges to their uses.

■=■

Continued on next page.

Quicknotes

RIGHT OF PUBLICITY   The right of a person to control the commercial exploitation of his name or likeness.

RIGHT TO PRIVACY   An individual's right to be protected against unwarranted interference in his personal affairs, falling into one of four categories: (1) appropriating the individual's likeness or name for commercial benefit; (2) intrusion into the individual's seclusion; (3) public disclosure of private facts regarding the individual; and (4) disclosure of facts placing the individual in a false light.

■═■

Louis Vuitton Malletier S.A. v. Warner Brothers Entertainment Inc.

High-fashion designer (P) v. Movie studio (D)

868 F. Supp. 2d 172 (S.D.N.Y. 2012).

NATURE OF CASE: Motion to dismiss in action for, inter alia, false designation of origin/unfair competition in violation of § 43(a) of the Lanham Act.

FACT SUMMARY: Louis Vuitton Malletier S.A. (Louis Vuitton) (P), a high-fashion designer, contended that movie studio Warner Brothers Entertainment Inc.'s (Warner Brothers') (D) use of a knockoff Louis Vuitton (P) travel bag, made by Diophy, in the film "The Hangover: Part II," violated Louis Vuitton's (P) trademarks by confusing the public into believing that the Diophy bag was an authentic Louis Vuitton (P) product and that Louis Vuitton (P) had sponsored and approved Warner Brothers' (D) use and misrepresentation of the infringing Diophy bag as a genuine product of Louis Vuitton (P). Warner Brothers (D) moved to dismiss for failure to state a claim.

🏛 **RULE OF LAW**

A trademark action under § 43(a) of the Lanham Act will be dismissed for failure to state a claim upon which relief can be granted where the defendant's use of the plaintiff's mark is made in an artistic work and is (1) "artistically relevant" to the work and (2) not "explicitly misleading" as to the source or content of the work.

FACTS: Warner Brothers Entertainment Inc. (Warner Brothers) (D), the venerable movie studio, used a knockoff Louis Vuitton (P) travel bag, made by Diophy, in the film "The Hangover: Part II." Louis Vuitton Malletier S.A. (Louis Vuitton) (P) is a high-fashion designer known for its distinctive Toile Monogram. Diophy is a company that creates products that use a monogram design that is a knockoff of the famous Toile Monogram (the "Knock-Off Monogram Design"). The Diophy products bearing the Knock-Off Monogram Design have been extensively distributed throughout the United States, causing enormous harm to Louis Vuitton (P). Despite the inferior quality of Diophy's products, demand for its products bearing the Knock-Off Monogram Design remains high because they are far less expensive than genuine Louis Vuitton (P) products. In "The Hangover: Part II," Alan, one of the characters, is carrying what appears to be a matching over-the-shoulder Louis Vuitton (P) "Keepall" bag, but it is actually an infringing Diophy bag. Moments later, Alan is seen sitting on a bench in the airport lounge and places his bag on the empty seat next to him. Another character, Stu, who is sitting in the chair to the other side of the bag, moves the bag, and Alan reacts by saying: "Careful that is . . . that is a Lewis Vuitton." No other reference to Louis

Vuitton (P) or the Diophy bag is made after this point. Louis Vuitton (P) sent Warner Brothers (D) a cease and desist letter noting its objection to the use of the Diophy bag in the movie, but Warner Brothers (D) did not stop its distribution of the movie. Louis Vuitton (P) then brought suit, asserting claims for, inter alia, false designation of origin/unfair competition in violation of § 43(a) of the Lanham Act. Specifically, Louis Vuitton (P) alleged that use of the Diophy bag in the film confused the public into believing that the Diophy bag was an authentic Louis Vuitton (P) product and that Louis Vuitton (P) had sponsored and approved Warner Brothers' (D) use and misrepresentation of the infringing Diophy bag as a genuine product of Louis Vuitton (P). Louis Vuitton (P) alleged that it had been harmed by the prominent use of the aforementioned scenes and its trademarks in commercials and advertisements for the movie, and that Alan's "Lewis Vuitton" line had "become an oft-repeated and hallmark quote from the movie." Louis Vuitton (P) presented evidence from what it claimed were representative Internet references and blog excerpts demonstrating that consumers mistakenly believed that the Diophy bag was a genuine Louis Vuitton (P) bag. Louis Vuitton (P) also asserted claims under the Lanham Act for tarnishment and dilution. Warner Brothers (D) moved to dismiss the complaint in its entirety, with prejudice, for failure to state a claim upon which relief could be granted on the grounds that its use of the Diophy bag in the film was protected by the First Amendment under the framework established by *Rogers v. Grimaldi*, 875 F.2d 994 (2d Cir. 1989). *Rogers* held that the Lanham Act is inapplicable to "artistic works" as long as the defendant's use of the mark is (1) "artistically relevant" to the work and (2) not "explicitly misleading" as to the source or content of the work. Louis Vuitton (P) objected to the Warner Brothers' (D) motion on the grounds that (1) whether, under *Rogers*, the use of the bag in the film was "artistically relevant" is an issue of fact that requires discovery; (2) the "explicitly misleading" prong of the *Rogers* test is not limited to confusion as to the source or content of the defendant's work; (3) Warner Brothers (D) is not afforded First Amendment protection for using an infringing product; and (4) disposing the case on a motion to dismiss is otherwise inappropriate.

ISSUE: Will a trademark action under § 43(a) of the Lanham Act be dismissed for failure to state a claim upon which relief can be granted where the defendant's use of the plaintiff's mark is made in an artistic work and is (1)

Continued on next page.

"artistically relevant" to the work and (2) not "explicitly misleading" as to the source or content of the work?

HOLDING AND DECISION: (Carter, J.) Yes. A trademark action under § 43(a) of the Lanham Act will be dismissed for failure to state a claim upon which relief can be granted where the defendant's use of the plaintiff's mark is made in an artistic work and is (1) "artistically relevant" to the work and (2) not "explicitly misleading" as to the source or content of the work. Here it is undisputed the movie is an artistic work for purposes of the *Rogers* test. The threshold for "artistic relevance" is low and will be satisfied unless the use has no artistic relevance to the underlying work whatsoever. The artistic relevance prong of the *Rogers* test ensures that the defendant intended an artistic—i.e., noncommercial—association with the plaintiff's mark, as opposed to one in which the defendant intends to associate with the mark to exploit the mark's popularity and goodwill. Here, the use of the Diophy bag is artistically relevant to the movie, since Alan's "Lewis Vuitton" remark comes across as snobbish only because the public signifies Louis Vuitton (P) with luxury and a high society lifestyle. His remark also comes across as funny because he mispronounces the French "Louis" like the English "Lewis," and ironic because he cannot correctly pronounce the brand name of one of his expensive possessions, adding to the image of Alan as a socially inept and comically misinformed character. Louis Vuitton (P) objects that this determination cannot be made on a motion to dismiss and must await discovery as to whether the movie's creators intended to use a genuine Louis Vuitton (P) bag or the knockoff. Louis Vuitton's (P) argument is unpersuasive, since regardless of whether a genuine or knockoff bag was used, the significance of the airport scene relies on Alan's bag looking like a Louis Vuitton (P) bag. Hence, discovery is not needed to resolve this prong of the *Rogers* test. Since using the Diophy bag has some relevance to the film, Warner Brothers' (D) use of it is unprotected only if it "explicitly misleads as to the source or the content of the work." The relevant question as to this second prong of the test is whether the defendant's use of the mark is misleading in the sense that it induces members of the public to believe the work was prepared or otherwise authorized by the plaintiff. To resolve this prong, the first step is to determine likelihood of confusion using the traditional multi-factor test for such confusion. The confusion, if any, must be in relation to the defendant's artistic work, and not to someone else's. Thus, the public's interest in free expression is accommodated by restricting its application to those situations that present the greatest risk of consumer confusion, i.e., when trademarks are used to dupe consumers into buying a product they mistakenly believe is sponsored by the trademark owner. When this concern is present it will generally outweigh the public's interest in free expression. If the defendant does not use the plaintiff's designation as defendant's own identifying trademark, then confusion will usually be unlikely, and

application of the Lanham Act is unnecessary. Here, Louis Vuitton's (P) allegations of confusion do not relate to Warner Brothers' (D) film, as Louis Vuitton (P) does not claim that the Diophy bag was used for the purpose of misleading consumers into believing that Louis Vuitton (P) produced or endorsed the film. Therefore, the complaint fails to even allege the type of confusion that could potentially overcome the *Rogers* protection. Accordingly, the use of the Diophy bag is not explicitly misleading, and the second prong of the *Rogers* test is met. Louis Vuitton (P) further argues that it is inappropriate to apply the *Rogers* test on a motion to dismiss; Louis Vuitton's (P) argument is rejected. Such an assessment can be made in the absence of discovery where the court is satisfied that the products or marks are so dissimilar that no question of fact is presented. Here, there is no likelihood of confusion that viewers would believe that the Diophy bag is a real Louis Vuitton (P) bag just because a fictional character made this claim in the context of a fictional movie. Neither is there a likelihood of confusion that this statement would cause viewers to believe that Louis Vuitton (P) approved of Warner Brothers' (D) use of the Diophy bag. Therefore, no amount of discovery will tilt the scales in favor of Louis Vuitton (P) at the expense of the public's right to free expression. Even assuming, arguendo, that Louis Vuitton (P) could state a cognizable claim of confusion, Warner Brothers' (D) use of the Diophy bag is protected under *Rogers* because it has some artistic relevance to the film and is not explicitly misleading. Motion to dismiss is granted.

ANALYSIS

Even if Louis Vuitton (P) did allege confusion as to the film, it is very unlikely that it would be able to demonstrate a likelihood of sponsorship confusion between the film and Louis Vuitton (P). The marks and products are entirely dissimilar; Louis Vuitton (P) and Warner Brothers (D) are in different industries and not in competition with each other; there is little chance that Louis Vuitton (P) would be able to "bridge the gap" to movie production; there was no claim that Warner Brothers (D) knowingly used a knockoff when filming the movie; and moviegoers are sophisticated enough to know that the mere presence of a brand name in a film, especially one that is briefly and intermittently shown, does not indicate that the brand sponsored the movie, and consumers of handbags are sophisticated enough to know the difference between a real bag and a knockoff. Thus, even assuming Louis Vuitton (P) could show some actual confusion, as this case illustrates, *Rogers* teaches that mark owner's must accept "some" confusion when outweighed by free speech interests.

E.S.S. Entertainment 2000, Inc. v. Rock Star Videos, Inc.

Strip club owner (P) v. Video game producer (D)

547 F.3d 1095 (9th Cir. 2008).

NATURE OF CASE: Appeal from dismissal on summary judgment of action for, inter alia, trade dress and trademark infringement and unfair competition under § 43(a) of the Lanham Act.

FACT SUMMARY: E.S.S. Entertainment 2000, Inc. (ESS) (P), the owner of the "Play Pen Gentlemen's Club" strip club in East Los Angeles, contended that Rockstar Games, Inc. (Rockstar) (D), the producer of the popular Grand Theft Auto video games, infringed ESS's (P) trade dress and trademark by including in its Grand Theft Auto: San Andreas game a strip club named the "Pig Pen" in a fictitious town called East Los Santos, which is based on East Los Angeles. Rockstar (D) moved for summary judgment on all of ESS's (P) claims, arguing that, inter alia, the First Amendment protected it against liability. The district court granted Rockstar's (D) motion.

> ## 🏛 RULE OF LAW
> A trademark action under § 43(a) of the Lanham Act will be dismissed on summary judgment where the defendant's use of the plaintiff's mark is made in an artistic work and is (1) "artistically relevant" to the work and (2) not "explicitly misleading" as to the source or content of the work.

FACTS: Rockstar Games, Inc. (Rockstar) (D), produces the popular Grand Theft Auto video games, including Grand Theft Auto: San Andreas (San Andreas). This series of video games is known for an irreverent and sometimes crass brand of humor, gratuitous violence and sex, and overall seediness. Each game in the series takes place in one or more dystopic, cartoonish cities modeled after actual American urban areas. The games always include a disclaimer stating that the locations depicted are fictional. The cities in San Andreas include Los Santos, which is modeled on Los Angeles. The neighborhoods in Los Santos mimic the look and feel of actual Los Angeles neighborhoods. These areas have been populated with virtual liquor stores, ammunition dealers, casinos, pawnshops, tattoo parlors, bars, and strip clubs. The brand names, business names, and other aspects of the locations have been changed to fit the irreverent "Los Santos" tone. East Los Santos contains variations on the businesses and architecture of the real thing, including a virtual, cartoon-style strip club known as the "Pig Pen." E.S.S. Entertainment 2000, Inc. (ESS) (P), the owner of the "Play Pen Gentlemen's Club" (Play Pen) strip club in East Los Angeles, brought suit against Rockstar (D) asserting claims for, inter alia, trademark and trade dress infringement and unfair competition under § 43(a) of the Lanham Act. The Play Pen's

"logo" consists of the words "the Play Pen" (and the lower- and upper-case letters forming those words) and the phrase "Totally Nude," with a silhouette of a nude female dancer inside the stem of the first "P." Although Rockstar's (D) artists took some inspiration from photographs of the Play Pen, they used photographs of other East Los Angeles locations to design certain aspects of the Pig Pen, and elements of the Play Pen's architecture are absent from the Pig Pen. The core of ESS's complaint (P) was that Rockstar (D) used Play Pen's distinctive logo and trade dress without its authorization and created a likelihood of confusion among consumers as to whether ESS (D) endorsed, or was associated with, the video depiction. Rockstar (D) moved for summary judgment on all of ESS's (P) claims, arguing that, inter alia, the First Amendment protected it against liability. The district court granted Rockstar's (D) motion on this ground. The court of appeals granted review.

ISSUE: Will a trademark action under § 43(a) of the Lanham Act be dismissed on summary judgment where the defendant's use of the plaintiff's mark is made in an artistic work and is (1) "artistically relevant" to the work and (2) not "explicitly misleading" as to the source or content of the work?

HOLDING AND DECISION: (O'Scannlain, J.) Yes. A trademark action under § 43(a) of the Lanham Act will be dismissed on summary judgment where the defendant's use of the plaintiff's mark is made in an artistic work and is (1) "artistically relevant" to the work and (2) not "explicitly misleading" as to the source or content of the work. In determining whether the First Amendment protects use of another's trademark in an artistic work, the basic policy is that the Lanham Act will apply only where the public interest in avoiding consumer confusion outweighs the public interest in free expression. The framework for determining this issue was established by *Rogers v. Grimaldi*, 875 F.2d 994 (2d Cir. 1989). *Rogers* held that the Lanham Act is inapplicable to "artistic works" as long as the defendant's use of the mark is (1) "artistically relevant" to the work and (2) not "explicitly misleading" as to the source or content of the work. Here it is undisputed that San Andreas is an artistic work. The first prong of the *Rogers* test is satisfied here because the use of a strip club in the game that mimics and parodies the strip clubs of East Los Angeles has some—i.e., more than zero—artistic relevance to the game. As with most urban neighborhoods, East Los Angeles' distinctiveness lies in its "look and feel,"

Continued on next page.

not in particular destinations, and distinct neighborhood, with all that characterizes it, is relevant to Rockstar's (D) artistic goal, which is to develop a cartoon-style parody of East Los Angeles. It does not matter, as ESS (P) argues, that the game is not "about" ESS's (P) Play Pen. The second prong is also satisfied. The relevant question as to this prong is whether San Andreas would confuse its players into thinking that the Play Pen is somehow behind the Pig Pen or that it sponsors Rockstar's (D) product. In answering this question it must be kept in mind that the mere use of a trademark alone cannot suffice to make such use explicitly misleading. There is nothing to indicate that consumers would reasonably believe that ESS (P) produced the video game or that Rockstar (D) operated a strip club. A player can enter the virtual Pig Pen strip club in Los Santos, but that setting is generic. It also seems far-fetched that someone playing San Andreas would think ESS (P) had provided whatever expertise, support, or unique strip-club knowledge it possesses to the production of the game, since the game does not revolve around running or patronizing a strip club, and whatever a player can do at the Pig Pen is incidental to the game's overall story. A reasonable consumer would not think a company that owns one strip club in East Los Angeles, which is not well known to the public at large, also produces a technologically sophisticated video game like San Andreas. Although ESS (P) is correct that players could chose to spend all their time at the Pig Pen, so that the Pig Pen can be considered a significant part of the game that misses the point; the chance to attend a virtual strip club is unambiguously not the game's main selling point. Thus, Rockstar's (D) modification of ESS's (P) trademark is not explicitly misleading and is protected by the First Amendment. The district court did not err, therefore, in dismissing ESS's (P) case on summary judgment. Affirmed.

▌ ANALYSIS

Rockstar (D) also asserted a nominative fair use defense, which the district court rejected. On appeal, Rockstar (D) argued that regardless of whether it infringed ESS's (P) trademark under the Lanham Act or related state law, it was entitled to a defense under the nominative fair use doctrine. Unlike a traditional fair use scenario, nominative fair use occurs when the defendant uses the trademarked term to describe not its own product, but the plaintiff's. The doctrine protects those who deliberately use another's trademark or trade dress for the "purposes of comparison, criticism, or point of reference." Here, however, Rockstar's (D) use of "Pig Pen" was not identical to the Play Pen mark and was not intended to comment on Play Pen per se. The court of appeals held that since Rockstar (D) did not use the trademarked logo to describe ESS's (P) strip club, the district court correctly held that the nominative fair use defense did not apply in this case.

Quicknotes

PARODY For purposes of trademark law, an amusing use of another's trademark that evokes the original trademark while simultaneously satirizing or criticizing the trademark, in a manner that either is likely to confuse the consuming public as to the use's source, sponsorship or approval, or not, but if the use is not likely to cause consumer confusion, it will not constitute trademark infringement.

SUMMARY JUDGMENT Judgment rendered by a court in response to a motion made by one of the parties, claiming that the lack of a question of material fact in respect to an issue warrants disposition of the issue without consideration by the jury.

TRADE DRESS The overall image of, or impression created by, a product that a court may enforce as a trademark if it determines that such image has acquired secondary meaning and that the public recognizes it as an indication of source.

TRADEMARK INFRINGEMENT The unauthorized use of another's trademark in such a manner as to cause a likelihood of confusion as to the source of the product or service in connection with which it is utilized.

Cliffs Notes, Inc. v. Bantam Doubleday Dell Publishing Group, Inc.

Mark holder (P) v. Parodist publisher (D)

886 F.2d 490 (2d Cir. 1989).

NATURE OF CASE: Appeal from injunction.

FACT SUMMARY: Bantam Doubleday Dell Publishing Group, Inc. (Bantam) (D) intended to publish *Spy Notes*, a parody of *Cliffs Notes*. Cliffs Notes, Inc. (CNI) (P) publishes *Cliffs Notes* and sued to enjoin Bantam's (D) publication as an infringement of CNI's (P) trademark.

🏛 RULE OF LAW
Parody is an expressive element deserving of greater protection than the mere labeling of a commercial product despite that product's trademark protection.

FACTS: Cliffs Notes, Inc. (CNI) (P) publishes *Cliffs Notes*, which are popular summaries of classic novels typically assigned in college-level English courses. CNI (P) has trademark protection for the cover of *Cliffs Notes*, which includes a diagonal yellow and black design, the name of the book being summarized, and a clay sculpture of a mountain. *Cliffs Notes* are particularly popular with college students. Bantam Doubleday Dell Publishing Group, Inc. (Bantam) (D) is a well-known publishing company that publishes *Spy Notes*. The other creator of Spy Notes is *Spy* magazine, a magazine publishing satirical political and social commentary. *Spy* magazine has become quite popular on college campuses and with the college-educated demographic. *Spy* magazine and Bantam (D) created *Spy Notes* to parody *Cliffs Notes*. The *Spy Notes* cover has a diagonal yellow and black design, the names of the three books being summarized, and a clay sculpture of New York City. Additionally, the word "satire" appears several times on the front and back covers, the *Spy* magazine logo is on the front lower corner, and the cover has phrasing in addition to the book's title. *Spy Notes* also includes an insert titled the "Spy Novel-O-Matic Fiction-Writing Device." The books being summarized are three contemporary novels *Cliffs Notes* has not and does not plan to summarize. Bantam (D) intended to package the *Spy Notes* in prepacks of 10. CNI (P) sued to enjoin Bantam (D) from publishing *Spy Notes* with the claim that *Spy Notes* would likely cause confusion that CNI (P) authorized or sponsored them. The district court granted the injunction. Bantam (D) appealed.

ISSUE: Is parody an expressive element deserving of greater protection than the mere labeling of a commercial product despite that product's trademark protection?

HOLDING AND DECISION: (Feinberg, J.) Parody is an expressive element deserving of greater protection

than the mere labeling of a commercial product despite that product's trademark protection. The First Amendment protects parody as a form of artistic expression but the parody cannot infringe upon trademark protections. The parody must evoke the original but not infringe upon its trademark, which is a delicate balance. *Rogers v. Grimaldi*, 875 F.2d 994, 997 (2d Cir. 1989), is applicable here although the facts were quite different. Rogers involved a title that was potentially misleading about the content and the *Rogers* holding was that the Lanham Act's prohibition against false advertising applies only if the title is explicitly misleading. The overall balancing approach in *Rogers*, in construing the Lanham Act narrowly with regard to First Amendment claims, is relevant here even if the holding is inapplicable. CNI (P) argues for the application of the "likelihood of confusion" eight-factor test set out in *Polaroid Corp. v. Polara Electronics Corp.*, 287 F. 2d 492 (2d Cir. 1961), but the balancing test is more appropriate because of the inherent tension between First Amendment rights and trademark property rights. Here, there is a great public interest in avoiding confusion over the contents of *Spy Notes* because consumers should not be misled over the products they purchase. The likelihood of confusion between *Cliffs Notes* and *Spy Notes* is slight. *Spy Notes* may not contain obvious visual gags, but sophisticated satire is not prohibited. The differences between the covers should alert the purchaser to the fact that CNI (P) is not involved in *Spy Notes*. The typical purchaser of *Cliffs Notes* is a college-attending or college-educated person who is likely to discern that *Spy Notes* is summarizing a trio of novels not covered in standard college literature courses and that the "Spy Novel-O-Matic Fiction-Writing Device" is not serious fare. *Spy Notes* does mimic the *Cliffs Notes* cover but it raises only a slight risk that someone would confuse *Spy Notes* for *Cliffs Notes*. The injunction is vacated. Reversed.

▶ *ANALYSIS*

The court pointed out the difficulty for satirists in striking that delicate balance necessary to evoke the original product without infringing its trademark. The parody must exaggerate or distort the original product to an extent the consumer is not likely confused but the parody does not have to be an obvious sight gag or expressly labeled as a parody. The humor can be sophisticated and protected expression.

Continued on next page.

Quicknotes

PARODY For purposes of trademark law, an amusing use of another's trademark that evokes the original trademark while simultaneously satirizing or criticizing the trademark, in a manner that either is likely to confuse the consuming public as to the use's source, sponsorship or approval, or not, but if the use is not likely to cause consumer confusion, it will not constitute trademark infringement.

TRADEMARK INFRINGEMENT The unauthorized use of another's trademark in such a manner as to cause a likelihood of confusion as to the source of the product or service in connection with which it is utilized.

Dr. Seuss Enterprises, L.P. v. Penguin Books USA, Inc.

Children's books series publisher (P) v. Book publisher (D)

109 F.3d 1394 (9th Cir. 1997).

NATURE OF CASE: Appeal from preliminary injunction in trademark and copyright action.

FACT SUMMARY: Dr. Seuss Enterprises, L.P. (Seuss) (P), which owned trademarks and copyrights in the well-known series of Dr. Seuss children's books, including *The Cat in the Hat,* sued Penguin Books USA, Inc. (Penguin) (D) (along with Dove (D), the distributor) for trademark and copyright infringement based on Penguin's (D) publishing a book titled *The Cat NOT in the Hat! A Parody by Dr. Juice,* which was purportedly a parody of *The Cat in the Hat* through a poetic and satiric retelling of the O.J. Simpson double murder trial. Seuss (P) obtained a preliminary injunction enjoining Penguin (D) and Dove (D) from distributing the book, and, as to the trademark infringement claim, Penguin (D) and Dove (D) contended that there was no likelihood of confusion, and that even if there was, Penguin's (D) book was protected by the work's parodic character.

🏛 RULE OF LAW
In a trademark infringement action, where the purportedly infringing work is a parody of the trademarked work, a preliminary injunction enjoining the distribution of the purportedly infringing work is appropriate where the factors for determining likelihood of confusion are indeterminate, it is not clear that the purported parody does not create consumer confusion as to source, sponsorship or approval, and the balance of hardships favors the mark holder.

FACTS: Dr. Seuss Enterprises, L.P. (Seuss) (P) owned trademarks and copyrights in the well-known series of Dr. Seuss children's illustrated books, including *The Cat in the Hat.* The principal character in that book is the Cat, who is almost always depicted with his distinctive scrunched and somewhat shabby red and white stove-pipe hat. Seuss (P) owns the common-law trademark rights to the words "Dr. Seuss" and "Cat in the Hat," as well as the character illustration of the Cat's stove-pipe hat. Seuss (P) had licensed the Dr. Seuss marks, including *The Cat in the Hat* character, for use on clothing, in interactive software, and in a theme park. Penguin Books USA, Inc. (Penguin) (D) published a book titled *The Cat NOT in the Hat! A Parody by Dr. Juice,* which was purportedly a parody of *The Cat in the Hat* through a poetic and satiric retelling of the O.J. Simpson double murder trial. Penguin (D) and Dove (D), the distributor, were neither licensed nor authorized to use any of the works, characters or illustrations owned by Seuss (P), nor did they seek permission from Seuss (P). Seuss (P) filed a complaint for copyright and trademark infringe-

ment, seeking a preliminary injunction, after seeing an advertisement promoting *The Cat NOT in the Hat!* prior to its publication. The district court granted Seuss's (P) request for a preliminary injunction. By that point, Penguin (D) had printed about 12,000 books at an expense of approximately $35,500, and those books were enjoined from distribution. In reaching its decision, the district court held that Penguin (D) and Dove (D) infringed Seuss's (P) copyright and that Penguin's (D) work was not a fair use parody. As to trademark infringement, the district court, applying an eight-factor test for likelihood of confusion, also concluded that most of the factors were indeterminate and posed serious questions for litigation. The eight factors are as follows: (1) strength of the mark; (2) proximity of the goods; (3) similarity of the marks; (4) evidence of actual confusion; (5) marketing channels used; (6) type of goods and the degree of care likely to be exercised by the purchaser; (7) defendant's intent in selecting the mark; (8) likelihood of expansion of the product lines. The court also concluded that the balance of hardships favored Seuss (P). Penguin (D) and Dove (D) appealed, contending that there was no likelihood of confusion, and that even if there was, Penguin's (D) book was protected by the work's parodic character. The court of appeals granted review.

ISSUE: In a trademark infringement action, where the purportedly infringing work is a parody of the trademarked work, is a preliminary injunction enjoining the distribution of the purportedly infringing work appropriate where the factors for determining likelihood of confusion are indeterminate, it is not clear that the purported parody does not create consumer confusion as to source, sponsorship or approval, and the balance of hardships favors the mark holder?

HOLDING AND DECISION: (O'Scannlain, J.) Yes. In a trademark infringement action, where the purportedly infringing work is a parody of the trademarked work, a preliminary injunction enjoining the distribution of the purportedly infringing work is appropriate where the factors for determining likelihood of confusion are indeterminate, it is not clear that the purported parody does not create consumer confusion as to source, sponsorship or approval, and the balance of hardships favors the mark holder. Here, the district court correctly determined that the majority of the eight factors for assessing likelihood of confusion were indeterminate and posed serious questions for litigation. As to the first factor, Seuss's (P) trademarks

Continued on next page.

are widely recognized. As to the second and third factors, the proximity and similarity between the marks and the infringing items was substantial. As to the fourth factor, there was no evidence of actual confusion, given that the distribution of the Penguin (D) book had been enjoined. As to the fifth factor, the marketing channels used were indeterminate. As to the sixth factor, the use of the Cat's stove-pipe hat or the confusingly similar title to capture initial consumer attention, even though no actual sales had been finally completed as a result of the confusion, could still be an infringement. As to the seventh factor, Penguin (D) and Dove's (D) likely intent in selecting the Seuss (P) marks was to draw consumer attention to what would otherwise be just one more book on the O.J. Simpson murder trial. Lastly, as to the eighth factor, the likelihood of expansion of the product lines was indeterminate. Penguin (D) and Dove (D) argued that even if Seuss (P) established a likelihood of confusion, their identical and confusingly similar use of Seuss's (P) marks was offset by the work's parodic character. However, in a trademark infringement suit founded on the likelihood of confusion rationale, the claim of parody is not truly a separate "defense" per se, but merely a way of phrasing the response that customers are not likely to be confused as to the source, sponsorship or approval of the purportedly infringing work. Parodies can be confusing or not confusing, but only the latter are noninfringing. Finally, here, the balance of hardship favors Seuss (P), as the goodwill and reputation associated with *The Cat in the Hat* character and title, the name "Dr. Seuss," and the Cat's Hat outweigh the $35,500 in expenses incurred by Penguin (D). Affirmed.

▶ ANALYSIS

As this case emphasizes, the fact that a purportedly infringing work is a parody is not dispositive as to whether it infringes or dilutes another's trademark. If the parody is confusing as to the source, sponsorship or approval of the purportedly infringing work, and not merely amusing, it will be found to be infringing. In several cases, the courts have held, in effect, that poking fun at a trademark is no joke and have issued injunctions. Examples include: a diaper bag with green and red bands and the wording "Gucchi Goo," allegedly poking fun at the well-known Gucci name and the design mark, *Gucci Shops, Inc. v. R.H. Macy & Co.*, 446 F. Supp. 838 (S.D.N.Y. 1977); the use of a competing meat sauce of the trademark "A.2" as a "pun" on the famous "A.1" trademark, *Nabisco Brands, Inc. v. Kaye,* 760 F. Supp. 25 (D. Conn. 1991). Stating that, whereas a true parody will be so obvious that a clear distinction is preserved between the source of the target and the source of the parody, a court found that the "Hard Rain" logo was an infringement of the "Hard Rock" logo. In such a case, the claim of parody is no defense "where the purpose of the similarity is to capitalize on a famous mark's popularity for the defendant's own commercial use." *Hard Rock Cafe*

Licensing Corp. v. Pacific Graphics, Inc., 776 F. Supp. 1454, 1462 (W.D. Wash. 1991).

Quicknotes

COPYRIGHT Refers to the exclusive rights granted to an artist pursuant to Article I, Section 8, clause 8 of the United States Constitution over the reproduction, display, performance, distribution, and adaptation of his work for a period prescribed by statute.

COPYRIGHT INFRINGEMENT A violation of one of the exclusive rights granted to an artist pursuant to Article I, Section 8, clause 8 of the United States Constitution over the reproduction, display, performance, distribution, and adaptation of his work for a period prescribed by statute.

ENJOIN The ordering of a party to cease the conduct of a specific activity.

PARODY For purposes of trademark law, an amusing use of another's trademark that evokes the original trademark while simultaneously satirizing or criticizing the trademark, in a manner that either is likely to confuse the consuming public as to the use's source, sponsorship or approval, or not, but if the use is not likely to cause consumer confusion, it will not constitute trademark infringement.

PRELIMINARY INJUNCTION A judicial mandate issued to require or restrain a party from certain conduct; used to preserve a trial's subject matter or to prevent threatened injury.

TRADEMARK INFRINGEMENT The unauthorized use of another's trademark in such a manner as to cause a likelihood of confusion as to the source of the product or service in connection with which it is utilized.

Dilution

Quick Reference Rules of Law

Ty Inc. v. Perryman

Manufacturer of Beanie Babies (P) v. Internet seller of second-hand beanbag stuffed animals (D)

306 F.3d 509 (7th Cir. 2002).

NATURE OF CASE: Appeal from grant of injunction in action for trademark infringement and dilution under the Lanham Act.

FACT SUMMARY: Perryman (D), who operated a website reselling beanbag stuffed animals, primarily Beanie Babies made by Ty Inc. (P), contended that her use of the term "Beanie" or "Beanies" did not infringe Ty's (P) trademark because the terms "beanies" had become a generic term, and that an injunction that prohibited her from using those terms within any business name, Internet domain name, trademark, or in connection with any non-Ty products was overbroad.

> ### 🏛 RULE OF LAW
> (1) A seller in a secondary market of a product does not infringe or dilute the manufacturer's trademark in that product by using the trademark in a business name or domain name.
> (2) A seller of products similar to a manufacturer's product infringes the manufacturer's trademark in that product by using the trademark to identify the similar products.

FACTS: Ty Inc. (P) manufactures Beanie Babies, a line of well-known beanbag stuffed animals. Ty's (P) marketing strategy is to deliberately produce a quantity of each Beanie Baby that fails to clear the market at the very low price that it charges for Beanie Babies. This has led to the creation of a secondary market for scarce Beanie Babies, in which prices are bid up to a market-clearing level. Perryman (D) is a middleman in this second market. She sells second-hand beanbag stuffed animals, primarily Beanie Babies, over the Internet on a website with the domain name <bargainbeanies.com>, where she clearly disclaims any affiliation with Ty (P). After listing various Beanie Babies for sale, she also has the caption "Other Beanies" and under that is a list of non-Ty products. Ty (P) brought suit for trademark infringement against Perryman (D) based on the antidilution statute, which protects "famous" marks from commercial uses that cause "dilution of the distinctive quality of the mark." The district court granted summary judgment to Ty (P) and entered an injunction that forbade Perryman (D) from using "Beanie" or "Beanies," whether alone or in combination with other terms, "within any business name, Internet domain name, or trademark, or in connection with any non-Ty products." Perryman (D) appealed, contending that "beanies" has become a generic term for beanbag stuffed animals, and

that the injunction was overbroad. The Seventh Circuit Court of Appeals granted review.

ISSUE:
(1) Does a seller in a secondary market of a product infringe or dilute the manufacturer's trademark in that product by using the trademark in a business name or domain name?
(2) Does a seller of products similar to a manufacturer's product infringe the manufacturer's trademark in that product by using the trademark to identify the similar products?

HOLDING AND DECISION: (Posner, J.)
(1) No. A seller in a secondary market of a product does not infringe or dilute the manufacturer's trademark in that product by using the trademark in a business name or domain name. As to the Beanie Babies that Perryman (D) sells, confusion is not an issue, since she is not a Ty (P) competitor, but sells Ty (P) products. Nonetheless, the antidilution statute is implicated, since "Beanie Babies" and "Beanies" are famous trademarks, which Perryman (D) used in interstate and foreign commerce for a commercial purpose. However, none of the theories of dilution supports Ty's (P) position as related to Perryman's (D) sale of Beanies. One such theory is blurring, where consumer search costs rise if a trademark becomes associated with a variety of unrelated products. A second theory is tarnishment, where the trademark is tarnished by having its distinctiveness reduced as a signifier of the trademarked product or service. A third is an expansive concept of dilution that provides the trademark holder the full benefit of its investment in the trademark by preventing use of the trademark even though the efficacy of the trademark will not be impaired. Because Perryman (D) is not producing a product or service that is distinct from any product or service, but rather is selling the very product to which the trademark sought to be protected is attached, there is no dilution. "You can't sell a branded product without using its brand name, that is, its trademark." Ty's (P) dilution argument is especially strained given its marketing strategy, which deliberately has created the secondary market. Trademark law does not enable producers to own their aftermarkets or to impede sellers in the aftermarket from marketing the trademarked product. If Ty (P) is attempting to extend antidilution law to prevent commercial uses from ac-

Continued on next page.

celerating the transition of its trademark to a generic term, it must assume the risk that its trademark, which describes a basic element of the product, will at some point become generic. At that point, Ty (P) will have to cast about for a different trademark. While the downside when a mark becomes generic is that the trademark owner must invest in a new trademark, the social upside is that there is an addition to ordinary language. In fact, a nontrivial number of words in common use began as trademarks. Thus, interpreting antidilution law to permit trademark owners to prevent uses of their marks, that while not confusing, threaten to render the mark generic, may therefore not be in the public interest. Accordingly, Ty (P) has not demonstrated any basis for enjoining Perryman (D) from using the terms at issue in any business name, Internet domain name, or trademark. Reversed and vacated as to this issue.

(2) Yes. A seller of products similar to a manufacturer's product infringes the manufacturer's trademark in that product by using the trademark to identify the similar products. As to the non-Ty products that Perryman (D) identifies with the caption "Other Beanies," such identification is misdescription and false advertising, and supports the injunction as to the prohibition on using the terms at issue in connection with non-Ty products. Therefore, this much of the injunction must stand. While an argument could be made that deleting "Other Beanies" is not enough, since consumers might assume that other beanbag stuffed animals which look like Ty's (P) are "Beanies," Ty (P) does not seem to be seeking to broaden the injunction to require a disclaimer as to the source of such non-Ty products. In any event, this part of the injunction can be addressed further on remand. Remanded.

▶ *ANALYSIS*

One significance of this decision is that Judge Posner has posited a sort of cognitive model of dilution that is based on internal search costs for consumers—whereby dilution makes it more difficult for consumers to recall or recognize the diluted trademark. For example, Posner's concept of blurring is one where a single term activates multiple, nonconfusing associations in the consumer's mind, increasing cognitive processing time and load. As Judge Posner puts it, "Consumers will have to think harder—incur as it were a higher imagination cost." Regarding tarnishment, his concept also involves interference with cognitive processing, whereby a reference to the senior user's trademark activates negative associations, thus decreasing the overall positive value associated with the trademark. Such a model of dilution, however, has been criticized as lacking sufficient empirical support to justify its adoption, since it is not clear exactly how consumers process trademarks in the marketplace.

■=■

Quicknotes

DISTINCTIVENESS A standard for trademark protection, whereby the more distinctive a mark is, the greater its eligibility for protection. Distinctive marks typically consist of terms that are fanciful or coined, arbitrary, or suggestive. If a mark is descriptive, it is not entitled to trademark protection unless it has acquired distinctiveness through consumer association of goods or services with the mark (such acquired distinctiveness is also known as secondary meaning).

GENERIC MEANING A term that encompasses a class of related products and lacks the requisite distinctiveness for federal trademark protection.

SUMMARY JUDGMENT Judgment rendered by a court in response to a motion made by one of the parties, claiming that the lack of a question of material fact in respect to an issue warrants disposition of the issue without consideration by the jury.

TRADEMARK DILUTION The diminishment of the capability of a trademark to identify and distinguish the particular good or service with which it is associated.

■=■

National Pork Board v. Supreme Lobster and Seafood Company

Pork industry organization (P) v. Seafood company (D)

96 U.S.P.Q.2d 1479 (T.T.A.B. 2010).

NATURE OF CASE: Appeal from order denying trademark registration on the grounds of likelihood of dilution.

FACT SUMMARY: National Pork Board (NPB) (P) opposed the registration by the Supreme Lobster and Seafood Company (Supreme Lobster) (D) of the trademark "THE OTHER RED MEAT" for salmon, contending that this mark would, inter alia, dilute NPB's (P) well-known mark "THE OTHER WHITE MEAT" for pork products in violation of § 43(c) of the Lanham Act.

🏛 RULE OF LAW
(1) For purposes of determining likelihood of dilution of a mark, survey questions that ask what the accused mark brings to mind have probative value as to dilution where otherwise the questions posed are clear and not leading and where the survey is conducted by qualified persons following proper interview procedures and in a manner that ensures objectivity.
(2) For purposes of determining likelihood of dilution of a mark, the mark is famous where a preponderance of the evidence shows that a substantial portion of the consuming population knows the mark.

FACTS: The Supreme Lobster and Seafood Company (Supreme Lobster) (D) applied for an intent-to-use registration of the trademark "THE OTHER RED MEAT" for fresh and frozen salmon. National Pork Board (NPB) (P), a pork products organization, opposed the registration on the grounds that this mark would, inter alia, dilute NPB's (P) well-known mark "THE OTHER WHITE MEAT" for pork products in violation of § 43(c) of the Lanham Act. "THE OTHER WHITE MEAT" was registered to promote the interests of the pork industry in connection with pork products, apparel, merchandise, and a website. NPB (P) and the pork industry, through an intensive national advertising campaign, spent millions of dollars ($500 million between 1987 and 2007) in promoting its trademark for the purpose of convincing consumers that chicken and fish are not the only choices for a reduced-fat, balanced diet, especially in light of the health concerns associated with eating red meat. This advertising campaign was waged in print and on radio, television, billboards, taxi cabs, and transit shelters. The campaign was supplemented by retailers and food manufacturers, which participated in co-branded advertising campaigns promoting "THE OTHER WHITE MEAT" mark in conjunction with their own products and/or services. In addition, supermarkets regularly and frequently advertised the mark in their regular weekly newspaper circulars. State pork producer associations also spent around $50 million to promote the mark. The mark also garnered media and celebrity attention and endorsement, and during the month of July 2007, the dominant website for the mark, "www.theotherwhitemeat.com", received almost 100,000 daily, unique visitors, with a total of almost 600,000 page views. NPB (P) also ran local and national advertising playing off the mark with tag-lines, e.g., "The Other Backyard Barbecue," that attempted to establish a close consumer perception around the phrase "The Other . . ." in connection with promotion of the pork industry. Surveys conducted semi-annually by independent research firms since 1987 consistently showed public awareness of the mark "THE OTHER WHITE MEAT" at or above 85% of consumers nationwide. A separate study (the Northwestern Study) concluded that the mark was the fifth most recognized advertising slogan in the United States among the general adult population at that time. In connection with its opposition, NPB (P) hired a research firm to conduct a survey (the Klein Dilution Survey) testing the likelihood of dilution caused by applicant's intended mark. This research purported to show that more than 35% of the respondents, in response to an unaided question, associated Supreme Lobster's (D) slogan with NPB's (P) slogan or the pork products it promotes. There was also evidence of extensive references to the mark in the popular culture, and the mark was discussed in third-party publications and college textbooks on advertising and marketing. Marketing professionals also testified that in light of the "phenomenal" degree of consumer recognition of the mark, the renown of this remarkable slogan makes it one of the most well-known and successful advertising slogans in modern times. Supreme Lobster (D) attacked, inter alia, the probative value of the Northwestern Study and the Klein Dilution Survey. For the Northwestern Study, respondents during a telephone survey were presented with 25 slogans and asked whether they recognized a slogan and whether they could correctly attribute it to a brand, product, or industry. Supreme Lobster (D) attacked the aided awareness questioning used during the telephone survey. For the Klein Dilution Survey, respondents were played Supreme Lobster's (D) slogan (THE OTHER RED MEAT) and were asked if any other advertising slogans or phrases came to mind, and, if yes, which other advertising slogan or phrase came to mind. At no point in the survey did the screener ever mention NPB's (P) mark or product. Supreme Lobster (D) attacked this methodology on the

Continued on next page.

grounds that it improperly suggested to survey respondents that another slogan or phrase existed that should have been brought to mind upon hearing its slogan. The examiner granted the opposition and denied the registration. The Trademark Trial and Appeal Board (the TTAB) granted review.

ISSUE:

(1) For purposes of determining likelihood of dilution of a mark, do survey questions that ask what the accused mark brings to mind have probative value as to dilution where otherwise the questions posed are clear and not leading, and the survey is conducted by qualified persons following proper interview procedures and in a manner that ensures objectivity?

(2) For purposes of determining likelihood of dilution of a mark, is the mark famous where a preponderance of the evidence shows that a substantial portion of the consuming population knows the mark?

HOLDING AND DECISION: (Bucher, J.)

(1) Yes. For purposes of determining likelihood of dilution of a mark, survey questions that ask what the accused mark brings to mind have probative value as to dilution where otherwise the questions posed are clear and not leading, and the survey is conducted by qualified persons following proper interview procedures and in a manner that ensures objectivity. The purpose of the Northwestern Study was to assess the strength of "THE OTHER WHITE MEAT" mark in comparison with other well-known slogans. The methodology of this study did not lead respondents to a desired result by using inherently suggestive questions, as the results relied on the respondents being able to make the correct association with a slogan completely on their own. Because this study was otherwise conducted in a manner to ensure objectivity, it has probative value on the question of the public perception of NPB's (P) claimed slogan, especially since it was conducted prior to Supreme Lobster (D) filing its application, and one of the elements that opposers must prove under the likelihood of dilution claim is whether the opposer's mark became famous prior to the filing date of applicant's application. As to the Klein Dilution Survey, the survey was intended to test the precise question of whether Supreme Lobster's (D) mark called to mind NPB's (P) mark or advertising campaigns. Accordingly, it seems that it was necessary to pose the question of whether this slogan brought to mind any other advertising slogans. The questions asked were not inappropriately leading questions, since an affirmative answer of another slogan was not presumed with the phrasing of ". . . do any other advertising slogans . . ." come to mind. Association queries, such as the ones posed by the study/survey at issue, are appropriate in light of the specific language of the current dilution provisions of the Lanham Act, which requires evidence of the association made in the consumer's mind between the

defendant's mark and the plaintiff's mark. Here, the questions posed were clear and not leading, and the survey was conducted properly in a manner that ensured objectivity. Finally, because Supreme Lobster's (D) mark was an intent-to-use slogan with virtually no actual presence in the marketplace, it was appropriate for NPB (P) to use a well-designed telephone survey in this context. For all these reasons, the survey evidence is probative on the issue of likelihood of dilution. [Affirmed as to this issue.]

(2) For purposes of determining likelihood of dilution of a mark, the mark is famous where a preponderance of the evidence shows that a substantial portion of the consuming population knows the mark. NPB's (P) mark is among the most well-known advertising slogans in the United States given awareness rates at 80 to 85% of the general adult population and rates of correct source recognition at nearly 70% of the population. Awareness and recognition at this level has supported a finding of fame in those rare instances a likelihood of dilution has been found. Here, the evidence also demonstrates that NPB (P) spent in the neighborhood of $25 million every year for almost 20 years on demand enhancement advertising and marketing prior to the filing of Supreme Lobster's (D) application. Additionally, the record shows an extensive amount of third-party advertising, in-store retail promotions, and unsolicited, national news media coverage and academic recognition. All of this evidence taken together supports the conclusion that the mark "THE OTHER WHITE MEAT" is famous among a broad spectrum of the general consuming public. Because the majority of the evidence in the record about the renown of this slogan predates Supreme Lobster's (D) application, the mark's fame was well-established prior to the date of that application. [The TTAB concluded that "THE OTHER RED MEAT" slogan was likely to dilute the famous "THE OTHER WHITE MEAT" slogan through blurring.] [Affirmed as to this issue.]

▌ ANALYSIS

Because the NPB's (P) services were "promoting the interests of members of the pork industry," it was not critical that consumers could identify NPB (P) as the source of the slogan. Rather, for the mark to be source-identifying, it was sufficient that consumers could associate the mark with a single, albeit anonymous source. Thus, the "THE OTHER WHITE MEAT" slogan did not have to identify the particular company or entity that was its source in the way, for example, that "Just Do It" identifies Nike as its source, or "Don't Leave Home Without It" identifies American Express as its source.

■=■

Continued on next page.

Quicknotes

INTER ALIA Among other things.

TRADEMARK DILUTION The diminishment of the capability of a trademark to identify and distinguish the particular good or service with which it is associated.

Visa International Service Association v. JSL Corp.

Financial services firm (P) v. Online multilingual education company (D)

610 F.3d 1088 (9th Cir. 2010).

NATURE OF CASE: Appeal from summary judgment enjoining the use of a mark on the grounds of trademark dilution by blurring.

FACT SUMMARY: Visa International Service Association (Visa) (P), the world's top brand in financial services, contended that the use by JSL Corp. (D) of the mark "eVisa" for online multilingual education would dilute the "Visa" mark by blurring. JSL (D) contended that its mark could not cause dilution by blurring since "visa" is an ordinary English word, so that Visa's (P) use of the word was insufficiently distinctive.

RULE OF LAW

A famous trademark that is comprised of an ordinary English word is susceptible of dilution by blurring where the way the trademark is used in a particular commercial context is unique, and the purportedly blurring mark is not being used for its literal dictionary definition, but rather creates a new meaning for the word in a different commercial context.

FACTS: Visa International Service Association (Visa) (P), which is the world's top brand in financial services through its issuance of credit cards, uses the "Visa" trademark. Its credit cards are used for online purchases almost as often as all other credit cards combined. JSL Corp. (D) started using the mark "eVisa" for online multilingual education after Visa's (P) mark had become famous. The name "eVisa" traced its origin back to an English language tutoring service called "Eikaiwa Visa" that JSL's (D) owner ran while living in Japan. "Eikaiwa" is Japanese for English conversation, and the "e" in "eVisa" is short for "Eikaiwa." The use of the word "visa" in both "eVisa" and "Eikaiwa Visa" was meant to suggest "the ability to travel, both linguistically and physically, through the English-speaking world." Visa (P) sued JSL (D), claiming that "eVisa" was likely to dilute the "Visa" trademark through blurring. The district court granted summary judgment for Visa (P), and JSL (D) appealed, arguing that its mark could not cause dilution since "visa" is an ordinary English word, so that Visa's (P) use of the word was insufficiently distinctive. The court of appeals granted review.

ISSUE: Is a famous trademark that is comprised of an ordinary English word susceptible of dilution by blurring where the way the trademark is used in a particular commercial context is unique, and the purportedly blurring mark is not being used for its literal dictionary definition, but rather creates a new meaning for the word in a different commercial context?

HOLDING AND DECISION: (Kozinski, C.J.) Yes. A famous trademark that is comprised of an ordinary English word is susceptible of dilution by blurring where the way the trademark is used in a particular commercial context is unique, and the purportedly blurring mark is not being used for its literal dictionary definition, but rather creates a new meaning for the word in a different commercial context. A plaintiff seeking relief under federal antidilution law must show that its mark is famous and distinctive, that defendant began using its mark in commerce after plaintiff's mark became famous and distinctive, and that defendant's mark is likely to dilute plaintiff's mark. Here it is undisputed that the "Visa" mark is famous and distinctive or that JSL began using the "eVisa" mark in commerce after "Visa" achieved its renown. JSL (D) claims only that the district court erred when it found as a matter of law that "eVisa" was likely to dilute the Visa trademark. Factors used to determine likelihood of dilution include the similarity between the two marks and the distinctiveness and recognition of the plaintiff's mark. Here, the marks are effectively identical, and "Visa" is a strong trademark. People ordinarily would not associate credit cards with visas if it weren't for the "Visa" brand. This suggests that any association is the result of goodwill and deserves broad protection from potential infringers. JSL (D) claims the "eVisa" mark cannot cause dilution because, in addition to being an electronic payment network, a visa is a travel document authorizing the bearer to enter a country's territory. When a trademark is also a word with a dictionary definition, it may be difficult to show that the trademark holder's use of the word is sufficiently distinctive to deserve antidilution protection because such a word is likely to be descriptive or suggestive of an essential attribute of the trademarked good. Moreover, such a word may already be in use as a mark by third parties. Here, however, Visa's (P) use of the word "visa" is sufficiently distinctive because it plays only weakly off the dictionary meaning of the term and there was no evidence that a third party has used the word as a mark. Merely because the mark is comprised of an ordinary English word does not necessarily undermine the uniqueness of the trademark. The question is not whether the word itself is common, but whether the way the word is used in commerce to identify a good or service is unique enough to warrant trademark protection. Despite widespread use of the word "visa" for its common English meaning, the introduction of the "eVisa" mark to the marketplace means that there are two products, and

Continued on next page.

not just one, competing for association with that word. This is the quintessential harm addressed by antidilution law. Further, JSL (D) is not using the word "visa" for its literal dictionary definition, so that it is not merely evoking the word's existing dictionary meaning, as to which no one may claim exclusivity. Instead, JSL (D) is using visa in a way that creates a new association for the word: to identify a "multilingual education and information business." This multiplication of meanings is the essence of dilution by blurring, and this is true even when use of the word also gestures at the word's dictionary definition, since blurring occurs when a mark previously associated with one product also becomes associated with a second, thus weakening the mark's ability to evoke the first product in the minds of consumers. Because dilution always involves use of a mark by a defendant that is "different" from the plaintiff's use, and the injury addressed by antidilution law in fact occurs when marks are placed in new and different contexts, thereby weakening the mark's ability to bring to mind the plaintiff's goods or services, the district court did not err in granting summary judgment to Visa (P) and enjoining JSL's (D) use of "eVisa." Affirmed.

▶ ANALYSIS

Whether a defendant's mark creates a likelihood of dilution is a factual question generally not appropriate for decision on summary judgment. Nevertheless, as this case demonstrates, summary judgment may be granted in a dilution case, as in any other, if no reasonable factfinder could fail to find a likelihood of dilution. Also, as happened in this case, in an appropriate case, the district court may conclusively determine one or more of the likelihood of dilution factors before trial.

Quicknotes

DISTINCTIVENESS A standard for trademark protection, whereby the more distinctive a mark is, the greater its eligibility for protection. Distinctive marks typically consist of terms that are fanciful or coined, arbitrary, or suggestive. If a mark is descriptive, it is not entitled to trademark protection unless it has acquired distinctiveness through consumer association of goods or services with the mark (such acquired distinctiveness is also known as secondary meaning).

SECONDARY MEANING A word or mark that becomes associated with a particular merchant or product as its source of origin.

TRADEMARK DILUTION The diminishment of the capability of a trademark to identify and distinguish the particular good or service with which it is associated.

Rolex Watch U.S.A., Inc. v. AFP Imaging Corporation

Watchmaker (P) v. X-ray table maker (D)

101 U.S.P.Q.2d 1188 (T.T.A.B. 2011), *later proceeding*, 468 Fed. Appx. 996 (Fed. Cir. 2012) (*appeal dismissed as moot*).

NATURE OF CASE: Opposition proceeding, based on dilution by blurring, in trademark registration action.

FACT SUMMARY: Rolex Watch U.S.A., Inc. (Rolex) (P) opposed the registration by AFP Imaging Corp. (AFP) (D) of the mark "ROLL-X" for rolling x-ray tables, contending that AFP's (D) mark would dilute by blurring Rolex's (P) "ROLEX" mark for watches. The Trademark Trial and Appeal Board assessed the statutory blurring factors to determine if there was a likelihood of dilution by blurring.

🏛 RULE OF LAW
A defendant's mark is not likely to dilute by blurring a plaintiff's famous mark where the degree of dissimilarity between the marks, conflicting survey results as to the degree of actual association between the marks, and lack of evidence that the defendant intended to create an association with the plaintiff's mark outweigh the recognition, distinctiveness, and substantially exclusive use of the plaintiff's mark.

FACTS: Rolex Watch U.S.A., Inc. (Rolex) (P) has been using the mark "ROLEX" for watches and timepieces for over 100 years, with annual sales in the hundreds of millions of dollars and annual U.S. advertising expenditures in the tens of millions of dollars. It is one of the world's top brands. AFP Imaging Corp. (AFP) (D) filed an intent-to-use application to register the mark "ROLL-X" for rolling x-ray tables to be used in the healthcare industry. Rolex (P) opposed on the grounds that AFP's (D) mark would dilute by blurring the "ROLEX" mark. As part of its opposition, Rolex (P) submitted survey evidence that involved veterinarians and other animal professionals who made x-ray table purchasing decisions. The survey used both a test cell bearing the "ROLL-X" and a control cell. Following a series of screening questions, the respondents shown the test cell "ROLL-X" were asked the following questions: "Assume for a moment that you were looking for a new x-ray table and you encountered one that uses this name . . . What, if anything, came to your mind when I first showed you the name of this x-ray table?" Of the test cell respondents, 82% replied that something came to mind. Of that 82%, 42% replied "Rolex/Watch," 32% replied "Portable/Movable/ Rolling," 18% replied "X-Ray Tables/Equipment" and 7% replied "X-Rays." AFP (D) did not present any evidence of third-party usage of the mark "ROLEX," or of use of phonetic equivalents. The Trademark Trial and Appeal Board assessed the statutory blurring factors to determine if there was a likelihood of dilution by blurring.

ISSUE: Is a defendant's mark likely to dilute by blurring a plaintiff's famous mark where the degree of

dissimilarity between the marks, conflicting survey results as to the degree of actual association between the marks, and lack of evidence that the defendant intended to create an association with the plaintiff's mark outweigh the recognition, distinctiveness, and substantially exclusive use of the plaintiff's mark?

HOLDING AND DECISION: (Lycos, J.) No. A defendant's mark is not likely to dilute by blurring a plaintiff's famous mark where the degree of dissimilarity between the marks, conflicting survey results as to the degree of actual association between the marks, and lack of evidence that the defendant intended to create an association with the plaintiff's mark outweigh the recognition, distinctiveness, and substantially exclusive use of the plaintiff's mark. The first factor to determine likelihood of dilution by blurring is the degree of similarity between the defendant's mark and the famous mark. Although "ROLEX" and "ROLL-X" are likely to be pronounced in an identical manner, the marks are spelled differently and, because of the spelling of "ROLL-X," it engenders a different appearance, meaning and commercial impression from "ROLEX." Because of the hyphen between "ROLL" and "X," consumers are likely to view the mark as consisting of the English word "ROLL," which has various meanings including "to move on rollers or wheels" and the letter "X," which, when the mark is used in connection with AFP's (D) goods, is likely to be perceived as suggesting the term "x-ray." Thus, this factor favors AFP (D). The second blurring factor is the distinctiveness of the famous mark. Here it is undisputed that "ROLEX" is distinctive since it is a coined, arbitrary term with no meaning other than as a trademark. The third factor is the degree to which the famous mark is used exclusively by the plaintiff. Here, there was no evidence that "ROLEX," or a phonetic equivalent, is used by any third party; this favors Rolex (P). The fourth factor is the degree of recognition of the famous mark, and here it is undisputed that "ROLEX" is a highly recognized mark; this favors Rolex (P). The fifth factor is the defendant's intent to create an association with the famous mark. Here, there was no evidence that AFP (D) intended to create an association of "ROLL-X" with "ROLEX." To the contrary, the "ROLL-X" name was intended to describe the attributes of AFP's (D) rolling x-ray tables. This factor thus favors AFP (D). The sixth factor is the degree of any actual association between the defendant's mark and the famous mark. Here, the survey evidence was not flawed. Contrary to AFP's (D) objections, the survey questions clearly communicated to respondents

Continued on next page.

the nature the AFP's (D) goods, for which there is no current market. Nonetheless, although 42% of the respondents who stated that when something came to mind, it was "Rolex/Watch," this level of "actual association" is insufficient to prove a likelihood of dilution between the marks at issue, given that a higher percentage, 50% of respondents who replied that something came to mind, thought of a feature of the goods (portable, rolling) or the actual goods themselves (x-ray tables/equipment). Moreover, the survey results, while showing an "actual association" between the marks, do not establish that such an association would impair the distinctiveness of Rolex's (P) famous mark. Thus, this factor favors AFP (D). Balancing these factors, the degree of dissimilarity between the marks, the conflicting results obtained from the survey, and lack of evidence that AFP (D) intended to create an association with "ROLEX" outweigh the recognition, distinctiveness and substantially exclusive use of the "ROLEX" trademark. Further, Rolex (P) has not presented any evidence that an association between the marks will impair the distinctiveness of "ROLEX." For all these reasons, Rolex (P) has failed to demonstrate that the registration of "ROLL-X" is likely to cause dilution by blurring of "ROLEX." Judgment for AFP (D).

▌ *ANALYSIS*

As this case illustrates, an owner of a famous mark must not only show that the purportedly blurring mark creates an association between the marks in consumers' minds arising from the similarity of the marks, but must also show whether such association is likely to impair the distinctiveness of the famous mark. The burden of proof on the famous mark's owner is higher when a market for the defendant's mark does not yet exist—as in this case where an intent-to-use registration was involved. That burden of proof can be satisfied, inter alia, through consumer survey or expert testimony evidence of the degree to which the famous mark's owner's marketing power would potentially be diminished by the intended use of the defendant's mark. Here, Rolex (P) failed to present such evidence, which reinforced the court's conclusion that there would be no dilution by blurring of "ROLEX" if the registration for "ROLL-X" were granted.

Quicknotes

DISTINCTIVENESS A standard for trademark protection, whereby the more distinctive a mark is, the greater its eligibility for protection. Distinctive marks typically consist of terms that are fanciful or coined, arbitrary, or suggestive. If a mark is descriptive, it is not entitled to trademark protection unless it has acquired distinctiveness through consumer association of goods or services with the mark (such acquired distinctiveness is also known as secondary meaning).

INTER ALIA Among other things.

SECONDARY MEANING A word or mark that becomes associated with a particular merchant or product as its source of origin.

TRADEMARK DILUTION The diminishment of the capability of a trademark to identify and distinguish the particular good or service with which it is associated.

Louis Vuitton Malletier S.A. v. Haute Diggity Dog, LLC

Luxury good manufacturer/Trademark owner (P) v. Pet products manufacturer (D)

507 F3d. 252 (4th Cir. 2007).

NATURE OF CASE: Appeal from summary judgment for defendant in action for, inter alia, trademark dilution.

FACT SUMMARY: Louis Vuitton Malletier S.A. (LVM) (P), a luxury goods manufacturer, claimed that Haute Diggity Dog., LLC (D), a pet products manufacturer, among other things, diluted LVM's (P) trademarks by creating and selling a line of "Chewy Vuiton" dog chew toys that spoofed LVM's (P) handbags and trademarked designs.

> ## 🏛 RULE OF LAW
> (1) Trademark dilution by blurring does not occur under the Trademark Dilution Revision Act of 2006 where a famous and distinctive mark is parodied, but the mark is only mimicked and not actually used.
> (2) Trademark dilution by tarnishment does not occur under the Trademark Dilution Revision Act of 2006 where harm to a famous mark is only speculative and without record support.

FACTS: Louis Vuitton Malletier S.A. (LVM) (P) is a well-known manufacturer and seller of various luxury goods, including ladies handbags, that has adopted trademarks and trade dress that are well recognized and have become famous and distinct. LVM (P) has registered trademarks for an entwined "LOUIS VUITTON," (the "LOUIS VUITTON mark"); and for a stylized monogram of "LV" (the "LV mark"); for a monogram canvas design consisting of a canvas with repetitions of the "LV" mark along with four-pointed stars, four-pointed stars inset in curved diamonds, and four-pointed flowers inset in circles (the "Monogram Canvas mark"). It also adopted a brightly colored version of the "Monogram Canvas" mark in which the "LV" mark and the designs were of various colors and the background was white (the "Multicolor design"). It also adopted another design consisting of a canvas with repetitions of the "LV" mark and smiling cherries on a brown background (the "Cherry design"). LVM's (P) products are very expensive usually costing hundreds or thousands of dollars. Although LVM (P) also markets a limited selection of luxury pet accessories, it does not make dog toys. Haute Diggity Dog, LLC (HDD) (D) manufactures and sells a line of pet chew toys and beds whose names parody elegant high-end brands of products. In particular, HDD (D) created a line of "Chewy Vuiton" chew toys that resembled LVM(P) handbags. The toys loosely resemble miniature handbags and undisputedly evoke LVM (P) handbags of similar shape, design, and

color. In lieu of the "LOUIS VUITTON" mark, the dog toy uses "Chewy Vuiton"; in lieu of the "LV" mark, it uses "CV"; and the other symbols and colors employed are imitations, but not exact ones, of those used in the "LVM Multicolor" and "Cherry" designs. The chew toys were sold mainly in pet stores and cost around $20. LVM (P) brought suit against HDD (D) for, inter alia, trademark dilution, claiming that HDD's (D) advertising, sale, and distribution of the "Chewy Vuiton" dog toys diluted its "LOUIS VUITTON," "LV" and "Monogram Canvas" marks, which are famous and distinctive, in violation of the Trademark Dilution Revision Act of 2006 (TDRA) (there were other copyright and trademark claims). On cross-motions for summary judgment, the district court concluded that HDD's (D) "Chewy Vuiton" dog toys were successful parodies of LVM's (P) trademarks, designs, and products, and on that basis, entered judgment in favor of HDD (PD) on all of LVM's (P) claims. The court of appeals granted review.

ISSUE:
(1) Does trademark dilution by blurring occur under the Trademark Dilution Revision Act of 2006 where a famous and distinctive mark is parodied, but the mark is only mimicked and not actually used?
(2) Does trademark dilution by tarnishment occur under the Trademark Dilution Revision Act of 2006 where harm to a famous mark is only speculative and without record support?

HOLDING AND DECISION: (Cacheris, J.)
(1) No. Trademark dilution by blurring does not occur under the Trademark Dilution Revision Act of 2006 (TDRA) where a famous and distinctive mark is parodied, but the mark is only mimicked and not actually used. To state a dilution claim under the TDRA, a plaintiff must show: (1) that the plaintiff owns a famous mark that is distinctive; (2) that the defendant has commenced using a mark in commerce that allegedly is diluting the famous mark; (3) that a similarity between the defendant's mark and the famous mark gives rise to an association between the marks; and (4) that the association is likely to impair the distinctiveness of the famous mark or likely to harm the reputation of the famous mark. In the context of blurring, distinctiveness refers to the ability of the famous mark uniquely to identify a single source and thus maintain its selling power. Here, the only statutory factor at issue is the fourth factor—whether the association between

Continued on next page.

HDD's (D) marks and LVM's (P) marks will impair the distinctiveness of LVM's (P) marks. LVM (P) suggests that any use by a third person of an imitation of its famous marks dilutes the famous marks as a matter of law. Such an interpretation, however, goes too far. The TDRA has six statutory factors that must be considered when determining if a junior mark has diluted a famous mark, but the district court did not consider these. The factors are: (i) the degree of similarity between the mark or trade name and the famous mark; (ii) the degree of inherent or acquired distinctiveness of the famous mark; (iii) the extent to which the owner of the famous mark is engaging in substantially exclusive use of the mark; (iv) the degree of recognition of the famous mark; (v) whether the user of the mark or trade name intended to create an association with the famous mark; and (vi) any actual association between the mark or trade name and the famous mark. Although the district court erred by not considering these factors, when they are considered, the conclusion is the same as that reached by the district court. Under the TDRA, which provides that fair use is a complete defense, parody is not automatically a complete defense to a claim of dilution by blurring where the defendant uses the parody as its own designation of source, i.e., as a trademark. Nevertheless, a court is directed by the TDRA to consider all relevant factors, so that a court may take into account the existence of a parody that is used as a trademark as part of the circumstances to be considered. A defendant's use of a mark as a parody is relevant to the overall question of whether the defendant's use is likely to impair the famous mark's distinctiveness, as well as to several of the listed factors. Regarding the fifth and sixth factors, a parody intentionally creates an association with the famous mark in order to be a parody, but also intentionally communicates, if it is successful, that it is not the famous mark, but rather a satire of the famous mark. The first, second, and fourth factors are also directly implicated when the defendant's use of the mark is a parody. In fact, a successful parody may render the famous mark even more distinctive. Thus, while a defendant's use of a parody as a mark does not support a "fair use" defense, it may be considered in determining whether the plaintiff has proved its claim that the defendant's use of a parody mark is likely to impair the distinctiveness of the famous mark. It is undisputed that LVM's (P) marks are distinctive, famous, and strong—even iconic. Accordingly, because these famous marks are particularly strong and distinctive, it becomes more likely that a parody will not impair their distinctiveness. That is the case here; because HDD's (D) "Chewy Vuiton" marks are a successful parody, they will not blur the distinctiveness of the famous marks as a unique identifier of their source. While this might not be true if the parody is so similar to the famous mark that it likely could be construed as actual use of the famous mark itself, here HDD (D)

mimicked the famous marks; it did not come so close to them as to destroy the success of its parody and, more importantly, to diminish the LVM (P) marks' capacity to identify a single source. The limitations by HDD (D) are intentionally imperfect so that it is clear that they are a parody. HDD (D) intentionally associated its marks, but only partially and imperfectly, so as to convey the simultaneous message that it was not in fact a source of LVM (P) products. Rather, as a parody, it separated itself from the LVM (P) marks in order to make fun of them. When all these factors are considered, it is clear that the distinctiveness of LVM's (P) marks will not likely be impaired by HDD's (D) marketing and sale of its "Chewy Vuiton" products. Affirmed as to this issue.

(2) No. Trademark dilution by tarnishment does not occur under the Trademark Dilution Revision Act of 2006 where harm to a famous mark is only speculative and without record support. To establish dilution by tarnishment, LVM (P) must prove that HDD's (D) use of the "Chewy Vuiton" mark on dog toys actually harmed the reputation of LVM's (P) marks. The only argument LVM (P) makes in this regard is that a dog could choke on a "Chewy Vuiton" toy, but LVM (P) presents no evidence that a dog has ever choked on one of these toys or that there is a likelihood that a dog ever will. Therefore, LVM (P) has failed to demonstrate a claim for dilution by tarnishment. Affirmed as to this issue.

▶ ANALYSIS

One of the effects of the Trademark Dilution Revision Act of 2006 (TDRA) was to overturn the United States Supreme Court decision in *Moseley v. V Secret Catalogue, Inc.,* 537 U.S. 418 (2003), which held a plaintiff needed to prove actual dilution under the Federal Trademark Dilution Act (FTDA). The TDRA revised the FTDA so that a plaintiff only needs to show the defendant's mark is likely to cause dilution, thus facilitating claims brought by owners of famous marks for dilution. However, the TDRA also limited famous marks to those that are "widely recognized by the general consuming public of the United States" and abolished the concept of niche fame, thus reducing the number of dilution claims that could be brought successfully.

Quicknotes

DISTINCTIVENESS A standard for trademark protection, whereby the more distinctive a mark is, the greater its eligibility for protection. Distinctive marks typically consist of terms that are fanciful or coined, arbitrary, or suggestive. If a mark is descriptive, it is not entitled to

Continued on next page.

trademark protection unless it has acquired distinctiveness through consumer association of goods or services with the mark (such acquired distinctiveness is also known as secondary meaning).

PARODY For purposes of trademark law, an amusing use of another's trademark that evokes the original trademark while simultaneously satirizing or criticizing the trademark, in a manner that either is likely to confuse the consuming public as to the use's source, sponsorship or approval, or not, but if the use is not likely to cause consumer confusion, it will not constitute trademark infringement.

SECONDARY MEANING A word or mark that becomes associated with a particular merchant or product as its source of origin.

TRADE DRESS The overall image of, or impression created by, a product that a court may enforce as a trademark if it determines that such image has acquired secondary meaning and that the public recognizes it as an indication of source.

TRADEMARK Any word, name, symbol, device or combination thereof that is either currently utilized, or which a person has a bona fide intent to utilize, in commerce in order to distinguish his goods from those of another.

TRADEMARK DILUTION The diminishment of the capability of a trademark to identify and distinguish the particular good or service with which it is associated.

TRADEMARK INFRINGEMENT The unauthorized use of another's trademark in such a manner as to cause a likelihood of confusion as to the source of the product or service in connection with which it is utilized.

Starbucks Corp. v. Wolfe's Borough Coffee, Inc.

Coffee company (P) v. Coffee company (D)

588 F.3d 97 (2d Cir. 2009).

NATURE OF CASE: Appeal from judgment for defendant in action asserting federal and state trademark and unfair competition claims.

FACT SUMMARY: Starbucks Corp. (P), an international coffee company, contended, inter alia, that its famous "Starbucks" mark would be diluted by blurring and tarnishment by the "Charbucks" mark used by Wolfe's Borough Coffee, Inc. d/b/a Black Bear Micro Roastery (Black Bear) (D), a small New England coffee company. After the district court rendered judgment for Black Bear (D), Starbucks (P) appealed, arguing as to blurring that there only had to be similarity between the marks, not "substantial" similarity; that a mere intent by Black Bear (D) to associate "Charbucks" with "Starbucks" was all that was needed, not a finding of bad intent; and that the absence of evidence of "actual confusion" between the marks was not dispositive as to whether there was a likelihood of dilution. As to tarnishment, Starbucks (P) argued that "Charbucks" damaged the positive reputation of Starbucks (P) by evoking both Starbucks (P) and negative impressions in consumers, including the image of bitter, over-roasted coffee. Black Bear (D) defended by claiming that even if the "Charbucks" mark diluted the "Starbucks" mark, by either blurring or tarnishment, its use of "Charbucks" was protected as a parody.

RULE OF LAW

(1) To prevail on a claim of dilution by blurring, a plaintiff is not required to show that the similarity between the junior mark and its famous mark is substantial.

(2) For purposes of determining likelihood of dilution by blurring, in determining whether the user of a junior mark intended to create an association with the famous mark, it is not appropriate to consider whether bad faith corresponds with that intent.

(3) For purposes of determining likelihood of dilution by blurring, the absence of actual or even of a likelihood of confusion does not undermine evidence of trademark dilution.

(4) Evidence that consumers may associate a negative-sounding junior mark with a famous mark by itself is not probative of trademark dilution by tarnishment.

(5) The use of a junior mark cannot qualify under the parody exception to trademark dilution where the junior mark is used as a designation of source for the defendant's own goods.

FACTS: Starbucks Corp. (P) is an international coffee company, with close to 9,000 retail locations throughout the world. It supplies its coffee to numerous third party vendors, e.g., restaurants, airlines, and it also maintains a well-frequented website. Starbucks (P) prominently displays its registered "Starbucks" marks on its products and areas of business. The Starbucks (P) marks include, inter alia, the tradename "Starbucks" and its logo, which is circular and generally contains a graphic of a mermaid-like siren encompassed by the phrase "Starbucks Coffee." Starbucks has been the subject of U.S. trademark registrations continuously since 1985 and has around 60 U.S. trademark registrations and numerous foreign trademark registrations. Starbucks (P) has spent hundreds of millions of dollars on advertising, promotion, and marketing, and has gained significant exposure through product placements in movies and television programs. Wolfe's Borough Coffee, Inc. d/b/a Black Bear Micro Roastery (Black Bear) (D), a small New England coffee company, began selling a dark roasted blend of coffee called "Charbucks Blend" and later "Mister Charbucks." Charbucks Blend was sold in a packaging that showed a picture of a black bear above the large font "BLACK BEAR MICRO ROASTERY." The package informed consumers that the coffee was roasted in New Hampshire and was dark. Mister Charbucks was sold in a packaging that showed a picture of a man walking above the large font "Mister Charbucks." The package also informed consumers that the coffee was roasted in New Hampshire by "The Black Bear Micro Roastery" and that the coffee was "ROASTED TO THE EXTREME . . . FOR THOSE WHO LIKE THE EXTREME." Starbucks (P) brought suit against Black Bear (D), asserting various federal and state trademark and unfair competition claims, including trademark dilution by blurring and by tarnishment. The district court rendered judgment for Black Bear (D), and Starbucks (P) appealed, arguing as to blurring that there only had to be similarity between the marks, not "substantial" similarity as the district court had ruled; that a mere intent by Black Bear (D) to associate "Charbucks" with "Starbucks" was all that was needed, not a finding of bad intent as the district court required; and that the absence of evidence of "actual confusion" between the marks was not dispositive as to whether there was a likelihood of dilution, so that the district court erred as to this factor. As to whether consumers associated the two marks, Starbucks (P) submitted the results of a telephone survey where 3.1% of 600 consumers responded that Starbucks (P) was the possible

Continued on next page.

source of "Charbucks." The survey also showed that 30.5% of consumers responded "Starbucks" to the question: "[w]hat is the first thing that comes to mind when you hear the name 'Charbucks.'" As to tarnishment, Starbucks (P) argued that "Charbucks" damaged the positive reputation of Starbucks (P) by evoking both Starbucks (P) and negative impressions in consumers, including the image of bitter, over-roasted coffee. Black Bear (D) defended by claiming that even if the "Charbucks" mark diluted the "Starbucks" mark, by either blurring or tarnishment, its use of "Charbucks" was protected as a parody. The court of appeals granted review.

ISSUE:

(1) To prevail on a claim of dilution by blurring, is a plaintiff required to show that the similarity between the junior mark and its famous mark is substantial?

(2) For purposes of determining likelihood of dilution by blurring, in determining whether the user of a junior mark intended to create an association with the famous mark, is it appropriate to consider whether bad faith corresponds with that intent?

(3) For purposes of determining likelihood of dilution by blurring, does the absence of actual or even of a likelihood of confusion undermine evidence of trademark dilution?

(4) Is evidence that consumers may associate a negative-sounding junior mark with a famous mark by itself probative of trademark dilution by tarnishment?

(5) Can the use of a junior mark qualify under the parody exception to trademark dilution where the junior mark is used as a designation of source for the defendant's own goods?

HOLDING AND DECISION: (Miner, J.)

(1) No. To prevail on a claim of dilution by blurring, a plaintiff is not required to show that the similarity between the junior mark and its famous mark is substantial. The first factor federal law specifies for determining likelihood of dilution by blurring is the similarity between the junior mark and the famous mark. Here, the district court did not clearly err in finding that the "Charbucks" marks were minimally similar to the "Starbucks" marks as presented to consumers. Although "Ch"arbucks is similar to "St"arbucks in sound and spelling, the Charbucks packaging makes clear that Black Bear (D) is the roaster and is a micro-roaster, and otherwise Black Bear's (D) packaging is different in imagery, color, and format from Starbucks' (P) logo and signage. Also, "Charbucks" is associated with Black Bear (D) on that company's website, and it is unlikely that "Charbucks" will appear to consumers outside the context of its normal use, since "Char-bucks" is not directly identifiable with the actual product, i.e., coffee beans. Moreover, it was not clearly erroneous for the district court to find that the "Mister" prefix or "Blend" suffix lessened the similarity between the "Charbucks" marks and the "Starbucks" marks in

the court's overall assessment of similarity. Starbucks (P) unconvincingly argues that the district court should have ignored these terms, as they are generic and too weak to aid in rendering the "Charbucks" marks distinctive. First, this argument to ignore relevant evidence is unfounded in the law, and, second, even if the core term "Charbucks" were used to identify a product as a stand-alone term, such finding would not be dispositive of the district court's overall assessment of the degree of similarity. Nevertheless, the district court did err in concluding that because there was no substantial similarity between the marks, this fact alone was sufficient to defeat Starbucks' (P) blurring claim. Thus, the district court may also have placed undue significance on the similarity factor in determining the likelihood of dilution in its alternative analysis. With the Trademark Dilution Revision Act of 200[6] (TDRA), Congress did not require a finding of substantial similarity between marks to support a blurring claim. Instead, only a finding of similarity is necessary to support such a claim. Although "similarity" is an integral element in the definition of "blurring," the TDRA does not use the words "very" or "substantial" in connection with the similarity factor to be considered in examining a federal dilution claim. The inquiry is made as to the degree of similarity, not whether there is substantial similarity. Additionally, if substantial similarity were a requirement for all dilution by blurring claims, the significance of the remaining five factors would be materially diminished because they would have no relevance unless the degree of similarity between the marks was initially determined to be "substantial." [Vacated and remanded as to this issue.]

(2) No. For purposes of determining likelihood of dilution by blurring, in determining whether the user of a junior mark intended to create an association with the famous mark, it is not appropriate to consider whether bad faith corresponds with that intent. The fifth factor federal law specifies for determining likelihood of dilution by blurring is whether the user of the junior mark intended to create an association with the famous mark. The district court erred in concluding that Black Bear (D) possessed the requisite intent to associate "Charbucks" with "Starbucks," but that this factor did not weigh in favor of Starbucks (P) because Black Bear (D) did not act in "bad faith." The statute simply does not refer to bad faith, but only requires consideration of an intent to associate the marks. Because Black Bear (D) intended to associate its marks with those of Starbucks (P), this factor weighs in favor of Starbucks (P). [Vacated and remanded as to this issue.]

(3) No. For purposes of determining likelihood of dilution by blurring, the absence of actual or even of a likelihood of confusion does not undermine evidence of trade-

Continued on next page.

mark dilution. The sixth factor federal law specifies for determining likelihood of dilution by blurring is whether there is any actual association between the junior mark and the famous mark. The district court rejected Starbucks' (P) claim of actual association, relying on the lack of evidence supporting "actual confusion." This was error, as the absence of actual or even of a likelihood of confusion does not undermine evidence of trademark dilution. Here, Starbucks (P) survey was evidence of some actual association between the marks, so it was error for the district court to reject that evidence on the basis that there was no evidence of confusion between the marks. [Vacated and remanded as to this issue.]

(4) No. Evidence that consumers may associate a negative-sounding junior mark with a famous mark by itself is not probative of trademark dilution by tarnishment. Dilution by tarnishment is an association arising from the similarity between a junior mark and a famous mark that harms the reputation of the famous mark. Starbucks (P) argues that the district court erred by failing to find that "Charbucks" damages the positive reputation of Starbucks (P) by evoking both "Starbucks" and negative impressions in consumers, including the image of bitter, over-roasted coffee. The results of Starbucks' (P) survey were that 30.5% of persons surveyed "immediately associated 'Charbucks' with 'Starbucks'"; and 62% of those surveyed who associated "Charbucks" with "Starbucks" "indicated that they would have a negative impression" of a "coffee named 'Charbucks.'" A mere association between "Charbucks" and "Starbucks," coupled with a negative impression of the name "Charbucks," is insufficient to establish a likelihood of dilution by tarnishment, since such an association is not indicative of whether consumers view the junior mark as harming the reputation of the famous mark. Hypothetically speaking, it is possible that it may even be that "Charbucks" would strengthen the positive impressions of Starbucks (P) because it brings to the attention of consumers that the "Char" is absent in "Star" bucks, and, therefore, of the two "bucks," Starbucks (P) is the "un-charred" and more appealing product. Unfortunately, Starbucks' (P) survey failed to ask the correct questions in this regard and to shed light on this issue. Additionally, although "Charbucks" may be in general be a pejorative term for Starbucks' (P) coffee, Black Bear (D) is not using that term pejoratively. To the contrary, Black Bear (D) is redefining "Charbucks" to promote a positive image for its brand of coffee, and therefore it cannot be said that the use is harming the reputation of Starbucks' (P) coffees—especially given that the "Charbucks" line of coffee is marketed as a product of very high quality. These factors undermine the argument that the use tarnishes Starbucks' (P) reputation. Although the similarity between "Charbucks" and "Starbucks" in that they are both very high quality coffees

may be relevant in determining dilution, such similarity undercuts the claim that "Charbucks" harms the reputation of Starbucks (P). For these reasons, the district court did not err in rejecting Starbucks' (P) claim of dilution by tarnishment. [Affirmed as to this issue.]

(5) No. The use of a junior mark cannot qualify under the parody exception to trademark dilution where the junior mark is used as a designation of source for the defendant's own goods. The TDRA added an exception to trademark dilution for a use that identifies and parodies, criticizes or comments upon the famous mark owner or the goods or services of the famous mark owner. Thus, under the TDRA, Black Bear's (D) use of the "Charbucks" marks cannot qualify under the parody exception because its marks are used to designate the source for its own goods. Black Bear's (D) use also cannot qualify as a parody that undermines a finding of dilution, because, at most, it is a subtle satire of Starbucks (P), and not a clear parody thereof. To the contrary, "Charbucks" is promoted not as a satire or irreverent commentary of Starbucks (P) but, rather, as a beacon to identify "Charbucks" as a coffee that competes at the same level and quality as Starbucks (P) in producing dark-roasted coffees. Because the "Charbucks" marks do not effect an increase in public identification of the "Starbucks" marks with Starbucks (P), the purported "Charbucks" parody plays no part in undermining a finding of dilution. Accordingly, the parody exception is of no help to Black Bear (D) in defending against Starbucks' (P) dilution claim. [Affirmed as to this issue.]

► ANALYSIS

In *Louis Vuitton Malletier S.A. v. Haute Diggity Dog, LLC*, 507 F.3d 252 (4th Cir. 2007), the Fourth Circuit ruled that although the fair use exception for parodies as specified in 15 U.S.C. § 1125(c)(3)(A) does not extend to parodies used as a trademark that serves as a designation of source for the person's own goods or services, the defendant's use of a parody may still be considered in determining whether the owner of a famous mark has proved its claim that the defendant's use of a parody mark is likely to impair the distinctiveness of the famous mark through blurring. The Second Circuit in this case, while noting that it did not need to adopt or reject the Fourth Circuit's holding, nonetheless concluded that Black Bear's (D) use of the "Charbucks" marks was not a parody of the kind that would favor Black Bear (D) in the dilution analysis even if it had adopted the Fourth Circuit's rule, since Black Bear (D) did not separate itself from the "Starbucks" marks in order to make fun of them, but used the association with Starbucks (P) to sell its own coffee. In such instances, where an alleged parody of a competitor's mark is used

Continued on next page.

to sell a competing product, parodic use is sharply restricted.

■══■

Quicknotes

PARODY   For purposes of trademark law, an amusing use of another's trademark that evokes the original trademark while simultaneously satirizing or criticizing the trademark, in a manner that either is likely to confuse the consuming public as to the use's source, sponsorship or approval, or not, but if the use is not likely to cause consumer confusion, it will not constitute trademark infringement.

■══■

The Hershey Company v. Art Van Furniture, Inc.

Chocolate and confectionery company (P) v. Furniture retailer (D)

2008 U.S. Dist. LEXIS 87509 (E.D. Mich. Oct. 24, 2008).

NATURE OF CASE: Motion for temporary restraining order and preliminary injunction in action for trademark and trade dress infringement and dilution.

FACT SUMMARY: The Hershey Company (Hershey) (P), the well-known chocolate and confectionery company, contended that Art Van Furniture, Inc. (Art Van) (D), a furniture retailer, infringed and diluted by blurring Hershey's (P) trademarks and trade dress for its candy bars by posting on Art Van's (D) website a decoration design for its delivery trucks that comprised an image of a brown sofa emerging from a candy wrapper, which was reminiscent of the trade dress for Hershey's (P) candy bars.

🏛 RULE OF LAW

(1) For purposes of obtaining a preliminary injunction enjoining the use of trade dress, an owner of a famous trade dress will not likely succeed on the merits of a likelihood-of-confusion claim where the allegedly infringing trade dress resembles the plaintiff's trade dress in some aspects, but not in others, and has significant generic aspects to it.

(2) For purposes of obtaining a preliminary injunction enjoining the use of trade dress, an owner of a famous trade dress will likely succeed on the merits of a likelihood-of-dilution-by-blurring claim where the allegedly infringing trade dress bears an unmistakable resemblance to the famous trade dress and the evidence supports an inference that the defendant intended to create an association with the plaintiff's trade dress.

(3) A defendant in a trade dress infringement and dilution action cannot prevail on a parody defense where the defendant's design is neither sufficiently similar to the famous trade dress nor sufficiently different to convey a satirical message.

FACTS: The Hershey Company (Hershey) (P) is a well-known chocolate and confectionery company that has been using the same trade dress for its candy bars for over 100 years. The trade dress is comprised of (1) a rectangular design; (2) silver, stylized lettering; (3) a brownish-maroon colored wrapper; (4) the name "Hershey's;" and (5) silver foil protruding from under the wrapper along the edges of the bar. Hershey (P) is one of the largest producers of chocolate and confectionery goods, its products are sold around the world, and it spends tens of millions of dollars annually to maintain and promote its products. Its Special

Dark candy bar has a reddish-burgundy colored wrapper. Art Van Furniture, Inc. (Art Van) (D) is a furniture retailer. At some point, it had an ad contest whereby it posted ten truck decorations on its website and invited visitors to vote for their favorite design. One design was an image of a brown sofa emerging from a red-burgundy candy wrapper, which was reminiscent of the trade dress for Hershey's (P) candy bars. This "couch bar's" packaging is torn open. The words "ART VAN," spelled in white, block lettering, appear in the middle of the wrapper, and on the bottom left of the wrapper, in smaller type, is written "Since 1959." On the right side of the image, where the sofa juts from the "candy bar," the torn wrapper has the appearance of crackled and ripped tinfoil. On the left, the same silver-colored foil is visible, protruding beneath the red and white wrapper. Hershey (P) brought suit for trademark and trade dress infringement and dilution by blurring, and Hershey (P) sought a temporary restraining order and preliminary injunction to enjoin Art Van (D) from using the "couch bar" image on its website and trucks. In addition to claiming that Hershey (P) could not show a likelihood of confusion, nor meet the statutory trademark dilution factors, Art Van (D) defended by claiming its mark was a parody of the Hershey (P) mark.

ISSUE:

(1) For purposes of obtaining a preliminary injunction enjoining the use of trade dress, will an owner of a famous trade dress likely succeed on the merits of a likelihood-of-confusion claim where the allegedly infringing trade dress resembles the plaintiff's trade dress in some aspects, but not in others, and has significant generic aspects to it?

(2) For purposes of obtaining a preliminary injunction enjoining the use of trade dress, will an owner of a famous trade dress likely succeed on the merits of a likelihood-of-dilution-by-blurring claim where the allegedly infringing trade dress bears an unmistakable resemblance to the famous trade dress and the evidence supports an inference that the defendant intended to create an association with the plaintiff's trade dress?

(3) Can a defendant in a trade dress infringement and dilution action prevail on a parody defense where the defendant's design is neither sufficiently similar to the famous trade dress nor sufficiently different to convey a satirical message?

HOLDING AND DECISION: (Roberts, J.)

(1) No. For purposes of obtaining a preliminary injunction enjoining the use of trade dress, an owner of a famous

Continued on next page.

trade dress will not likely succeed on the merits of a likelihood-of-confusion claim where the allegedly infringing trade dress resembles the plaintiff's trade dress in some aspects, but not in others, and has significant generic aspects to it. As a threshold matter, Art Van (D) argues that Hershey's (P) trade dress is famous only if it includes the name "Hershey's," since without it the trade dress is much weaker, as the plethora of brown-colored, rectangular-shaped candy bars on the market indicates. However, the trade dress of a product is the result of "its total image and overall appearance" not one or more isolated elements of its packaging. Here, the strength of Hershey's (P) trade dress comes from the combination of its features and its historical presence in the marketplace, strengthened by decades of advertising. Thus, Hershey's (P) trade dress is highly distinctive and famous, and this factor strongly suggests a likelihood of confusion. Here, Art Van's "couch bar" clearly evokes Hershey's (P) candy bars, especially Hershey's (P) Special Dark bar, and is identical insofar as each wrapper is composed of two distinct elements, a silver foil containing the actual product, and a slightly narrower "sleeve" inscribed with the company name. Other aspects are similar, but not identical. The words "HERSHEY'S" and "ART VAN" are both printed in stylized block lettering; however, their font, color and positioning are different: the letters on Hershey's (P) iconic chocolate bar are silver and occupy the upper half of the wrapper, whereas Art Van's (D) letters are white and sit squarely in the middle. Other similarities are so generic that their impact on the overall analysis is minimal: both designs are rectangular in shape, but the relevance of this element is limited, since most candy bars share this characteristic. Likewise, Art Van's (D) brown-colored sofa evokes chocolate in general, not specifically Hershey's (P) chocolate, much less Hershey's (P) trademark or trade dress. On balance, consumers are unlikely to confuse the "couch bar" with Hershey's (P) iconic chocolate bar. Therefore, Hershey (P) will unlikely succeed on the merits of a likelihood-of-confusion claim.

(2) Yes. For purposes of obtaining a preliminary injunction enjoining the use of trade dress, an owner of a famous trade dress will likely succeed on the merits of a likelihood-of-dilution-by-blurring claim where the allegedly infringing trade dress bears an unmistakable resemblance to the famous trade dress and the evidence supports an inference that the defendant intended to create an association with the plaintiff's trade dress. There are six nonexclusive statutory factors for courts to consider when analyzing whether a mark or trade name is likely to cause dilution by blurring. Here, the second factor (the degree of inherent or acquired distinctiveness of the famous mark) and the third factor (the extent to which the owner of the famous mark is engaging in substantially exclusive use of the mark) are easily met by Hershey (P). The evidence supports an inference

that Art Van (D) intended to "create an association" with Hershey's (P) trade dress (fifth factor), but whether such an association has actually been made is unclear (sixth factor). Finally, Art Van's (D) "couch bar" design, with its stylized block lettering, its packaging in two elements, and especially its silver foil visible beneath the wrapper's sleeve, bears an unmistakable resemblance to some of Hershey's (P) candy bars. Accordingly, Hershey (P) has sustained its burden to show a reasonable likelihood of succeeding on the merits of its dilution-by-blurring claim.

(3) No. A defendant in a trade dress infringement and dilution action cannot prevail on a parody defense where the defendant's design is neither sufficiently similar to the famous trade dress nor sufficiently different to convey a satirical message. Art Van (D) contends that its "couch bar" design is a parody, and, therefore, is protected under the parody exception to trade dress infringement and dilution claims. However, a parody must convey two simultaneous and contradictory messages: that it is the original, but also that it is not the original and is instead a parody. This second message must not only differentiate the alleged parody from the original but must also communicate some articulable element of satire, ridicule, joking, or amusement. Here, Art Van's (D) design is neither similar nor different enough from Hershey's (P) trade dress to convey a satirical message, so that its design does not qualify as a parody, and it cannot prevail on its parody defense. Injunction granted.

▶ *ANALYSIS*

This case illustrates that junior trade dress has to have some similarity to famous trade dress to be found to be dilutive by blurring. This comports with the statutory language of 15 U.S.C. § 1125(c)(2)(B), which provides that "'[D]ilution by blurring' is association arising from the similarity between a mark or trade name and a famous mark." Thus, a plaintiff does not have to establish that the trade dress is identical, nearly identical, or substantially similar to the famous trade dress in order to obtain injunctive relief—provided, of course, that the plaintiff can also show that the junior trade dress will likely impair the distinctiveness of the famous trade dress.

■=■

Quicknotes

DISTINCTIVENESS A standard for trademark protection, whereby the more distinctive a mark is, the greater its eligibility for protection. Distinctive marks typically consist of terms that are fanciful or coined, arbitrary, or suggestive. If a mark is descriptive, it is not entitled to trademark protection unless it has acquired distinc-

Continued on next page.

tiveness through consumer association of goods or services with the mark (such acquired distinctiveness is also known as secondary meaning).

INJUNCTIVE RELIEF A court order issued as a remedy, requiring a person to do, or prohibiting that person from doing, a specific act.

PARODY For purposes of trademark law, an amusing use of another's trademark that evokes the original trademark while simultaneously satirizing or criticizing the trademark, in a manner that either is likely to confuse the consuming public as to the use's source, sponsorship or approval, or not, but if the use is not likely to cause consumer confusion, it will not constitute trademark infringement.

TRADE DRESS The overall image of, or impression created by, a product that a court may enforce as a trademark if it determines that such image has acquired secondary meaning and that the public recognizes it as an indication of source.

TRADEMARK Any word, name, symbol, device or combination thereof that is either currently utilized, or which a person has a bona fide intent to utilize, in commerce in order to distinguish his goods from those of another.

TRADEMARK DILUTION The diminishment of the capability of a trademark to identify and distinguish the particular good or service with which it is associated.

TRADEMARK INFRINGEMENT The unauthorized use of another's trademark in such a manner as to cause a likelihood of confusion as to the source of the product or service in connection with which it is utilized.

MasterCard International Inc. v. Nader 2000 Primary Committee, Inc.

Mark holder (P) v. Presidential election committee (D)

70 U.S.P.Q.2d (BNA) 1046 (S.D.N.Y. 2004).

NATURE OF CASE: Motion for summary judgment in trademark infringement and dilution case.

FACT SUMMARY: MasterCard International, Inc. (MasterCard) (P) has the registered trademarks to "PRICELESS" and "THERE ARE SOME THINGS MONEY CAN'T BUY. FOR EVERYTHING ELSE THERE'S MASTERCARD." Nader 2000 Primary Committee, Inc. (Nader) (D) used the marks in its political ads during the presidential primary. MasterCard (P) sought to enjoin the use.

> **RULE OF LAW**
> Communicative political messages employing another's marks are permissible where the message communicated is not commercial or likely to cause confusion.

FACTS: MasterCard International, Inc. (MasterCard) (P) regularly used advertisements identifying the price of certain goods and then an intangible with the voiceover "Priceless. There are some things money can't buy, for everything else there's MasterCard." It registered the trademarks "PRICELESS" and "THERE ARE SOME THINGS MONEY CAN'T BUY. FOR EVERYTHING ELSE THERE'S MASTERCARD." During the 2000 presidential primary, Nader 2000 Primary Committee, Inc. (Nader) (D) aired advertisements identifying the price of items other politicians accepted from wealthy contributors and the tagline "finding out the truth: priceless. There are some things money can't buy." MasterCard (P) contacted Nader (D) to ask it to air "more original" ads, but the two could not come to an agreement. MasterCard (P) filed suit against Nader (D) on claims of trademark infringement and dilution. MasterCard (P) also sought a preliminary injunction against Nader (D) airing the ads during the primary season, but the court denied the injunction. Nader (D) moved for summary judgment.

ISSUE: Are communicative political messages employing another's marks permissible where the message communicated is not commercial or likely to cause confusion?

HOLDING AND DECISION: (Daniels, J.) Yes. Communicative political messages employing another's marks are permissible where the message communicated is not commercial or likely to cause confusion. MasterCard (P) first argued the likelihood of consumer confusion that MasterCard (P) endorsed Nader (D)'s candidate, Ralph Nader, for president and thus sponsored the ads. The court applies the *Polaroid Corp. v. Polorad Elecs., Corp.*,

287 F.2d 492 (2d Cir. 1961), balancing test to determine the likelihood of confusion. Analysis of the *Polaroid* factors shows little likelihood of confusion, although Nader (D) employed MasterCard's (P) strong marks in a very similar fashion. Consumers were not likely to confuse a political ad with a commercial and Nader (D) testified it did not intend to imply a relationship. MasterCard (P) next argued dilution of its marks. The Federal Trademark Dilution Act (FTDA) specifically exempts noncommercial use from its coverage. MasterCard (P) argued the Nader (D) ads are commercial because donations to Nader (D) increased significantly after the ads ran. MasterCard (P) fails, however, to establish a causal connection. Even if the causal connection could be shown, the speech is political rather than "commercial." Political speech bringing to mind another's mark is permissible, expressive speech. Further, Nader's (D) use of the marks did not dilute them. MasterCard (P) admitted it continued to air the commercials even after Nader's (D) ads and there was no evidence the effectiveness of the marks was lessened. Claims dismissed.

▌ANALYSIS

The court determined Nader's (D) ads were a parody of the MasterCard (P) ads and not likely to cause confusion in the minds of the consumer. MasterCard (P) was vilified by critics for keeping the politician in litigation for over four years over a political speech use of its trademarks. It is important to consider, however, the effect of the four-year battle for MasterCard, because while it lost, another individual may think twice before creating ads employing MasterCard's "Priceless Advertising" technique if the result is four years of litigation time and expense. The balancing act between protecting a trademark and encouraging free expression is a constant tension for the courts.

■=■

Quicknotes

PARODY For purposes of trademark law, an amusing use of another's trademark that evokes the original trademark while simultaneously satirizing or criticizing the trademark, in a manner that either is likely to confuse the consuming public as to the use's source, sponsorship or approval, or not, but if the use is not likely to cause consumer confusion, it will not constitute trademark infringement.

Continued on next page.

POLITICAL SPEECH Speech pertaining to the political process that is afforded the greatest amount of protection under the First Amendment.

TRADEMARK DILUTION The diminishment of the capability of a trademark to identify and distinguish the particular good or service with which it is associated.

TRADEMARK INFRINGEMENT The unauthorized use of another's trademark in such a manner as to cause a likelihood of confusion as to the source of the product or service in connection with which it is utilized.

■═■

False Advertising

Quick Reference Rules of Law

Fashion Boutique of Short Hills, Inc. v. Fendi USA, Inc.

Seller of exclusive line of Fendi products (P) v. Seller of exclusive line of Fendi products (D)

314 F.3d 48 (2d Cir. 2002).

NATURE OF CASE: Appeal from grant of summary judgment to defendant in action under § 43(a)(1)(B) of the Lanham Act, which prohibits misrepresentation of another person's goods or services in commercial advertising or promotion.

FACT SUMMARY: Fashion Boutique of Short Hills, Inc. (Fashion Boutique) (P), which had sold Fendi USA, Inc.'s (Fendi's) (D) international line of products, contended that it lost its business once Fendi (D) opened a store in the area that also carried the international line and made isolated disparaging remarks about Fashion Boutique's (P) products, and that these actions by Fendi (D) violated § 43(a)(1)(B) of the Lanham Act, which prohibits misrepresentation of another person's goods or services in commercial advertising or promotion.

🏛 RULE OF LAW
Under § 43(a)(1)(B) of the Lanham Act, isolated instances of disparaging remarks made by a competitor do not constitute "commercial advertising or promotion" sufficient to sustain a claim under that statute where those remarks are not made as part of an organized campaign designed to penetrate the relevant market.

FACTS: For several years, Fashion Boutique of Short Hills, Inc. (Fashion Boutique) (P) was the only store in the New York City area that carried the international line of products bearing the famous Fendi trademark. Fendi USA, Inc.'s (Fendi's) (D) international line was an exclusive line that was superior in quality to Fendi's (D) domestic line sold in department stores. Then Fendi (D) opened a store in Manhattan that also sold the international line, and Fashion Boutique's (P) business dropped precipitously thereafter. Eventually, Fashion Boutique (P) went out of business. Fashion Boutique (P) brought suit against Fendi (D) asserting, inter alia, claims under § 43(a)(1)(B) of the Lanham Act, which prohibits misrepresentation of another person's goods or services in commercial advertising or promotion. Fashion Boutique's (P) principal theory was that Fendi (D) had a corporate policy to misrepresent the quality and authenticity of the products sold at Fashion Boutique (P). Although Fashion Boutique (P) could not show that many of its customers heard disparaging statements first-hand at Fendi's (D) store, it theorized that Fendi (D) employees made misrepresentations to some customers at Fendi's (D) store, those customers relayed the comments to others, and the false rumors were thus spread throughout Fashion Boutique's (P) customer base. Specifically, Fashion Boutique (P) adduced evidence from

undercover agents posing as shopper that employees at the Fendi (D) store made disparaging remarks about the quality of merchandise at Fashion Boutique (P), but only after the undercover agents initiated conversations with comments about Fashion Boutique (P); there was no evidence that the Fendi (D) employee proactively initiated such conversations. There was also evidence that Fendi (D) employees told a total of 11 customers that Fashion Boutique (P) carried an inferior, "department store" line of products or that Fashion Boutique (P) sold "fake" or "bogus" merchandise. In addition, Fendi (D) employees made critical comments about the customer service at Fashion Boutique (P) to six investigators and one customer, and 16 Fashion Boutique (P) customers reported having heard rumors, after the Fendi (D) store opened, that Fashion Boutique (P) sold fake Fendi (D) merchandise. Eight customers identified similar statements made after Fashion Boutique (P) went out of business. Further, a former Fendi (D) employee testified that although her superiors never explicitly told her of a policy to disparage Fashion Boutique (P), she learned from speaking to managers and salespersons at Fendi's (D) store that salespersons followed a practice of disparaging the customer service at Fashion Boutique (P). The district court ruled that this evidence did not support Fashion Boutique's (P) Lanham Act claim, as Fendi's (D) actions did not fall within the meaning of "commercial advertising or promotion." The district court held that the Lanham Act is violated when defendants proactively pursue customer contacts and disparage the plaintiff's goods or services, and found that Fendi's (D) employees' actions were reactive rather than proactive. In addition, the district court held that the Lanham Act requires sufficient dissemination of the disparaging comments to the relevant purchasing public, and found that there was no such dissemination here. For these reasons, the district court granted summary judgment to Fendi (D) on Fashion Boutique's (P) Lanham Act claim. The court of appeals granted review.

ISSUE: Under § 43(a)(1)(B) of the Lanham Act, do isolated instances of disparaging remarks made by a competitor constitute "commercial advertising or promotion" sufficient to sustain a claim under that statute where those remarks are not made as part of an organized campaign designed to penetrate the relevant market?

HOLDING AND DECISION: (Walker, C.J.) No. Under § 43(a)(1)(B) of the Lanham Act, isolated instances

Continued on next page.

of disparaging remarks made by a competitor do not constitute "commercial advertising or promotion" sufficient to sustain a claim under that statute where those remarks are not made as part of an organized campaign designed to penetrate the relevant market. Fashion Boutique's (P) evidence of several disparaging comments by Fendi (D), together with evidence of rumors that Fashion Boutique (P) sold fake or inferior merchandise, does not fall into the category "commercial advertising or promotion." While the Lanham Act encompasses more than the traditional advertising campaign, the language of the Act cannot be stretched so broadly as to encompass all commercial speech. The touchstone of whether a defendant's actions may be considered "commercial advertising or promotion" under the Lanham Act is that the contested representations are part of an organized campaign to penetrate the relevant market. Proof of widespread dissemination within the relevant industry is a normal concomitant of meeting this requirement. Thus, businesses harmed by isolated disparaging statements do not have redress under the Lanham Act, and they must seek redress under state-law causes of action. The proactive-reactive distinction used by the district court is instructive as to whether a defendant's misrepresentations are designed to reach the public, but not necessarily dispositive, since there is a possibility that merely reactive disparaging remarks could be part of an orchestrated campaign intended to reach many customers. Applying these principles here, Fashion Boutique (P) failed to adduce sufficient evidence that Fendi's (D) actions constituted "commercial advertising or promotion." The district court did not abuse its discretion in excluding the evidence of rumors, as that evidence was more prejudicial than it was probative, and there was no evidence to suggest that the remaining statements were part of an organized campaign to penetrate the marketplace. Fashion Boutique (P) presented a total of 27 oral statements regarding its products in a marketplace of thousands of customers. Such evidence is insufficient to satisfy the requirement that representations be disseminated widely in order to constitute "commercial advertising or promotion." Affirmed.

▶ ANALYSIS

Although the statute does not define the phrase "commercial advertising or promotion," in determining whether representations qualify as "commercial advertising or promotion," most courts have adopted the four-part test set forth in *Gordon & Breach Sci. Publishers S.A. v. Am. Inst. of Physics, 859 F. Supp. 1521, (S.D.N.Y. 1994) ("Gordon & Breach I")*. Under the test, in order to qualify as "commercial advertising or promotion," the contested representations must be "(1) commercial speech; (2) by a defendant who is in commercial competition with plaintiff; (3) for the purpose of influencing consumers to buy defendant's goods or services"; and, (4) although representations less formal than those made as part of a classic advertising campaign may suffice, they must be dissemi-

nated sufficiently to the relevant purchasing public. Here, the court adopted the first, third, and fourth elements of the *Gordon & Breach* test.

Quicknotes

SUMMARY JUDGMENT Judgment rendered by a court in response to a motion made by one of the parties, claiming that the lack of a question of material fact in respect to an issue warrants disposition of the issue without consideration by the jury.

Coca-Cola Co. v. Tropicana Products, Inc.

Orange juice manufacturer (P) v. Orange juice manufacturer (D)

690 F.2d 312 (2d Cir. 1982).

NATURE OF CASE: Appeal from denial of preliminary injunction in action for false advertising under the Lanham Act.

FACT SUMMARY: Coca-Cola Co. (Coke) (P), an orange juice manufacturer, claimed that it would suffer irreparable harm from a television ad by Tropicana Products, Inc. (Tropicana) (D) that showed fresh-squeezed orange juice being poured into a bottle with a voice-over saying that juice was pure, whereas in truth Tropicana's (D) juice was pasteurized and sometimes frozen prior to packaging.

RULE OF LAW
Advertising that is false will be enjoined under the Lanham Act where a plaintiff presents proof that there is reasonable basis for believing that it will be injured as a result of the false advertising and shows that the advertising is explicitly false.

FACTS: Tropicana Products, Inc. (Tropicana) (D) aired a television ad that showed Bruce Jenner, a renowned Olympic athlete, squeezing an orange while saying "It's pure, pasteurized juice as it comes from the orange." The ad then showed Jenner pouring the fresh-squeezed juice into a Tropicana (D) container while the audio stated "It's the only leading brand not made with concentrate and water." Coca-Cola Co. (Coke) (P), an orange juice manufacturer, brought suit for false advertising against Tropicana (D), on the basis of the ad, under § 43(a) of the Lanham Act, and sought to preliminarily enjoin further broadcast of the ad. Coke (P) claimed that the ad was false because Tropicana's (D) juice was pasteurized through heating and sometimes frozen prior to packaging. The district court denied the requested preliminary injunction. The Second Circuit Court of Appeals granted review.

ISSUE: Will advertising that is false be enjoined under the Lanham Act where a plaintiff presents proof that there is reasonable basis for believing that it will be injured as a result of the false advertising and shows that the advertising is explicitly false?

HOLDING AND DECISION: (Cardamone, J.) Yes. Advertising that is false will be enjoined under the Lanham Act where a plaintiff presents proof that there is reasonable basis for believing that it will be injured as a result of the false advertising and shows that the advertising is explicitly false. To obtain an injunction, a plaintiff must show likelihood that he will suffer irreparable harm in the absence of the injunction. This is one of the most difficult elements of a false advertising claim to prove. A plaintiff

who can prove actual lost sales is entitled to an injunction. On the other hand something more than a mere subjective belief must be demonstrated. The plaintiff must submit proof that provides a reasonable basis for believing that it is likely that the plaintiff will be harmed by the false ad. Where products compete head-to-head, as here, a preliminary injunction will issue where the advertising tends to mislead consumers, as supported by market studies. The market studies supply the causative link between the advertising and the plaintiff's potential lost sales. If Coke (P) can show that Tropicana's (D) advertising misleads consumers into believing that its product is a more desirable product, then it is likely that Coke (P) will lose a portion of market share and suffer irreparable injury. Here, the record supports the conclusion that consumer are likely to be misled in this manner, based on a consumer reaction survey, which although flawed in some respects, clearly showed that at least a small number of interviewees were clearly deceived. Coke (P), therefore, has demonstrated that it is likely to suffer irreparable harm. Moreover, Coke (P) is likely to succeed on the merits of its claim because the ad is facially false since it makes the explicit representation that the Tropicana (D) product is produced by squeezing oranges and pouring the resulting juice into the carton. Also, the audio component of the ad is blatantly false when it says that the product is "pasteurized juice as it comes from the orange;" pasteurized juice does not come from oranges, but must be heated significantly. The district court's conclusion to the contrary was erroneous. Therefore, Coke (P) is likely to succeed in arguing that Tropicana's (D) ad was false, as the purpose of the Lanham Act is to ensure truthfulness in advertising and to eliminate misrepresentations with reference to the inherent quality or characteristic of a product. Tropicana's (D) claim that its product contains only fresh-squeezed, unprocessed juice is clearly a misrepresentation. Broadcast of the ad must be enjoined. Reversed and remanded.

▶ ANALYSIS

When a merchandising statement or representation is literally or explicitly false, the court may grant relief without reference to the advertisement's impact on the buying public. When the challenged advertisement is implicitly rather than explicitly false, its tendency to violate the Lanham Act by misleading, confusing or deceiving should be tested by public reaction. To satisfy its burden, the plaintiff must show how consumers have actually reacted to the

Continued on next page.

challenged advertisement rather than merely demonstrating how they could have reacted.

■■■

Quicknotes

ENJOIN The ordering of a party to cease the conduct of a specific activity.

LANHAM ACT, § 43(a) Federal trademark infringement statute.

MISREPRESENTATION A statement or conduct by one party to another that constitutes a false representation of fact.

■■■

Clorox Co. Puerto Rico v. Proctor & Gamble Commercial Co.

Detergent manufacturer (P) v. Detergent manufacturer (D)

228 F.3d 24 (1st Cir. 2000).

NATURE OF CASE: Appeal from dismissal of action asserting false advertising violations of § 43(a) of the Lanham Act.

FACT SUMMARY: The Clorox Company Puerto Rico (Clorox) (P), which produces chlorine bleach, sought to enjoin Proctor and Gamble Commercial Company's (Proctor & Gamble) (D) use in Puerto Rico of an ad for detergent, "Ace con Blanqueador" (Ace with whitener), contending that the ad, and a subsequently revised ad, which claimed that "mas no se puede" (whiter is not possible) constituted false advertising because, Clorox (P) asserted, no detergent brings out the white like a chlorine bleach when used with a detergent.

RULE OF LAW

A plaintiff states claims under § 43(a) of the Lanham Act where the plaintiff adduces evidence that a defendant's advertising is literally false, is misleading to consumers, and is not mere puffery.

FACTS: Proctor and Gamble Commercial Company (Proctor & Gamble) (D) sells in Puerto Rico a powdered detergent that contains a non-chlorine whitening agent, which it markets as "Ace con Blanqueador" (Ace with whitener) (Ace). It also sells a liquid detergent under the same name that does not contain an actual whitener. Proctor & Gamble (D) sought to convince the public that it was not necessary to use chlorine bleach to get clothes white, and that Ace was better than using a cheaper detergent along with chlorine. To achieve this goal, Proctor & Gamble (D) broadcast a series of television ads that showed women in their homes praising Ace after they switched to it without using chlorine, after they were "dared" to do so. The overriding theme of the ads was that chlorine bleach was not necessary to whiten clothes if washed with Ace. Some of the commercials also suggested that eliminating chlorine from the laundry process would save consumers time or money, or curtail the negative side effects of washing clothes with chlorine. Each ad closed with the tag line "Whiter is not possible." Proctor & Gamble (D) also sent a promotional brochure and product samples to consumers in Puerto Rico. Again, this promotional material dared consumers to use Ace without chlorine, and closed with the tag line "Whiter is not possible!" The Clorox Company Puerto Rico (Clorox) (P), which markets chlorine-based liquid bleach called Clorox, demanded that Proctor & Gamble (D) stop running the ads because they were false and misleading. Although Proctor & Gamble (D) did not change the theme of its ads, it added before its tag line the qualification "compare with your detergent." Clorox (P)

was not satisfied by this addition, and brought suit under § 43(a) of the Lanham Act for, inter alia, false advertising, seeking to permanently enjoin Proctor & Gamble (D) from making any claims that Ace gets clothes the whitest possible without the use of chlorine bleach. It contended that Proctor & Gambles (D) claim that using Ace alone whitened better than using detergent with chlorine was literally false because tests prove that chlorine bleach whitens better than detergents used alone. Clorox (P) also contended that the name, "Ace con Blanqueador" was literally false respecting Ace liquid detergent because it falsely suggested that Ace liquid contained whitener or bleach. Clorox (P) also asserted that the Ace advertising campaign was misleading, because even if literally true or ambiguous, it made an implied claim that misled consumers. It supported this claim with a survey that showed consumers were deceived into believing that Ace possessed the same qualities and characteristics as a detergent used with chlorine bleach. Finally, Clorox (P) claimed that the statements "Compare with your detergent. . . . Whiter is not possible" were not non-actionable puffery. It also sought damages, attorneys' fees, and a preliminary injunction. Relevant evidence, including consumer surveys, experts' statements, and testimony of witnesses was presented to the district court, which, however did not hear oral argument and which ultimately dismissed the Lanham Act claim sua sponte. The First Circuit Court of Appeals granted review.

ISSUE: Does a plaintiff state claims under § 43(a) of the Lanham Act where the plaintiff adduces evidence that a defendant's advertising is literally false, is misleading to consumers, and is not mere puffery?

HOLDING AND DECISION: (Lipez, J.) Yes. A plaintiff states claims under § 43(a) of the Lanham Act where the plaintiff adduces evidence that a defendant's advertising is literally false, is misleading to consumers, and is not mere puffery. With respect to Clorox's (P) claims of literal falsity respecting the ad campaign, a fact finder must first determine the claim that has been conveyed by the challenged advertising, and then must determine whether that claim is false. Clorox (P) presented evidence that chlorine bleach produces whiter results than Ace alone, and such evidence must be accepted as true given the procedural posture of the motion to dismiss— in fact, Proctor & Gamble (D) does not challenge the veracity of this evidence. Therefore, any claim to the contrary would be literally false. However, the parties dispute primarily whether the ads made a claim of whitening

Continued on next page.

superiority over chlorine bleach. In considering this issue, any implicit claims made by the advertisement may also be taken into account. A claim is conveyed by necessary implication when, considering the advertisement in its entirety, the audience would recognize the claim as readily as if it had been explicitly stated. Here, Clorox (P) has stated a claim that the Proctor & Gamble (D) commercials were literally false because a fact finder could reasonably conclude that the commercials claimed that Ace was equal or superior in whitening ability to a detergent and bleach combination. The advertising campaign, as modified with the addition of the words "Compare your detergent," while rendering the comparative claim of the ads more ambiguous, nevertheless implied the superiority of Ace over chlorine bleach. Therefore, the district court erred in dismissing Clorox's (P) literal falsity claims with respect to the advertising campaigns. With regard to Clorox's (P) literal falsity claim respecting the name "Ace con Blanqueador" as applied to liquid Ace, Clorox's (P) allegation that Ace liquid does not contain any "whiteners" but only contains "color enhancers" must be credited. Therefore, the district court erred in dismissing this claim, because if Clorox (P) succeeds in proving that liquid Ace contains only an "enhancer," rather than a "whitener," and if it further establishes the other elements of a false advertising claim, it will be entitled to relief since Proctor & Gamble's (D) designation of Ace liquid detergent as "Ace con Blanqueador" would be literally false. Clorox's (P) next liability theory is based on misleading advertising, which is independent of literal falsity. Under this theory, Clorox (P) must prove that a substantial portion of the audience for the ad was actually misled. A survey conducted by an independent third party indicated that a significant percentage (up to 47%) had been deceived into believing that with Ace, there is no need to use other products for maximum whitening performance. This survey, and Clorox's (P) allegations that flow therefrom, must be credited. Whether a message conveyed by advertising is misleading is determined by public reaction, not by judicial evaluation. Thus, because Clorox's (P) consumer survey data showed that the ads deceived a substantial portion of the intended audience, it was error to dismiss Clorox's (P) misleading advertising claim. Finally, the statements "Compare with your detergent. . . . Whiter is not possible" and "Whiter is not possible," are not non-actionable puffing. Puffery or puffing is exaggerated advertising that no reasonable consumer would rely on. However, a specific and measurable advertisement claim of product superiority, as opposed to bluster and boasting, is not puffery. Proctor & Gamble's (D) ad claim is specific and measurable, and is not the kind of subjective statement that characterizes puffery. The statement "Whiter is not possible," taken alone, might constitute an unspecified boast, and thus puffery. However, when this statement is preceded by the statement "Compare with your detergent," the statement invites consumers to make a comparison. Despite any ambiguity, the claim is specific and measure, and hence not puffing. Because

Clorox (P) has stated a claim for literal falsity relating to the name of the Ace liquid detergent, "Ace con Blanqueador," as well as claims for literal falsity and for misleading advertising with respect to the commercials aired in both the original and modified advertising campaigns, as well as the promotional brochure, the district court erred by dismissing these claims. Vacated and remanded.

▶ *ANALYSIS*

It should be kept in mind that the court here is not ruling on the merits of Clorox's (P) claim, but is only determining whether its claims should have survived a motion to dismiss pursuant to Fed. R Civ. P. Rule 12(b)(6). For the purposes of a motion to dismiss, a court must credit the type of allegations of misleading advertising that Clorox (P) set forth here. Obviously, if confronted with a motion for summary judgment, the plaintiff can no longer rest on the allegations in the complaint. For example, Proctor & Gamble (D) vigorously disputed the validity of Clorox's (P) survey, but the court expressed no view on the merits of Proctor & Gamble's (D) arguments, since the probative value of a consumer survey is a highly fact-specific determination and is not the type of determination that a court may make as a matter of law upon review of a motion to dismiss.

■=■

Quicknotes

FED. R. CIV. P. 12(b)(6) Defense of failure to state a claim upon which relief can be granted shall be asserted in the responsive pleading or by motion.

INTER ALIA Among other things.

MOTION TO DISMISS Motion to terminate an action based on the adequacy of the pleadings, improper service or venue, etc.

PUFFING The communication of an opinion not intended as a representation of fact and upon which an action for fraud or misrepresentation cannot be based.

SUA SPONTE An action taken by the court by its own motion and without the suggestion of one of the parties.

■=■

Church & Dwight Co. v. The Clorox Company

Cat litter manufacturer (P) v. Cat litter manufacturer (D)

102 U.S.P.Q.2d 1453 (S.D.N.Y. 2012).

NATURE OF CASE: Motion for injunction in action for false advertisement under § 43(a) of the Lanham Act.

FACT SUMMARY: Church & Dwight Co. (P) brought suit under § 43(a) of the Lanham Act seeking, among other things, to preliminarily enjoin Clorox Pet Products Company (D) from airing a commercial that made allegedly misleading claims about the respective merits of each party's cat litter.

🏛 RULE OF LAW
A plaintiff is likely to succeed on the merits of a false advertising claim made under § 43(a) of the Lanham Act where the plaintiff can show that the scientific evidence supporting the defendant's advertising claims is not sufficiently reliable, or, even if it is reliable, it cannot possibly support the defendant's implied claims.

FACTS: Church & Dwight Co. (C & D) (P) manufactures a variety of cat litters that use Arm & Hammer baking soda under the "Arm & Hammer" trademark, including Arm & Hammer Double Duty Clumping Litter (Double Duty) and Arm & Hammer Super Scoop Clumping Litter (Super Scoop). Clorox Pet Products Company (Clorox) (D) also manufactures cat litter under the "Fresh Step" brand, but instead of using baking soda, Clorox (D) uses carbon for odor elimination. Clorox (D) started airing certain commercials that represented that Fresh Step litter with carbon was better at eliminating odors than Super Scoop litter with baking soda. C & D commissioned a test that tested the veracity of Clorox's (D) claims. The test results showed that less than 4% of cats rejected Super Scoop litter, whereas 5% rejected Fresh Step litter. Consequently, C & D (P) filed a complaint against Clorox (D), claiming that the Clorox (D) commercials were literally false. Clorox (D) agreed to permanently discontinue the commercials, and C & D (P) voluntarily dismissed the complaint. Not even two weeks later, Clorox (D) started airing a new commercial. This time, Clorox (D)—which in all its commercials stated that cats are smart, and that's why they choose Fresh Step—displayed two laboratory beakers. One beaker was represented as Fresh Step and the bottom of it was filled with a black substance labeled "carbon." The other beaker was filled with a white substance labeled "baking soda." While the second beaker was not identified as any specific brand of cat litter, Arm & Hammer is the only major cat litter brand that uses baking soda. Green gas was then shown floating through the beakers and the voiceover said: "So we make Fresh Step

scoopable litter with carbon, which is more effective at absorbing odors than baking soda." The green gas in the Fresh Step beaker then rapidly evaporated while the gas level in the baking soda beaker barely changed. During this dramatization, small text appeared at the bottom of the screen informing the viewer that Clorox's (D) claims were based on a sensory lab test. In response to this commercial, C & D (P) brought suit under § 43(a) of the Lanham Act seeking, among other things, to preliminarily enjoin Clorox (D) from airing the commercial on the grounds that the new commercial contained several false messages, including, inter alia, that cat litter products made with baking soda do not eliminate odors well and that cat litter products made with baking soda are less effective at eliminating odors than Clorox's (D) Fresh Step cat litter. To support its claim that carbon better eliminates cat malodor than baking soda, Clorox (D) conducted an in-house test called the "Jar Test," which used separate sealed containers of: (i) fresh cat feces covered with carbon; (ii) fresh cat urine covered with carbon; (iii) fresh cat feces covered with baking soda; (iv) fresh cat urine covered with baking soda; (v) uncovered feces; and (vi) uncovered urine. After letting the sealed containers sit between 22 and 26 hours, the containers were placed in three sensory testing booths—one containing the carbon samples, one containing the baking soda samples, and one containing the uncovered feces and urine as a control—and 11 panelists rated the samples on a 0 to 15 scale, with 0 representing no odor. This experiment was repeated four times, for a total of 44 samplings. Carbon was found to reduce odor from 2.72 to 0 while baking soda was found to reduce odor only from 2.72 to 1.85. Reducing odor from 2.72 to 1.85 represents a 32% decrease, precisely the decrease that was represented in the demonstration shown in Clorox's (D) commercial. Clorox (D) trained the 11 panelists used in the Jar Test to evaluate odors on a specific scale. Clorox (D) claimed that its sensory evaluation methodology was peer-reviewed and technically sound. Over the course of their training, panelists smelled identical smells at different levels of intensity in order to develop a common metric for pungency. Panelists also smelled different litter products, both with and without cat excrement, in order to learn to discriminate between cat malodor and other odors present in litter. All panelists gave a malodor rating of zero whenever cat excrement was treated with carbon, resulting in a score of zero for each of the 44 trials. C & D (P) criticized the reliability of the Jar Test. First, it argued that Clorox's (D) commercial broadly claimed that Fresh Step cat litter

Continued on next page.

outperforms C & D's (P) products in eliminating odor, a claim the Jar Test cannot support. Second, it argued that certain aspects of the Jar Test—particularly the uniformity of the panelists' findings that carbon completely eliminates cat malodor—were so suspicious as to render the Jar Test unreliable even for the narrower proposition that carbon better eliminates odor than baking soda. Third, it argued that the Jar Test was unreliable because it failed to use a ratio scale to compare degrees of malodor. In conjunction with these criticisms, C & D (P) pointed out that humans are "noisy instruments," meaning that, for neurological and psychological reasons, they perceive the exact same thing differently at different times and report the presence of olfactory stimuli even where they do not exist. C & D (P) noted that Clorox's (D) own studies supported this observation. First, in an internal panel validation test report involving cat litter, Clorox's (D) panelists gave an average malodor score of greater than zero to a box of litter that admittedly contained no cat excrement. Second, in an earlier iteration of the Jar Test, 18% of trials resulted in a report of some malodor in jars of excrement treated with carbon. The district court considered C & D's motion.

ISSUE: Is a plaintiff likely to succeed on the merits of a false advertising claim made under § 43(a) of the Lanham Act where the plaintiff can show that the scientific evidence supporting the defendant's advertising claims is not sufficiently reliable, or, even if it is reliable, it cannot possibly support the defendant's implied claims?

HOLDING AND DECISION: (Rakoff, J.) Yes. A plaintiff is likely to succeed on the merits of a false advertising claim made under § 43(a) of the Lanham Act where the plaintiff can show that the scientific evidence supporting the defendant's advertising claims is not sufficiently reliable, or, even if it is reliable, it cannot possibly support the defendant's implied claims. To succeed on the merits under § 43(a), a plaintiff must demonstrate that the challenged advertisement is either (1) literally false, i.e., false on its face, or (2) while not literally false, nevertheless likely to mislead or confuse consumers. Where, as here, scientific or technical evidence is said to establish an advertiser's claim (a so-called "establishment claim"), a plaintiff can prove literal falsity by showing that the test does not establish the proposition for which it is cited, because it is either not sufficiently reliable, or because it is simply irrelevant. Here, C & D's (P) first two criticisms of Clorox's (D) Jar Test are meritorious, and, thus, the court does not need to reach the third criticism. Under the doctrine of "falsity by necessary implication," a company's claims about particular aspects of its product may necessarily imply more sweeping claims about that product, and these implied claims may be "literally false" when the disputed message is analyzed in its full context. C & D (P) argues that under this doctrine, Clorox's (D) claims about the superiority of carbon to baking soda necessarily imply that Fresh Step cat litter better eliminates odors than do Arm & Hammer litters that use baking soda. While Clorox (D) responds that

one could reasonably interpret its commercial as simply comparing the general odor-reducing properties of carbon and baking soda, Clorox (D) has not identified any basis for believing that any consumer who pays attention to its commercial reasonably cares about how effectively carbon works compared with baking soda outside the context of cat litter and competing litter products. Given this necessary implication of Clorox's (D) commercial, the Jar Test cannot support this implication. Clorox (D) sealed the jars of cat waste 22 to 26 hours before subjecting them to testing. In actual practice, however, cats do not seal their waste, and smells offend as much during the first 22 hours as they do afterwards. Thus, the Jar Test says little, if anything, about how carbon performs in cat litter under real-life conditions. Moreover, to substantiate the commercial's implied claims, the Jar Test must prove not only that carbon eliminates odors in open cat litter (as opposed to sealed jars), but also (1) that it outperforms baking soda in that task and (2) that baking soda eliminates only 32% of odors, the amount by which, in the commercial, the gas dissipated in the beaker labeled "baking soda." Given that the Jar Test says little about how substances perform in litter as opposed to jars, it cannot possibly support Clorox's (D) very specific claims with regard to litter, and, consequently, the necessarily contrary implication of Clorox's (D) commercials is literally false. As to C & D's (P) second criticism—casting doubt on the plausibility of the uniformity of the panelists' results—it is true that humans are "noisy instruments," and given the variation even among the same person's reports at different times, and that even trained panelists report smells even when none are present, as demonstrated by Clorox's (D) in-house tests and earlier iterations of the Jar Test, it is highly implausible that 11 panelists would stick their noses in jars of excrement and report 44 independent times that they smelled nothing unpleasant. Accordingly, the results of the Jar Test are not sufficiently reliable to permit one to conclude with reasonable certainty that they established the proposition for which they were cited in Clorox's (D) commercial. For these reasons, Clorox's (D) claims are literally false, and C & D (P) is likely to succeed on the merits of its claim, thus supporting the issuance of an injunction. Further, C & D (P) has proved a likelihood of irreparable harm since consumers shopping for cat litter overwhelmingly identify baking soda with C & D's (P) Arm & Hammer cat litter products, and Clorox's (D) commercial makes false statements about the odor-fighting abilities of baking soda. Finally, the commercial at issue shares themes with Clorox's (D) former commercials—e.g., reference to cats' intelligence and cleverness—recalling those former commercials' explicit mention of C & D's (P) products. Given the literal falsity of the commercial, it may be inferred that Clorox (D) is likely to divert customers from C & D's (P) products to its own unless the offending commercial is

Continued on next page.

enjoined. Therefore, C & D's (P) motion for an injunction is granted. Judgment for C & D (P).

▶ ANALYSIS

Under the doctrine of "falsity by necessary implication," because an implication must be necessary in order to render the commercial's claims false, if the language or graphic is susceptible to more than one reasonable interpretation, the advertisement cannot be literally false. In addition, in cases of literal falsity, the likelihood of irreparable harm may be presumed where the plaintiff demonstrates a likelihood of success in showing that the defendant's comparative advertisement is literally false and that given the nature of the market, it would be obvious to the viewing audience that the advertisement is targeted at the plaintiff, even though the plaintiff is not identified by name. Here, the court did not rely on this presumption, but independently determined that C & D (P) had successfully shown a high likelihood of irreparable harm.

■■■■

Quicknotes

LANHAM ACT, § 43(a) Federal trademark infringement statute.

■■■■

Innovation Ventures, LLC v. N.V.E., Inc.

Energy drink producer (P) v. Energy drink producer (D)

694 F.3d 723 (6th Cir. 2012).

NATURE OF CASE: Appeal from grant of summary judgment on claim of trademark infringement and on counterclaim for false advertising.

FACT SUMMARY: After Innovation Ventures, LLC, d/b/a Living Essentials (LE) (P), creator of the "5-hour ENERGY" energy shot, asserted that N.V.E. Inc. (NVE) (D), creator of the "6 Hour POWER" energy shot, infringed its trademark, in violation of § 43(a) the Lanham Act, NVE (D) counterclaimed that a recall notice that LE (P) had sent regarding a recall of a product called "6 Hour Energy Shot," which was produced by a third party, constituted false advertising under the Lanham Act, because, NVE (D) asserted, the recall notice was both literally false and ambiguous, and actually created confusion in the marketplace as to which product had been recalled.

🏛 RULE OF LAW

It is not appropriate to grant summary judgment on a false advertising claim under the Lanham Act where the communication at issue can be construed as grammatically or descriptively ambiguous or literally false, and where there is evidence that the communication has created actual confusion in the marketplace.

FACTS: Innovation Ventures, LLC, d/b/a Living Essentials (LE) (P), creator of the "5-hour ENERGY" energy shot, asserted that N.V.E. Inc. (NVE) (D), creator of the "6 Hour POWER" energy shot, infringed its trademark, in violation of § 43(a) the Lanham Act. In a different case, LE (P) had obtained a trade dress infringement decision in its favor against a different competitor (N2G), which made the "6 Hour Energy Shot" energy shot. In that case, the court ordered an injunction and recall. Concerned that the recall notice did not adequately reach customers who may have purchased "6 Hour Energy Shot" through resellers, LE (P) distributed its own "recall notice" to over 100,000 retailers nationwide. The notice was titled "RECALL OF "6 HOUR" SHOT ORDERED." The first paragraph stated "Court orders immediate stop to manufacturing, distribution and sale of 6 Hour Energy shot." The body of the notice stated that a "6 Hour" product had been recalled. It claimed that LE (P) had "won a decision against a "6 Hour" energy shot. The notice did not, however, specify which "6 Hour" product was the subject of the recall. In addition, the notice said: "If you have any of the '6 Hour' energy shots in your store(s) or warehouse(s) contact the product's manufacturer or your distributor to return the product immediately." At the time, there were

several other energy shots, in addition to NVE's (D), with the phrase "6 Hour" in the title. Following the recall, NVE (D) and its distributors received numerous calls from convenience stores and truck stop retailers—the very people that received the recall notice—who wanted to return "6 Hour POWER." Based on the language of the notice, and the impact it had on its recipients, NVE (D) counterclaimed that the LE (P) recall notice constituted false advertising in violation of the Lanham Act. The district court granted cross-motions for summary judgment, dismissing the claims. The district court found that a likelihood of confusion did not exist between "6 Hour POWER" and "5-hour ENERGY," and then held that the recall notice did not constitute false advertising, concluding that the notice was neither literally false nor misleading. The court of appeals granted review, and reversed as to LE's (P) trademark infringement claim because the factors indicative of likelihood of confusion were evenly balanced, which the court of appeals held counseled against a finding of summary judgment, as it meant there were genuine issues of material fact that had to be decided. The court of appeals then considered whether the district court had appropriately granted summary judgment as to NVE's (D) false advertising claim.

ISSUE: Is it appropriate to grant summary judgment on a false advertising claim under the Lanham Act where the communication at issue can be construed as grammatically or descriptively ambiguous or literally false, and where there is evidence that the communication has created actual confusion in the marketplace?

HOLDING AND DECISION: (Boggs, J.) No. It is not appropriate to grant summary judgment on a false advertising claim under the Lanham Act where the communication at issue can be construed as grammatically or descriptively ambiguous or literally false, and where there is evidence that the communication has created actual confusion in the marketplace. The Lanham Act prohibits "[a]ny person [from] . . . us[ing] in commerce any word, term, name, symbol, or device . . . which . . . in commercial advertising or promotion, misrepresents the nature, characteristics, qualities, or geographic origin of his or her or another person's goods, services, or commercial activities. Liability arises if the commercial message or statement is either (1) literally false or (2) literally true or ambiguous, but has the tendency to deceive consumers. A literally false message may be either explicit or conveyed by necessary implication when, considering the advertisement in its entirety, the audience would recognize the claim as readily as if

Continued on next page.

it had been explicitly stated. However, the greater the degree to which a message relies upon the viewer or consumer to integrate its components and draw the apparent conclusion, the less likely it is that a finding of literal falsity will be supported. Here, LE's (P) recall notice teeters on the cusp between ambiguity and literal falsity in two main respects—descriptive and grammatical. Read broadly, the notice could be considered ambiguous, as it does not specify which product was the subject of the recall. Read narrowly, the notice could be literally false, since only a product specifically called "6 Hour Energy Shot" was recalled, not any energy shot whose name contained the words "6 Hour." This is especially true given that, at the time, there were several energy shots whose name contained "6 Hour." Relatedly, LE (P) wrote in its notice that it "w[o]n a decision against a '6 Hour' energy shot." This statement is not literally true, since LE (P) won a decision against N2G's use of its trade dress, which was confusingly similar to LE's (P) overall product image. Grammatically, the notice used different prefatory articles to introduce the recalled product—"a," "any," and "the." The use of "a" suggests that there may be more than one possible product at issue. By saying "any" of the shots, the notice suggests that any shot bearing the name "6 Hour" was subject to recall. By using "the," the notice suggests that there is only one specific product at issue, though the statement as a whole fails to specify exactly what product. The meaning of these articles must be determined in the context they are made, so that their meaning depends on that context. Because such a determination must be made, a finding of literal falsity as a matter of law cannot be made on the face of the notice, since only an unambiguous message can be literally false. While it is a close question whether the notice is literally false, it cannot be said that it is unambiguously so. Likewise, there is a genuine issue of material fact as to whether the notice was misleading and tended to deceive its intended audience. The district court erroneously dismissed documentary and testimonial evidence from NVE (D), distributors, and brokers showing confusion as to whether NVE's (D) product, "6 Hour POWER," had been recalled when it excluded as inadmissible hearsay all evidence introduced by NVE (D) to show that "various unidentified retailers contacted them because they were confused by the legal notice." The numerous phone calls received by NVE (D) were not relied on to show the content of the conversations, but rather were introduced merely to show that the conversations occurred and the state of mind of the declarants. The fact that so many people called NVE (D) immediately after receiving the notice at the very least raises a genuine issue of material fact as to whether a significant portion of the recipients were misled. Moreover, contrary to LE's (P) characterization, the phone calls were not mere inquiries, but, to the contrary, many distributors called to stop buying "6 Hour POWER" after the notice was issued. NVE (D) claimed that after the recall, its sales growth for 6 Hour POWER dropped from 13.7% to 1.1%, and NVE's (D) damages expert estimated that NVE (D) lost $3.4 million in sales as a result of the recall notice. A jury could find that

these were not just inquiries, but were calls that resulted in lost sales. All these calls evidence a belief that "6 Hour POWER" had been recalled, since had the callers lacked such a mistaken belief, such phone calls would not have occurred. Additionally, evidence of corrective notices sent by NVE (D) and its distributors should have been admitted and considered, since such evidence about these corrective notices was introduced not for the truth of the matters asserted therein but rather to provide circumstantial evidence that some retailers believed that there was in fact a recall on "any of the '6 Hour' shots in your store," including "6 Hour POWER," and that NVE (D) took actions to alleviate these concerns. For all these reasons, there is more than enough evidence to survive summary judgment, and whether the evidence shows that the retailers were tricked into believing an untruth about "6 Hour POWER" is an issue that must be resolved at trial. [Reversed and remanded as to this issue.]

▶ ANALYSIS

For purposes of a Lanham Act false advertisement claim, where statements are literally true yet deceptive or too ambiguous to support a finding of literal falsity, a violation can only be established by proof of actual deception. A plaintiff relying on statements that are literally true yet misleading cannot obtain relief by arguing how consumers could react; it must show how consumers actually do react. Thus, if on remand a jury determined that the recall notice was too ambiguous to support a finding of literal falsity, NVE (D) would have to adduce evidence of actual deception. On the other hand, where statements are literally false, a violation may be established without evidence that the statements actually misled consumers.

■=■

Quicknotes

LANHAM ACT, § 43(a) Federal trademark infringement statute.

MATERIAL FACT A fact without the existence of which a contract would not have been entered.

SUMMARY JUDGMENT Judgment rendered by a court in response to a motion made by one of the parties, claiming that the lack of a question of material fact in respect to an issue warrants disposition of the issue without consideration by the jury.

TRADEMARK Any word, name, symbol, device or combination thereof that is either currently utilized, or which a person has a bona fide intent to utilize, in commerce in order to distinguish his goods from those of another.

TRADEMARK INFRINGEMENT The unauthorized use of another's trademark in such a manner as to cause a

Continued on next page.

likelihood of confusion as to the source of the product or service in connection with which it is utilized.

■━■

Coors Brewing Co. v. Anheuser-Busch Co.

Beer company (P) v. Beer company (D)

802 F. Supp. 965 (S.D.N.Y. 1992).

NATURE OF CASE: Application for a preliminary injunction in action under § 43(a) of the Lanham Act for false or misleading advertising based on both literal and implied falsehoods.

FACT SUMMARY: Coors Brewing Company (Coors) (P), a beer brewer, contended that a television commercial by Anheuser-Busch Companies, Inc. (Anheuser-Busch) (D), also a beer brewer, violated § 43(a) of the Lanham Act because it constituted false or misleading advertising that contained both literal and implied falsehoods as to how Coors' (P) beer, Coors Light, was manufactured and how it differed from Anheuser-Busch's (D) competing beer, Natural Light. Coors (P) applied for a preliminary injunction to prohibit Anheuser-Busch (D) from broadcasting the ad.

RULE OF LAW

Injunctive relief will not be granted against an allegedly false or misleading advertising claim pursuant to § 43(a) of the Lanham Act where the plaintiff can demonstrate neither that the challenged advertising is literally false nor that, although literally true, the advertisement is likely to mislead and confuse consumers through implied falsehoods.

FACTS: Coors Brewing Company (Coors) (P), a beer brewer, sued Anheuser-Busch Companies, Inc. (Anheuser-Busch) (D), also a beer brewer, claiming that an Anheuser-Busch's (D) television ad violated § 43(a) of the Lanham Act and seeking a preliminary injunction to prohibit Anheuser-Busch (D) from broadcasting the ad. Coors (P) makes a beer called Coors Light using a "high gravity" process that involves cooling the brew, filtering it, further cooling it, and then blending it with water so its alcohol level meets statutory standards. Most Coors Light is brewed, blended, and bottled, in Colorado. However, somewhere between 65% and 85% of the Coors Light beer supplied to the Northeast is blended and bottled in Virginia. Using special insulated railcars, Coors (P) transports the high gravity brew from Colorado to Virginia, where Virginia water is added to the brew, which, after further filtering, is bottled and distributed. Anheuser-Busch (D) produces a competing beer called Natural Light, which is also produced by a "high gravity" brewing process, but which, unlike Coors Light, is pasteurized at high temperatures and is entirely processed—brewed, blended, and bottled—in regional Anheuser-Busch (D) breweries. In the challenged ad, Anheuser-Busch (D) shows a railroad tanker and a can of Coors Light with voice over saying: "This is a railroad tanker. [flash, the image of a railway tanker] This is the taste of the Rockies. [flash, the image of

a can of Coors Light] Tanker. [image of a railway tanker] Rockies. [image of a can of Coors Light]." The narrative continues as follows: "Actually, a concentrated form of Coors Light leaves Colorado in a tanker and travels to Virginia, where local water dilutes the Rockies concentrate before it's sent to you. So what's it gonna be, the Rockies concentrate or an ice cold Natural Light that leaves our local breweries fresh and ready to drink? Like this [picture of a Natural Light delivery truck], not like this [picture of railway tanker]. So drink fresh, cold Natural Light and don't be railroaded." Radio ads and printed materials by Anheuser-Busch (D) contained a similar message and included the phrase "Don't be railroaded." Coors (P), in its own ads, had emphasized that its beer was made with water from the Rocky Mountains. Coors (P) contended that the Natural Light ads implied that differences in production make Natural Light "fresh" in a way in which Coors Light is not, by implying that Natural Light is "fresher" than Coors Light because Natural Light leaves the factory ready to drink while Coors Light leaves Colorado in a "concentrate" form, which is diluted when it reaches Coors' plant in Virginia. Coors (P) also contended that by broadcasting nationally the Natural Light advertisements, Anheuser-Busch (D) lead consumers outside the Northeast to believe erroneously that their Coors Light was shipped to Virginia to be diluted before being shipped to their regional retailers. Coors (P) contended that the challenged advertisements contained two literal falsehoods: (1) that "Coors Light is made from 'concentrate' that is 'diluted' with water" and (2) that "Coors Light travels to Virginia 'before it's sent to you.'" Coors (P) also contended that by repeatedly stating that Coors Light is made from concentrate and is diluted, and by showing Coors Light being shipped from Colorado in railway cars while stating that Natural Light leaves Anheuser-Busch (D) factories fresh and ready to drink, Anheuser-Busch's (D) commercial implied three falsehoods: (1) that Natural Light is not also made by a process of "high gravity" brewing; (2) that all of the Coors Light sold in the Northeast has been "blended" with Virginia water; and (3) that there is a difference between Colorado Coors and Virginia Coors. Coors (P) presented survey evidence in support of its implied falsehood claims. The survey firm (Shapiro) conducted consumer surveys in shopping malls located in Boston, Philadelphia, Washington, D.C., New York, Los Angeles, and Kansas City. In all, Shapiro interviewed 200 men and 100 women who were over 21 years old and who had consumed beer in the preceding four weeks, with 50

Continued on next page.

individuals interviewed in each location. The survey respondents were shown the challenged ad and then were asked two questions:

Question 2a: Now, tell me what you recall about the commercial I just showed you?

Question 2b: And, what was the central theme or message in this commercial? What were they trying to tell you?

The ad was shown again after the respondents answered the questions, and then they were asked six more questions. One of these, Question 5, was as follows:

Question 5: Based on this commercial, do you believe that Coors Light and Natural Light are made the same way, or are they made differently? If different: In what way is Coors Light made differently than Natural Light?

In response to this question, 67% of all respondents answered that they believed the two beers were made in different ways while 21% of all respondents answered that they believed the two beers were made the same way. Of those respondents who answered that the two beers were made in different ways, (1) 29% stated that they believed that "Coors is diluted/watered down/Natural Light is not," (2) 25% stated that "Coors/Coors Light made from concentrate/Natural Light is not," and (3) 13% stated that "Coors made in two places/Natural Light from one place." From this, Coors (P) argued that 67% of all respondents falsely believed, based on the ad, Natural Light and Coors Light are made differently. The total percentage of the 67% of respondents who had been misled by the commercial into thinking that Natural Light is not made by a process of high gravity brewing was 54%, and thus, 36.18% of all respondents were misled by the commercial as to the differences between how the two beers are made. In response to Question 2a, however, the bulk of respondents indicated that Coors Light is made from concentrate (20%), is "diluted/watered down" (32%), is transported by railway tanker (26%), and travels a long distance before it reaches customers (20%).

ISSUE:
Will injunctive relief be granted against an allegedly false or misleading advertising claim pursuant to § 43(a) of the Lanham Act where the plaintiff can demonstrate neither that the challenged advertising is literally false nor that, although literally true, the advertisement is likely to mislead and confuse consumers through implied falsehoods?

HOLDING AND DECISION:
(Mukaskey, J.) No. Injunctive relief will not be granted against an allegedly false or misleading advertising claim pursuant to § 43(a) of the Lanham Act where the plaintiff can demonstrate neither that the challenged advertising is literally false nor that, although literally true, the advertisement is likely to

mislead and confuse consumers through implied falsehoods. To prevail on its application for a preliminary injunction, Coors (P) must show either that the ad is literally false or that, although literally true, it is likely to mislead and confuse customers. The first alleged literal falsehood asserted by Coors (P) is that the ad indicates that Coors Light is made from "concentrate" that is diluted with water. Coors (P) fails as to this claim. The word "concentrate" can mean, as claimed by Coors (P), a substance from which water has been removed. However, an equally plausible definition is that it means a concentrated substance. Because the term "concentrate" is equally susceptible to either definition, the ad is ambiguous, at most. Therefore, the ad's use of "concentrate" is not literally false. The second alleged literal falsehood is that the ad claims that Coors Light is diluted. Because it is true that water is added to the Coors Light concentrate to make it less concentrated, the use of this term is also not literally false. Coors (P) also claims that except as applied to the Northeast, the ad's claim that Coors Light travels to Virginia before being distributed is also literally false. However, because Anheuser-Busch (D) represents that it will only broadcast the commercials in the Northeast, this claim is moot. As to Coors' (P) implied falsehood claims, these must be proven by evidence of consumer confusion. Coors (P) attempts to satisfy its burden with the Shapiro survey, but fails to do so. Coors' (P) reliance on the survey respondents' answers to Question 5 is misplaced because that question is leading and thus produced unreliable results. The question assumes that the ad conveys some message comparing how the two beers are made, but, in response to the open-ended questions presented in Questions 2a and 2b, a statistically insignificant number of respondents noted differences between the processes by which the two beers are made. Question 5 is also leading because it itself suggests that the ad implies a difference in the way the two beers are made, given that it invidiously compares one product with another. The question also failed to inform respondents that they could answer that they did not know if the commercial implied that the two beers are made by different processes. For these reasons, Question 5 does not have probative value. On the other hand, Questions 2a and 2b are generally reliable because they were not leading and were, instead, open-ended. In response to Question 2a, because Shapiro lumped together the percentage of respondents who said that Coors Light is diluted and the percentage of respondents who said that Coors Light is watered down, the 32% figure combining both answers is uninformative. While it is literally true that in one sense Coors Light is "diluted," Coors Light does not appear to be "watered down," in the sense of containing more water than beer should or than Natural Light does. However, because there is no way of knowing what percentage of respondents said that Coors Light is diluted and

Continued on next page.

what percentage said that Coors Light is watered down, this category of responses has no probative value. Based on the lack of probative value of the answers to Question 5, and on the ambiguous or statistically insignificant answers to Questions 2a and 2b, Coors (P) has failed to carry its burden of proving that the ad is likely to mislead consumers into believing that Coors Light, as opposed to Natural Light, is not made by "high gravity" brewing. The survey also does not address Coors (P) other implied falsehood claims—that all of the Coors Light sold in the Northeast has been "blended" with Virginia water and that there is a difference between Colorado Coors and Virginia Coors—and Coors (P) has otherwise not supported these claims with extrinsic evidence. Moreover, Coors (P) is estopped from asserting the last claim because, after having advertised for years that Coors (P) beers taste better because they are made with Rocky Mountain water, Coors (P) now cannot seek an equitable remedy that would prohibit Anheuser-Busch (D) from hoisting Coors (P) by its own petard. The implied falsehoods claim must fail as unsubstantiated with reliable extrinsic evidence. Finally, the balance of hardships between the parties is evenly balanced. The application for a preliminary injunction is denied.

▶ ANALYSIS

As the decision in this case illustrates, the evidentiary value of a survey's results rests upon the underlying objectivity of the survey itself. That objectivity is measured by such factors as whether the survey was properly filtered to screen out those who got no message from the advertisement, whether the questions are directed to the real issues, and whether the questions are leading or suggestive.

■■■■

Quicknotes

EXTRINSIC EVIDENCE Evidence that is not contained within the text of a document or contract, but which is derived from the parties' statements or the circumstances under which the agreement was made.

OBJECTIVE STANDARD A standard that is not personal to an individual, but is dependent on some external source.

PRELIMINARY INJUNCTION A judicial mandate issued to require or restrain a party from certain conduct; used to preserve a trial's subject matter or to prevent threatened injury.

■■■■

McNeil-PPC, Inc. v. Pfizer, Inc.

Dental floss manufacturer (P) v. Mouthwash manufacturer (D)

351 F. Supp. 2d 226 (S.D.N.Y. 2005).

NATURE OF CASE: Motion for a preliminary injunction in action under § 43(a) of the Lanham Act for false or misleading advertising based on both literal and implied falsehoods.

FACT SUMMARY: McNeil-PPC, Inc. (PPC) (P), the leading dental floss seller, contended that Pfizer Inc.'s (D) ads for Pfizer's (D) mouthwash, Listerine Antiseptic Mouthrinse (Listerine), were false and misleading because the ads claimed that Listerine is as effective as dental floss at combating plaque and gingivitis.

🏛 RULE OF LAW

Injunctive relief will be granted against an allegedly false or misleading advertising claim pursuant to § 43(a) of the Lanham Act where the plaintiff can demonstrate that the challenged advertising is literally false and that, even if literally true, the advertisement is likely to mislead and confuse consumers through implied falsehoods.

FACTS: Pfizer Inc. (D) launched a consumer advertising campaign for its mouthwash, Listerine Antiseptic Mouthrinse (Listerine). Print ads and hang tags featured an image of a Listerine bottle balanced on a scale against a white container of dental floss. A television commercial called the "Big Bang" announced that "Listerine's as effective as floss at fighting plaque and gingivitis. Clinical studies prove it." Although the commercial cautioned that "there's no replacement for flossing," the commercial repeated two more times the message that Listerine is "as effective as flossing against plaque and gingivitis." The commercial also showed a narrow stream of blue liquid flowing out of a Listerine bottle, then tracking a piece of dental floss being pulled from a white floss container, and then swirling around and between teeth—bringing to mind an image of liquid floss. Pfizer (D) also featured the "as effective as flossing" claim on its website for Listerine. In all the ads, in small print, or in a Q&A section of its website, Pfizer (D) indicated that Listerine was not a replacement for floss. McNeil-PPC, Inc. (PPC) (P), the leading dental floss seller, brought suit under § 43(a) of the Lanham Act, claiming that Pfizer's (D) ads were false and misleading. PPC (P) contended that Pfizer's (D) literal claim that "clinical studies prove" that Listerine is "as effective as floss against plaque and gingivitis" was false and that Pfizer's (D) ads also implicitly were claiming that Listerine is a replacement for floss, and that this implied message was also false and misleading. PPC (P) moved for a preliminary injunction to prohibit Pfizer (D) from making these claims in its ads. Plaque is a biofilm of bacteria that can lead to gingivitis, the inflammation of the superficial gum tissue, and to periodontitis, an inflammation of deeper tissues and bone. Plaque removal is key to preventing these dental ailments, as well as preventing or reducing cavities. For most people, toothbrushing alone cannot effectively control plaque. The most widely recommended device for supplementing toothbrushing to remove plaque is floss. Around 87% of consumers, however, floss either infrequently or not at all, and although dentists and dental hygienists regularly tell their patients to floss, most consumers do not floss or rarely floss because it is a difficult and time-consuming process. Thus, the 87% of consumers who do not floss represents a very large untapped market. If these reluctant flossers can be convinced to floss, sales of floss will rise dramatically; if they can be convinced that Listerine is as good as flossing without the accompanying hassles, sales of Listerine will rise dramatically. Thus, Pfizer (D) and PPC (P) were competing for this market. Pfizer (D) sponsored two studies (Sharma and Bauroth studies) that purported to compare the efficacy of Listerine against dental floss in controlling plaque and gingivitis, but only used subjects with mild to moderate gingivitis. Although after six months Listerine results were better than those for subjects who only had been asked to floss and those who had been given a placebo mouthwash, the authors of both studies suggested that the most probable reason was that the subjects failed to floss consistently in the later months of the study. Neither study purported to examine whether Listerine could replace floss. In connection with the case, PPC (P) had an independent survey firm (Ridgway) conduct three surveys throughout the country. The first survey sought to determine the message consumers took away from Pfizer's (D) Big Bang commercial. The second sought to determine the message consumers took away from Listerine's printed labels; and the third—a control study—sought to determine the pre-existing beliefs of consumers regarding the use of Listerine and floss. The first survey concluded that 50% of the respondents took away the message that floss can be replaced by Listerine. The second survey concluded that 45% of the respondents took away this same message. The third study concluded that 19% of those who had not seen the ads believed that Listerine could be used in place of floss. Taking the surveys together, the surveyors subtracted the 19% figure from the 50% and 45% figures, respectively, and concluded that 31% of those who saw the commercial and 26% of those who viewed the shoulder label took away a replacement message.

ISSUE: Will injunctive relief be granted against an allegedly false or misleading advertising claim pursuant to

Continued on next page.

§ 43(a) of the Lanham Act where the plaintiff can demonstrate that the challenged advertising is literally false and that, even if literally true, the advertisement is likely to mislead and confuse consumers through implied falsehoods?

HOLDING AND DECISION: (Chin, J.) Yes. Injunctive relief will be granted against an allegedly false or misleading advertising claim pursuant to § 43(a) of the Lanham Act where the plaintiff can demonstrate that the challenged advertising is literally false and that, even if literally true, the advertisement is likely to mislead and confuse consumers through implied falsehoods. As to the claim of literal falsity, PPC (P) only needs to prove that the "clinical studies" referred to in the ads were not sufficiently reliable to permit one to conclude with reasonable certainty that they established the proposition for which they were cited. In this regard, the Sharma and Bauroth studies do not stand for the proposition that "Listerine is as effective as floss against plaque and gingivitis." That is because the studies excluded individuals with severe gingivitis or any degree of periodontitis. Therefore, Pfizer's (D) claim is overbroad, as the ads do not specify that the claim is limited to those with mild to moderate gingivitis. Consumers with more severe conditions would thus be misled into believing that Listerine would be just as effective as floss to help them fight plaque, whereas the studies do not stand for that proposition. Second, the studies were not sufficiently reliable to permit the conclusion that Listerine is as effective as floss in fighting plaque and gingivitis, regardless of who is involved, since the studies only showed that Listerine is as effective as floss only when flossing is not properly executed. In fact, the authors of the studies said as much. Pfizer (D) argues that the studies were reliable because they reflected "real-world" conditions, but the ads do not limit their claim to "real-world" situations by indicating that Listerine is as effective as floss only when people do not floss or floss improperly. For these reasons, PPC (P) is likely to prevail on its claim of literal falsity. Regarding the implied falsity claims, the first step is to determine the message that consumers take away from the challenged ad, and the second is to determine whether that message is false. Here, the ads send an implicit message that Listerine is a suitable replacement for floss. The words and images of the ads convey the message that Listerine is the equal to floss. Also the Ridgway survey, which was convincing and was conducted in an objective and fair manner, shows that up to 31% of consumers took away the message that "you can replace floss with Listerine." This shows that a substantial percentage of the consumers who saw the advertisements took away a replacement message. For these reasons, the ads send an implicit message that Listerine is a replacement for floss. This message is false. Pfizer (D) argues, to the contrary, that the message is true: Listerine provides all the benefits of flossing. It bases this argument on the Sharma and Bauroth studies and on its contention that no clinical proof shows that flossing

provides any benefit other than fighting plaque and gingivitis. It also claims that there is no proof that reducing plaque will reduce cavities or periodontitis. From this Pfizer (D) reasons that because Listerine does everything that floss can do, it provides all the benefits of floss, and the implied message of the ad claims is therefore not false. This line of reasoning must be rejected because, first, Pfizer's (D) initial premise is wrong. As indicated before, the Sharma and Bauroth studies do not prove that Listerine is just as effective as floss in fighting plaque and gingivitis. The second premise is also wrong, since there is substantial, convincing clinical, medical, and other proof that flossing does fight tooth decay and periodontitis, and since flossing provides benefits that Listerine does not. Other substantial evidence also demonstrates, overwhelmingly, that flossing is important in reducing tooth decay and periodontitis and that it cannot be replaced by rinsing with a mouthwash. Therefore, Pfizer's (D) implicit message that Listerine can replace floss is false and misleading. PPC (P), which has thus demonstrated a likelihood of success on its literal falsity and implied falsity claims, and which will suffer irreparable harm if a preliminary injunction is not issued, is granted such injunction. The ads will also be enjoined because they pose a public health risk, as they present a danger of undermining the efforts of dental professionals and the American Dental Association (ADA) to convince consumers to floss daily. Motion for a preliminary injunction is granted.

▌ *ANALYSIS*

Pfizer's (D) use of disclaimer and cautionary language telling consumers to "floss daily," urging them to consult their dentists, and noting that "there's no replacement for flossing" does not negate the implied replacement message. Notwithstanding the disclaimer language, Pfizer's (D) ads clearly suggested to consumers, through their overall words and images, that if the consumers did not have the time or desire to floss, they could rinse with Listerine instead, for Listerine is just "as effective as floss." The few words of disclaimer are lost when the ads are considered as a whole. After all, the point of an implied falsity claim is that even though an advertisement "is literally true it is nevertheless likely to mislead or confuse consumers."

■=■

Quicknotes

INJUNCTIVE RELIEF A court order issued as a remedy, requiring a person to do, or prohibiting that person from doing, a specific act.

LANHAM ACT, § 43(a) Federal trademark infringement statute.

Continued on next page.

PRELIMINARY INJUNCTION A judicial mandate issued to require or restrain a party from certain conduct; used to preserve a trial's subject matter or to prevent threatened injury.

■═■

Internet Domain Names

Quick Reference Rules of Law

Fagnelli Plumbing Company v. Gillece Plumbing and Heating, Inc.

Plumbing, heating and cooling company (P) v. Plumbing, heating and cooling company (D)

98 U.S.P.Q.2d 1997 (W.D. Pa. 2011).

NATURE OF CASE: Cross-motions for summary judgment in action for, inter alia, cybersquatting in violation of the Anticybersquatting Consumer Protection Act.

FACT SUMMARY: Fagnelli Plumbing Company (Fagnelli) (P) contended that its direct competitor, Gillece Plumbing and Heating, Inc. (Gillece) (D), violated the Anticybersquatting Consumer Protection Act by obtaining the domain name "www.fagnelli.com" without Fagnelli's (P) knowledge or permission, and having that domain name redirect internet traffic to Gillece's (D) website.

RULE OF LAW

A plaintiff will prevail, as a matter of law, on a claim that a defendant has cybersquatted in violation of the Anticybersquatting Consumer Protection Act where the plaintiff proves (1) that its name is a distinctive mark entitled to protection; (2) the defendant's registration of a domain name is identical or confusingly similar to the plaintiff's mark; and (3) the defendant registered the domain name with the bad-faith intent to profit from it.

FACTS: Fagnelli Plumbing Company (Fagnelli) (P) and Gillece Plumbing and Heating, Inc. (Gillece) (D) were direct competitors in the same geographic area for plumbing, heating and cooling services. Fagnelli (P) was the registrant of the domain name "www.fagnelliplumbing .com." Gillece (D) obtained the domain name "www .fagnelli.com" ("fagnelli.com") without Fagnelli's (P) knowledge or permission, and had that domain name redirect internet traffic to Gillece's (D) website. Gillece (D) has similarly registered close to 100 other domain names containing in whole or in part the names of many other plumbing, heating, cooling, and electrical contractors in the region, without those companies' permission or knowledge. After Fagnelli (P) learned of this situation, it demanded that Gillece (D) cease and desist from having "fagnelli.com" redirect internet traffic to its website and that Gillece (D) transfer ownership and registration of "fagnelli.com" to Fagnelli (P). Redirection of internet traffic from "fagnelli.com" ceased promptly, but Gillece (D) refused to transfer ownership and registration of "fagnelli .com" to Fagnelli (P). Fagnelli (P) then brought suit in district court against Gillece (D), claiming, inter alia, that Gillece's (D) actions constituted cybersquatting in violation of the Anticybersquatting Consumer Protection Act (the ACPA). Both parties moved for summary judgment.

ISSUE: Will a plaintiff prevail, as a matter of law, on a claim that a defendant has cybersquatted in violation of the

Anticybersquatting Consumer Protection Act where the plaintiff proves (1) that its name is a distinctive mark entitled to protection; (2) the defendant's registration of a domain name is identical or confusingly similar to the plaintiff's mark; and (3) the defendant registered the domain name with the bad-faith intent to profit from it?

HOLDING AND DECISION: (Schwab, J.) Yes. A plaintiff will prevail, as a matter of law, on a claim that a defendant has cybersquatted in violation of the Anticybersquatting Consumer Protection Act (the ACPA) where the plaintiff proves (1) that its name is a distinctive mark entitled to protection; (2) the defendant's registration of a domain name is identical or confusingly similar to the plaintiff's mark; and (3) the defendant registered the domain name with the bad-faith intent to profit from it. Here, Fagnelli's (P) name is distinctive when assessed by a multifactor distinctiveness test. Fagnelli (P) had been using its name for more than 50 years, and it had spent tens of thousands of dollars to advertise its name in different media well before Gillece (D) registered the domain name at issue. There was evidence from customers and plumbing inspectors that the Fagnelli (P) name was well-known in the area and was associated with plumbing, heating, and cooling services—which indicates that its mark had acquired distinctiveness as well as being inherently distinctive. For these reasons, "Fagnelli" is a distinctive mark entitled to protection. Here there is also a great likelihood that registration of "fagnelli.com" is confusingly similar to Fagnelli's (P) mark. There was testimony from a long-time customer that he was confused when trying to access Fagnelli's (P) contact information online. This is not surprising, given that "fagnelli.com" is similar in sight and meaning to the "Fagnelli" mark, and could be confused by potential customers attempting to access Fagnelli's (P) official website. The likelihood of confusion is increased because potential customers were, at one point, redirected to another plumbing company advertising many of the same services to the same geographic area. Therefore, Fagnelli (P) has met its burden to demonstrate that its mark and Gillece's (D) domain are so similar in sight, sound or meaning that they could be confused. As to the last factor, whether Gillece (D) acted in bad faith to profit from registration of the "fagnelli.com" domain name, the court may use a nonexhaustive statutory list of nine factors to assess this issue. Here, the overwhelming number of the nine factors weigh in Fagnelli's (P) favor. First, Gillece (D) has no trademark or other intellectual property rights in the "fagnelli.com" domain name and such domain name is

Continued on next page.

not consistent with Gillece's (D) name, nor has Gillece (D) legitimately used the domain name in connection with offering its services. Further, Gillece's (D) of the Fagnelli domain name has not been used in a noncommercial or fair use in a site accessible through fagnelliplumbing.com. Gillece's (D) argument that ACPA was intended to cover only profiteering through extortion is not supported by the legislative history, which shows that ACPA was intended to also cover the registration of domain names to divert customers from the mark owner's site to the cybersquatter's site. The fact that Gillece (D) registered so many of its competitors' names as domain names establishes a pattern of behavior that may have kept potential customers from accessing the legitimate websites of competing businesses and diverted customers to its own website. Gillece (D) failed to provide any other bona fide reason for its actions other than to limit the parties' direct competition. Thus, the evidence clearly demonstrates Gillece's (D) bad faith intent to profit from Fagnelli's (P) goodwill, either for its own commercial gain or to deprive Fagnelli (P) of potential customers. Because the record establishes the three elements of a cybersquatting claim under ACPA, Fagnelli (P) is entitled to summary judgment. Summary judgment for Fagnelli (P).

▶ *ANALYSIS*

The Lanham Act, 15 U.S.C. § 1125(d)(1)(B)(i), provides a nonexhaustive list of nine factors that courts may use to determine if a defendant acted with a bad faith intent to profit. These factors are: (1) the trademark or other intellectual property rights of the person, if any, in the domain name; (2) the extent to which the domain name consists of the legal name of the person or a name that is otherwise commonly used to identify that person; (3) the person's prior use, if any, of the domain name in connection with the bona fide offering of any goods or services; (4) the person's bona fide noncommercial or fair use of the mark in a site accessible under the domain name; (5) the person's intent to divert customers from the mark owner's online location to a site accessible under the domain name that could harm the goodwill represented by the mark, either for commercial gain or with the intent to tarnish or disparage the mark, by creating a likelihood of confusion as to the source, sponsorship, affiliation, or endorsement of the site; (6) the person's offer to transfer, sell, or otherwise assign the domain name to the mark owner or any third party for financial gain without having used, or having an intent to use, the domain name in the bona fide offering of any goods or services, or the person's prior conduct indicating a pattern of such conduct; (7) the person's provision of material and misleading false contact information when applying for the registration of the domain name, the person's intentional failure to maintain accurate contact information, or the person's prior conduct indicating a pattern of such conduct; (8) the person's registration or acquisition of multiple domain names

which the person knows are identical or confusingly similar to marks of others that are distinctive at the time of registration of such domain names, or dilutive of famous marks of others that are famous at the time of registration of such domain names, without regard to the goods or services of the parties; and (9) the extent to which the mark incorporated in the person's domain name registration is or is not distinctive and famous. Here, the court found that these factors overwhelmingly demonstrated bad intent to profit on Gillece's (D) part.

■=■

Quicknotes

BAD FAITH Conduct that is intentionally misleading or deceptive.

GOODWILL An intangible asset reflecting a corporation's favor with the public and expectation of continued patronage.

SUMMARY JUDGMENT Judgment rendered by a court in response to a motion made by one of the parties, claiming that the lack of a question of material fact in respect to an issue warrants disposition of the issue without consideration by the jury.

■=■

GoPets Ltd. v. Hise

Video game producer (P) v. Domain name owner (D)

657 F.3d 1024 (9th Cir. 2011).

NATURE OF CASE: Appeal from judgment for plaintiff in action for, inter alia, cybersquatting under the Anticybersquatting Consumer Protection Act, and for service mark infringement under the Lanham Act.

FACT SUMMARY: The Hises and their company, Digital Overture (collectively, "the Hises") (D), contended that they did not violate the Anticybersquatting Consumer Protection Act (the ACPA) or the Lanham Act by re-registering "gopets.com," a domain name they owned, the original registration of which did not violate the ACPA, and they also contended that they did not violate the ACPA or the Lanham Act by registering other domain names that were close variants of "gopets.com" ("Additional Domains"), notwithstanding that at the time of the re-registration and the Additional Domains registrations GoPets Ltd. (P) owned a distinctive service mark for "GoPets."

RULE OF LAW

(1) The Anticybersquatting Consumer Protection Act does not apply to a re-registration of a currently registered domain name by a new registrant.

(2) Where an initial domain name registration does not violate the Anticybersquatting Consumer Protection Act (the ACPA), additional domain name registrations that are similar variants of the initial domain name will violate the ACPA where those additional registrations are confusingly similar to a distinctive trademark or service mark not owned by the registrant and the registrations are made in bad faith.

FACTS: In 1999, Edward Hise (D) registered the domain name "gopets.com," intending to use it for a pets-related website. Edward Hise (Edward) (D) also owned Digital Signatures (D), a domain name registration company, with his brother, Joseph Hise (Joseph) (D). (The Hises (D) and Digital Signatures (D) are collectively referred to as "the Hises" (D).) In 2004, Bethke founded the company GoPets Ltd. (P), which created a computer game called "GoPets." GoPets (P) obtained a service mark for "GoPets" in 2006. Beginning in 2004, Bethke made several unsuccessful attempts to purchase the "gopets.com" domain name from the Hises (D). After Bethke reached out to Edward (D), he started adding content to the "gopets. com" site. In May 2006, GoPets (P) filed a complaint against Edward (D) with the World Intellectual Property Organization (WIPO), which administers the Internet Corporation for Assigned Names and Numbers' (ICANN's)

dispute resolution policy. WIPO held for Edward (D), finding that he had not registered the "gopets.com" domain name in bad faith. After the WIPO decision, Bethke kept raising his offer price for "gopets.com"—from a few hundred dollars to $40,000—but his offers were rejected. In December 2006, Edward (D) offered to sell "gopets.com" to GoPets (P) for $5 million. After sending this offer, Edward (D) transferred the registration of "gopets.com" from himself to Digital Overture (D). By January 2007, the site contained a link to the GoPets.com WIPO arbitration decision. By March 2007, the site contained a "GoPets.com" logo and text saying "Welcome to **goPets**.com the official online website. goAhead [sic] pet lovers tell your friends that **GoPets**.com will be arriving soon!" Also, soon after the WIPO decision in their favor, the Hises (D) began registering domain names ("Additional Domains") similar to "gopets.com" (e.g., "gopet.biz," "gopet.org," "egopets. com," "gopets.bz," etc.). GoPets (P) then sued the Hises (D) alleging claims for, inter alia, cybersquatting under the Anticybersquatting Consumer Protection Act, and service mark infringement and unfair competition under the Lanham Act. The district court rendered judgment for GoPets (P), finding that the Hises' (D) re-registration of gopets. com, and their registration of the Additional Domains, was in bad faith. The district court based its finding in part on the fact that the Hises (D) had used the Additional Domains as leverage to increase the price they could obtain for gopets.com. The court of appeals granted review.

ISSUE:

(1) Does the Anticybersquatting Consumer Protection Act apply to a re-registration of a currently registered domain name by a new registrant?

(2) Where an initial domain name registration does not violate the Anticybersquatting Consumer Protection Act (the ACPA), will additional domain name registrations that are similar variants of the initial domain name violate ACPA where those additional registrations are confusingly similar to a distinctive trademark or service mark not owned by the registrant and the registrations are made in bad faith?

(3) May a defendant's addition of text to a website that creates a likelihood of confusion with a trademark or service mark constitute a violation of the Lanham Act?

HOLDING AND DECISION: (Fletcher, J.)

(1) No. The Anticybersquatting Consumer Protection Act (the ACPA) does not apply to a re-registration of a currently registered domain name by a new registrant.

Continued on next page.

To prevail on an ACPA claim, a plaintiff must show (1) registration of a domain name, (2) that was "identical or confusingly similar to" a mark that was distinctive at the time of registration, and (3) "bad-faith intent" at the time of registration. The issue presented here is whether re-registration of a registration that does not violate ACPA falls within ACPA's definition of "registration," which is undefined in the statute. A number of actions taken by a domain name owner subsequent to an initial registration conceivably could also qualify as registrations—e.g., renewal, switching to private registration, updating, etc.—but the legislative history indicates that Congress intended that "registration" refer only to the initial registration. A registrant can retain all of his rights to a domain name indefinitely if he maintains the registration of the domain name in his own name, and there is no basis in the ACPA to conclude that a right that belongs to an initial registrant of a currently registered domain name is lost when that name is transferred to another owner. A general rule of property law is that a property owner may sell all of the rights he holds in property. If re-registration through an assignment could subject the transferee to the ACPA, that would make rights to many domain names effectively inalienable, whether the alienation is by gift, inheritance, sale, or other form of transfer. Nothing in the text or structure of the statute indicates that Congress intended that rights in domain names should be inalienable, and, therefore, Digital Overture's (D) re-registration of "gopets.com" was not a registration within the meaning of the ACPA. Because Edward's (D) initial registration did not violate the ACPA, Digital Overture's (D) re-registration and continued ownership of "gopets.com" also does not violate the ACPA. [Reversed as to this issue.]

(2) Yes. Where an initial domain name registration does not violate the ACPA, additional domain name registrations that are similar variants of the initial domain name will violate the ACPA where those additional registrations are confusingly similar to a distinctive trademark or service mark not owned by the registrant and the registrations are made in bad faith. Here, the Additional Domains were registered at a time when the "GoPets" mark was distinctive. Thus, the question is whether they were registered in bad faith. The district court found bad faith in part on the fact that the Hises (D) used the Additional Domains as leverage to increase the price they could obtain for "gopets.com." This conclusion is amply supported by the record, notwithstanding that the re-registration of "gopets.com" did not violate the ACPA. For purposes of determining bad faith under the ACPA, a court may consider nine non-exhaustive statutory factors. Two factors are key here: the defendant's registration of multiple domain names that the defendant knows are identical or confusingly similar to marks of others that are distinctive at the time of registration of such domain names, and the

defendant's intent to divert consumers from the mark owner's online location to a site accessible under the domain name that could harm the goodwill represented by the mark for commercial gain by creating a likelihood of confusion as to the source, sponsorship, affiliation, or endorsement of the site. Here, it is undisputed that the service mark "GoPets" was distinctive at the time of registration of the Additional Domains, and the Hises (D) have adduced no evidence that the Additional Domains were not confusingly similar to the GoPets mark. This factor weighs in favor of a bad-faith finding. Additionally, it is clear that the Hises (D) intended the Additional Domains to divert consumers from GoPets' (P) online location to sites accessible under their domain names by creating a likelihood of confusion. It is also clear that the registration of the Additional Domains was intended to achieve "commercial gain" by confusing consumers and diverting them from the website they intended to access. The Hises (D) argue that they qualify for the ACPA's safe harbor for registrants who "believed and had reasonable grounds to believe that the use of the domain name was a fair use or otherwise lawful." They allege that their victory in the WIPO arbitration led them to believe that their registration of the domain name "gopets.com" was proper. However, the WIPO decision gave the Hises (D) no reason to believe they had the right to register additional domain names that were identical or confusingly similar to "GoPets," especially since that decision made clear that the Hises (D) prevailed only because the service mark "GoPets" had not been registered when Edward (D) registered "gopets.com." Because the Additional Domains were registered well after "GoPets" was registered as a service mark, the Hises (D) violated the ACPA when they registered the Additional Domains. Affirmed as to this issue.

(3) Yes. A defendant's addition of text to a website that creates a likelihood of confusion with a trademark or service mark may constitute a violation of the Lanham Act. Mere registration of a domain name does not constitute service mark or trademark infringement, so with respect to the Additional Domains, the Hises (D), who did nothing more than register the Additional Domains, did not violate the Lanham Act. However, they did more than merely register "gopets.com"; they added text to the website that indicated that it was "GoPets.com the official online website." The district court thus properly held that in so doing the Hises (D) violated the Lanham Act. [Affirmed as to this issue.]

▶ *ANALYSIS*

As this case demonstrates, the safe harbor defense under the Anticybersquatting Consumer Protection Act, for regis-

Continued on next page.

trants who believed and had reasonable grounds to believe that the use of the domain name was a fair use or otherwise lawful, is difficult to prove. The courts have cautioned that the safe harbor defense should be invoked very sparingly and only in the most unusual cases. Moreover, a defendant who acts even partially in bad faith cannot successfully assert a safe harbor defense.

■══■

Quicknotes

BAD FAITH Conduct that is intentionally misleading or deceptive.

SERVICE MARK A word, symbol, device or combination thereof used in conjunction with a particular service so as to distinguish that service from those of others.

TRADEMARK Any word, name, symbol, device or combination thereof that is either currently utilized, or which a person has a bona fide intent to utilize, in commerce in order to distinguish his goods from those of another.

■══■

Lucas Nursery and Landscaping, Inc v. Grosse

Bad landscaper (P) v. Website operator (D)

359 F.3d 806 (6th Cir. 2004).

NATURE OF CASE: Appeal from denial of summary judgment.

FACT SUMMARY: Lucas Nursery and Landscaping, Inc. (Lucas Nursery) (P) did some landscaping for Michelle Grosse (D), who thought Lucas Nursery (P) did a terrible job. She registered the domain name "lucasnursery.com" and told her story on the website. Lucas Nursery (P) sued under the Anticybersquatting Consumer Protection Act.

🏛 RULE OF LAW
The Anticybersquatting Consumer Protection Act is not intended to prevent "cybergripers."

FACTS: Michelle Grosse (D) had a swale in her front yard and Lucas Nursery and Landscaping, Inc. (Lucas Nursery) (P) said it could repair it with topsoil. Grosse (D) was unhappy with the work done by Lucas Nursery (P) and complained repeatedly to the company. Lucas Nursery (P) refused to address her concerns, so Grosse (D) filed a complaint with the Better Business Bureau (BBB). The BBB closed its investigation without making a recommendation, which frustrated Grosse (D). She registered the domain name "lucasnursery.com" and used the website to publish her story. Counsel for Lucas Nursery (P) sent a cease and desist letter to Grosse (D), who then took down the website. She confirmed with the U.S. Patent & Trademark Office that Lucas Nursery (P) had no registered trademark and subsequently put her site back up with the story narrative. Lucas Nursery (P) sued Grosse (D); both parties filed summary judgment. The district court denied summary judgment to Lucas Nursery (P) and granted summary judgment to Grosse (D). Lucas Nursery (P) appealed.

ISSUE: Is the Anticybersquatting Consumer Protection Act intended to prevent "cybergripers"?

HOLDING AND DECISION: (Cole, J.) No. The Anticybersquatting Consumer Protection Act (the ACPA) is not intended to prevent "cybergripers." Lucas Nursery (P) accused Grosse (D) of acting with bad faith when she registered the "lucasnursery.com" domain name only to publish complaints about the company's service. The ACPA lists nine factors the court must consider in determining whether a party acted with "bad faith." Grosse (D) does not hold an intellectual property right in the domain name, the domain name does not consist of her legal name, and she has not used it in connection with offering goods or services. The site was not used for commercial purposes, though, so the fourth factor is in Grosse's (D) favor. None of the remaining factors cut against Grosse (D), however, because Grosse (D) was not trying to mislead consumers. Lucas Nursery (P) did not have an online presence, Grosse (D) never offered to sell the site to Lucas Nursery (P), she did not provide misleading contact information, and she did not acquire other domain names. The case law upon which Lucas Nursery (P) heavily relied involved a defendant who registered 16 other domain names that intentionally misled consumers about the name of the entity they sought. Grosse's (D) intent of informing consumers about her experience with a service provider is not inconsistent with the ideal of the ACPA. Affirmed.

▶ ANALYSIS

"Cybercomplaint" sites grew exponentially in the 1990s as consumers became more Internet-savvy and used the web to express displeasure with particular companies. Blogs in the 2000s then became the more popular forums for criticisms as litigation over the cybercomplaint sites increased. As long as the registrant does not improperly use the mark holder's trademark, the cybercomplaint site is permissible.

■=■

Quicknotes

TRADEMARK INFRINGEMENT The unauthorized use of another's trademark in such a manner as to cause a likelihood of confusion as to the source of the product or service in connection with which it is utilized.

■=■

People for the Ethical Treatment of Animals v. Doughney

Animal rights group (P) v. Individual's web site (D)

263 F.3d 359 (4th Cir. 2001).

NATURE OF CASE: Appeal of an anticybersquatting trademark infringement decision.

FACT SUMMARY: Doughney (D) created a web page entitled "People Eating Tasty Animals," which was a parody of the website run by the People for the Ethical Treatment of Animals (P).

🏛 RULE OF LAW
To establish an Anticybersquatting Consumer Protection Act violation, it must be proved there was bad-faith intent to profit from using the parodied domain name and that the domain name is identical or confusingly similar to, or dilutive of, the distinctive and famous mark.

FACTS: People for the Ethical Treatment of Animals (PETA) is an advocacy group opposed to eating meat, wearing fur, and conducting research on animals. PETA has an Internet web site of "peta.com." Doughney (D) registered an Internet domain with the name "peta.org" and set up a page entitled "People Eating Tasty Animals," which he intended to use as a parody of PETA (P) and its goals and beliefs. PETA (P) sued Doughney (D) over the registration of that domain name.

ISSUE: To establish an Anticybersquatting Consumer Protection Act violation, must it be proved there was bad-faith intent to profit from using the parodied domain name and that the domain name is identical or confusingly similar to, or dilutive of, the distinctive and famous mark?

HOLDING AND DECISION: (Gregory, J.) Yes. To establish an Anticybersquatting Consumer Protection Act (ACPA) violation, it must be proved there was bad-faith intent to profit from using the parodied domain name and that the domain name is identical or confusingly similar to, or dilutive of, the distinctive and famous mark. To establish a violation under the ACPA, PETA (P) must prove that: (1) Doughney (D) had a bad-faith intent to profit from the use of peta.org and (2) that this domain name "is identical or confusingly similar to, or dilutive of," the distinctive and more famous PETA (P) trademark. The lower court had found that PETA (P) met both of the above requirements. Doughney (D) made several arguments and concluded that he is entitled to protection under the ACPA's safe harbor provision, allowing protection of a website if the person believes or has reasonable grounds to believe that use of the domain name was fair or lawful. Doughney's (D) arguments refuting PETA's (P) suit included: (1) that the ACPA, effective in 1999, cannot be applied to events of 1995 and 1996 because it was not meant to be retroactive; in fact the ACPA explicitly stated that it applies to "domain names registered before, on, or after the date of enactment." (2) Doughney (D) stated that he did not seek any financial gain from the use of PETA's (P) trademark; there is no dispute that Doughney (D) made numerous statements, both on the website and to the press, suggesting that PETA (P) pay him to shut down the site. (3) Doughney (D) claimed that he did not act in bad faith, a claim that this court finds unavailing because of the fact that Doughney (D), when registering his domain name, made false statements and knew that he was registering a name identical to PETA (P). Doughney (D) also had registered other domain names similar or identical to the trademarks or names of other organizations and famous people. Finally, the court finds that Doughney (D) "clearly intended to confuse Internet users into accessing his website." Doughney (D) did not establish that he had "reasonable grounds to believe" that his use of PETA's (P) trademark was lawful; merely "thinking" it to be lawful does not make that belief reasonable. For the above stated reasons, Doughney (D) is not entitled to relief under the safe harbor provision of the ACPA. Affirmed.

▶ ANALYSIS

Parody can be protected against claims of infringement; however, it is not an absolute protection against an infringement charge. The fact that Doughney (D) suggested that PETA (P) settle with him undercut his good faith argument. And the fact that Doughney (D) lied when he registered his web site undercuts his argument that he reasonably believed he had a lawful right to parody PETA (P).

Quicknotes

BAD FAITH Conduct that is intentionally misleading or deceptive.

PARODY Affirmative defense to an action for copyright infringement under the fair use doctrine that the infringer's use of the copyrighted material was permissible for the purpose of criticism or satire.

TRADEMARK Any word, name, symbol, device or combination thereof that is either currently utilized, or which a person has a bona fide intent to utilize, in commerce in order to distinguish his goods from those of another.

Continued on next page.

TRADEMARK INFRINGEMENT The unauthorized use of another's trademark in such a manner as to cause a likelihood of confusion as to the source of the product or service in connection with which it is utilized.

■═■

Lamparello v. Falwell

Cybergriper (P) v. Mark holder (D)

420 F.3d 309 (4th Cir. 2005).

NATURE OF CASE: Cross appeals in cybergripe case.

FACT SUMMARY: Christopher Lamparello (P) registered the domain name "www.fallwell.com" and operated a site as a critique and complaint site about the Reverend Jerry Falwell (D). Falwell (D), a well-known minister active in political areas, had common-law trademarks in his name "Jerry Falwell" and "Falwell." He sought to enjoin Lamparello's (P) use of the site and requested the domain name transferred to him.

🏛 RULE OF LAW
The "initial interest confusion" doctrine, which the Fourth Circuit has not adopted, requires the mark user to lure consumers from the actual producer by use of the mark to sell its goods or services, which is a violation of the Lanham Act even if the confusion is dispelled by the time the sale is consummated.

FACTS: Reverent Jerry Falwell (D) is a nationally known minister with sometimes controversial opinions on politics, religion, and public life. He holds common-law trademarks in his name "Jerry Falwell" and "Falwell." He registered and operated "www.falwell.com" website, which received 9,000 hits daily. Christopher Lamparello (P) disagreed with statements Falwell (D) made about homosexuals and homosexuality, so he registered the domain name "www.fallwell.com" to operate a cybergripe site. He published critiques of Falwell's (D) comments and citations to support his beliefs in contradiction to those of Falwell (D). The homepage of Lamparello's (P) site contained a disclaimer that the site was not affiliated with or authorized by Falwell (D) and it included a link to Falwell's (D) site. Lamparello (P) did not sell goods or services on the site. The site received about 200 hits daily. Falwell (D) sent Lamparello (P) cease and desist letters and demanded the transfer of the domain name. Lamparello (P) filed suit against Falwell (D) for a declaration of noninfringement. The parties filed cross motions for summary judgment. The district court granted Falwell's (D) motion and ordered the transfer of the domain name. The district court denied Falwell's (D) request for statutory damages and attorney fees. Lamparello (P) appealed the summary judgment and Falwell (D) appealed the denial of damages and fees.

ISSUE: Does the "initial interest confusion" doctrine, which the Fourth Circuit has not adopted, require the mark user to lure consumers from the actual producer by use of the mark to sell its goods or services, which is a violation of the Lanham Act even if the confusion is dispelled by the time the sale is consummated?

HOLDING AND DECISION: (Motz, J.) Yes. The "initial interest confusion" doctrine, which the Fourth Circuit has not adopted, requires the mark user to lure consumers from the actual producer by use of the mark to sell its goods or services, which is a violation of the Lanham Act even if the confusion is dispelled by the time the sale is consummated. Trademark law is intended to identify the producer of goods or services but it is not intended to provide rights to control language. Lamparello (P) argues the Lanham Act must be restricted to commercial speech, which other circuits have endorsed. Congressional enactment of the Federal Trademark Dilution Act of 1995 and the Anticybersquatting Consumer Protection Act of 1999 leaves little doubt Congress did not intend trademark protection to impinge upon First Amendment free expression. "Noncommercial" language is expressly protected. The Lanham Act's trademark infringement and false designation of origin prohibitions, however, do not use the word "noncommercial" but they do only pertain to the use of the mark related to goods and services offered for sale. The Second Circuit has explained that the term "services" is defined broadly. The court does not need to determine whether Lamparello's (P) speech constitutes "noncommercial" speech as understood in the Lanham Act because Falwell's (D) claims fail because there is no likelihood of confusion. Lamparello (P) may use Falwell's mark if there is no likelihood of confusion. Falwell's (D) mark is distinctive and the domain name closely resembles it, but the websites do not resemble one another in the slightest nor do they offer similar goods or services. Anyone accessing Lamparello's (P) site would quickly ascertain it is not sponsored by or affiliated with Falwell (D) because the opinions espoused on the site are completely antithetical to those of Falwell (D). Falwell (D) next argued he prevails under the "initial interest confusion" doctrine, which is the doctrine that a mark user cannot lure consumers from the trademark holder by initially passing its goods off as the producer's even if that confusion is dispelled by the time the sale is consummated. This circuit has never adopted that doctrine and the assertion that this court did in *People for the Ethical Treatment of Animals v. Doughney*, 263 F.3d 359 (4th Cir. 2001), (PETA) is incorrect. The issue in PETA was whether the website hosted at "www.peta.org" was a successful parody of the actual PETA organization. The site's content made it clear it was not related to PETA, but that message was not conveyed with the initial message that implied it was PETA's official website, so the court rejected the registrant's parody de-

Continued on next page.

fense. PETA did not adopt the "initial interest confusion" doctrine but expressly stated the court should consider the use in its entirety causes confusion rather than a fragment of a given use. Further, the doctrine requires the user to financially capitalize on the use of the mark. Here, the alleged infringer operates a gripe site with no financial benefit to the mark holder. The Lanham Act does not shield a trademark holder from criticism. Reversed and remanded for entry of judgment in favor of Lamparello (P).

▶ ANALYSIS

The "initial interest confusion" doctrine was sporadically employed by courts in the early days of internet litigation under the assumption consumers were easily confused by domain names and the producers of those websites. The trademark laws were intended to protect against confusion by the reasonable consumer rather than confusion by a careless or unsophisticated consumer, so critics of the "initial interest confusion" doctrine were pleased by the Fourth Circuit's opinion noting the flaws in the doctrine.

■■■■

Quicknotes

LANHAM ACT Name of the Trademark Act of 1946 that governs federal law regarding trademarks.

TRADEMARK INFRINGEMENT The unauthorized use of another's trademark in such a manner as to cause a likelihood of confusion as to the source of the product or service in connection with which it is utilized.

■■■■

Solid Host, NL v. NameCheap, Inc.

Internet-related services provider (P) v. Domain name registrar (D)

652 F. Supp. 2d 1092 (C.D. Cal. 2009).

NATURE OF CASE: Motion to dismiss action for contributory liability for cybersquatting under the Anticybersquatting Consumer Protection Act.

FACT SUMMARY: After Solid Host, NL's (P) domain name was stolen by a hacker, and through the anonymous domain name registration services of NameCheap, Inc. (D) the domain name was re-registered and linked to the hacker's website, which ransomed the domain name, Solid Host (P) brought suit against NameCheap (D) for, inter alia, contributory liability for cybersquatting under the Anticybersquatting Consumer Protection Act because NameCheap (D) refused to reveal the hacker's identity.

🏛 RULE OF LAW
A defendant may be found liable for contributory cybersquatting under the Anticybersquatting Consumer Protection Act where the defendant directly controls and monitors the instrumentality used by a hacker to engage in domain name piracy and cybersquatting, through the defendant's ability to identify the hacker and return the domain name to its rightful owner, and has knowledge of such cybersquatting.

FACTS: Solid Host, NL (P) had registered the domain name "solidhost.com" through eNom, a domain name registrar. Due to a security breach at eNom, a hacker (Doe) was able to steal the registration information for "solidhost.com," and was able to move the domain name to another registration at eNom. The IP address associated with the name was changed so that Internet users accessing "solidhost.com" viewed a website controlled by Doe rather than Solid Host's site. Doe's website stated that the domain name was for sale, essentially ransoming the domain name for $12,000. NameCheap, Inc. (D) is a domain name registrar that also provides an anonymity service known as "WhoisGuard," whereby NameCheap (D) becomes the registered owner of a domain name desired by a customer, and licenses the domain name to the customer, thus preserving the customer's anonymity. Doe and NameCheap (D) entered into a contract for this anonymity service, and NameCheap (D) became the stolen domain name's registrant, after which Solid Host (P) could no longer alter the IP address associated with the domain name to re-direct internet traffic to Solid Host's (P) website. Although Doe controlled his website, NameCheap (D) had the ability to transfer the domain name to Solid Host (P) or to reveal Doe's identity. Despite being presented with evidence that Solid Host's (P) domain name had been stolen and re-registered by a hacker, NameCheap (D) refused to reveal

Doe's identity or restore the registration to Solid Host (P). Solid Host (P) then brought suit against NameCheap (D) for, inter alia, cybersquatting under the Anticybersquatting Consumer Protection Act, on a theory of contributory liability. NameCheap (D) moved to dismiss the action.

ISSUE: May a defendant be found liable for contributory cybersquatting under the Anticybersquatting Consumer Protection Act where the defendant directly controls and monitors the instrumentality used by a hacker to engage in domain name piracy and cybersquatting, through the defendant's ability to identify the hacker and return the domain name to its rightful owner, and has knowledge of such cybersquatting?

HOLDING AND DECISION: (Morrow, J.) Yes. A defendant may be found liable for contributory cybersquatting under the Anticybersquatting Consumer Protection Act (the ACPA) where the defendant directly controls and monitors the instrumentality used by a hacker to engage in domain name piracy and cybersquatting, through the defendant's ability to identify the hacker and return the domain name to its rightful owner, and has knowledge of such cybersquatting. The ACPA's scope is narrow, designed to counter cybersquatting, a narrow class of wrongdoing defined as registering, trafficking in, or using domain names "similar to trademarks with the bad-faith intent to profit from the goodwill of the trademarks." Here, the case differs from the paradigmatic cybersquatting case. First, in the typical case, the cybersquatter registers a well-known trademark as a domain name before the trademark owner is able to register it, hoping to capitalize on the value of the domain name to the trademark owner. Here, Doe stole the domain name after it had been in use for several years, and then tried to ransom it. Thus, after obtaining the registration, Doe proceeded as a typical cybersquatter would, attempting to ransom the domain name to Solid Host (P). Second, although Doe's liability for cybersquatting is clear, the issue here is not Doe's liability, but whether NameCheap (D) can be held contributorily liable for Doe's cybersquatting. In general, contributory trademark infringement occurs when the defendant either intentionally induces a third party to infringe the plaintiff's mark or supplies a product or service to a third party with actual or constructive knowledge that the product or service is being used to infringe the mark. Here, it is undisputed that NameCheap (D) did not induce Doe to engage in cybersquatting. Where the defendant supplies the infringer with a service rather than a product—as here—courts consider the extent of control exercised by the defendant over

Continued on next page.

the third party's means of infringement in analyzing whether a claim for contributory infringement lies. To prove sufficient control, a plaintiff must prove that the defendant had knowledge and direct control and monitoring of the instrumentality used by the third party to infringe the plaintiff's mark. Courts that have addressed this issue in the context of cybersquatting have held that merely serving as a registrar does not render the defendant contributorily liable for cybersquatting. Here, however, NameCheap (D) also had the ability to transfer the domain name to Solid Host (P) or to reveal Doe's identity, so that arguably NameCheap (D) had a greater degree of control and monitoring than a mere registrar. In other words, Solid Host (P) has alleged sufficient facts that NameCheap (D) was the "cyber-landlord" of the Internet real estate stolen by Doe, i.e., the domain name. NameCheap's (D) anonymity service was central to Doe's cybersquatting scheme, but if NameCheap (D) had returned the domain name to Solid Host (P), Doe's illegal activity would have ceased. This crucial factor distinguishes NameCheap (D) from defendants who merely receive link traffic from an infringing website, or from a registrar that provides nothing more than a registration service. Accordingly, the direct control and monitoring requirement necessary to plead a contributory liability claim is satisfied. Additionally, Solid Host (P) must also allege that NameCheap (D) knew of Doe's cybersquatting, which involves a bad-faith intent to profit from the domain name. Because a defendant in NameCheap's (D) position may not easily be able to ascertain a customer's good or bad faith, "exceptional circumstances" must be shown to prove the degree of knowledge required to impose contributory liability for cybersquatting. Here, Solid Host (P) alleged that Solid Host (P) gave NameCheap (D) evidence that would have led a normal and prudent person to conclude that the domain it registered had been stolen. Based on this allegation, the court cannot conclude, as matter of law, that Solid Host (P) will be unable to prove exceptional circumstances satisfying the knowledge requirement for contributory liability. What constitutes exceptional circumstances, and whether they can be proved in this case are matters that can only be addressed on a more fully developed factual record. Demand from a party such as Solid Host (P) is by itself insufficient to constitute exceptional circumstances, but where such demand is accompanied by sufficient evidence of a violation, the defendant may have a duty to investigate. The extent of that duty, however, will be circumscribed by the relative difficulty of confirming or denying the accusation under the facts of a particular case. For these reasons, Solid Host (P), at this stage of the litigation, has alleged sufficient facts to plead a claim for contributory liability for cybersquatting. Consequently, NameCheap's (D) motion to dismiss is denied.

⏵ *ANALYSIS*

The direct control and monitoring rule in service-based contributory infringement cases evolved in the context of

renting booth space at a flea market. In *Hard Rock Cafe Licensing Corp. v. Concession Servs., Inc.,* 955 F.2d 1143 (7th Cir. 1992), the Seventh Circuit concluded that a flea market operator could be held liable for the sale of infringing products at the market, citing the close comparison between the legal duty owed by a landlord to control illegal activities on his or her premises and by a manufacturer to control illegal use of his or her product. Although the "flea market" analysis generally has been applied in the infringement context, the court here found that a similar standard arguably could be applied to allegations of cybersquatting. However, because the Anticybersquatting Consumer Protection Act (the ACPA) requires a showing of bad-faith intent—a subjective element not required under traditional infringement, unfair competition, or dilution claims—the standard would be somewhat heightened. It would be insufficient that an entity were merely aware that domain names identical or similar to protected marks were being sold over its website, or that third parties were using its registration services to register such marks. Rather, because legitimate uses of others marks are protected under the ACPA, a plaintiff would have to demonstrate that the "cyber-landlord" knew or should have known that its vendors or registrants had no legitimate reason for having registered the disputed domain names in the first place. Because an entity such as NameCheap (D) could not be expected to ascertain the good- or bad-faith intent of those using its services, contributory liability would apply, if at all, in only "exceptional circumstances." Here, the court concluded that Solid Host (P) had alleged sufficient facts that, at trial, could show such exceptional circumstances.

■▬■

Quicknotes

BAD FAITH Conduct that is intentionally misleading or deceptive.

CONTRIBUTORY INFRINGEMENT The intentional assisting of another in the unlawful appropriation of a patented work.

DILUTION The diminishment of the capability of a trademark to identify and distinguish the particular good or service with which it is associated.

GOOD FAITH An honest intention to abstain from taking advantage of another.

UNFAIR COMPETITION Any dishonest or fraudulent rivalry in trade and commerce, particularly imitation and counterfeiting.

■▬■

Cable News Network L.P. v. CNNews.com

U.S.-based news company (P) v. Chinese-based news company (D)

177 F. Supp. 2d 506 (E.D. Va. 2001).

NATURE OF CASE: Cross-motions for summary judgment in an in rem action under the Anticybersquatting Consumer Protection Act.

FACT SUMMARY: Cable News Network L.P. (CNN) (P), a U.S.-based news company, contended that the registration by the Chinese-based news company Maya Online Broadband Network (HK) Co. Ltd. (Maya HK) (D) and its parent, Shanghai Online Broadband Network Co. Ltd (Shanghai Maya) (D) of the domain name "cnnews.com" constituted a violation of the in rem provisions of the Anticybersquatting Consumer Protection Act, because, according to CNN (P), the "cnnews.com" domain name infringed and diluted its rights to the "CNN"mark, in violation of the Lanham Act and the Federal Trademark Dilution Act, and because Shanghai Maya (D) and Maya HK (D) acted in bad faith in registering the offending domain name.

🏛 RULE OF LAW
To prevail on an in rem action under the Anticybersquatting Consumer Protection Act, a plaintiff must prove, as one of the elements of the action, that the registrant or user of the offending domain name acted in bad faith in registering or using the offending domain name.

FACTS: Cable News Network L.P. (CNN) (P) is a U.S.-based news company that provides news and information services throughout the world via a variety of electronic media. It is also the owner of the trademark "CNN," which it has registered in the United States as well as in China. CNN's (P) services are accessible worldwide via the Internet at the domain name cnn.com, and its "CNN" mark is well-known throughout Asia, including China. Maya Online Broadband Network (HK) Co. Ltd. (Maya HK) (D) and its Chinese parent, Shanghai Online Broadband Network Co. Ltd (Shanghai Maya) (D), registered the domain name "cnnews.com" through a Virginia registrar. The cnnews.com website was designed and operated by Shanghai Maya (D) to provide news and information to Chinese-speaking individuals worldwide. Shanghai Maya's (D) main website, cnmaya.com, makes significant use of the terms "cnnews" and "cnnews.com" as brand names, including use of logos that CNN (P) contends resemble its logos. Among the news articles posted on the cnnews.com and cnmaya.com websites are numerous articles that reference the CNN mark and CNN's (P) news reports and stories. Shanghai Maya (D) admitted that "cnnews" stands for "China Network News," the abbreviation for which is "CNN." Thus, it seemed that Shanghai Maya (D) intended

consumers to view the "cnnews.com" domain name as including the "CNN" mark in the form of "cnn-news.com," rather than as "cn-news.com." Although Maya HK (D) asserted that most people who access the cnnews.com website in China likely have never heard of CNN (P), it is clear that many Chinese-speaking people worldwide, including residents of China, have access to CNN's (P) television station as well as to the cnn.com website and its subsites. CNN (P) brought suit against Shanghai Maya (D) and Maya HK (D), alleging that they violated the in rem provisions of the Anticybersquatting Consumer Protection Act (the ACPA), on the grounds that the cnnews.com domain name infringed and diluted its rights to the "CNN" mark, in violation of the Lanham Act and the Federal Trademark Dilution Act. To prevail on such an action, a plaintiff must establish, inter alia, that the suit was brought in the jurisdiction where the registrar, registry, or registrar certificate for the infringing domain name is located; that in personam jurisdiction over a person or entity who would have been a defendant in an in personam civil action does not exist; and that each of the elements of trademark infringement, pursuant to the Lanham Act, or, alternatively, trademark dilution, pursuant to the Federal Trademark Dilution Act are established in the factual record as a matter of law. However, it is unclear whether bad faith is a requirement for the ACPA in rem actions. The parties cross-moved for summary judgment.

ISSUE: To prevail on an in rem action under the Anticybersquatting Consumer Protection Act, must a plaintiff prove, as one of the elements of the action, that the registrant or user of the offending domain name acted in bad faith in registering or using the offending domain name?

HOLDING AND DECISION: (Ellis, J.) Yes. To prevail on an in rem action under the Anticybersquatting Consumer Protection Act (the ACPA), a plaintiff must prove, as one of the elements of the action, that the registrant or user of the offending domain name acted in bad faith in registering or using the offending domain name. Here, it is clear that the first two elements of the in rem action are satisfied, since "cnnews.com" was registered in Virginia, and it has been established that the court does not have in personam jurisdiction over Shanghai Maya (D) and Maya HK (D), or any of their agents. As to the third element, "cnnews.com" was used in commerce, and an application of the multifactor test for likelihood of confusion in violation of the Lanham Act weighs in favor of a finding of likelihood of confusion. This satisfies the third element of the in rem ACPA action, notwithstanding that

Continued on next page.

CNN (P) has failed to show a likelihood of dilution in violation of the Federal Trademark Dilution Act. The final question that needs to be resolved is whether an ACPA in rem action requires a showing that the registrant or user of an offending domain name acted in bad faith. Some courts and have held that such a showing is necessary, whereas other courts and commentators have indicated their belief that it is not. Arguably, the ACPA is ambiguous on this point. However, because the purpose of the ACPA is to deter, prohibit and remedy "cyberpiracy," which is defined in the legislative history as the bad-faith registration or use of a domain name, and because bad faith is an explicit requirement of the ACPA in personam actions, resolution of the ACPA's ambiguity to require a showing of bad faith furthers the ACPA's purpose and design. For these reasons, the ACPA should be read, as most courts have, to incorporate a bad-faith requirement into the in rem section of the ACPA and not merely to define the circumstances in which an in rem proceeding is appropriate. Balancing the nine non-exclusive statutory factors for determining bad faith, in this case leads to the conclusion that "cnnews.com" was registered in bad faith. Additionally, the actions of Shanghai Maya (D) and Maya HK (D) do not fall within the ACPA's safe harbor for registrants who believe and have reasonable grounds to believe that the use of the domain name was a fair use or otherwise lawful. Finally, contrary to Shanghai Maya (D) and Maya HK's (D) argument that it would unconstitutionally violate due process to transfer the certificate of the "cnnews.com" domain name to CNN (P), because doing so would impermissibly interfere with the contract of two foreign entities, Maya HK (D) and its foreign registrar, such transfer does not violate due process. Because the certificate for the "cnnews.com" domain name is deposited with this court and the registry for the domain name is located within this judicial district, the situs of the domain name is in this district and the application of U.S. substantive law to it is consistent with due process. Further, in true in rem actions, there is no requirement that the owner or claimant of the res have minimum contacts with the forum, and it is not necessary that the allegedly infringing registrant have minimum contacts with the forum. Summary judgment is granted in favor of CNN (P), and Maya HK's (D) motion for summary judgment is denied.

▶ ANALYSIS

Whereas the court in this case held that proof of bad faith is an element of an in rem ACPA action, proponents of the contrary view argue that an in rem action focuses on the name itself, not the acts of the registrant or user. The court found that this conclusionary argument was unpersuasive, as it assumed the point in issue, namely what the focus is of an ACPA in rem action. Proponents of the contrary view also argue that requiring a bad faith showing in an in rem action places an unreasonable burden on plaintiffs in such actions in the event, as may often occur, that the registrant or user of the offending domain name is not available or

amenable to discovery. The court here also found this argument to be unpersuasive, reasoning that the absence of a registrant or user may hinder or conceivably aid a plaintiff's efforts to show bad faith in various cases, but in no event is proof of bad faith absolutely precluded or impossible simply because the matter proceeds in rem. Moreover, the court concluded that the speculative prospect of an increased difficulty of proof in some cases cannot trump what the statute is ultimately construed to require, nor is it a sound basis or guide for statutory construction.

Quicknotes

DILUTION The diminishment of the capability of a trademark to identify and distinguish the particular good or service with which it is associated.

IN REM An action against property.

MINIMUM CONTACTS The minimum degree of contact necessary in order to sustain a cause of action within a particular forum, consistent with the requirements of due process.

RES Thing; subject matter of a dispute to establish rights therein.

SUMMARY JUDGMENT Judgment rendered by a court in response to a motion made by one of the parties, claiming that the lack of a question of material fact in respect to an issue warrants disposition of the issue without consideration by the jury.

TRADEMARK INFRINGEMENT The unauthorized use of another's trademark in such a manner as to cause a likelihood of confusion as to the source of the product or service in connection with which it is utilized.

Dial-A-Mattress Operating Corp. v. Christopher E. Moakely

Corporation (P) v. Cybersquatter (D)

WIPO Arbitration and Mediation Center Case No. D2005-0471 (July 1, 2005).

NATURE OF CASE: Panel review of domain name registration complaint.

FACT SUMMARY: Christopher E. Moakely (D), a former employee of Dial-A-Mattress Operating Corp. (DialAMattress) (P), registered the domain name "1-800mattress.com." DialAMattress (P) owned the "1-800-Mattress" service mark. DialAMattress (P) filed a complaint with the World Intellectual Property Organization's Arbitration and Mediation Center to have the domain name transferred to it.

🏛 RULE OF LAW
A party may have a domain name in a suspected cybersquatting case cancelled or transferred via an arbitration decision if the party proves (1) the domain name is identical or confusingly similar to complainant's mark; (2) respondent has no rights or legitimate interests with the domain name; and (3) the domain name is registered and used in bad faith.

FACTS: Dial-A-Mattress Operating Corp. (DialAMattress) (P) operated a telemarketing mattress sales company and then expanded into online sales at www.mattress.com. On December 22, 1990, it registered the service mark "1-800-MATTRES, AND LEAVE OFF THE LAST S THAT'S THE S FOR SAVINGS." On December 31, 1995, it began using the mark "1-800-MATTRESS" in commerce and registered that service mark on January 4, 2005. Christopher E. Moakely (D) and his wife were former DialAMattress (P) employees when Moakely (D) registered "www.1-800mattress.com" on February 7, 2000. Moakely (D) did not set up a web presence, but merely parked the domain site with the web host. DialAMattress (P) filed this complaint with the World Intellectual Property Organization's Arbitration and Mediation Center (the Center), asking the Center to order the transfer of the domain name from Moakely (D) to DialAMattress (P).

ISSUE: May a party have a domain name in a suspected cybersquatting case cancelled or transferred via an arbitration decision if the party proves (1) the domain name is identical or confusingly similar to complainant's mark; (2) respondent has no rights or legitimate interests with the domain name; and (3) the domain name is registered and used in bad faith?

HOLDING AND DECISION: (Towns, Panelist) Yes. A party may have a domain name in a suspected cybersquatting case cancelled or transferred via an arbitration decision if the party proves (1) the domain name is identical or confusingly similar to complainant's mark; (2)

respondent has no rights or legitimate interests with the domain name; and (3) the domain name is registered and used in bad faith. The World Intellectual Property Organization's (WIPO's) Arbitration and Mediation Center (the Center) panel is limited to decisions involving cybersquatting. Here, Moakely (D) failed to file a response to the complaint so the Panel takes all allegations as true as it evaluates whether DialAMattress (P) proved all three elements. The domain name is confusingly similar to DialAMattress's (P) service mark "1-800-MATTRESS." The service mark was registered after the domain name was registered, but it was first used in commerce years prior. Moakely (D), as a former employee, would have been familiar with the mark. Nothing indicates DialAMattress (P) authorized Moakely (D) to register its mark or use its mark in the domain name. No evidence suggests Moakely (D) has any rights or interest in the domain name. He does not even use the site for commercial or noncommercial purposes; it is merely parked with the web host. Finally, *Telstra Corporation Limited v. Nuclear Marshmallows*, WIPO Case No. D2000-0003, sets forth requirements to show bad faith registration, which includes no plausible actual or contemplated active use of the dispute domain name that would not be illegitimate. Moakely (D) does not use the site and was aware of the marks prior to registering the domain name. The Panel cannot conceive of Moakely's (D) legitimate use for the site. This is a classic case of cybersquatting. The Panel orders the transfer of the domain name "1-800mattress.com" to complainant DialAMattress (P).

▶ ANALYSIS

The elements a complainant must prove are set forth in the Uniform Domain Name Dispute Resolution Policy promulgated by the International Corporation for Assigned Names and Numbers (ICANN). ICANN issued the Policy to provide a standard, lower-cost method to adjudicate domain name disputes because the Internet crosses geopolitical boundaries. Registrants of any nationality registered through any registration company in the world can take their disputes to the World Intellectual Property Organization's Arbitration and Mediation Center and apply the Policy elements.

■━■

Quicknotes

BAD FAITH Conduct that is intentionally misleading or deceptive.

Continued on next page.

TRADEMARK INFRINGEMENT The unauthorized use of another's trademark in such a manner as to cause a likelihood of confusion as to the source of the product or service in connection with which it is utilized.

UNFAIR COMPETITION Any dishonest or fraudulent rivalry in trade and commerce, particularly imitation and counterfeiting.

The Orange Bowl Committee, Inc. v. Front and Center Tickets, Inc./Front and Center Entertainment

Football tournament sponsor (P) v. Ticket seller (D)

WIPO Arbitration and Mediation Center Case No. D2004-0947 (January 20, 2005).

NATURE OF CASE: Request to transfer domain name.

FACT SUMMARY: Front and Center Tickets, Inc./Front and Center Entertainment (FCE) (D) registered two domain names containing the name "Orange Bowl" for the online resale of sporting and entertainment tickets. The Orange Bowl Committee, Inc. (Orange Bowl) (P) sought the transfer of those domain names to it because of a concern of trademark dilution.

🏛 RULE OF LAW
The addition of a generic word or term descriptive of the service offered is insufficient to avoid likelihood for confusion with the mark used in the domain name.

FACTS: The Orange Bowl Committee, Inc. (Orange Bowl) (P) has used the "ORANGE BOWL" mark since 1935 for one of the nation's best-known college football tournaments. The mark is now on merchandise, other sports tournaments, and millions of tickets. It garners significant media attention. Orange Bowl (P) registered its mark in 1995, inadvertently let the registration lapse in September 2002, and re-applied for federal registration in December 2002. Respondent Front and Center Tickets, Inc./Front and Center Entertainment (FCE) (D) concedes "ORANGE BOWL" is a famous name. FCE (D) registered "orangebowl.net" and "orangebowltickets.net" in 1999 for the online resale of sporting and entertainment tickets, including tickets to the Orange Bowl. Orange Bowl (P) sought the transfer of those domain names to it. FCE (D) deactivated the orangebowl.net site and put a large disclaimer on the other site that it was not affiliated with or authorized by Orange Bowl (P).

ISSUE: Is the addition of a generic word or term descriptive of the service offered insufficient to avoid likelihood for confusion with the mark used in the domain name?

HOLDING AND DECISION: (Partridge, Panelist) Yes. The addition of a generic word or term descriptive of the service offered is insufficient to avoid likelihood for confusion with the mark used in the domain name. FCE (D) concedes it has no argument for retaining "orangebowl.net" and agrees to transfer that domain name to Orange Bowl (P). Orange Bowl (P) must now prove the following three elements to achieve the transfer of "orangebowltickets.net": (1) FCE's (D) domain name is identical or confusingly similar to Orange Bowl's (P) mark; (2) FCE

(D) has no rights or legitimate interests in the domain name; and (3) the domain name was registered and used in bad faith. FCE (D) argued the addition of "tickets" removed any confusion between the domain name and the mark. "Tickets" is a generic word, however, and merely describes the service offered, so it is not distinctive enough to separate the domain name from the mark. Orange Bowl (P) has satisfied the first element. Orange Bowl (P) argued FCE (D) has no rights or legitimate interests in the domain name because it has no authorization from Orange Bowl (P) for the mark's use and FCE's (D) legal name does not include "ORANGE BOWL." FCE (D) argued it is using the site for the bona fide offering of Orange Bowl tickets. The issue becomes whether FCE's (D) admitted use of the mark is infringing. It does not meet the test for fair use because the use is to get consumer attention for the sale of many different kinds of tickets, not just Orange Bowl tickets. Orange Bowl (P) satisfied element two. Finally, FCE (D) conceded it registered and used the site with the mark as a method of enticing consumers to its site to sell them a variety of tickets for commercial gain. FCE (D) placed a large disclaimer on its site in an attempt to dispel confusion. The problem is, however, the consumer was already confused by the domain name and might believe Orange Bowl (P) authorized the use of "ORANGE BOWL" in the name and therefore authorized the ticket sales. Further, the disclaimer was confusing about whether FCE (D) was an authorized ticket reseller for Orange Bowl tickets. The risk of consumer confusion and FCE's (D) intentional use of the mark to create that confusion demonstrated bad faith registration and use. The domain name "orangebowltickets.net" is to be transferred to Orange Bowl (P).

DISSENT: (Smith, Panelist) "Tickets" is a sufficiently distinct term to remove the chance of confusion between the domain name and the mark. The Orange Bowl itself is too difficult to describe without using the words "Orange Bowl" because it changes dates, days, and is one of several "bowl" games in any given year. The domain name is for a site that sells tickets to that particular event and it has placed a prominent disclaimer on its site decrying any association with Orange Bowl (P). Further, the Orange Bowl is now known as the "FedEx Orange Bowl," so confusion is even less likely and FCE's (D) use of the mark "ORANGE BOWL" without the corporate sponsor name less damaging.

Continued on next page.

▶ *ANALYSIS*

FCE (D) conceded it was trying to attract consumers to its site with use of Orange Bowl's (P) trademark. Its site was arguably valid even though it was not an authorized ticket sales agent for Orange Bowl (P), so it should have operated under a domain name that was more closely linked to FCE's (D) name than Orange Bowl's (P). The dissent, however, shows the difficult evaluation courts and the WIPO Panel must make when differentiating one domain name from another. Is the word "tickets" too generic? The Panel argued it was also simply descriptive of the service offered. Perhaps FCE (D) could have sold Orange Bowl memorabilia instead of tickets and kept the domain name.

■══■

Quicknotes

TRADEMARK Any word, name, symbol, device or combination thereof that is either currently utilized, or which a person has a bona fide intent to utilize, in commerce in order to distinguish his goods from those of another.

TRADEMARK INFRINGEMENT The unauthorized use of another's trademark in such a manner as to cause a likelihood of confusion as to the source of the product or service in connection with which it is utilized.

■══■

Barcelona.com, Inc. v. Excelentisimo Ayuntamiento de Barcelona

Registrant (D) v. Barcelona City Council (P)

330 F.3d 617 (4th Cir. 2003).

NATURE OF CASE: Appeal from declaratory judgment.

FACT SUMMARY: Barcelona.com, Inc. (Bcom) (D) owns and operates barcelona.com, intended to be a tourist site. Excelentisimo Ayuntamiento de Barcelona (City Council) (P), which is the City Council of Barcelona, Spain, sought the transfer of the domain name to it.

🏛 RULE OF LAW
A U.S. party may appeal the transfer of its domain name in federal court with no deference given to a Uniform Domain Name Dispute Resolution Policy decision and the court must apply U.S. law even to a foreign mark holder.

FACTS: Mr. Joan NoguerasCobo, a Spanish citizen, registered "Barcelona.com" with Network Solutions, Inc., in Virginia and began seeking investors for the site. Mr. Cobo and his wife partnered with Mr. ShahabHanif, a British citizen, to form Barcelona.com, Inc. (Bcom) (D), a Delaware corporation. Bcom (D) owned and operated the website and the individuals continued to look, unsuccessfully, for financing. Eventually, Mr. Cobo offered to sell the domain name to ExcelentisimoAyuntamiento de Barcelona (City Council) (P), but received no response to his offer. City Council (P) owns numerous trademarks, most of which incorporate the name "Barcelona." After a year, City Council (P) demanded Bcom (D) transfer the domain name, but Bcom (D) refused. City Council (P) then filed a complaint with the World Intellectual Property Organization's (the WIPO's) Arbitration and Mediation Center pursuant to the Uniform Domain Name Dispute Resolution Policy (UDRP) promulgated by the Internet Corporation for Assigned Names and Numbers (ICANN). The WIPO panelist found in favor of City Council (P) and ordered Bcom (D) to transfer the domain name. Bcom (D) timely filed its appeal from the Panel decision in Virginia district court seeking a declaratory judgment under the Anticybersquatting Consumer Protection Act, which authorizes a registrant to seek recovery or restoration of its domain name if the trademark holder overstepped its authority in causing the domain name to be disabled, suspended, or transferred. The district court followed the WIPO decision and applied Spanish law in finding for City Council (P) and ordering the domain name transferred. Bcom (D) appealed.

ISSUE: May a U.S. party appeal the transfer of its domain name in federal court with no deference given to a Uniform Domain Name Dispute Resolution Policy decision and must the court apply U.S. law even to a foreign mark holder?

HOLDING AND DECISION: (Niemeyer, J.) Yes. A U.S. party may appeal the transfer of its domain name in federal court with no deference given to a Uniform Domain Name Dispute Resolution (UDRP) Policy decision and the court must apply U.S. law even to a foreign mark holder. A decision pursuant to the UDRP is given no deference under the Anticybersquatting Consumer Protection Act(the ACPA) because it is nothing more than an agreed-upon administrative decision that could apply foreign law that conflicts with U.S. law. The ACPA requires the application of the Lanham Act. Here, the district court stated it gave no weight to the World Intellectual Property Organization's finding, but then proceeded to adopt the findings. Further, the district court applied Spanish law in determining City Council (P) had a registered trademark in the name "Barcelona." Bcom (D) argued it is entitled to relief under the ACPA's reverse hijacking provision because it can establish (1) it is a domain name registrant; (2) its domain name was suspended, disabled, or transferred under a statutory policy implemented by a registrar; (3) the owner of the mark that prompted the reverse hijacking had notice of the action by service or otherwise; and (4) the registration or use of the domain name was not unlawful under the Lanham Act. Bcom (D) appealed on the basis of the last issue because the district court applied Spanish law instead of the Lanham Act. City Council (P) does not have a registered trademark in "Barcelona" in the United States. That application of Spanish law shows it arguably has a trademark in Spain, is irrelevant. The district court should have applied the Lanham Act, and such application shows Bcom's (D) registration and use of the name "Barcelona" is not unlawful. Bcom (D) is entitled to relief under the reverse hijacking provision of the ACPA and the district court's judgment is reversed. Reversed and remanded.

▶ ANALYSIS

The Uniform Domain Name Dispute Resolution (UDRP) is an administrative body formed to issue opinions on domain name disputes as a means of avoiding more costly litigation or conflicting countries' laws. The United States, however, provides no deference to UDRP decisions once a party files a claim for protection under U.S. laws. A registrant and/or mark holder cannot argue application of another country's laws in a U.S. court, while it can argue such application in a UDRP proceeding, so the proceeding

Continued on next page.

could be particularly beneficial to a mark holder lacking
U.S. registration but having protection in its home country.

■══■

Quicknotes

LANHAM ACT Name of the Trademark Act of 1946 that
governs federal law regarding trademarks.

■══■

Remedies

Quick Reference Rules of Law

Nova Wines, Inc. v. Adler Fels Winery LLC

Trademark holder (P) v. Competitor wine seller (D)

467 F. Supp. 2d 965 (N.D. Cal. 2006).

NATURE OF CASE: Motion for preliminary injunction in trademark infringement case.

FACT SUMMARY: Nova Wines, Inc. (Nova) (P) is the exclusive licensee for the use of Marilyn Monroe's name, image, and likeness on wine. Adler Fels Winery LLC (Adler Fels) (D) purchased a license from a third party to apply a particular photograph of Marilyn Monroe to its wine bottles. Nova (P) sought to prohibit the marketing and distribution of the Adler Fels (D) wine.

🏛 RULE OF LAW

A party seeking an injunction in a trademark infringement case, needs to prove that either (1) it will prove by a preponderance of the evidence the likelihood of consumer confusion and suffer irreparable injury absent the injunction; or (2) serious questions exist about the merits of the case and the balance of hardships tips sharply in plaintiff's favor.

FACTS: Marilyn Monroe's estate granted Nova Wines, Inc. (Nova) (P) an exclusive license to use her name, image, and likeness on its wine bottles. It developed, marketed, and sold various Monroe wines such as Marilyn Merlot, Marilyn Cabernet, and the Velvet Collection since 1987. During Marilyn Monroe's lifetime, she posed for nude photographs for Tom Kelley, Sr., who obtained a model's release from Ms. Monroe permitting him to use her name, portrait, and pictures from that photo session. Kelley used Saal Brown, Inc. d/b/a Pacific Licensing (Pacific Licensing) as its licensing agent for the photographs. Pacific Licensing offered a license to Nova (P) for use of one of the photos. After working with the Tobacco Tax and Trade Bureau (TTTB) to develop a "modesty overlay" for Ms. Monroe's breasts and buttocks, Pacific Licensing was able to provide a TTTB-approved photo to Nova (P) for its wine label. The parties' relationship deteriorated, however, and Pacific Licensing informed Nova (P) it would find a new licensee. Pacific Licensing sold its license to Adler Fels Winery LLC (Adler Fels) (D), a competitor of Nova's (P). Nova (P) learned of Adler Fels' (D) plan to market a wine bearing the Monroe photograph and it sent a cease and desist letter to Adler Fels (D). Adler Fels (D) refused to comply and began a marketing campaign in earnest for its intended fall release of the Monroe wine label. Nova (P) learned of the intended fall release and filed suit for trademark infringement, trade dress infringement, unfair competition, and passing off. Nova (P) seeks a preliminary injunction to prohibit Adler Fels (D) releasing and selling the wine with the Monroe photograph on the label.

ISSUE: Will a party seeking an injunction in a trademark infringement case need to prove that either (1) it will prove by a preponderance of the evidence the likelihood of consumer confusion and suffer irreparable injury absent the injunction; or (2) serious questions exist about the merits of the case and the balance of hardships tips sharply in plaintiff's favor?

HOLDING AND DECISION: (Patel, J.) Yes. A party seeking an injunction in a trademark infringement case, needs to prove that either (1) it will prove by a preponderance of the evidence the likelihood of consumer confusion and suffer irreparable injury absent the injunction; or (2) serious questions exist about the merits of the case and the balance of hardships tips sharply in plaintiff's favor. A preliminary injunction is intended to preserve the status quo pending resolution of the litigation. In a trademark infringement case, the plaintiff must demonstrate at trial the likelihood of confusion, so the possibility of irreparable injury is presumed absent an injunction. The Court applied the Sleekcraft factors to determine the strength of the Marilyn wines trade dress, the relatedness of the goods, and the degree of care the product purchasers will use all weigh in plaintiff's favor. The plaintiff will likely be able to prove a likelihood of confusion at trial. That alone is sufficient to warrant injunctive relief. The Court, however, also finds the second basis for injunctive relief is present. Nova (P) has spent years as the sole purveyor of Marilyn wines and would suffer irreparable injury if another winery could sell nearly identical wine labels outside Nova's (P) control. In contrast, Adler Fels (D) has failed to provide evidence it would suffer at all if prohibited from marketing and selling its Marilyn-labeled wine. It claims it would lose $4 million because of the loss of marketing time and inability to take advantage of pre-holiday sales. The wine is not yet in the market, however, so nothing needs to be withdrawn and it has a variety of other wines in the marketplace to make up for this missing wine. Further, it has plenty of non-trademarked labels from which to choose for this new wine. The balance of hardships tips sharply in Nova's (P) favor. Preliminary injunction granted.

▶ ANALYSIS

The Velvet Collection was a series of photographs of a nude Marilyn Monroe (at the time an unknown aspiring model and actress) posing on a red velvet drape. One of the photographs became the centerfold of the very first "Playboy" magazine in 1953. The photographer of the now-

Continued on next page.

famous Velvet Collection series was Tom Kelley, Sr. who had a registered copyright in the photographs. He licensed that copyright to various entities, including "Playboy," over the years. This case is important because it is the first case that demonstrates a tension between copyright law and trademark law where trademark might trump. Judge Hall Patel opined the broad trade dress protection afforded Nova (P) because of its decades as the sole purveyor of wine with Marilyn Monroe on its label was stronger than the copyright protection Kelley enjoyed in any one particular photograph that had been used in a variety of settings.

■===■

Quicknotes

COPYRIGHT LAW   Refers to the exclusive rights granted to an artist pursuant to Article I, Section 8, clause 8 of the United States Constitution over the reproduction, display, performance, distribution, and adaptation of his work for a period prescribed by statute.

PRELIMINARY INJUNCTION   A judicial mandate issued to require or restrain a party from certain conduct; used to preserve a trial's subject matter or to prevent threatened injury.

TRADE DRESS   The overall image of, or impression created by, a product that a court may enforce as a trademark if it determines that such image has acquired secondary meaning and that the public recognizes it as an indication of source.

TRADEMARK INFRINGEMENT   The unauthorized use of another's trademark in such a manner as to cause a likelihood of confusion as to the source of the product or service in connection with which it is utilized.

■===■

Home Box Office v. Showtime

Mark holder (P) v. Advertising competitor (D)

832 F.2d 1311 (2d Cir. 1987).

NATURE OF CASE: Cross-appeal from injunction entered in trademark infringement action.

FACT SUMMARY: Showtime (D) used Home Box Office's (HBO) (P) trademark, HBO, in its advertising. HBO (P) sought to enjoin the use.

🏛 RULE OF LAW
The infringing user has the burden of proof to demonstrate its disclaimer is effective in preventing the likelihood of consumer confusion.

FACTS: Home Box Office (HBO) (P) and Showtime (D) compete in the field of subscription television. At the 1987 cable television industry trade show, Showtime (D) unveiled a new slogan "SHOWTIME & HBO. It's Not Either/Or Anymore" in addition to other ads using HBO. Small disclaimers on some of the ad materials stated Showtime (D) and HBO (P) were separate entities. HBO (P) objected to the use of its trademark in Showtime's advertisements and sought to enjoin the use. HBO (P) claimed the use was confusing because it implied HBO (P) and Showtime (D) joined forces. HBO (P) introduced evidence of that consumer confusion in the form of Showtime (D) promotional materials used at the convention, a newspaper article discussing the confusion the materials engendered, and a four-city survey result. Showtime (D) argued it used the trademark to show the two entities are different and Showtime (D) offers films HBO (P) does not. Showtime's (D) intention was to advertise people can order both instead of one or the other. It also relied on its disclaimers. Showtime (D) produced new promotional materials at the trial that included more prominent disclaimers. The district court enjoined the use of the promotional materials that were used at the convention but expressly exempted the new promotional materials with the more prominent disclaimers. HBO (P) filed for an expedited appeal and Showtime (D) cross-appealed.

ISSUE: Does the infringing user have the burden of proof to demonstrate its disclaimer is effective in preventing the likelihood of consumer confusion?

HOLDING AND DECISION: (Lumbard, J.) Yes. The infringing user has the burden of proof to demonstrate its disclaimer is effective in preventing the likelihood of consumer confusion. The district court correctly applied the likelihood of confusion factors to the Showtime (D) promotional materials and found the materials caused consumer confusion. The district court did not, however, correctly evaluate the disclaimers. Showtime's (D) disclaimers were not located closely enough to the infringing material to be sufficient. It was Showtime's (D) burden to show the effectiveness of the disclaimers used and that burden was not met here. A full hearing should be held on the effectiveness of the disclaimers. This is particularly important because many disclaimers employing brief negator words such as "no" or "not" simply are not effective. Showtime (D) can seek relief from the injunction by noticing a hearing to HBO (P) and producing evidence of its disclaimers' effectiveness. The burden of proof on Showtime (D) is appropriate because it demonstrates (1) HBO (P) met its burden in proving likelihood of consumer confusion; (2) Showtime's (D) use of the marks as at the convention was an infringing use and Showtime (D) must demonstrate a change of use to be no longer infringing; and (3) HBO (P) does not have to catch up to Showtime's (D) use by showing each new infringement causes consumer confusion. Affirmed as to the injunction but vacated as to the exemption for the new promotional materials and if a disclaimer is used. Showtime's (D) cross-appeal is denied. Remanded.

▶ ANALYSIS

Disclaimers are permitted as a defense to trademark infringement where the disclaimers used are effective in preventing consumer confusion. The disclaimers are evaluated on a case-by-case basis, however, because the effectiveness may depend on the wording, placement, font, size of text, or other factors. Courts that do permit an infringing use typically require strong disclaimers as part of a limited injunction.

■═■

Quicknotes

BURDEN OF PROOF The duty of a party to introduce evidence to support a fact that is in dispute in an action.

DISCLAIMER Renunciation of a right or interest.

INFRINGEMENT Conduct in violation of a statute or contract that interferes with another's rights pursuant to law.

INJUNCTION A court order requiring a person to do, or prohibiting that person from doing, a specific act.

■═■

Perfect Fit Indus. v. Acme Quilting Co.

Mattress pad manufacturer (P) v. Infringer (D)

646 F.2d 800 (2d Cir. 1981).

NATURE OF CASE: Appeal from order for recall in unfair competition case.

FACT SUMMARY: The district court ordered Acme Quilting Co. (Acme) (D) to request its customers return the labels from Acme's (D) products. Acme (D) objected to the recall order based on a claim of undue burden.

🏛 RULE OF LAW
A district court should weigh the benefit to the plaintiff against the burden and expense to the defendant when ordering a recall as part of a remedy.

FACTS: Perfect Fit Indus. (Perfect Fit) (P) filed suit against Acme Quilting Co. (Acme) (D) for violating its state law unfair competition rights. Acme's (D) product and trade dress exactly copied Perfect Fit's (P), so the district court found in favor of Perfect Fit (P). It ordered Acme (D) to deliver all offending product to Perfect Fit (P) for destruction. It further ordered Acme (D) to notify all customers from the last six months that the customers should return the inserts from the Acme (D) products. Acme (D) objected based on projected costs and undue burden. Acme (D) appealed.

ISSUE: Should a district court weigh the benefit to the plaintiff against the burden and expense to the defendant when ordering a recall as part of a remedy?

HOLDING AND DECISION: (Kearse, J.) Yes. A district court should weigh the benefit to the plaintiff against the burden and expense to the defendant when ordering a recall as part of a remedy. After weighing, a district court may mold its order to best suit the particular facts of a specific case. Acme (D) argued the recall order placed an undue burden on it and will be too costly. Acme (D) did not, however, provide convincing evidence of the projected cost. Acme's (D) estimate assumed each of its customers would return the entire product at Acme's (D) expense. The district court merely ordered Acme (D) to notify its customers one time and request the return of the product inserts. Not all customers will comply. The order is consistent with the holding of *Kiki Undies Corp. v. Promenade Hosiery Mills, Inc.*, 308 F. Supp. 489 (S.D.N.Y. 1969). The district court here, as in *Kiki*, reviewed the facts of the case and fashioned an appropriate remedy. It was Acme's (D) burden to show the district court abused its discretion and it did not meet that burden. Affirmed.

▶ ANALYSIS

Courts are cautioned to use a recall as a remedy in a sparing, judicious manner. (See, *Oral Research Laboratories, Inc. v. L. Perrigo Company*, 864 F.2d 149 (Fed. Cir. 1988), which overturned a recall remedy as unnecessary and overly burdensome to the defendant). A recall always involves some burden to the defendant but may be the most appropriate remedy if the benefit to the plaintiff outweighs that burden. Here, the court noted the extent of defendant's attempts to replicate plaintiff's product as well as the delay in court proceedings, which increased the harm to plaintiff. The defendant failed to prove it would suffer unduly by the recall, so the benefit to the plaintiff in immediately addressing the consumer confusion far outweighed the de minimis burden to defendant in notifying its customers and paying for a few returns of labels.

■═■

Quicknotes

DE MINIMIS Insignificant; trivial; not of sufficient significance to require legal action.

TRADE DRESS The overall image of, or impression created by, a product that a court may enforce as a trademark if it determines that such image has acquired secondary meaning and that the public recognizes it as an indication of source.

UNFAIR COMPETITION Any dishonest or fraudulent rivalry in trade and commerce, particularly imitation and counterfeiting.

■═■

Gucci America, Inc. v. Daffy's, Inc.

Mark holder (P) v. Infringer (D)

354 F.3d 228 (3d Cir. 2003).

NATURE OF CASE: Appeal from recall and injunction denial in trademark infringement case.

FACT SUMMARY: Daffy's, Inc. (D) sold high-quality counterfeit handbags with the Gucci America, Inc. (Gucci) (P) label without confirming authenticity. Gucci (P) filed suit for trademark infringement, requested a recall of the counterfeit bags, and sought an injunction against future sales of the counterfeit bags.

🏛 RULE OF LAW
A recall is appropriate if (1) the defendant's infringement was willful or intentional; (2) the risk of public confusion and trademark owner injury is greater than the recall burden to the defendant; and (3) the defendant's infringement causes substantial risk of danger to the public.

FACTS: Daffy's, Inc. (D), a discount retail store, accepted a shipment of Gucci America, Inc. (Gucci) (P) label handbags without the usual indicia of authenticity. A Daffy's (D) employee took one of the bags to a Gucci (P) retail store and the Gucci (P) employee confirmed it was authentic. Daffy's (D) also sent one of the bags to Gucci (P) for repair and the bag was repaired without comment. Daffy's (D) sold several hundred of the bags before Gucci (P) determined the bags were counterfeit and sent a cease and desist letter to Daffy's (D). Daffy's (D) immediately pulled the remaining bags and issued a policy of no longer selling Gucci (P) products. Gucci (P) filed suit for trademark infringement and sought an injunction and a recall of the sold bags. The district court found Daffy's (D) liable for unintentional trademark infringement but denied the injunction and the recall. Gucci (P) appealed.

ISSUE: Is a recall appropriate if (1) the defendant's infringement was willful or intentional; (2) the risk of public confusion and trademark owner injury is greater than the recall burden to the defendant; and (3) the defendant's infringement causes substantial risk of danger to the public?

HOLDING AND DECISION: (McKee, J.) Yes. A recall is appropriate if (1) the defendant's infringement was willful or intentional; (2) the risk of public confusion and trademark owner injury is greater than the recall burden to the defendant; and (3) the defendant's infringement causes substantial risk of danger to the public. The denial of the recall is reviewed for abuse of discretion. The court below focused on the balancing of harms elements because Gucci (P) conceded the infringement was unintentional and there was no danger to the public. The district court correctly

determined the burden to Daffy's (D) far outweighed the benefit to Gucci (P). The counterfeit bags were of such high quality that Daffy's (D) customers are unlikely to believe Gucci (P) created an inferior product. Gucci (P) argued the consumer was harmed because the consumer believed he or she owned an authentic Gucci (P) bag when it was counterfeit. The district court considered this but did not find it justified the burden of a recall. The potential damage to Duffy's (D) is greater because consumers might believe the infringement was intentional. The district court also denied Gucci's (P) request for an injunction. The moving party must show: (1) actual success on the merits; (2) movant will be irreparably harmed absent injunctive relief; (3) the defendant will not suffer even greater harm; and (4) the injunction is in the public's interest. This court has previously stated trademark infringement is irreparable harm as a matter of law. The infringement creates a loss of control for the trademark holder over its own trademark and could result in damage to its reputation. Here, however, Gucci (P) failed to argue loss of control until appeal and has thus waived that argument. The district court could only look to actual harm to Gucci's (P) reputation in the absence of a loss of control argument. The district court reasonably concluded Gucci (P) had not suffered harm to its reputation or goodwill. Affirmed.

DISSENT: (Rosenn, J.) The trademark statute is meant to protect the holder from injury to its reputation and to protect the consumer from deceit. Daffy's (D) would not stipulate that it will not sell Gucci (P) products in the future, so Gucci (P) is left with no protection from a future unintentional infringement by Daffy's (D). Gucci (P) should not have to prove trademark infringement again and should have been granted an injunction against future infringement. Gucci (P) proved infringement, so it proved irreparable injury as a matter of law. Daffy's (D) then had the burden to prove the injury will not recur. The majority improperly shifts that burden to Gucci (P). The denial of the injunction was reversible error.

▶ ANALYSIS

Gucci sought an injunction and a recall to protect its reputation for quality products. The court did not review Gucci's argument for an injunction because of Gucci's procedural error in failing to preserve the issue for appeal, but injunctions against future infringement are a common remedy in trademark infringement cases. It prevents the burden of the plaintiff having to return to court time and

Continued on next page.

again in cases of repeat infringement to prove actual infringement. The plaintiff's burden is lowered to mere proof of violation of the injunction. As the dissent in Gucci argues, Gucci now has to bear the burden of a return trip to court if Daffy's again infringes, intentionally or not, Gucci's trademark.

■■■

Quicknotes

DISCRETION The authority conferred upon a public official to act reasonably in accordance with his own judgment under certain circumstances.

GOODWILL An intangible asset reflecting a corporation's favor with the public and expectation of continued patronage.

IRREPARABLE INJURY Such harm that because it is either too great, too small or of a continuing character that it cannot be properly compensated in damages, and the remedy for which is typically injunctive relief.

■■■

Taco Cabana Int'l, Inc. v. Two Pesos, Inc.

Trade dress holder (P) v. Infringer (D)

932 F.2d 1113 (5th Cir. 1991), *aff'd*, 505 U.S. 763 (1992).

NATURE OF CASE: Appeal from monetary award in trade dress infringement case.

FACT SUMMARY: Taco Cabana, Int'l Inc. (P) had a chain of Mexican restaurants in Texas in a "day-glo" colorful style that it claimed was copied by Two Pesos, Inc. (D).

🏛 RULE OF LAW
A prevailing plaintiff in a trade dress infringement case may recover (1) defendant's profits; (2) plaintiff's damages; and (3) costs of the action and the court may enter judgment for up to three times the actual damages so long as the damage award is compensatory and not punitive.

FACTS: In 1978, Taco Cabana Int'l, Inc. (P) began its Mexican restaurant empire in San Antonio, adopting as its motif an atmosphere of gaudy interior and exterior seating with colorful murals and ersatz artifacts. In 1985, a Two Pesos, Inc. (D) restaurant in Houston put forth an appearance that was suspiciously similar. In 1986, Taco Cabana (P) made a push into the Houston market, saw Two Pesos' (D) setup and sued Two Pesos (D) for trade dress infringement under § 43(a) of the Lanham Act and theft of trade secrets under Texas common law. Responding to five questions from the judge, a jury concluded that Taco Cabana (P) had a trade dress that was nonfunctional and inherently distinctive, that the trade dress had not acquired secondary meaning in Texas, and that the alleged infringement created a likelihood of confusion in the public as to the source or association of the two restaurant chains. The Fifth Circuit affirmed, holding the evidence was sufficient for the jury's findings and rejecting Two Pesos' (D) contention that secondary meaning must be shown to protect unregistered trade dress. Their position was supported by the rulings of the Second Circuit (alone). The United States Supreme Court granted certiorari to resolve the split among the circuits.

ISSUE: May a prevailing plaintiff in a trade dress infringement case recover (1) defendant's profits; (2) plaintiff's damages; and (3) costs of the action and may the court enter judgment for up to three times the actual damages so long as the damage award is compensatory and not punitive?

HOLDING AND DECISION: (Reavley, J.) Yes. A prevailing plaintiff in a trade dress infringement case may recover (1) defendant's profits; (2) plaintiff's damages; and (3) costs of the action and the court may enter judgment for up to three times the actual damages so long as the

damage award is compensatory and not punitive. Here, the jury awarded monetary damages to Taco Cabana Int'l, Inc. (Taco Cabana) (P) for lost profits and lost income. The judge determined Two Pesos, Inc.'s (D) infringement was intentional and deliberate, so the district court doubled the jury's monetary award to Taco Cabana (P). At trial, Taco Cabana (P) argued it suffered under the "headstart" theory which recognizes an infringer's preemption of a market to the detriment of the mark holder. The jury heard abundant testimony about Taco Cabana's (P) losses and the damage figures well over the jury's eventual award. Two Pesos (D) argued the proper damages were diverted sales after proof of actual confusion. This court does not agree and the precedent runs against Two Pesos' (D) argument. Taco Cabana's (P) "headstart" theory is sufficient to support the award of monetary damages. Given the evidence of millions in damages, the jury's award of hundreds of thousands was reasonable. The district court judge, Judge Singleton, then doubled the jury award based on the testimony and evidence of intentional, willful, and deliberate infringement. Section 35 endows the district court with considerable discretion to fashion an appropriate remedy so long as an enhancement of damages is compensatory and not punitive. This is particularly appropriate where imprecise damage models fail to provide just compensation to a damaged plaintiff, such as here. Judge Singleton acted consistent with the principles of equity and this court cannot say he abused his discretion. Affirmed.

▶ ANALYSIS

The Ninth Circuit in *Maier Brewing Co. v. Fleischmann Distilling Corp.*, 390 F.2d 117 (9th Cir. 1968), held the trial court's primary function should be to make infringement unprofitable to the infringing party. If the jury's award due to imprecise damage models cannot adequately compensate a damaged plaintiff, it is the trial judge's opportunity, arguably obligation, to compensate the plaintiff by enhancing the damage award. The difficulty arises when all plaintiffs seek treble damages as a starting point instead of presenting adequate damage models for the jury to make an appropriate award at the start.

■▬■

Quicknotes

COMPENSATORY DAMAGES Measure of damages necessary to compensate victim for actual injuries suffered.

Continued on next page.

DISCRETION The authority conferred upon a public official to act reasonably in accordance with his own judgment under certain circumstances.

SECONDARY MEANING A word or mark that becomes associated with a particular merchant or product as its source of origin.

TRADE DRESS The overall image of, or impression created by, a product that a court may enforce as a trademark if it determines that such image has acquired secondary meaning and that the public recognizes it as an indication of source.

TRADE SECRET Consists of any formula, pattern, plan, process, or device known only to its owner and business which gives an advantage over competitors; a secret formula used in the manufacture of a particular product that is not known to the general public.

Banjo Buddies, Inc. v. Renosky

Mark holder (P) v. Infringer (D)

399 F.3d 168 (3d Cir. 2005).

NATURE OF CASE: Appeal from damages award in trademark infringement case.

FACT SUMMARY: Joseph Renosky (Renosky) (D) was a board member of Banjo Buddies, Inc. (BBI) (P) when he decided to develop and sell independently a "new and improved" BBI (P) product. BBI (P) filed a trademark infringement suit against Renosky (D) and recovered Renosky's (D) profits.

🏛 RULE OF LAW
Factors the court considers in determining whether a trademark infringer's profits should be disgorged to the mark holder include (1) the defendant had the intent to confuse or deceive; (2) sales have been diverted; (3) other remedies are inadequate; (4) the plaintiff engaged in no unreasonable delay in asserting its rights; (5) the public has an interest in making the misconduct unprofitable; and (6) the case involves "palming off."

FACTS: Joseph Renosky (Renosky) (D) was a Banjo Buddies, Inc. (BBI) (P) board member for several years when the most profitable BBI (P) product was the fishing lure called the "Banjo Minnow." BBI (P) sold the lure through infomercials but eventually hired another company, Tristar Products, Inc. (Tristar) to continue the marketing and sales of the lure. Tristar paid BBI (P) 48 percent of Tristar's net profits. Renosky (D) had his own corporation, Renosky Lures, Inc., through which he sold the lure kit for the Banjo Minnow and he agreed to continue selling the kits to Tristar and BBI (P) for a reasonable price in exchange for BBI (P) shares. Renosky (D) presented a "new and improved" version of the Banjo Minnow to the BBI (P) board, but the board took no action. Renosky (D) determined to market and sell, this "Bionic Minnow" through Renosky Lures, Inc. despite board opposition. After Renosky (D) began selling the Bionic Minnow through infomercials, BBI (P) sent him a cease and desist letter. Renosky (D) ignored the letter, so BBI (P) filed suit for trademark infringement in violation of section 43(a) of the Lanham Act alleging consumers would be deceived that the Bionic Minnow was a BBI (P) product. The district court found Renosky (D) was liable for "false destination of origin." The court ordered Renosky (D) to disgorge his profits and produce verified financial records to support the profit amount. Renosky (D) did not produce the records so the court accepted Renosky's (D) independent financial analysis to establish the Bionic Minnow's total sales and then relied on Renosky Lures, Inc.'s business manager's testimony that the company typically

saw a 15–17 percent profit. The court used the manager's testimony to multiply the total sales by 16 percent and order that amount disgorged as profit. The court also ordered Renosky (D) should disgorge all distributions made to him as a shareholder in BBI (P). The total award was $1,589,155. Renosky (D) appealed.

ISSUE: Should the court, in determining whether a trademark infringer's profits should be disgorged to the mark holder, consider whether (1) the defendant had the intent to confuse or deceive; (2) sales have been diverted; (3) other remedies are inadequate; (4) the plaintiff engaged in no unreasonable delay in asserting its rights; (5) the public has an interest in making the misconduct unprofitable; and (6) the case involves "palming off"?

HOLDING AND DECISION: (Roth, J.) Yes. Factors the court considers in determining whether a trademark infringer's profits should be disgorged to the mark holder include (1) the defendant had the intent to confuse or deceive; (2) sales have been diverted; (3) other remedies are inadequate; (4) the plaintiff engaged in no unreasonable delay in asserting its rights; (5) the public has an interest in making the misconduct unprofitable; and (6) the case involves "palming off." Renosky (D) first argued the district court erred because it did not find his trademark infringement was willful, which is a prerequisite to disgorge of profits. Renosky (D) relied on *SecuraComm Consulting, Inc. v. Securacom, Inc.*, 166 F.3d 182 (3d Cir. 1999). The bright-line willfulness test articulated in *Securacom* has been superseded by statute, so the district court did not need to find willfulness. Congress amended Section 43(a) of the Lanham Act to read disgorge of profits is appropriate where there is a "violation under section 43(a), or a willful violation under section 43(c)." Congress surely was aware courts interpreted a willfulness requirement in the statute and the deliberate inclusion of the word "willful" only with regard to section 43(c) superseded the courts' interpretation. The Fifth Circuit, the only other circuit to address this issue, used similar reasoning and developed its six-factor based approach to determine the appropriateness of ordering disgorgement. Applying the six factors, the district court did not abuse its discretion in ordering disgorgement even when the first factor, willfulness, was not demonstrated. Renosky (D) next argued the district court erred in developing the profits figure because his corporation actually suffered a loss on the sales of the Bionic Minnow. It was Renosky's (D) burden, however, to prove losses and costs and he failed to produce verified

Continued on next page.

financial records or credible testimony about a loss. The district court had no alternative but to use another method to calculate the sales, so it relied on Renosky's (D) own financial analysis and the testimony of his corporation's business manager. Renosky (D) went on to argue BBI (P) should only recover 48 percent of the profits because that is all they would expect given the deal they had made with Tristar. The court cannot analyze this factual issue and determine whether Renosky (D) would have struck a better deal with BBI (P) than the deal Tristar made. Finally, there is no requirement for the defendant's profits to approximate the plaintiff's damages. Congress intended to make infringement unprofitable and permitting Renosky (D) to keep over half of his ill-gotten profits would not serve that goal. It is better for BBI (P) to receive a windfall than for Renosky (D) to keep his profits. Renosky's (D) final argument was that the district court erred in awarding a disgorgement of his shareholder dividends in addition to his profits. This argument succeeds because those dividends already were included in the court's estimation of profits. Affirmed in part and reversed in part.

▶ ANALYSIS

Until Congress amended the Lanham Act in 1999, trademark infringers could avoid disgorging profits by successfully proving the infringement was "innocent" rather than willful. Now the willfulness of the infringement is just one of several factors for the court to consider in determining whether the infringer was unjustly enriched through his infringing actions. It appears to be much more difficult for defendants to successfully argue against the public policy inherent in the factor-based analysis than to demonstrate "innocent" infringement.

■══■

Quicknotes

INFRINGEMENT Conduct in violation of a statute or contract that interferes with another's rights pursuant to law.

PALMING OFF/PASSING OFF Conducting business or selling goods in a manner so as to mislead potential clients or consumers into believing they are doing business with, or purchasing goods from, another entity.

■══■

Big O Tire Dealers, Inc. v. Goodyear Tire & Rubber Co.

Tire dealer (P) v. Tire manufacturer (D)

561 F.2d 1365 (10th Cir. 1977).

NATURE OF CASE: Appeal from an order awarding damages and an injunction in a trademark infringement case.

FACT SUMMARY: Reverse confusion was claimed not to be actionable if Goodyear Tire & Rubber Co.'s (D) second use of Big O Tire Dealers' (P) trademark merely created likelihood of confusion concerning the source of Big O Tire Dealers' (P) "Big Foot" tires.

RULE OF LAW
The second use of a trademark is actionable if it merely creates a likelihood of confusion concerning the source of the first user's product.

FACTS: Big O Tire Dealers, Inc. (P) asserted claims of unfair competition against Goodyear Tire & Rubber Co. (Goodyear) (D) based upon false designation of origin and common-law trademark infringement. The jury found that Goodyear (D) was liable only for trademark infringement and trademark disparagement and awarded general compensatory and punitive damages. The district court permanently enjoined Goodyear (D) from infringing on Big O Tire Dealers' (P) "Big Foot" trademark. Goodyear (D) appealed, arguing that its second use of the "Bigfoot" trademark was not actionable if it merely created a likelihood of confusion concerning the source of the first user's product.

ISSUE: Is the second use of a trademark actionable if it merely creates a likelihood of confusion concerning the source of the first user's product?

HOLDING AND DECISION: (Lewis, C.J.) Yes. The second use of a trademark is actionable if it merely creates a likelihood of confusion concerning the source of the first user's product. The Colorado courts, if given the opportunity, would extend their common-law trademark infringement actions to include reverse confusion situations. The jury could have reasonably inferred a likelihood of confusion from witnesses' testimony of actual confusion. Affirmed.

► ANALYSIS

The court also ruled that Goodyear (D) had to pay money damages for the cost of corrective advertising to undo the damage done when it had used the trademark name. That Goodyear (D) did not intend to trade on the good will of Big O Tire Dealers (P) or to palm off its products was irrelevant in this case. The court found that Colorado's policy was to widen the scope of its policy of protecting trade names and preventing public confusion.

■━■

Quicknotes

DAMAGES Monetary compensation, that may be awarded, by the court to a party, who has sustained injury or loss to his or her person, property or rights due to another party's unlawful act, omission or negligence.

INJUNCTION A remedy imposed by the court ordering a party to cease the conduct of a specific activity.

TRADEMARK INFRINGEMENT The unauthorized use of another's trademark in such a manner as to cause a likelihood of confusion as to the source of the product or service in connection with which it is utilized.

■━■

U-Haul International, Inc. v. Jartran, Inc.

Original self-mover (P) v. Comparative self-mover (D)

793 F.2d 1034 (9th Cir. 1986).

NATURE OF CASE: Appeal from damages awarded in false comparative advertising case.

FACT SUMMARY: Jartran, Inc. (D) spent millions of dollars on an advertising campaign comparing itself to U-Haul International, Inc. (U-Haul) (P) and significantly increased its profits while damaging U-Haul's (P) profits. U-Haul (P) sued Jartran (D) for false comparative advertising.

🏛 RULE OF LAW
The district court has the discretion to award actual corrective advertising expenditures in a false comparative advertising case even when the original advertising expenditures were less than half of the eventual award.

FACTS: U-Haul International, Inc. (U-Haul) (P) was the dominant self-move consumer rental company for years when Jartran, Inc. (D) decided to enter the national market. Jartran (D) launched an advertising campaign that compared itself favorably with U-Haul (P). Jartran's (D) profits skyrocketed from $7 million annually to $80 million annually while U-Haul's (P) decreased for the first time ever. Jartran (D) was awarded a "Gold Effie" award by the American Marketing Association for its effective advertising campaign. U-Haul (P) filed suit against Jartran (D) alleging false comparative advertising. The district court found Jartran (D) liable and awarded U-Haul (P) the cost of the advertising campaign to Jartran (D), the cost of U-Haul's (P) corrective advertising campaign, and then doubled that award amount under section 35 of the Lanham Act for a total damages award of $40 million and attorneys' fees. Jartran (D) appealed.

ISSUE: Does the district court have the discretion to award actual corrective advertising expenditures in a false comparative advertising case even when the original advertising expenditures were less than half of the eventual award?

HOLDING AND DECISION: (Sneed, J.) Yes. The district court has the discretion to award actual corrective advertising expenditures in a false comparative advertising case even when the original advertising expenditures were less than half of the eventual award. Jartran (D) argued U-Haul's (P) injury was insufficiently direct to recover under the Lanham Act; only surveys of actual consumers could prove actual deception and consumer reliance; and the court should not have presumed actual deception from proof of Jartran's (D) intent to deceive. This court rejects the first and third challenges so need not

consider the second. First, the district court properly held the publication of deliberately false comparative claims gives rise to a presumption of actual deception and reliance. Jartran (D) argued the precedent upon which U-Haul (P) relied involved an injunction case with a lower burden of proof and two factually distinguishable "palming off" cases. The differences in the cases, however, do not justify overturning the district court decision. Jartran (D) cannot argue it should not bear the burden of a presumption when it deliberately deceived with its false advertising. This is in keeping with earlier "palming off" cases. Next, Jartran (D) argued the district court did not have the discretion to award over twice the amount of its original advertising expenditures. The case on which it relied however, is not applicable, because that case did not include actual corrective advertising expenditures when the court stated the plaintiff could only recover 25 percent of the original advertising expenditures. Here, U-Haul (P) had and proved actual corrective advertising expenditures. The district court rejected Jartran's (D) claims that the corrective advertising was unnecessary. Affirmed.

▶ ANALYSIS

A group of law school students introduced the idea of corrective advertising in 1970 to the Federal Trade Commission (FTC) in an FTC complaint involving the Campbell Soup Company. Federal courts soon adapted the corrective advertising remedy to provide monetary damages to corporations suffering after false advertising by a competitor or infringer. While the federal courts do not order corrective advertising like the FTC might do, they do compensate companies who engage in it. Scholars still debate the effectiveness of corrective advertising and are wary of rewarding those who engage in it in case the expenditures are incurred merely to "up the ante" owed when the infringement and/or false advertising case gets to the remedy stage.

■=■

Quicknotes

DECEIT A false statement made either knowingly or with reckless disregard as to its truth and which is intended to induce the plaintiff to act in reliance thereon to his detriment.

DISCRETION The authority conferred upon a public official to act reasonably in accordance with his own judgment under certain circumstances.

Continued on next page.

RELIANCE Dependence on a fact that causes a party to act or refrain from acting.

Nightingale Home Healthcare, Inc. v. Anodyne Therapy, LLC

Provider of home healthcare services (P) v. Seller of medical devices (D)

626 F.3d 958 (7th Cir. 2010).

NATURE OF CASE: Appeal from award of attorneys' fees to defendant in action under the Lanham Act (Act), where such fees were awarded pursuant to the Act's provision for attorneys' fees in exceptional cases.

FACT SUMMARY: Nightingale Home Healthcare, Inc. (Nightingale) (P) contended that Anodyne Therapy, LLC (Anodyne) (D) was not entitled to attorneys' fees under the Lanham Act's provision of such fees to the prevailing party in exceptional cases, because, notwithstanding that Nightingale (P) had instituted its suit for the purpose of extracting a price reduction from Anodyne (D), the case was not "exceptional."

RULE OF LAW
A case under the Lanham Act is "exceptional," in the sense of warranting an award of reasonable attorneys' fees to the winning party, if the losing party was the plaintiff and was guilty of abuse of process in suing, or if the losing party was the defendant and had no defense yet persisted in the trademark infringement or false advertising for which he was being sued, in order to impose costs on his opponent.

FACTS: Nightingale Home Healthcare, Inc. (Nightingale) (P), a home healthcare services provider, purchased several infrared lamps from Anodyne Therapy, LLC (Anodyne) (D). Nightingale (P) told its patients that Anodyne's (D) lamps were intended for treating peripheral neuropathy. The lamps had been approved by the Food and Drug Administration (FDA) and were intended for the treatment of peripheral neuropathy. Although the FDA had not approved the lamps for that purpose, this did not preclude a physician or other healthcare provider, such as Nightingale (P), from prescribing the lamps to patients as a treatment for that condition. Unhappy with the price Anodyne (D) charged for the lamps, Nightingale (P) sued Anodyne (D) under the Lanham Act, claiming that Anodyne's (D) sales representative had falsely represented that the lamps had been approved by the FDA for treatment of peripheral neuropathy. When Nightingale (P) replaced Anodyne's (D) lamps with the virtually identical lamps of another company (apparently for reasons of price, unrelated to the scope of the FDA's approval), it advertised them just as it had advertised Anodyne's (D) lamps—as devices for the treatment of peripheral neuropathy. At no time did Nightingale (P) indicate that the FDA had approved the lamps for that particular purpose. The district court found that Nightingale's (P) suit lacked merit, and that Nightingale (P) had brought the suit in an attempt to coerce a

price reduction from Anodyne (D). Accordingly, the district court granted summary judgment to Anodyne (D) early in the proceedings. In addition, the district court awarded Anodyne (D) attorneys' fees in the amount of $72,747, based on the Lanham Act's provision for such fees to the prevailing party in exceptional cases. Nightingale (P) argued that that no award of attorneys' fees was justified, because the case was not "exceptional." The court of appeals granted review.

ISSUE: Is a case under the Lanham Act "exceptional," in the sense of warranting an award of reasonable attorneys' fees to the winning party, if the losing party was the plaintiff and was guilty of abuse of process in suing, or if the losing party was the defendant and had no defense yet persisted in the trademark infringement or false advertising for which he was being sued, in order to impose costs on his opponent?

HOLDING AND DECISION: (Posner, J.) Yes. A case under the Lanham Act is "exceptional," in the sense of warranting an award of reasonable attorneys' fees to the winning party, if the losing party was the plaintiff and was guilty of abuse of process in suing, or if the losing party was the defendant and had no defense yet persisted in the trademark infringement or false advertising for which he was being sued, in order to impose costs on his opponent. The circuits are split as to what constitutes an exceptional case under the Lanham Act. Some of the circuits apply different tests of exceptionality depending on whether it was the plaintiff or the defendant who prevailed; some do not make this distinction. Some circuits require some sort of bad faith; others do not. Some leave the determination to the court's discretion, whereas others provide certain standards involving oppression, fraud, meritless suits, etc. In this circuit, prior decisions have held that an exceptional case exists, in the case of a winning defendant, where the conduct of the party from which the payment of attorneys' fees was sought had been "oppressive," and that "whether the plaintiff's suit was oppressive" turned on whether the suit "was something that might be described not just as a losing suit but as a suit that had elements of an abuse of process, whether or not it had all the elements of the tort." If the plaintiff had prevailed, the focus was on whether the defendant had lacked a solid justification for the defense or had put the plaintiff to an unreasonable expense in suing. Later cases ruled that "vexatious litigation conduct" by the losing party could justify the award of attorneys' fees to the winner, regardless of which side engaged in such conduct, as long as it was the losing side. To formulate an appropri-

Continued on next page.

ate test, it is helpful to consider why the Lanham Act makes a narrow exception to the "American" rule that forbids shifting the litigation expenses of the prevailing party to the loser. One reason is to provide a complete remedy including attorneys' fees for acts that courts have characterized as malicious, fraudulent, deliberate, and willful. Such a remedy makes a trademark owner whole in enforcing his mark against willful infringers, and it gives defendants a remedy against unfounded suits. Additionally, such an award addresses the potential for businesses to use Lanham Act litigation for strategic purposes, not to obtain a judgment or defeat a claim but to obtain a competitive advantage independent of the outcome of the case by piling litigation costs on a competitor. For example, a large firm sued for trademark infringement by a small one might mount a scorched-earth defense to a meritorious claim in the hope of imposing prohibitive litigation costs on the plaintiff. It is these types of cases, in the trademark litigation context, that are "exceptional." This is the case where the plaintiff engages in abuse of process, which is the use of the litigation process for an improper purpose, whether or not the claim is colorable. Likewise, where a defendant's trademark infringement or other trademark violation is abundantly clear, the defendant's insistence on mounting a costly defense is the same misconduct as a plaintiff's bringing a case (frivolous or not) not in order to obtain a favorable judgment but instead to burden the defendant with costs likely to drive it out of the market. Based on these considerations, a case under the Lanham Act is "exceptional," in the sense of warranting an award of reasonable attorneys' fees to the winning party, if the losing party was the plaintiff and was guilty of abuse of process in suing, or if the losing party was the defendant and had no defense yet persisted in the trademark infringement or false advertising for which he was being sued, in order to impose costs on his opponent. Such a general rule is warranted regardless of whether the winning party is the plaintiff or the defendant, because most parties to Lanham Act trademark suits are businesses. Although the businesses may be very different in size, that is not a reason for a general rule favoring prevailing plaintiffs or prevailing defendants, because there is no correlation between the size of a party and which side of the litigation the party is on. Disparity in size will often be relevant in evaluating the legitimacy of the suit or defense, but it is as likely to favor the defendant as the plaintiff. Because federal courts already have the power, independent of the Lanham Act, to award attorneys' fees when a party has acted in bad faith, vexatiously, wantonly, or for oppressive reasons, it seems that the Lanham Act's provision for attorneys' fees in exceptional cases is superfluous. However, the reason Congress included the provision in the Lanham Act was that prior to the provision's inclusion, the United States Supreme Court had held that attorneys' fees could not be awarded in cases under the Act; it was that decision that prompted Congress to add the fee-shifting provision. This history lends support to an approach that incorporates the same substantive content

as the inherent power held inapplicable to Lanham Act cases by the United States Supreme Court. Finally, in considering whether a case is exceptional, the inquiry should be whether the party seeking the award can show that his opponent's claim or defense was objectively unreasonable, i.e., was a claim or defense that a rational litigant would pursue only because it would impose disproportionate costs on his opponent. The application of this test and principles here leads to the conclusion that Nightingale (P) engaged in an abuse of process, by bringing a frivolous claim against Anodyne (D) in order to obtain an advantage unrelated to obtaining a favorable judgment. Nightingale (P) argues that even if Anodyne (D) is entitled to reimbursement for some of the attorneys' fees that it incurred, the district court's award was excessive because it included fees for defending against claims that were based on state law rather than the Lanham Act. However, Anodyne (D) showed that the work that its lawyers had performed in defending against the Lanham Act claim could not be separated from their work in defending against the other claims, so Nightingale's (P) argument is rejected. Given Nightingale's (P) persistent frivolous litigation tactics, not only is an award of attorneys' fees affirmed, but fees for this appeal are also granted to Anodyne (D). Affirmed.

▶ *ANALYSIS*

As the court intimates, trademark suits, like much other commercial litigation, often are characterized by firms' desire to heap costs on their rivals, imposing marketplace losses out of proportion to the legal merits. The increased ease of bringing suit in federal court and the greater availability of remedies may extend the competitive battlefield beyond supermarket shelves and into the halls of the courthouse. Commentators have already suggested that the availability of large damage awards will motivate firms to litigate false advertising suits aggressively in the hope of winning large damage awards and impairing the competitiveness of a business rival, particularly a new entrant. See, e.g., James B. Kobak Jr. & Mary K. Fleck, "Commercial Defamation Claim Added to Revised Lanham Act," *Nat'l L.J.*, Oct. 30, 1989, p. 33. Given these economic realities and motivators, the decision in this case is designed to ensure that aggressive trademark litigation does not cross over into abuse of process or an unjustified exaction of litigation costs.

■■■

Quicknotes

ABUSE OF PROCESS The unlawful use of the legal process after it has been granted.

BAD FAITH Conduct that is intentionally misleading or deceptive.

Continued on next page.

FRAUD A false representation of facts with the intent that another will rely on the misrepresentation to his detriment.

TRADEMARK INFRINGEMENT The unauthorized use of another's trademark in such a manner as to cause a likelihood of confusion as to the source of the product or service in connection with which it is utilized.

Rolex Watch, U.S.A., Inc. v. Michel Co.

Mark holder (P) v. Infringer (D)

179 F.3d 704 (9th Cir. 1999).

NATURE OF CASE: Appeal from injunctive relief and denial of attorneys' fees in trademark infringement and counterfeiting case.

FACT SUMMARY: Micha Mottale d/b/a Michel Co. (Michel) (D) reconditioned authentic Rolex watches by replacing parts with unauthorized parts, adding unauthorized designs, and performing unauthorized repairs. The reconditioned watches retained the Rolex mark and Michel (D) did not provide full disclosure to purchasers of the used and unauthorized replacement parts. Rolex Watch, U.S.A., Inc. (P) filed suit.

🏛 RULE OF LAW
Trademark counterfeiting may occur without duplication of the mark, and if the original mark is retained, when the product is reconditioned or altered to the point it becomes a different product requiring a different mark.

FACTS: Micha Mottale d/b/a Michel Co. (Michel) (D) sells jewelry and luxury watches at wholesale and reconditions luxury watches for retail customers. He sells used Rolex watches, reconditioned or customized Rolex watches with unauthorized replacement parts, and Rolex watches with used or otherwise unauthorized replacement parts. The altered Rolex watches retain the Rolex mark. Rolex Watch, U.S.A., Inc. (Rolex) (P) sued Michel (D) for counterfeit trademark use. The district court found Michel (D) liable and issued a permanent injunction requiring Michel (D) to place a permanent, independent mark on the replacement parts and include written disclosure on his tags, promotions, and advertisements. The district court also denied Rolex's (P) motion for attorneys' fees. Rolex (P) appealed.

ISSUE: May trademark counterfeiting occur without duplication of the mark, and if the original mark is retained, when the product is reconditioned or altered to the point it becomes a different product requiring a different mark?

HOLDING AND DECISION: (Tashima, J.) Yes. Trademark counterfeiting may occur without duplication of the mark, and if the original mark is retained, when the product is reconditioned or altered to the point it becomes a different product requiring a different mark. The district court followed this court's holding in *Westinghouse Electric Corp. v. General Circuit Breaker & Electric Supply Inc.*, 106 F.3d 894 (9th Cir. 1997). *Westinghouse* involved reconditioned circuit breakers that retained the original circuit-breaker's mark and this court held that duplication of a mark is not necessary for trademark counterfeiting. Similarly here, Michel (D) did not duplicate the Rolex mark but retained the original on unauthorized products. Rolex (P) now seeks greater injunctive relief than that afforded by the district court's ruling. The analysis begins with *Champion Spark Plug Co. v. Sanders*, 331 U.S. 125 (1947). The United States Supreme Court in *Champion* permitted reconditioned products to retain the original mark so long as the words "Used" or "Repaired" were added because the reconditioning was not extensive. The *Champion* facts, however, differ from the facts here. Here, the products were given a new design, altering the original to such an extent that it became a new product, and retaining the original mark could bring an association between the Rolex mark and inferior quality. The district court's requirement of an independent mark is insufficient. Relying on *Champion*, the district court erred in not completely enjoining the use of Rolex's (P) marks. Rolex (P) next argued it is entitled to an award of attorneys' fees. The district court determined the facts of the case were not exceptional to justify the award of fees. The district court did not, however, determine if fees could be awarded pursuant to § 1117(b) for violation of the trademark counterfeiting prohibitions of § 1114(1)(a). This court will not decide whether attorneys' fees are appropriate. Reversed and remanded.

▶ ANALYSIS

Consumers may not be aware they have purchased a reconditioned/altered product bearing the original brand-name product's mark. This can cause problems ranging from a misperception about the quality of the brand-name product to the fact a brand-name producer rarely services a reconditioned counterfeit product even if the consumer believes the product is covered by a warranty. Even the addition of "used" or "repaired" to the brand name could imply authorized parts remain in the brand-name product. Courts must carefully fashion remedies to avoid infringing upon the rights and profits of legitimate second market merchants while protecting the consumers from counterfeit confusion.

Quicknotes

TRADEMARK Any word, name, symbol, device or combination thereof that is either currently utilized, or which a person has a bona fide intent to utilize, in commerce in order to distinguish his goods from those of another.

United States v. Torkington

Federal government (P) v. Counterfeit watch salesman (D)

812 F.2d 1347 (11th Cir. 1987).

NATURE OF CASE: Appeal from dismissal of criminal indictment in counterfeit goods case.

FACT SUMMARY: John Torkington (D) sold counterfeit Rolex watches for $27 at a flea market stand in Florida. A Rolex investigator discovered the counterfeit goods and the Government (P) sought to indict Torkington (D) on charges of trafficking and attempting to traffic in counterfeit goods.

🏛 **RULE OF LAW**
The Trademark Counterfeiting Act of 1984 requires a showing that members of the purchasing public, not only direct purchasers, would likely be confused, mistaken, or deceived, including in the post-sale context.

FACTS: John Torkington (D) operated a booth at an indoor flea market in Florida. He did not display, but did offer for sale, counterfeit Rolex watches virtually indistinguishable from the real thing. The fake watches had the Rolex mark, the look of Rolex, and the Rolex name but did not have the Rolex price. A private investigator for Rolex observed Torkington (D) demonstrating the watches for potential purchasers and asked to view them himself. He then purchased a faux Rolex for $27. The Government (P) indicted Torkington (D) on charges of trafficking and attempting to traffic in counterfeit goods. The district court dismissed the indictment because the direct purchasers of the fake watches were not likely to be confused, deceived, or misled that the fake watches were the real thing given the huge price difference, and therefore, the mark was not "counterfeit." The Government (P) appealed.

ISSUE: Does the Trademark Counterfeiting Act of 1984 require a showing that members of the purchasing public, not only direct purchasers, would likely be confused, mistaken, or deceived, including in the post-sale context?

HOLDING AND DECISION: (Kravitch, J.) Yes. The Trademark Counterfeiting Act of 1984 (the Act) requires a showing that members of the purchasing public, not only direct purchasers, would likely be confused, mistaken, or deceived, including in the post-sale context. The district court defined "counterfeit" to require a showing that only direct purchasers would be confused, mistaken, or deceived. The language of the Act and the legislative history do not support this conclusion. The wording of the Act is broad and should not be read to be restricted to direct purchasers. The district court further concluded post-sale inquiry was irrelevant to its analysis, but this is also error. Potential purchasers could encounter the coun-

terfeit good in the possession of a direct purchaser and be confused over its origin. The policy of the Act supports the conclusion that the post-sale context is relevant to the analysis because the Act is meant to protect a mark holder's ability to identify itself and relate the mark to its good reputation. Reversed and remanded.

▶ **ANALYSIS**

Few are fooled into believing the $5 watch that looks exactly like the $2,000 brand-name watch is actually the real thing because most people know a heavily discounted price creates questions of authenticity. The "counterfeit" analysis becomes important when the purchaser of the $5 watch shows it to other potential purchasers who might believe it is the $2,000 brand-name watch because the purchase price is unknown to them. When the $5 watch falls apart in a few months, the potential purchasers could now believe the brand-name is associated with cheap quality. The district court in *Torkington* left the brand-name producers with little protection for their hard work and reputation for good products. The direct consumer might not have been fooled, but potential consumers could have been confused.

■■■

Quicknotes

TRADEMARK Any word, name, symbol, device or combination thereof that is either currently utilized, or which a person has a bona fide intent to utilize, in commerce in order to distinguish his goods from those of another.

■■■

Waco International, Inc. v. KHK Scaffolding Houston Inc.

Mark holder (P) v. Infringer (D)

278 F.3d 523 (5th Cir. 2002).

NATURE OF CASE: Appeal of liability and attorneys' fee award in wrongful seizure case.

FACT SUMMARY: Waco International, Inc. (Waco) (P) alleged KHK Scaffolding Houston Inc. (KHK) (D) infringed upon its trademark and Waco (P) obtained an ex parte seizure order. KHK (D) filed a counterclaim for compensatory and punitive damages based on wrongful seizure. The jury awarded attorneys' fees and punitive damages but found KHK (D) suffered no loss of profit or goodwill.

🏛 RULE OF LAW
A seizure of goods may be wrongful if the seizure order was sought in bad faith, or even if it was sought in good faith, if the seized goods are predominantly non-infringing.

FACTS: Waco International, Inc. (Waco) (P) manufactures scaffolding and owns the federally registered trademarks "WACO" and "HI-LOAD." Its products carry a decal with its WACO mark. KHK Scaffolding Houston Inc. (KHK) (D) manufactures scaffolding products compatible with Waco (P) products. Waco (P) learned KHK (D) was marketing WACO products. Waco's (P) investigator received a sales receipt from KHK (D) identifying the purchased product as WACO frames. Further, KHK (D) admitted its salesperson identified WACO products to potential customers. Waco (P) filed suit against KHK (D) for trademark infringement and obtained an ex parte seizure order. Waco (P) raided KHK (D) warehouses and seized KHK (D) products and certain business records. The magistrate recommended dissolving the seizure order because the seized products did not carry a counterfeit mark. She recommended injunctive relief prohibiting KHK (D) from quoting, describing, or purporting to sell Waco (D) products but no injunction to prohibit KHK (D) from using Waco's (P) marks in describing the style or compatibility of KHK (D) products. The district court adopted the magistrate's recommendations in full. KHK (D) filed a counterclaim for compensatory and punitive damages for wrongful seizure. The magistrate recommended the court grant the claim because the seized products were "legitimate non-infringing merchandise" but deny the damages claim because the alleged damage amount was disputed. The district court adopted the recommendations in full. The jury subsequently found KHK (D) liable for infringement but that the use constituted "fair use," that KHK (D) had not used a counterfeit mark, and that Waco (P) acted in bad faith in seeking the seizure order which resulted in the seizure of non-infring-

ing products. Waco (P) appealed the finding of wrongful seizure and the award of attorneys' fees to KHK (D).

ISSUE: May a seizure of goods be wrongful if the seizure order was sought in bad faith, or even if it was sought in good faith, if the seized goods are predominantly non-infringing?

HOLDING AND DECISION: (Restani, J.) Yes. A seizure of goods may be wrongful if the seizure order was sought in bad faith, or even if it was sought in good faith, if the seized goods are predominantly non-infringing. "Wrongful seizure" is determined on a case-by-case basis but Congress did provide guidelines for making the determination. Wrongful seizure may occur when the order was sought in bad faith or if the goods are non-infringing even if the order was sought in good faith. Waco (P) argued the goods seized were counterfeit goods because the sales receipt issued in connection with the goods identified them as Waco (P) products and carried the "WACO" mark. KHK's (D) liability is not the same as justification for seizure of its goods. Further, the focus of the ex parte seizure order is the goods rather than the business practice or representation accompanying the goods. Finally, the jury found KHK (D) did not use a counterfeit mark in connection with its goods. This court will not second-guess the jury's factual finding. Waco (P) next argued KHK (D) did not suffer loss of profit or goodwill so the seizure could not be found wrongful. Lost profits or goodwill is not a prerequisite to wrongful seizure. The wronged party is entitled to recover damages proved, which may include attorneys' fees, lost profits, and/or loss of goodwill. Waco (P) wrongly asserts the statute limits recovery to "actual" damage but the wrongful seizure claimant is entitled to be compensated for the wrongful seizure even in the absence of lost profits or goodwill. Waco (P) finally argued attorneys' fees are not appropriate because KHK (D) acted in bad faith during the litigation. The district court did not have an affirmative obligation to find that the actions constituted "extenuating circumstances" excusing the award of attorneys' fees. Affirmed.

▶ ANALYSIS

An award of attorneys' fees is often considered an extraordinary remedy or in line with punitive damages. In the case of compensating the wronged party in a seizure order, attorneys' fees are considered compensatory for actual damages suffered. The theory is the party would not have had to file a counterclaim incurring attorneys' fees but for

Continued on next page.

the wrongful actions of the party seeking the seizure order in bad faith. Rather than intended solely to deter the future similar conduct of the bad faith party, it fully compensates the wronged party.

■═■

Quicknotes

BAD FAITH Conduct that is intentionally misleading or deceptive.

EX PARTE A proceeding commenced by one party.

FAIR USE An affirmative defense to a claim of copyright infringement providing an exception from the copyright owner's exclusive rights in a work for the purposes of criticism, comment, news reporting, teaching, scholarship or research.

PUNITIVE DAMAGES Damages exceeding the actual injury suffered for the purposes of punishment of the defendant, deterrence of the wrongful behavior or comfort to the plaintiff.

SEIZURE The taking of property by unlawful activity or in satisfaction of a judgment entered by the court.

■═■

Skierkewiecz v. Gonzalez

[Parties not identified.]

711 F. Supp. 931 (N.D. Ill. 1989).

NATURE OF CASE: Motion to dismiss in wrongful seizure and abuse of process case.

FACT SUMMARY: The Defendant Attorneys obtained an ex parte seizure order and seized the Plaintiffs' goods. The Plaintiffs later filed a complaint for wrongful seizure against the Defendant Attorneys.

🏛 RULE OF LAW
A party prejudiced by an order obtained in bad faith may seek remedies from the movant even if the prejudiced party is liable to the movant on another basis.

FACTS: The Defendant Attorneys appeared before Judge Parsons on an ex parte motion for seizure of the Plaintiffs' goods. Judge Parsons granted the motion based upon the representations of the Defendant Attorneys. The Defendants executed on the seizure order and raided the Plaintiffs' warehouse. The Plaintiffs filed to vacate the Order and Judge Parsons was very disturbed by the number of misrepresentations the Defendant Attorneys made to get the Order. Nevertheless, Judge Parsons issued an injunction to prohibit the Plaintiffs from selling tennis rackets bearing the name "Panther" or marketing hang tags with a panther on them. The Plaintiffs subsequently filed a Complaint in which they alleged wrongful seizure, abuse of process, trespass to chattel, and trespass to land. The Defendant Attorneys filed a motion to dismiss for failure to state a claim upon which relief can be granted.

ISSUE: May a party, prejudiced by an order obtained in bad faith, seek remedies from the movant even if the prejudiced party is liable to the movant on another basis?

HOLDING AND DECISION: (Kocoras, J.) Yes. A party prejudiced by an order obtained in bad faith may seek remedies from the movant even if the prejudiced party is liable to the movant on another basis. Here, the Defendant Attorneys are alleged to have obtained an ex parte seizure order in bad faith but the Court also found the Plaintiffs liable for trademark infringement. The Defendant Attorneys first argued the count for wrongful seizure must be dismissed because it only seeks to recover for representations made to the Court in the course of zealous representation of their clients in a trademark infringement case. The Defendant Attorneys argued the Plaintiffs cannot show malice on the part of the attorneys or the clients' desire to harm. The Plaintiffs argued the Defendant Attorneys sought the seizure order pursuant to the federal statute and now wrongly read into it a conditional privilege for attorneys who obtain a wrongful seizure. Section 15

USC 1116(d) permits the seizure of counterfeit marks but only in extreme circumstances and if the courts use extreme caution. If the seizure order is sought in bad faith, the federal statute provides monetary damages to the injured party. No conditional privilege recognized by Illinois courts applies to the federal statute. The allegations of the first count are sufficient to survive the motion to dismiss. The Defendants next argued Counts III and IV must be dismissed because the Defendant Attorneys were on the Plaintiffs' property and seized the Plaintiffs' property pursuant to a valid seizure order. This is accurate if the court order is obtained in good faith, which was not the case here. The Complaint alleges the seizure order was obtained in bad faith, so the Counts will not be dismissed. Further, the Defendants acted outside the scope of the seizure order when they remained on Plaintiffs' property once the U.S. Marshals left. The Order specifically provided for the presence of the U.S. Marshal. Granted in part and denied in part.

▶ ANALYSIS

The intent behind the seizure remedy in the federal statute is to permit trademark holders to seize counterfeit goods before the counterfeiters destroy the evidence. Congress did not, however, ignore the possibility that this remedy could result in abuse by trademark holders who might routinely seek an ex parte order to avoid due process owed to the defendants. The result is an available remedy to trademark holders that requires significant court investigation and oversight. Congress did not provide much guidance into what constitutes "wrongful seizure" so the courts are left to determine on a case-by-case basis.

■■■

Quicknotes

ABUSE OF PROCESS The unlawful use of the legal process after it has been granted.

COMPLAINT The initial pleading commencing litigation that sets forth a claim for relief.

EX PARTE A proceeding commenced by one party.

GOOD FAITH An honest intention to abstain from taking advantage of another.

SEIZURE The taking of property by unlawful activity or in satisfaction of a judgment entered by the court.

■■■

Chanel, Inc. v. Italian Activewear of Florida, Inc.

Mark holder (P) v. Infringer (D)

931 F.2d 1472 (11th Cir. 1991).

NATURE OF CASE: Appeal from grant of summary judgment in trademark infringement case.

FACT SUMMARY: Italian Activewear of Florida, Inc. (Italian Activewear) (D) and its principal, Mervyn Brody (Brody) (D), sold luxury goods, including Chanel, Inc.'s (P) goods. Italian Activewear (D) acquired and sold counterfeit Chanel (P) goods, and Chanel (P) filed suit for trademark infringement.

🏛 RULE OF LAW
Plaintiff must prove intent to counterfeit a trademarked good to recover mandated treble damages and attorneys' fees pursuant to 15 U.S.C.A. § 1117(b).

FACTS: Italian Activewear of Florida, Inc. (Italian Activewear) (D) sold luxury goods, including Chanel, Inc.'s (P) goods. Its principal, Mervyn Brody (Brody) (D), acquired a shipment of supposed Chanel, Inc. (P) goods for Italian Activewear (D). Brody (D) was aware these goods did not contain the usual indicia of authenticity and he did not verify origin with the seller, but he compared them to authentic Chanel (P) product to ensure the goods were genuine. Part of the shipment was immediately sold to some California businessmen. The goods were counterfeit. Chanel (P) learned of the counterfeit goods and executed a seizure order against the product in California. Brody's (D) friend, Myron Greenberg (D), occasionally watched Italian Activewear's (D) retail store for Brody (D) when Brody (D) was out of town. Greenberg (D) learned of the seizure and immediately sent a fax to Brody (D) informing him of the seizure and his belief the authorities were on their way to Italian Activewear (D). Greenberg (D) then took the remaining counterfeit Chanel (P) product out of the store, put it into the trunk of a car, and parked the car several blocks away. Chanel (P) filed suit against Italian Activewear (D) and Brody (D) for trademark infringement and later added Greenberg (D) as a defendant. The district court granted Chanel's (P) motion for summary judgment, finding the defendants liable for infringement and that the infringement was intentional. It awarded treble damages and attorneys' fees for the violation of 15 U.S.C.A. § 1114(a)(1). Italian Activewear (D), Brody (D), and Greenberg (D) appealed.

ISSUE: Must plaintiff prove intent to counterfeit a trademarked good to recover mandated treble damages and attorneys' fees pursuant to 15 U.S.C.A. § 1117(b)?

HOLDING AND DECISION: (Edmonson, J.) Yes. Plaintiff must prove intent to counterfeit a trademarked good to recover mandated treble damages and attorneys' fees

pursuant to 15 U.S.C.A. § 1117(b). The Lanham Act prohibits the use of a counterfeit trademark if it is likely to cause consumer confusion. The remedies for such a use include injunctive relief, recovery of defendant's profits, and costs of the action. The court may award treble damages, and in exceptional cases, attorney fees. If the infringement is intentional, however, § 1117(b) applies and treble damages and attorney fees are mandated. The plaintiff must prove intent to recover mandatory treble damages and attorney fees. The district court held Brody (D) was willfully blind because (1) the counterfeit goods lacked indicia of authenticity, which Brody (D) knew should accompany the goods; and (2) Brody (D) failed to ask the seller the origin of the products. The question of whether willful blindness constitutes "intent" is a fact question. Chanel (P) argues Brody (D) was previously involved in trademark infringement litigation and Greenberg (D) hid the product after sending a warning fax to Brody (D). These facts strengthen the inference of intent or might provide evidence of defendants' lack of intent. Brody (D) was previously involved in litigation, which supports his argument he tried to ensure the products were genuine. Greenberg (D) engaged in those actions after the infringement occurred and might have been attempting to minimize the damage. Chanel (P) further argued defendants failed to provide sufficient evidence of a triable issue of fact. That is true only when the movant has satisfied its burden of proving no genuine dispute on any reasonable fact. Chanel (P) did not meet that burden, so defendants' response was sufficient. Affirmed in part, vacated in part, and remanded.

▶ ANALYSIS

The purpose for treble damages is to deter counterfeiters who might otherwise offend again if they simply had to disgorge profits from getting caught once. A counterfeiter cannot avoid treble damages by claiming "willful blindness" because that would encourage counterfeiters to avoid asking the origin of items if they were afraid of the answer. This case, however, reinforces the policy of a required finding of intent or "willful blindness" rather than circumstantial facts that suggest that is more likely than not.

■=■

Quicknotes

INTENT The state of mind that exists when one's purpose is to commit a criminal act.

Continued on next page.

SUMMARY JUDGMENT Judgment rendered by a court in response to a motion made by one of the parties, claiming that the lack of a question of material fact in respect to an issue warrants disposition of the issue without consideration by the jury.

TRADEMARK INFRINGEMENT The unauthorized use of another's trademark in such a manner as to cause a likelihood of confusion as to the source of the product or service in connection with which it is utilized.

TREBLE DAMAGES An award of damages triple of the amount awarded by the jury, provided for by statute for violation of certain offenses.

WILLFUL BLINDNESS Deliberately avoiding knowledge of a crime, particularly by not making a reasonable inquiry about suspected wrongdoing despite being aware that wrongdoing is highly probable.

Lorillard Tobacco Co., Inc. v. A&E Oil, Inc.

Cigarette manufacturer (P) v. Gas station company (D)

503 F.3d 588 (7th Cir. 2007).

NATURE OF CASE: Appeal from mandatory attorneys' fees awarded under 15 U.S.C. § 1117(b) in a trademark infringement action under the Lanham Act.

FACT SUMMARY: A&E Oil, Inc. (D), a gas station company, and its agents, Kuruvilla (D), Kurian (D), and Joseph (D), contended that they presented sufficient evidence that they neither knowingly or willfully sold counterfeit cigarettes in violation of Lorillard Tobacco Co., Inc.'s (P) trademark, so that the district court erred in granting a mandatory award for attorneys' fees under the Lanham Act, 15 U.S.C. § 1117(b) on summary judgment.

🏛 RULE OF LAW
The mandatory award for attorneys' fees under the Lanham Act, 15 U.S.C. § 1117(b), may be granted on summary judgment where a defendant has failed to present more than a scintilla of evidence that the defendant did not act knowingly, either with actual knowledge or willful blindness.

FACTS: Lorillard Tobacco Co., Inc. (Lorillard's) (P), a cigarette producer, discovered that A&E Oil, Inc. (A&E) (D), a gas station company, and its agents, Kuruvilla (D), Kurian (D), and Joseph (D), had sold counterfeit Lorillard (P) cigarettes. Lorillard (P) initiated a Lanham Act action against them, and prevailed on summary judgment. The district court granted mandatory attorneys' fees under the Lanham Act, 15 U.S.C. § 1117(b), finding that A&E (D) and its agents (D) had knowingly sold the counterfeit cigarettes. The evidence showed that the counterfeit cigarette packets bore fake tax stamps that were noticeably fraudulent. At deposition, Kuruvilla (D) testified that he examined each packet's tax stamp, but never noticed anything amiss. Later, in an affidavit opposing summary judgment, he denied checking tax stamps "most of the time," thus contradicting his deposition testimony. There was also contradictory evidence from Kuruvilla (D) and his brother, Kurian (D), about the source of the counterfeit cigarettes. Lorillard (P) presented evidence that the counterfeit cigarettes came from U.S.A. Cigarettes, a supplier connected to counterfeit cigarettes. A&E (D) presented no evidence to rebut this. Although A&E (D) and its agents (D) denied in depositions ever purchasing cigarettes from U.S.A. Cigarettes, they admitted that they could have done so, and they acknowledged that they did purchase other products from this company. One check written by A&E (D) to U.S.A. Cigarettes bore the endorsement of Amin Arba, an alias for Amin Umar, a known source for counterfeit Lorillard (P) cigarettes. Joseph (D) also did business with U.S.A. Cigarettes at his other gas stations and,

although Joseph (D) denied ever speaking to Umar, Umar's telephone records indicated that he placed a call to Joseph's (D) telephone number. Finally, A&E (D) did not produce the checks written to U.S.A. Cigarettes until after A&E (D) had inaccurately represented to the district court that Lorillard (P) already possessed "all business records in Defendant's possession." From this, the district court concluded that A&E's (D) conduct during discovery suggested that it knew about the counterfeit cigarettes. On appeal, A&E (D) and its agents (D) challenged the district court's decision determining Lorillard's (P) entitlement to attorneys' fees. The court of appeals granted review.

ISSUE: May the mandatory award for attorneys' fees under the Lanham Act, 15 U.S.C. § 1117(b), be granted on summary judgment where a defendant has failed to present more than a scintilla of evidence that the defendant did not act knowingly, either with actual knowledge or willful blindness?

HOLDING AND DECISION: (Manion, J.) Yes. The mandatory award for attorneys' fees under the Lanham Act, 15 U.S.C. § 1117(b), may be granted on summary judgment where a defendant has failed to present more than a scintilla of evidence that the defendant did not act knowingly, either with actual knowledge or willful blindness. To prove knowledge of the counterfeiting, Lorillard (P) was not required to prove A&E's (D) actual knowledge; knowledge includes a willful blindness or a failure to investigate because one "was afraid of what the inquiry would yield." Absent extenuating circumstances, willful blindness is sufficient to trigger the mandatory attorneys' fees provision. Here, the evidence demonstrates that A&E (D) and its agents (D) acted with knowledge or willful blindness. Kuruvilla's (D) conflicting statements regarding the tax stamps is an attempt to create sham issues of fact, which negates his feigned ignorance. The contradictory statements by Kuruvilla (D) and Kurian (D) also create a sham issue of fact. There was simply no evidence in the record to support A&E's (D) claims of an innocent source for the counterfeit cigarettes. A&E (D) also failed to present any evidence that the counterfeit cigarettes came for U.S.A. Cigarettes. In determining whether a party acted with knowledge, typically an inquiry into the party's state of mind must be made. However, denials supported by a mere scintilla of evidence are insufficient to create a genuine triable issue. Here, A&E (D) and its agents (D) must do more than baldly deny the reasonable inferences and facts presented by Lorillard (P) to avoid the conclusion that they knowingly sold counterfeit cigarettes, but they have failed to do,

Continued on next page.

so. They have offered no plausible explanation for the presence of the counterfeit cigarettes, the failure to notice the tax stamps when checked, implausible denials of knowledge of known counterfeit trafficker Umar and U.S.A. Cigarettes, and questionable discovery practices. All they have offered are bald denials of knowledge, unsupported by sufficient evidence to permit a jury to render a verdict in their favor. For these reasons, the district court did not err as a matter of law in determining that defendants knowingly sold counterfeit cigarettes and, that, therefore, the mandatory award for attorneys' fees applied. [Affirmed.]

▶ ANALYSIS

The award of fees in this case was not made in the discretion of the district court, but rather followed from statutory language requiring the award of attorneys' fees under 15 U.S.C. § 1117(b) if the defendants knowingly used a counterfeit mark. Section 1117(b) states that "... the court shall, unless the court finds extenuating circumstances, enter judgment for three times such profits or damages, whichever is greater, together with a reasonable attorney's fee ...." Accordingly, the court of appeals here did not review the district court's decision for an abuse of discretion, but rather reviewed the district court's application of the statute de novo as a question of law. In effect, this standard required the court of appeals to consider whether the evidence, when viewed in the light most favorable to the defendants, demonstrated that A&E (D) knowingly sold counterfeit cigarettes (a determination made by the district court in its summary judgment ruling), even though the defendants limited their appeal to the attorneys' fee award and did not appeal the summary judgment against them.

■▬■

Quicknotes

ACTUAL KNOWLEDGE Knowledge that presently and objectively exists.

SCINTILLA Doctrine whereby if there is the least bit of evidence regarding a material question of fact then that issue should be left for determination by the jury.

TRADEMARK INFRINGEMENT The unauthorized use of another's trademark in such a manner as to cause a likelihood of confusion as to the source of the product or service in connection with which it is utilized.

WILLFUL BLINDNESS Deliberately avoiding knowledge of a crime, particularly by not making a reasonable inquiry about suspected wrongdoing despite being aware that wrongdoing is highly probable.

■▬■

K Mart Corp. v. Cartier, Inc.

Intervening defendant (D) v. Party not identified (P)

486 U.S. 281 (1988).

NATURE OF CASE: Certiorari to resolve conflict among courts of appeal concerning Customs regulation interpreting § 526 of the Tariff Act of 1930.

FACT SUMMARY: The Secretary of the Treasury issued a regulation permitting importation of certain gray-market goods.

> 🏛 **RULE OF LAW**
> The importation of gray-market goods is permissible in the context where both the U.S. trademark or trade name holder and the foreign person or entity are subject to common ownership or control.

FACTS: The gray market arises in one of three contexts: (1) domestic company buys the rights to register and use an independent foreign company's mark in the United States and the foreign company imports its goods to the United States causing intrabrand competition; (2a) domestic company registers its trademark for foreign-manufactured goods and the foreign manufacturer incorporates a domestic subsidiary and registers its own U.S. trademark identical to the parent's; (2b) domestic company forms a foreign subsidiary and sells its trademarked goods abroad which compete with its domestic sales; (2c) domestic company forms foreign unincorporated manufacturing division to produce its U.S. trademarked goods and then imports them while the foreign division sells abroad; (3) U.S. trademark holder authorizes foreign entity to use it abroad but then the entity imports into the United States and competes in sales. In 1922, gray-market importation was not prohibited and the courts refused to enjoin importation of a context 1 situation. Congress immediately enacted § 526 of the Tariff Act of 1922, which was later reenacted in identical form as § 526 of the 1930 Tariff Act. Section 526 prohibits the importation of most gray-market goods. The Customs Service in its regulations implementing § 526 excepts goods under "common-control." The regulation states prohibition does not apply when the same person or entity owns the foreign and U.S. trademark or trade name or they are parent and subsidiary companies subject to common ownership or control. The regulation further permits importation of gray-market goods when the trademark or trade name is applied under authorization of the U.S. owner. An association of U.S. trademark holders sought to have the regulation declared invalid and unenforceable as inconsistent with § 526. The district court upheld the regulation and the court of appeals reversed. This Court granted certiorari to resolve a conflict among the courts of appeal.

ISSUE: Is the importation of gray-market goods permissible in the context where both the U.S. trademark or trade name holder and the foreign person or entity are subject to common ownership or control?

HOLDING AND DECISION: (Kennedy, J.) Yes. The importation of gray-market goods is permissible in the context where both the U.S. trademark or trade name holder and the foreign person or entity are subject to common ownership or control. The Court first analyzed the language of the regulation to determine if it was consistent with the language of the statute. If the language did not conflict, the Court must give deference to the agency interpretation. Here, the Customs Service language as far as the "common-control" regulation deserves deference. The language "owned by" is ambiguous when the domestic subsidiary is wholly owned by the foreign parent, so it is difficult to determine who "owns" the U.S. trademark. Further, "merchandise of foreign manufacture" could mean (1) goods manufactured in a foreign country; (2) goods manufactured by a foreign entity; or (3) goods manufactured in a foreign country by a foreign entity. The agency can interpret the statutory language to read goods manufactured by a foreign subsidiary of a domestic entity are not goods "of foreign manufacture." The "authorized use" interpretation, however, is not valid. This regulation addresses goods made in a foreign country by an independent foreign manufacturer that could then be permitted to import the goods domestically and compete with the U.S. trademark or trade name holder. No reasonable construction of the statutory language permits such importation. This part of the regulation is severable, so it alone is invalidated. Reversed as to invalidation of the "common-control" sections of the regulation; affirmed as to the "authorized use" invalidation.

▌ *ANALYSIS*

The gray market differs from the black market in that gray-market goods are legal and authorized goods that are in the country under suspicious circumstances. Black-market goods are illegal, typically counterfeit, goods that should not be sold anywhere. Gray-market goods cause problems for trademark holders because they cause intra-entity competition where none should exist.

■=■

Bourdeau Bros. v. ITC

Importers (D) v. Federal government agency (P)

444 F.3d 1317 (Fed. Cir. 2006).

NATURE OF CASE: Appeal from an International Trade Commission general exclusion order and cease and desist orders in importation case.

FACT SUMMARY: The International Trade Commission (P) recommended exclusion and cease and desist orders against Bourdeau Bros. (D) and other defendants based on their importation into the United States of Deere & Co. trademarked forage harvesters manufactured for sale in Europe.

🏛 RULE OF LAW
The importation and sale of a trademarked good of domestic manufacture, produced solely for sale abroad and not authorized by the owner of the trademark for sale in the United States, may violate § 1337 if the imported good is materially different from all or substantially all of those goods bearing the same trademark that are authorized for sale in the United States.

FACTS: Bourdeau Bros. (D) and others imported forage harvesters into the United States. These forage harvesters legally bore the Deere & Co. (Deere) trademark but they were manufactured solely for sale in Europe. Deere objected to their importation into the United States and the competition with Deere-mark forage harvesters manufactured for sale in the United States. Deere filed a complaint with the International Trade Commission (ITC) (P). The investigating Administrative Law Judge (ALJ) subsequently recommended an exclusion order and cease and desist orders against the importers, and the ITC adopted the recommendation in full and issued the orders. Bourdeau Bros. (D) and other importers appealed.

ISSUE: May the importation and sale of a trademarked good of domestic manufacture, produced solely for sale abroad and not authorized by the owner of the trademark for sale in the United States, violate § 1337 if the imported good is materially different from all or substantially all of those goods bearing the same trademark that are authorized for sale in the United States?

HOLDING AND DECISION: (Clevenger, J.) Yes. The importation and sale of a trademarked good of domestic manufacture, produced solely for sale abroad and not authorized by the owner of the trademark for sale in the United States, may violate 19 U.S.C. § 1337 if the imported good is materially different from all or substantially all of those goods bearing the same trademark that are authorized for sale in the United States. Section 1337(a)(1)(c) expressly forbids importation of articles that infringe a valid, enforceable, and registered U.S. trademark. Goods often falling within the § 1337 prohibition are "gray-market goods." The question with a gray-market good is not whether the trademark is validly affixed to the good but whether there are differences between the domestic goods and the imported goods bearing the trademark. If there are differences, the analysis becomes whether the differences are material. The threshold for materiality is a low one. Appellants first argue the goods are not "gray-market goods" because they were manufactured in the United States, and therefore, *K Mart Corp v. Cartier, Inc.*, 486 U.S. 281 (1987), permits their import. *K Mart* did not address § 1337, however, and further, should not be read to limit gray-market theory to goods of foreign manufacture. Section 1337 does not distinguish between goods of domestic or foreign manufacture. Here, several differences exist between the European and the American forage harvesters, including safety warnings and manuals. Substantial evidence supports the finding that the differences are material. Vacated and remanded [for determination whether Deere itself sold the European forage harvesters in the United States].

▶ ANALYSIS

On remand, the administrative law judge again found a violation of § 1337, but the International Trade Commission (ITC) reversed its determination. Deere & Co. appealed again to the Federal Circuit based in part on an allegation the ITC erred in determining Deere's sales in the United States were not all or substantially all of the North American-version forage harvester. The Federal Circuit heard oral argument on January 4, 2010. The Federal Circuit has not yet issued its ruling.

■═■

Quicknotes

CEASE AND DESIST ORDER An order from a court or administrative agency prohibiting a person or business from continuing a particular course of conduct.

■═■

Common Latin Words and Phrases Encountered in the Law

A FORTIORI: Because one fact exists or has been proven, therefore a second fact that is related to the first fact must also exist.

A PRIORI: From the cause to the effect. A term of logic used to denote that when one generally accepted truth is shown to be a cause, another particular effect must necessarily follow.

AB INITIO: From the beginning; a condition which has existed throughout, as in a marriage which was void ab initio.

ACTUS REUS: The wrongful act; in criminal law, such action sufficient to trigger criminal liability.

AD VALOREM: According to value; an ad valorem tax is imposed upon an item located within the taxing jurisdiction calculated by the value of such item.

AMICUS CURIAE: Friend of the court. Its most common usage takes the form of an amicus curiae brief, filed by a person who is not a party to an action but is nonetheless allowed to offer an argument supporting his legal interests.

ARGUENDO: In arguing. A statement, possibly hypothetical, made for the purpose of argument, is one made arguendo.

BILL QUIA TIMET: A bill to quiet title (establish ownership) to real property.

BONA FIDE: True, honest, or genuine. May refer to a person's legal position based on good faith or lacking notice of fraud (such as a bona fide purchaser for value) or to the authenticity of a particular document (such as a bona fide last will and testament).

CAUSA MORTIS: With approaching death in mind. A gift causa mortis is a gift given by a party who feels certain that death is imminent.

CAVEAT EMPTOR: Let the buyer beware. This maxim is reflected in the rule of law that a buyer purchases at his own risk because it is his responsibility to examine, judge, test, and otherwise inspect what he is buying.

CERTIORARI: A writ of review. Petitions for review of a case by the United States Supreme Court are most often done by means of a writ of certiorari.

CONTRA: On the other hand. Opposite. Contrary to.

CORAM NOBIS: Before us; writs of error directed to the court that originally rendered the judgment.

CORAM VOBIS: Before you; writs of error directed by an appellate court to a lower court to correct a factual error.

CORPUS DELICTI: The body of the crime; the requisite elements of a crime amounting to objective proof that a crime has been committed.

CUM TESTAMENTO ANNEXO, ADMINISTRATOR (ADMINISTRATOR C.T.A.): With will annexed; an administrator c.t.a. settles an estate pursuant to a will in which he is not appointed.

DE BONIS NON, ADMINISTRATOR (ADMINISTRATOR D.B.N.): Of goods not administered; an administrator d.b.n. settles a partially settled estate.

DE FACTO: In fact; in reality; actually. Existing in fact but not officially approved or engendered.

DE JURE: By right; lawful. Describes a condition that is legitimate "as a matter of law," in contrast to the term "de facto," which connotes something existing in fact but not legally sanctioned or authorized. For example, de facto segregation refers to segregation brought about by housing patterns, etc., whereas de jure segregation refers to segregation created by law.

DE MINIMIS: Of minimal importance; insignificant; a trifle; not worth bothering about.

DE NOVO: Anew; a second time; afresh. A trial de novo is a new trial held at the appellate level as if the case originated there and the trial at a lower level had not taken place.

DICTA: Generally used as an abbreviated form of obiter dicta, a term describing those portions of a judicial opinion incidental or not necessary to resolution of the specific question before the court. Such nonessential statements and remarks are not considered to be binding precedent.

DUCES TECUM: Refers to a particular type of writ or subpoena requesting a party or organization to produce certain documents in their possession.

EN BANC: Full bench. Where a court sits with all justices present rather than the usual quorum.

EX PARTE: For one side or one party only. An ex parte proceeding is one undertaken for the benefit of only one party, without notice to, or an appearance by, an adverse party.

EX POST FACTO: After the fact. An ex post facto law is a law that retroactively changes the consequences of a prior act.

EX REL.: Abbreviated form of the term "ex relatione," meaning upon relation or information. When the state brings an action in which it has no interest against an individual at the instigation of one who has a private interest in the matter.

FORUM NON CONVENIENS: Inconvenient forum. Although a court may have jurisdiction over the case, the action should be tried in a more conveniently located court, one to which parties and witnesses may more easily travel, for example.

GUARDIAN AD LITEM: A guardian of an infant as to litigation, appointed to represent the infant and pursue his/her rights.

HABEAS CORPUS: You have the body. The modern writ of habeas corpus is a writ directing that a person (body) being detained (such as a prisoner) be brought before the court so that the legality of his detention can be judicially ascertained.

IN CAMERA: In private, in chambers. When a hearing is held before a judge in his chambers or when all spectators are excluded from the courtroom.

IN FORMA PAUPERIS: In the manner of a pauper. A party who proceeds in forma pauperis because of his poverty is one who is allowed to bring suit without liability for costs.

INFRA: Below, under. A word referring the reader to a later part of a book. (The opposite of supra.)

IN LOCO PARENTIS: In the place of a parent.

IN PARI DELICTO: Equally wrong; a court of equity will not grant requested relief to an applicant who is in pari delicto, or as much at fault in the transactions giving rise to the controversy as is the opponent of the applicant.

IN PARI MATERIA: On like subject matter or upon the same matter. Statutes relating to the same person or things are said to be in pari materia. It is a general rule of statutory construction that such statutes should be construed together, i.e., looked at as if they together constituted one law.

IN PERSONAM: Against the person. Jurisdiction over the person of an individual.

IN RE: In the matter of. Used to designate a proceeding involving an estate or other property.

IN REM: A term that signifies an action against the res, or thing. An action in rem is basically one that is taken directly against property, as distinguished from an action in personam, i.e., against the person.

INTER ALIA: Among other things. Used to show that the whole of a statement, pleading, list, statute, etc., has not been set forth in its entirety.

INTER PARTES: Between the parties. May refer to contracts, conveyances or other transactions having legal significance.

INTER VIVOS: Between the living. An inter vivos gift is a gift made by a living grantor, as distinguished from bequests contained in a will, which pass upon the death of the testator.

IPSO FACTO: By the mere fact itself.

JUS: Law or the entire body of law.

LEX LOCI: The law of the place; the notion that the rights of parties to a legal proceeding are governed by the law of the place where those rights arose.

MALUM IN SE: Evil or wrong in and of itself; inherently wrong. This term describes an act that is wrong by its very nature, as opposed to one which would not be wrong but for the fact that there is a specific legal prohibition against it (malum prohibitum).

MALUM PROHIBITUM: Wrong because prohibited, but not inherently evil. Used to describe something that is wrong because it is expressly forbidden by law but that is not in and of itself evil, e.g., speeding.

MANDAMUS: We command. A writ directing an official to take a certain action.

MENS REA: A guilty mind; a criminal intent. A term used to signify the mental state that accompanies a crime or other prohibited act. Some crimes require only a general mens rea (general intent to do the prohibited act), but others, like assault with intent to murder, require the existence of a specific mens rea.

MODUS OPERANDI: Method of operating; generally refers to the manner or style of a criminal in committing crimes, admissible in appropriate cases as evidence of the identity of a defendant.

NEXUS: A connection to.

NISI PRIUS: A court of first impression. A nisi prius court is one where issues of fact are tried before a judge or jury.

N.O.V. (NON OBSTANTE VEREDICTO): Notwithstanding the verdict. A judgment n.o.v. is a judgment given in favor of one party despite the fact that a verdict was returned in favor of the other party, the justification being that the verdict either had no reasonable support in fact or was contrary to law.

NUNC PRO TUNC: Now for then. This phrase refers to actions that may be taken and will then have full retroactive effect.

PENDENTE LITE: Pending the suit; pending litigation under way.

PER CAPITA: By head; beneficiaries of an estate, if they take in equal shares, take per capita.

PER CURIAM: By the court; signifies an opinion ostensibly written "by the whole court" and with no identified author.

PER SE: By itself, in itself; inherently.

PER STIRPES: By representation. Used primarily in the law of wills to describe the method of distribution where a person, generally because of death, is unable to take that which is left to him by the will of another, and therefore his heirs divide such property between them rather than take under the will individually.

PRIMA FACIE: On its face, at first sight. A prima facie case is one that is sufficient on its face, meaning that the evidence supporting it is adequate to establish the case until contradicted or overcome by other evidence.

PRO TANTO: For so much; as far as it goes. Often used in eminent domain cases when a property owner receives partial payment for his land without prejudice to his right to bring suit for the full amount he claims his land to be worth.

QUANTUM MERUIT: As much as he deserves. Refers to recovery based on the doctrine of unjust enrichment in those cases in which a party has rendered valuable services or furnished materials that were accepted and enjoyed by another under circumstances that would reasonably notify the recipient that the rendering party expected to be paid. In essence, the law implies a contract to pay the reasonable value of the services or materials furnished.

QUASI: Almost like; as if; nearly. This term is essentially used to signify that one subject or thing is almost analogous to another but that material differences between them do exist. For example, a quasi-criminal proceeding is one that is not strictly criminal but shares enough of the same characteristics to require some of the same safeguards (e.g., procedural due process must be followed in a parole hearing).

QUID PRO QUO: Something for something. In contract law, the consideration, something of value, passed between the parties to render the contract binding.

RES GESTAE: Things done; in evidence law, this principle justifies the admission of a statement that would otherwise be hearsay when it is made so closely to the event in question as to be said to be a part of it, or with such spontaneity as not to have the possibility of falsehood.

RES IPSA LOQUITUR: The thing speaks for itself. This doctrine gives rise to a rebuttable presumption of negligence when the instrumentality causing the injury was within the exclusive control of the defendant, and the injury was one that does not normally occur unless a person has been negligent.

RES JUDICATA: A matter adjudged. Doctrine which provides that once a court of competent jurisdiction has rendered a final judgment or decree on the merits, that judgment or decree is conclusive upon the parties to the case and prevents them from engaging in any other litigation on the points and issues determined therein.

RESPONDEAT SUPERIOR: Let the master reply. This doctrine holds the master liable for the wrongful acts of his servant (or the principal for his agent) in those cases in which the servant (or agent) was acting within the scope of his authority at the time of the injury.

STARE DECISIS: To stand by or adhere to that which has been decided. The common law doctrine of stare decisis attempts to give security and certainty to the law by following the policy that once a principle of law as applicable to a certain set of facts has been set forth in a decision, it forms a precedent which will subsequently be followed, even though a different decision might be made were it the first time the question had arisen. Of course, stare decisis is not an inviolable principle and is departed from in instances where there is good cause (e.g., considerations of public policy led the Supreme Court to disregard prior decisions sanctioning segregation).

SUPRA: Above. A word referring a reader to an earlier part of a book.

ULTRA VIRES: Beyond the power. This phrase is most commonly used to refer to actions taken by a corporation that are beyond the power or legal authority of the corporation.

Addendum of French Derivatives

IN PAIS: Not pursuant to legal proceedings.

CHATTEL: Tangible personal property.

CY PRES: Doctrine permitting courts to apply trust funds to purposes not expressed in the trust but necessary to carry out the settlor's intent.

PER AUTRE VIE: For another's life; during another's life. In property law, an estate may be granted that will terminate upon the death of someone other than the grantee.

PROFIT A PRENDRE: A license to remove minerals or other produce from land.

VOIR DIRE: Process of questioning jurors as to their predispositions about the case or parties to a proceeding in order to identify those jurors displaying bias or prejudice.

Casenote® Legal Briefs